The Consequences of Loyalism

The CONSEQUENCES of LOYALISM

Essays in Honor of Robert M. Calhoon

Edited by

REBECCA BRANNON and JOSEPH S. MOORE

The University of South Carolina Press

© 2019 University of South Carolina

Published by the University of South Carolina Press
Columbia, South Carolina 29208
www.sc.edu/uscpress

Manufactured in the United States of America

28 27 26 25 24 23 22 21 20 19
10 9 8 7 6 5 4 3 2 1

Library of Congress Cataloging-in-Publication Data
can be found at http://catalog.loc.gov/.

ISBN: 978-1-61117-950-7 (hardcover)
ISBN: 978-1-61117-951-4 (ebook)

For Robert M. Calhoon
a generous scholar, collaborator, and mentor

Contents

List of Illustrations

Preface

"You're not going to work on the Loyalists. Nobody does the Loyalists anymore."

Thus began the first conversation with my doctoral mentor in 2005. I had moved to North Carolina to work with Robert M. "Bob" Calhoon, whose seminal book *The Loyalists in Revolutionary America* (1973) reshaped the study of Loyalist ideology. He had agreed to take one last doctoral student, and I was that student. I now had no idea why.

Bob had read my application closely. He rightly determined that I was not nearly as well equipped to reexamine Loyalist ideologies as I was the mixture of religion, race, and transatlantic communities inhabiting the southern backcountry that happened to include some Loyalists. Unbeknownst to me, sitting on his desk at the time was a note to coordinate funding for a doctoral dissertation on a virtually unknown antislavery group in backcountry South Carolina who fit that bill. When he read my application, he later told me, "I took the note, crumpled it up, and threw it in the wastebasket." This was why he had accepted that last doctoral student. Bob sent me on a journey for which I will be forever grateful, away from the Loyalists and toward the antislavery southern moderates who dominated the next decade of my intellectual life.

Later Bob admitted that he was, if not lying, at least protecting me from the hard truth. "There were too many people who were too far ahead of you," he said, "and they were all really, *really* good." As his bibliographical essay in *Tory Insurgents* (2010) made clear, Bob kept abreast of every word written on the subject; he was aware of, excited about, and encouraging toward an emerging wave of scholarship on the Revolutionary Loyalists he felt would form the new consensus to replace his. He understood the time was right for books that moved in different directions than his ideological tome had taken. The surest sign you had done something right was that the field needed to move past your questions to answer different ones; he felt good about handing the baton to the bevy of scholars who were doing just that.

Time quickly proved Bob right. In short order the works he referenced materialized, and they have reshaped Loyalist scholarship as he predicted they would. Jim Piecuch's *Three Peoples, One King* (2008), Ruma Chopra's *Unnatural Rebellion* (2011), and Maya Jasanoff's *Liberty's Exiles* (2011) each arrived as Bob supervised my dissertation. Two other dissertations, by Rebecca Brannon and Aaron Nathan Coleman, had him particularly sure that all the good ground was being covered.

If Loyalist scholarship sprang off of and moved beyond Bob's work, so did he. For nearly forty years after 1973 he groped for what might be described as

Loyalism's missing ideological link. Following Bob's lead, scholars now note the striking similarities between the king's friends and their Patriot antagonists. He was certain that these enemies did, at times, sense the opportunity and danger in each other's closeness. His forays through the 1980s and 1990s into American religious history provided close but still unsatisfying answers. Finally he struck upon the idea of historic moderation, not a trimming of sails or avoidance of conflict but principled partisanship wise enough to fear its own excess. A blend of classicism and Calvinism, historic moderation was Bob's best way to understand the tortured sense of history that kept some committed Loyalists and Whigs humble about their own commitments, careful about the alienation of enemies, and fearful of their own allies. Such beliefs might help explain why certain Patriots and Loyalists at times resembled each other more than their own side. Bob summarized this concept as "humility in the face of the past" in *Political Moderation in America's First Two Centuries* (2009).

This edited collection seeks to honor Calhoon and the themes that emerged in his fifty-year career. Ideology (which he labeled "perceptions"), religion, the backcountry, and moderation shaped the four waves of his writing. But embedded in each was Bob's refusal to take part in the intellectual balkanization of scholarly discourse that seemed to grow inexorably during his tenure as the dean of American Loyalist studies. A promiscuous reader of social science theory, he was never afraid to utilize innovations in other disciplines to reimagine past societies. Aaron Nathan Coleman and Rebecca Brannon's engagement with systems of transitional justice were just the kind of cross-disciplinary work he applauded. In honor of Bob's career trajectory, this book is broken into two sections. "Perceptions" evokes his concern with Loyalist ideologies and conceptions of self, while "Moderation" probes the depths of what it meant to resolve conflicted identities in the wake of unfathomable trouble and loss. Within each section are explorations of religion, gender, race, refugee status, memory, and geography that inform our conversations anew and would delight him.

This book honors Bob's career in another way by celebrating his generosity of spirit to generations of young scholars trying to make their way in conferences, journals, books, fellowships, and tenure applications. Early in his career, Bob passed up the opportunity to leave his adopted North Carolina home and take on doctoral students at the University of Connecticut. Not until the early twenty-first century did UNC-Greensboro begin admitting doctoral students; he officially oversaw just three dissertations. Bob filled this void with an inveterate encouragement of young Loyalist scholars across academia. Possessed of a curious mind coupled to an encyclopedic memory of the *William and Mary Quarterly*, he seems to know what everyone in the field is doing and to find it all endlessly inspiring. Bob loves the life of the mind, and he loves living it with others. This book says thank you for the cumulative effect of that scholarship, mentorship, and friendship in the best way we know how: by keeping the conversation going.

Acknowledgments

We thank the many scholars who collaborated on this project. The Ulster American Heritage Symposium sponsored and the University of Georgia hosted a panel where many of the contributors here made contact and the idea for a common understanding of this nature first took form. From there we recruited contributors whose work supported this vision, and we thank them for their willingness to come on board. Joseph especially thanks Rebecca for breathing new life into the project by transitioning from contributor to coeditor. Our families were very patient and forgiving in allowing us to pile one more project onto already overcrowded calendars. For that we thank Mary Julia, Charlotte, Joan, Seth, and Ziva.

And, of course, thanks to Robert M. Calhoon. He encouraged the work of countless future historians with his boundless enthusiasm for scholarship and his sage advice to eschew obfuscation.

Introduction

I keep hearing from other historians that the Loyalists are "in again." The truth is, in a nationalist history, the Loyalists never were and never will be "cool." It is only when we step outside the sureties of nationalism and its historical-meaning imperative that we can understand the Loyalists better. And frankly some of them were never cool. Period. A few burned with ideological fervor, but they never did it with as much style as Thomas Paine. Others were deeply pragmatic individuals—the moderates that Robert M. Calhoon celebrated but few others have or will. They were the kind of men and women we know, or are ourselves, but not the kind of people who normally make the history books.

As long as we try to understand the American Revolution, and the concomitant creation of an American nation-state, the Loyalists and their fate will be important—and will continue to slip from our grasp. As Ruma Chopra has pointed out, "intractable issues vex" the study of the Loyalists.[1] The Loyalists are a perpetual enigma, and they are the foil onto which generations of scholars have foisted conflicting values and aspirations. As history's losers, they have been cast as history's whiners.

We cannot even agree how many Loyalists there were—let alone what motivated them. Estimates of Loyalists have varied widely, then and now. John Adams famously estimated "that one full third were averse to the Revolution." Henry Laurens, a negotiator of the peace treaty ending the war, denied British estimates of ten thousand Loyalist refugees, arguing, "there is no such number nor any thing near it." Of course he had every reason to downplay the total number of dispossessed Loyalists in the context of discussing who was going to pay to support them.[2] Calhoon in his *The Loyalists in Revolutionary America* estimated that eighty thousand Loyalists became refugees, and as many as four hundred thousand had been Loyalists but remained in the United States after the war. Within five years of Calhoon's work, Paul Smith calculated that Loyalists, including men, women, and children, comprised as many as five hundred thousand individuals, or 19 percent of the white population.[3] Both men worked to consider the entire number of what we might now call the disaffected and did not only consider those whose Loyalism forced them into expulsion and diaspora at the end of the war. More recently Maya Jasanoff estimated some sixty thousand Loyalist refugees left after the Revolution, although Philip Ranlet has persuasively argued this is almost certainly too high. Ranlet himself refused to calculate a specific number but would probably put it at closer to twenty thousand adult refugees.[4] Yet in the end, does it really matter whether there were twenty or sixty or five hundred thousand Loyalists, depending on how we count? We are seeking to show their importance. A cursory examination of the concerted effort Patriot supporters made from the 1760s on to suppress dissent and limit public disaffection against the Revolution makes it clear Patriots thought the Loyalists were numerous enough and important enough to complicate their efforts.

We also argue over what motivated the Loyalists and what they sought in choosing the king's side. Scholars have at various times argued that the Loyalists were unlike their fellow colonial Americans—different somehow by religion, region, occupation, or intrinsic psychological makeup. Other scholars have shown again and again that this is not true. Loyalists came from every region, every religious group, and every occupation. Nor were they uniformly more conservative, cantankerous, or lacking in courage—or more courageous—than anyone else. We veer back and forth between trapping them in the scholarly apparatus of the nation-state that was only beginning to form in their age and their own age's still-coalescing goal of global empire. They ultimately served the goal of empire but were not well served by it. It is not clear, reading the Loyalists themselves, that any of these categories really fits their thinking—let alone their actions. To understand the Loyalists, we have to explain their motivations and actions without either celebrating or pathologizing them.

Today we are in a historiographical moment when we are ready to recognize there was widespread disaffection from the project of the Revolution and that the umbrella term of *disaffected* in fact covers a wide variety of people with varied motivations. They disliked the direction the American Revolution was taking by the time it came to blows, but their experiences during and after the Revolution showed how varied their thinking really was. Some became the troublesome refugees British royal governors complained about, while others became the reintegrated Loyalists who took their seats in state legislatures and became invested in the nasty political squabbles of the early Republic with little but occasional whispers about their Loyalist pasts. Such divergent fates and attitudes can in part be explained by the incredible diversity of issues that brought these disaffected people into the "Loyalist fold" to begin with.

A new generation of scholars have rediscovered the civil war at the heart of the American Revolution, and in so doing have had to grapple with the Loyalists anew. Scholars of European revolutions, also tired of and displeased with overarching narratives of nation-state and empire, are also newly emphasizing civil wars as a way of understanding the reality of the momentous changes set in motion in the eighteenth century. To understand the reality of civil war is to put the Loyalists back into the frame. It is also to grapple seriously with the reality that our American nation was born in violence. After all, it was an eight-year war that brought America its independence, not politely worded remonstrances.[5]

We have also spent a generation rediscovering the diversity of our nation from early America to today, and rediscovering the incredible diversity of Loyalists has been part of that process. Once pilloried by nationalistic, Cold War–era American historians as an aristocratic elite out of step with an evolving American identity and democratic society, Loyalists have come to show us the multiplicity of experiences and desires of all early Americans. The "new" social history established the importance of being attentive to the experiences of African Americans, women, and Native Americans. Historians of the American Revolution realized that Native Americans were a vital part of the war effort on both sides, and their military support made them eagerly sought allies by both sides. They were a vital part of the British "Loyalist" coalition in many places, but their motivations revolved around their own desires for independence, not notions of political loyalty to outsiders. In a different vein, Jim Piecuch argues that while black people and Native Americans were willing to offer substantial military support to the British cause in the Revolution, white Loyalists and white British commanders were too pig-headed in their lack of faith in nonwhite peoples to take full advantage of their help, and that therefore racism helped seal the fate of white Loyalists.[6] Black Loyalists began to find the historical spotlight they long deserved, as we historians uncovered the reality that the Patriot revolutionaries were not liberators to a substantial part of the population. Instead some twenty thousand enslaved people worked to free themselves by fleeing their masters for the British army lines. While a handful of free blacks found freedom fighting for the Patriots, many more found themselves cast on the mercy of the British and their white American allies. In the British Maritimes after the Revolution, many former slaves found that white Loyalists were not willing to embrace them as fellow members of society. They also found that the institution of slavery was so vital to British interests that it continued not only in the lucrative Caribbean colonies but also in Nova Scotia. Ultimately more than one thousand discouraged black Loyalists in Nova Scotia left for Sierra Leone.[7]

Yet Loyalist scholarship has also come to muddy important distinctions between the decisions people made (even with imperfect information) and those that were made for them. Crucial lines between self-determination and the way others labeled disaffected people, including neutrals, have been erased. All of these have been dumped under the capaciously large category of Loyalism—from Native Americans concerned with tribal advantage, to enslaved people seeking freedom for their families, to white artisans seeking temporary advantage in the face of British army occupation. Some historians call a wide variety of people with limited self-determination Loyalists. Jasanoff, for example, deals with the sad fates of children whose fathers' political decisions had made them refugees. Loyalism irrevocably changed their lives, but they were not the ones with the agency. At some level Native Americans and African American "Loyalists" were merely wartime allies and, like all allies, were motivated by very different considerations than those recruiting them to the cause. So too neutrals, such as pacifists, were slapped with the Loyalist label regardless of what they really felt. They paid the price, and that means we analyze them as Loyalists, yet they hardly had the same outlook on life and politics as an Anglican minister who chose to preach against the Revolution's ideology.

A new generation of historians is rediscovering the experiences of the majority of American Loyalists while at the same time honoring the experiences of the minority. Robert Calhoon himself pointed out that as many as four hundred thousand Loyalists stayed in the United States, and that their experiences were therefore important to understanding them and the early nation. Calhoon took up the question explicitly in his essay "The Reintegration of the Loyalists and the Disaffected." David Maas argued for the importance of understanding the reintegration of the Loyalists and the question of amnesty in the era of the Constitution, but unfortunately his work was mostly ignored. Calhoon took notice, however, and included him in an edited collection in 1994.[8] Despite their efforts to bring the question of reintegration of the many disaffected, historians concerned with the rise of the American democratic state and the nationalism needed to support it understandably ignored the sizable disaffected population who were still very much part of the postwar country. The global turn in scholarship made Loyalists the bleeding edge of a cosmopolitan vision of an ever-growing British empire and, understandably, turned attention away from the Loyalists who chose a pragmatic effort at reintegration in the place they knew well over a romantic but sometimes ill-fated journey across the world. And in national histories, where the intention of the revolutionaries is measured so often by the Constitution, the disaffected have became those upset at the power grab of the Constitutional Convention. Social and political reintegration after civil war disappeared in the mad rush to the constitutional settlement. It is notable how many scholars in early American history have moved from emphasizing the coming of the Revolution, the dominant field in the 1960s and 1970s, to focusing on the aftermath of the American Revolution in the last two decades.[9] The growing movement in Loyalist studies to focus on the Revolutionary War and the consequences of that war for all disaffected people is both part of this trend in early American historiography, and a recognition of how complicated the issue of peace-making really is. Perhaps as our generation of scholars who are developing historical careers in an age post 9/11, endless war in the Middle East, and terrorism around the world will reinvigorate the study of reconciliations and the creation of peaceful settlements in all kinds of historical epochs. The civil war of the Revolution is ripe for reconsideration from the vantage of peace studies.

Robert Calhoon was the leading voice on interpreting the American Loyalists in American historiography for more than a generation. This collection of essays is what we might call a festschrift-lite. Normally such festschrifts are the product of generations of graduate students. Yet Calhoon did not have his own graduate students until the end of his teaching career. Joseph S. Moore was his last graduate student and is the only contributor with that direct connection to Calhoon. This homage to the man and his work brings together scholars at different stages of their career around the issues of the Loyalists—the people Calhoon spent a career working to understand. This is the ultimate honor—an intellectual homage by scholars brought together by the work, not by the obligations to a good dissertation chair. As Moore and I pursued contributors, it became clear that Calhoon is not only an intellectual inspiration to scholars of the Loyalists but also a light in the sometimes dark groves of academe. Several scholars agreed to contribute because Calhoon had gone out of his way for them and smoothed their path into the profession at a moment when they were new and vulnerable. In addition Warren Hofstra and Carole Troxler, two long-established scholars and personal friends of Calhoon, also agreed early on to contribute to this volume on his behalf. Robert Calhoon is a fine scholar and a true gentleman, and we therefore offer this in his honor.

The contributions to this volume are original, research-driven essays on different aspects of the role of Loyalists before, during, and after the American Revolution. The editors have divided the work into two sections: "Perceptions" and "Moderation." "Perceptions" deals with the way Loyalists self-identified and, in consequence, the choices they made. As Moore notes in his preface, *perception* is the term Calhoon preferred, and it works well for the Loyalists, who found themselves in the midst of a civil war where no one ever had entirely good information. So they made their choices based on their perceptions of both what was right and what seemed wise given the limited information anyone had in an eighteenth-century war zone, let alone a civil war in which many people had every reason to hide their own thinking from others.

Taylor Stoermer pays a fitting intellectual homage to Calhoon's final work on moderation in early American life with his work on the Augustan, metropolitan way of thinking that led some Virginia planters to become moderate Loyalists. In his examination of the diverging fates of John Randolph and his cousin Thomas Jefferson, Stoermer finds a compelling window into the competing constitutional views of Virginians who were otherwise very similar, yet destined to choose opposing sides in the civil war. Kacy Tillman's work on Quaker women writers shows the diffuse nature of the sentiments that could make up a Loyalist, pacifist, or disaffected identity. Her delicate probing of the rhetorical strategies Quaker women used in their letters illuminates the performance of Loyalist feelings under the constraint of wartime. For her, self-perceptions are key to understanding the multiplicity of ways in which a Loyalist identity could be constructed and displayed. Christopher Sparshott uses the tools of political science studies of refugee camps today to cast a new light on the Loyalist experience in occupied New York. He finds that refugee Loyalism, as he terms it, was forged in the sometimes desperate circumstances of the refugee experience, where refugees found practical benefit in defining themselves to the British as ever faithful. Gradually this performance of their constancy convinced even them.

Several authors concentrate on the conduct of the war itself, with attention to those who took up arms in the king's defense. Christopher Minty wades into the fray, considering the panoply of American Loyalists in New York through his intensive and impressive prosopographical analysis. He proves that Loyalists were not oddballs or pampered elites but instead represent a persuasive cross-section of all colonial Americans. The American Revolution swept through all of American society, and all of society split in the civil war. Carole Troxler draws on her long career researching backcountry southern Loyalists to analyze Lord Cornwallis's disdain for Loyalist recruiting, and indeed the persistence of this disdain in historical memory. In exploring the contexts of six Loyalist recruiters in the western Carolinas she urges scholars to search beyond static perceptions of commanders in order to grasp the local and temporal dynamics of allegiance. Her work suggests that careful attention to the sources surrounding Loyalist recruiters helps historians recognize local revolutionary attempts to create hegemonies, and the fresh tensions those attempts aroused. C. L. Bragg shows the many ups and downs in the path of a committed Loyalist commander in the militia-led civil war in South Carolina. Alexander Chesney fought for the king's cause in several important battles over several years, ultimately left South Carolina with other refugee Loyalists, and fought for the British army in later campaigns in Ireland.

Loyalists came to straddle communities, nations, and even continents and oceans. Their history has long been central to Canadian history, but that robust scholarship has long been overlooked by generations of American historians. For too long I too was one of them. Loyalists were disproportionately influential in the politics of eastern Canada over generations, where they had outsized influence in the creation of a Canadian identity. Fittingly, therefore, two Canadian authors turn our attention to the vision Loyalist refugees had in remaking their lives in Nova Scotia after the war. Loyalists came with vague bromides about their place in the greater empire but refined these hazy ideas into clear visions of the Loyalist role in the British empire—a role that suggested that Britain's own interests were naturally aligned with rising prosperity for their loyal, or at least for their white, supporters. Bonnie Huskins shows the dreams of Loyalists who sought to remake their lives in British-held Shelburne, Nova Scotia, after the war. In Huskins's hands William Booth's journal depicts the dreams for upward mobility of both white and black Loyalists and the way in which their hopes were dashed by British aims for a stable and profitable empire. Catherine M.A. Cottreau-Robins uses both archaeological and written evidence to overturn the idea that all black people in Nova Scotia were free black Loyalists. Instead she shows how white Loyalists brought their slaves with them to Nova Scotia and re-creates the reality of their enslaved lives. White Loyalists used enslaved labor to construct their dream of an imperial landscape with ordered prosperity.

The second section of this book offers contemporary understandings of moderation—the subject of Calhoon's final book—with an eye to understanding how Loyalists dealt with the outcomes of their own actions and their inability to win the war. In a way these authors answer the oblique call Calhoon himself made in 1965 when he noted that his field-defining study of the Loyalists did not examine the "longer-term effect of the Revolution on the Loyalists—the exile experiences of perhaps 80,000 Loyalists and their dependents who departed or the adaptation of as many as 400,000 who remained in the United States—or the role of the Loyalists in the post-Revolutionary settlement."[10] It turns out that Americans were willing to offer reconciliation to the majority of Loyalists after the war, and Loyalists were willing to make the effort in order to heal society. Calhoon's *Political Moderation in America's First Two Centuries* argues for a long-standing moderate strain in American politics.[11] Moderation was a choice to deal with each other with empathy in the service of a lasting nation.

Our authors take up this challenge. Sally Hadden considers the approaches lawyers took to help relatives and other Loyalist clients regain their confiscated property in the United States. The attorneys found it to be personally lucrative even though many of their clients only regained a fraction of their total net worth. Then again, only Loyalists with difficult cases were likely to engage such high-powered legal help. Gregory Knouff deftly shows the complexity of Loyalist motivations, ideology, and postwar reintegration strategies through his evocative handling of Breed and Ruth Batcheller's experiences of New Hampshire Loyalism. Knouff argues that Breed Batcheller maneuvered through attempts at neutralism and efforts to preserve his relationships with those on the Patriot side. In the end his wife remained at home after the war, while he had to leave.

Brett Palfreyman shows the wide variety of people tagged with Loyalism who were able to reintegrate successfully into the United States. He argues that pacifist nonjurors were reconciled with other Pennsylvanians by the end of the 1780s, regaining their property, full citizenship, and social standing. Aaron N. Coleman and Rebecca Brannon both apply the recent political science field of transitional justice to understanding the way in which Loyalists were reintegrated into the United States and why. Coleman argues that transitional justice scholars should pay more attention to historical examples, both to make their models more flexible and to consider the role of contingency in reconciliation. He shows how the American revolutionaries brought about reconciliation with many former Loyalists within a decade of the end of the fighting. Brannon applies transitional justice thinking to argue that the United States engaged in a deliberate national wartime policy to purge Loyalists but that after the war every state moved from purges and reparations to ending most restrictions on Loyalists, leading to a de facto policy of national reconciliation. All three authors, Palfreyman, Coleman, and Brannon, agree that the substantial majority of Loyalists were reincorporated into the body politic within a decade of the end of the War for Independence and under generous terms.

Eileen Cheng shows how nationalist historian David Ramsay plagiarized a large segment of his history of South Carolina from Alexander Hewatt, a Loyalist. In doing so he created a vision of a cosmopolitan country with an exceptional role to play in the world. Loyalist ideologies helped create a thoroughly nationalist history. Ruma Chopra argues that the Loyalists who resettled in the Canadian Maritime provinces pursued a vision of both a unified empire—commercially and politically—that also benefited from governing unions within the empire in order to create a strong, stable antidote to the new United States. Victory after the fact would come from Loyalists' helping create an empire that would far outstrip the United States in wealth and power.

In conclusion Warren Hofstra places Calhoon's career and intellectual evolution into the perspective of the influence of Greensboro and its prominence in the American civil rights movement. Calhoon's own lifelong admiration for courageous, inclusive moderates sprang from his increasing immersion in Greensboro's and the university's efforts to make racial justice a reality.

All together we seek to honor Robert M. Calhoon's career as not only a Loyalist scholar but a man who epitomizes intellectual life as a joyous enterprise always open to new people and new conversations. We differ in methods and approaches, but all showcase the devotion to thorough research and flexible thinking that shaped Calhoon's own work. May others come behind us and lay down new pathways for Loyalist studies.

PART ONE

Perceptions

Taylor Stoermer

"The Success of either lies in the Womb of Time"

The Politics of Loyalty in the Revolutionary Chesapeake

"We both of us seem to be steering opposite Courses; the Success of either lies in the Womb of Time," John Randolph wrote to his cousin Thomas Jefferson in the late summer of 1775.[1] Randolph's insight was both literally and figuratively true. Their "opposite courses" were then about to lead Randolph, his wife, and both of his young daughters (but, tellingly, not his son) to board a ship bound for England, while Jefferson would soon be on his way to Philadelphia to attend the Continental Congress. However great the physical distance ahead of them, though, the miles could not compare with the schism that divided their perceptions of the political world and how it worked. For more than a century, that world had been woven together by powerful transatlantic webs of interests, but those ties began to fray in the middle of the eighteenth century, subtly dividing a once-coherent Chesapeake community into competitive political economies. Different political histories and separate constitutional languages left people such as Randolph and Jefferson as possessors of slightly but distinctly contrasting political persuasions. They employed the same Whiggish vocabulary and even shared that dominant ideology, but by the outbreak of the American War for Independence, the words they had once used in common—such as *Patriot, Loyalist,* and *Tory*—came to mean quite different things to them and those around them. Between 1745 and 1775, the differences in those political persuasions—one Augustan and metropolitan, the other Georgian and cosmopolitan, but both Whig and transatlantic—drove the British world apart, just as they were separating Jefferson and Randolph on that day in August 1775.

Randolph was almost certain that Jefferson was on a fool's errand. The British constitution was, indeed, broken, in real need of meaningful reform, but experience showed that it was not so far gone as to be in need of replacement. Quite to the contrary, there was enough empirical proof for the keenest Lockean observer that the constitution could be reformed without resort to such drastic measures as Jefferson's compatriots appeared inclined to take. The old, personal ties, Randolph fervently believed, could be stitched back together once again, but using more reliable thread than political economics: sentiment and a sense of history were the right stuff. A restoration, of sorts, of the salient elements of their common English identity was in order, reflecting a century of friendship and shared interests, but it depended on their common loyalty to the only revolutionary settlement that really mattered, that of 1688, and the robust, Augustan political culture of constitutional sense that it produced, along with unprecedented prosperity for many, although admittedly not all, of George III's subjects. For Randolph and his fellow constitutional Loyalists, that polite political persuasion hung, crucially, on the presumption that the supremacy of the people's representatives in Parliament, combined with a commitment to moderation in political practice, was the only effective means of preserving British liberty and securing any hope of its future expansion.

Jefferson, of course, saw things quite differently. His persuasion, dependent more on sensibility than sense, had little use for the revolutionary events of 1688, which only the most chauvinistic Englishman could call "glorious" and mean it. Instead they looked to a more British, even global, history, one that revealed a single, tenuous transatlantic tie that connected Virginia and the other American colonies to Britain—and it ran through the Crown. Consequently, so Jefferson's argument went, the wearer of that crown held the only possible power to strengthen those ties or sever them altogether. Parliament was nothing to the sensible Americans. As Lord North was said to have reflected at the time, it was a fabulist argument that only a Tory could love.

Either way, moderation under such circumstances as they found themselves in 1775 was out of the question. Jefferson was loyal to the belief that one should never compromise one's principles, especially when liberty was at stake. Randolph, however, maintained loyalty to the principle that to compromise was the only way to guarantee liberty and found ludicrous the notion that any British monarch had the authority to endanger it—even if he wanted to. Such mutually exclusive loyalties were the opposite courses down which Randolph and Jefferson were traveling in 1775, and it is no small matter that led one back to the old English metropolis and an attempt to reconcile the American colonies with Britain while the other went to a new American metropolis to encourage their separation.

How could two men with, on the face of things, so much in common develop such different, even mutually exclusive, constitutional identities? Jefferson blamed "the unnatural contest" over loyalties on the fact that British ministers had no idea what was really going on in the American colonies. "I wish they were thoroughly and minutely acquainted with every circumstance relative to America as it exists in truth." If they had accurate information about the sense and sensibility of colonists, then the ministry would not see "American opposition as that of a small faction" but understand that it was a widespread movement. "Even those in parliament who are called friends to America seem to know nothing of our real determinations," Jefferson lamented.[2] Randolph could not help but agree. "The people of England," he wrote in 1774, "on whom we so much rely, think that our Murmurs have no real Foundation."[3]

By virtue of their situation at the center of the political economy that had long bound the Virginia Tidewater to London, constitutional Loyalists such as John Randolph were able to weave a "tender band of amity"[4] that transformed the distance between imperial hub and provincial rim into a transatlantic community maintained by robust ties of friendship, kinship, commerce, and a common sense of their shared history. By rescuing moderates and their history from relative obscurity, we can recover the experience of a group of men and women who were integral to the British Atlantic empire in the eighteenth century. They not only created a community that existed for decades as a virtual public but also were the framers of British Virginia as a chauvinistic reflection of fundamental Britishness. For decades moderates effectively mediated the perceptions of political actors on both sides of the Atlantic, augmenting and informing the more impersonal and indirect mediums of discourse that grew in number over the century. They provided a critical text of transatlantic political communication that was simultaneously public and private, formal and informal, and that crucially kept any one connection or set of correspondents from exploiting the distance by dominating, and potentially manipulating, the flow of information. The consistent exchange effectively made the three thousand miles separating London from Virginia little more than a geographical detail. It made Virginia less a far-off colony than something closer to a Home County that merely happened to be separated from London by water instead of land. Yet when moderates have been considered at all, they have been dismissed inaccurately as "Tories" or anachronistically as conservatives. And the world they created, one ultimately divided by transatlantic communities with competing definitions of Britishness, has been largely lost.

In the first half of the eighteenth century, a tender band of amity developed into a "sacred knot"[5] of Britishness as these moderates, acting as political mediators and cultural brokers on both sides of the Atlantic, established for themselves a constitutional identity that made sense of the nature of the British Empire in Virginia and of Virginia in the empire. Their strong identification with an Anglocentric, Augustan Britishness as a fundamental commitment to parliamentary sovereignty and political moderation as the only practical means of keeping it safe from political and ideological extremism, dominated political praxis and culture in the Chesapeake for much of the period between the creation of the British state in 1707 and American independence in 1776.[6]

It is in this chauvinistic, constitutional sense that moderates made Virginia British and succeeded in keeping it that way for decades. Contemporaries viewed in them an "almost idolatrous deference to the mother country."[7] As active members of a coherent transatlantic community, they played a vital imperial role connecting the metropolitan hub to an expanding provincial rim.[8] Although they existed in other colonies, in Virginia the community was based on the template of relationships provided by the political economy in sweet-scented tobacco, and moderates were able to foster a community in which news, questions, and ideas could be constructed, circulated, contested, and resolved.[9] Consequently they succeeded in accommodating differences and facilitating relationships of all sorts.

As the Westminster Parliament came to be increasingly perceived as a threat to liberty and prosperity among provincials whose experience with the metropolis was of a decidedly different sort, so too did the presumptions that had underlain Augustan political culture. Those like John Randolph who continued to espouse the foundational importance of parliamentary supremacy and constitutional sense were increasingly targeted as enemies to liberty. Moderates faced the loss of their "lives, fortunes, and sacred honor" as a result of the "violence, passion, and intemperance" of "false Patriots" as the constitutional crisis reached its zenith in the mid-1770s.[10] Many of them were eventually hounded into quiescence or aggressively purged from the body politic by their less temperate revolutionary counterparts.

The clearest path to understanding the experience of moderates lies in recovering their salient characteristic, something historians have largely overlooked: the persistence of their attachment to what one contemporary called "the spirit of moderation," the political face of the Augustan ethos of politeness that gave such a distinctive cast to the eighteenth century.[11] By the revolutionary crisis, Augustan moderation remained a positive, vital political persuasion as clearly emblazoned on the period's politics as politeness was on its culture. And it possessed the same transatlantic scope.[12]

An Augustan political culture so dependent on a common sense of historical purpose could not forever provide a firm foundation for political discourse among peoples with increasingly diverse historical experiences. By the 1760s, after decades of social and economic change around the Atlantic world and the beginning of a cultural shift from sense to sensibility, the reasonable world of Robert Walpole, David Hume, and Sir John Randolph began to give way to the sensitive one of Horace Walpole, Laurence Sterne, and Thomas Jefferson. A political arena that had once been a forum for polite conversation was, it seemed to moderates, quickly and unaccountably transformed into one of outright combat.[13] Augustan historical consciousness remained largely uncontested for much of the period, until the transformation of that world first challenged and then overwhelmed it, drowning sense in sensibility and leading to a rupture in British political culture of such force that it carried off many (but not all) of the constituent imperial relationships.[14]

When we attempt to recover the Augustan constitutional sense that defined the moderates, we see that it was based on several fundamental and complementary assumptions: a commitment to political moderation as the antidote to party violence; unwavering support for the constitution that emerged from the settlement of 1688; an understanding of the British empire as a community of shared interests;

and a reliance on friendship as the most effective means to pursue those interests. The symbiosis among those fundamentals created a character that distinguished the moderates and their worldview. They carried with them that spirit of moderation that informed the eighteenth century with its distinctive ethos of sense and accommodation and stands in stark contrast to the decades of ideological extremes that preceded it and the "age of passion" that followed.[15] Understanding them, therefore, sheds new light on the sources of tension, fear, and conflict that emerged in the British Atlantic after the Seven Years' War, during its transformation from a political culture of constitutional sense to one of revolutionary sensibility.[16]

Political moderation, however, was not simply the result of the operation of unseen cultural forces. It was a powerful, positive idea. The most erudite thinkers, writers, and politicians of the age were its practitioners, and their works wended their way into Chesapeake coffeehouses, libraries, and correspondence with phenomenal frequency. The philosopher of the Augustan spirit of moderation, if not its secular patron saint, was David Hume. Interestingly enough, where a Virginian stood on Hume's work might be seen as a reliable indicator of the extent to which one could be considered a proper moderate.[17] The Scottish thinker's life, from 1711 to 1776, also tracks the age of constitutional sense as neatly as does his work. Like many adherents to Augustan moderation, Hume was a freethinker in religion, an avowed anti-Jacobite (and anti-Tory), an advocate of Enlightenment values, an epistemological skeptic, and a self-described moderate.[18] Using human nature as his starting point for moral and political thinking, Hume argued that experience proved that passion, not reason, was the dominant force in human psychology and, therefore, political behavior. The challenge facing political actors was to make men passionate for stability, security, and good government, to find ways in which self-interest and desire might be channeled to promote the common good.[19] Republican virtue, Hume might say, is all well and good, but is not a basis for a government that can be relied on to protect the liberty of its citizens. To accomplish that aim, he argued, parties of interest, such as the Whigs, should be preferred to parties of principle, such as the Tories, because adherents to the latter rarely compromised and tended to try to destroy their opponents, characteristics antithetical to the preservation of stability.[20]

And what of kings? A limited monarchy was necessary for constitutional moderation, Hume wrote, because it helped provide the balance between liberty and authority that gave the British constitution its distinctive strength. Of course, every moderate was, by definition, an enemy of royal authority but also had little to fear under Parliament's ostensibly benign rule because "the mere name of king commands little respect; and to talk of a king as GOD's viceregent on earth, or to give him any of those magnificent titles, which formerly dazzled mankind, would but excite laughter in everyone."[21] As much in Hume's political thought as in John Randolph's Virginia political practice, the keys to stability in government were moderation and compromise; vigilance against political excess, the active avoidance of extremes, and a commitment to the balanced, mixed constitution were the keys to moderation.

But what did the spirit of Augustan moderation mean for a province in the midst of almost constant social and economic expansion in the eighteenth century? Between 1710 and 1770, Virginians experienced considerable demographic change, yet politics at every level remained relatively free from conflict.[22] The colony somehow maintained the reputation it earned throughout the British world for its "cool and deliberate"[23] political temperament. Sir John Randolph's statement to the House of Burgesses in August 1734 that the colony had "none of the perturbations which we see every where else arising from the different Views and designs of Factions and Parties" appears to have remained true until the 1760s.[24] Edmund Randolph echoed the memory of Virginia's Augustan political culture in the next century when he wrote that before the revolution in Virginia it was unwise "ever to push to extremity any theory which by practical relations may not be accommodated."[25]

Cracks in the Augustans' hold on the political culture began to appear on both sides of the Atlantic following the suppression of the Jacobite rebellion of 1745.[26] After the defeat of Charles Edward Stuart at Culloden, what might be seen as a transatlantic epistemological crisis appears to have settled on the British world. A writer in 1751 observed that "the very Idea of a common Danger" ought to have constituted "a common Cause" among Britons everywhere to attend to threats to their constitutional rights and liberty, now that they had been returned to a proper appreciation of them, in no small measure by the efforts of Anglican worthies such as the Rev. William Stith and the Rev. Andrew Trebeck in providing them with lessons from the pulpit. The anonymous author observed that it had "become apparent from many Years Experience, that the whole Study of Those in Power, (next to the keeping the Hold they have got) is to empoverish, harass, and over-awe their Fellow-Subject." Employing the iconography of the English past, the author opined that the 1745 rebellion should have been "like the firing of the Beacons along the Coast; and accordingly the whole Nation ought to take the Alarm," but, instead, the result has been "our own Numbness, Coldness and Deadness in whatever related to the Public; our own impolitic and ruinous Distrust of each other."[27] Another writer reported that "Political Lying" had reached a stage of high development in which it was then "hardened to that unblushing Assurance, that can support being detected, and laugh at the Weakness, that believed it."[28] Faith in reason as the bastion of veracity appeared to erode rapidly. As Horace Walpole explained to a friend, "Man can give an appearance of reason to every thing he says. He can lend falsehood the semblance of Truth; he can establish false principles, draw false conclusions, form false hypotheses, and yet continue to seem a rational Being. One cause of these deceptions is the mysterious & fugitive nature of Truth."[29] Charges of corruption and illegitimacy, of falsehood and immorality, were levied at political leaders with increasing frequency.

The growth of distrust was, in reality, a tool of the cosmopolitan and country opposition to the ministry in the years immediately before the rebellion of '45, when Sir Robert Walpole found himself savagely lampooned on London streets and in provincial coffeehouses. Jonathan Swift, Alexander Pope, and John Gay all aimed their pens at "the skreenmaster" as the personification of a world in which morality was seen by some as increasingly at a discount. Walpole's resignation in 1742 was taken by some to herald the end of the ossified politeness that had obscured the real motivations in politics. As William Beverley, the son of the historian Robert Beverley and a provincial merchant-planter in Virginia, observed to a English correspondent in August 1742, "Walpole & his party have had a long reign of it, to ye great prejudice of ye Kingdom, & now ye Country party have prevailed[.] I hope ye affairs will soon take another turn."[30] Beverley pointed out the distinctions between himself and those in the province who had remained Walpole's supporters, echoing the observation of his correspondent, Lord Thomas Fairfax, that the change in government "will not be pleasing to some of our Gentry here."[31] One of those supporters, the twenty-year-old Peyton Randolph, who was in London at the time of the resignation of Walpole, to whom Randolph's father owed a great deal, airily reported to John Custis in Virginia that "we see all the Courts of Europe in an Uproar, & grand Revolutions in many of them. Here has been a very great one, as little expected before the Sitting of the Parliament, as that I shall come to be Grand Signor. Sr Robert being no longer able to keep a Majority in the House, was obliged voluntarily to give up all his Places; which was the most honorable Way of parting with them."[32] Radical Virginians later found their own illustration of Walpolean political corruption in Speaker of the House of Burgesses John Robinson ("the Big man" in the words of one planter), whose death in 1766 revealed that, as treasurer of the colony, he had lent, mostly on bond, almost £100,000 in public funds to more than two hundred people, including William Byrd III (the largest recipient at almost £15,000), Peter Jefferson (£52.12.0), and Patrick Henry (£11.6.8).[33]

This opposition critique of "false Patriots" dovetailed with, and was reinforced by, the cultural turn to sensibility.[34] Decades of political politeness and mistrust of passion began to give way to a growing reliance on feeling as a more accurate barometer of morality and truth than was sense and reason.[35] Provincial Virginians such as Patrick Henry and Thomas Jefferson, men who spent little time outside of the colony and dealt mainly with Scottish merchants and their cosmopolitan financiers, might have stood for similar Whiggish principles to their metropolitan compatriots, but their increasingly vehement and forceful denunciations of moderation and parliamentary sovereignty as the only tried and true means of protecting those principles owed more to the Earl of Shaftesbury and Frances Hutcheson than to moderates Joseph Addison and David Hume.[36] As one historian put it, for provincials such as Henry and Jefferson, "the empire was more remote" as they were "more likely to deal with resident factors at Scottish stores in their own neighborhoods and in a relationship based more on suspicion than on longtime confidence. When they became concerned with imperial issues, their response stood to be quick, direct, and not especially subtle."[37] It placed them on the opposite side of a growing divide in constitutional identities that ran through the British world. Just as Sterne, Edmund Burke, and Horace Walpole argued for a greater recognition of "a moral sense grounded in shared feeling," Richard Henry Lee and Landon Carter attacked moderates as traitors and Tories because they lobbied for stability, tranquility, and compromise of imperial political differences.[38]

Our modern understanding of "Tories" and "Loyalists" in Revolutionary Virginia is a relic of the eighteenth-century cultural turn to sensibility and the meanings that nineteenth-century romantic writers later heaped upon them.[39] To understand them as they saw themselves unfurls a rather different historical narrative. For most of the Anglophone world, *Tory* became, after the Augustan overhaul of political culture in the early part of the century, little more than an epithet used to tar one's political opponents, without any concrete attachment to a constitutional persuasion. The term gained currency throughout the American colonies in the 1770s when the self-described "real" Whigs, those for whom sensibility was a key element of their personal and political character, applied it promiscuously to anyone who did not cooperate with their political program—for instance by speaking out for compromise with the British ministry or by failing to sign nonimportation agreements.[40] In the revolutionary crisis, the term seems to have first appeared in the *Virginia Gazette* in 1774 and 1775 when coupled with thinly veiled, and quite impolite, threats of physical violence against constitutional moderates such as John Randolph and Ralph Wormeley. "Patriot" polemicists branded Randolph, Wormeley, and others as the ultimate anti-Whigs, whose mere presence in the province represented a threat to liberty.[41] There is no evidence that either Randolph or Wormeley, or any other Virginian who remained committed to Augustan moderation, ever seriously described himself or herself as a Tory. To do so would have been a rank betrayal of their constitutional sense of fundamental Britishness. John Randolph's son, Edmund, acknowledged as much when he later reflected on the "multitudes" that "could now be cited, who . . . were branded as Tories, though spotless as to treason even in thought; who could not comprehend what was to be the issue of provoking the fury of the British nation and were yet innocent even as to wishes of harm to their country; who believed in a chance of reconciliation, if excesses were spared; who might feel sufficient irritation at the distant danger of an abstract principle."[42] It is highly unlikely that a proper Tory existed anywhere in Virginia.

Yet the term stuck. Used so often by Patriots against their opponents as a convenient way to paint over the complexity of the issues at stake in the constitutional crisis and bolster their claims of American unity, the fiction was enshrined in the first histories of the Revolution, resurrected in the party battles of the Early Republic, celebrated on Cambridge's "Tory Row" in post-Revolution Massachusetts, and further embellished by Whig historians.[43] A Tory myth was created by historians to reinforce the fiction of unified colonial opposition to British tyranny and became so firmly entrenched in the historiography of the Revolution that, despite the work of modern historians, few scholars have bothered to question it.[44]

Historiographical misunderstandings of the term *Loyalist* are somewhat easier to understand and therefore rather more difficult to recover, because the term was embraced by so many moderates and others who opposed the Patriot movement.[45] Clouding the matter is the fact that Loyalists often spoke of their own cause in terms of support for the king or the authority of the Crown. Samuel Johnson unhelpfully defined *Loyalist* in 1756 as "one who professes uncommon adherence to his king."[46] Horace Walpole reflected similarly on the whole concept of loyalty. "Loyalty is a word I do not find either in the Bible or the statute book. It is a French word & conveys a French Idea: but ought to have a reciprocal signification. It comes from *Loy,* the Law, but is now confounded with *Royauté* but ought to imply only Attachment to the Laws, & then Loyalty wd be as much a Duty from the King to the people as from the people to the King."[47] For a Whig of any persuasion, support for a "British king" or for the "Hanoverian Succession" was actually a celebration of Parliament, for what else was a British monarch but a sovereign whose authority, whose very position, was circumscribed by the mixed constitution in which the representatives of the people reigned supreme?

Along with the social and economic changes that transformed British Virginia in the eighteenth century came the development of a new constitutional identity, a revolutionary sensibility more universal and cosmopolitan than its metropolitan shade because not tied to English political history. The disconnection from the history laid out by thinkers such as Hume created a different effective truth that was more accessible, and therefore more inclusive, to people who were products of different political histories that reached beyond 1688 to the Magna Carta or even further, to a natural law that came from the very beginning of time itself. It was this constitutional identity, largely made possible by striking shifts in transatlantic political economies and the relationships that overlaid them, that shaped the political thought of "provincial cosmopolitans" such as Thomas Jefferson.

In feeling, and being, disconnected from metropolitan Britain, Jefferson was hardly unique among his contemporaries. He was of the growing sort, unlike Randolph and his moderate compatriots who had spent important parts of their lives in England and retained vital ties to it, who stood in no need of "anglicization." In the absence of a more direct alternative, Jefferson's political experience, and the abstract, idealized imperial relationship he and many of his provincial compatriots envisioned, was a persuasion of an empire that, in an oft-employed phrase that Adam Smith used to criticize the British ministry in 1774, "existed in imagination."[48] Jefferson's vision of the imperial relationship was a far cry from the mixed constitution and unseverable authority of king, lords, and commons understood and, more important, practiced by John Randolph, who described himself as "nurtured" in such "mixed Principles."[49] Their competing visions of the imperial tie could not be reconciled without a framework for mediation and accommodation of differences. The absence of such a framework at the imperial level was the sine qua non in creating political and ideological conditions ripe for separation.

In 1775 Jefferson was a reputable but not terribly well-known lawyer and member of the House of Burgesses. He was thirty-two years old, had been married to Martha Wayles Skelton for four years, and was the father of two daughters, Martha and Jane. The small family lived in a half-finished house on top of Jefferson's "little mountain," Monticello. He had only recently become a member of the exclusive club that comprised Albemarle County's largest slaveholders and landowners as the result of a bequest to his wife from the estate of her late father, John Wayles.[50]

Jefferson's view of the world in which he lived, however, was not, or at least not yet, from the perspective of his mountaintop retreat. His understanding of Virginia's place in the British world, and his place in both, was formed where he had spent most of his life before 1775, only a few miles down the mountain from Monticello, at Shadwell, a two-story, wood-framed house situated on a slight rise next to the Rivanna River. He was born there in 1743, and the house remained home for his mother, four of his sisters, and his younger brother.[51] He was not yet the iconic cosmopolitan statesman, philosopher, architect, and gardener, thoughtfully considering his world from atop his mountain. Shadwell was the symbol of his early outlook on the world. In other words in 1775 there was much more Shadwell than sage in Jefferson. To understand that place, how he got there, and what he saw from there is to have a clearer understanding of the factors that shaped the provincial perception of the relationship between Virginia and Britain he shared with so many of his contemporaries.

The Jefferson family's journey to Shadwell began in the 1720s when Thomas's father, Peter Jefferson, settled at Fine Creek in Goochland County, a few miles above the falls of the James River, on land inherited from his own father.[52] To trek that far west in the second decade of the eighteenth century was to fall, almost literally, off the British imperial map. A drawing of the province reprinted in 1723 depicted British Virginia as a thirty-mile-wide zone of settlement that hugged one hundred miles of the western edge of the Chesapeake Bay. The part of Henrico County that would become Goochland in 1727 was a blank expanse of land so irrelevant to the cartographer that he used it as space for the royal coat of arms of George I.[53] The only space in British Virginia that seemed to matter to the cartographer was found along the rivers and coastline. Williamsburg and James Town—each a day's ride from Goochland—were the only towns "in the whole Country," the rest of the colony consisting of a number of plantations separated from each other by substantial distances.[54]

The most conspicuous absence in these visual and written early eighteenth-century representations of Virginia is that of almost any evidence of imperial authority. The government maintained no military presence in Virginia and, according to the accounts of the Treasury, spent almost no money there.[55] If one adds to this absence of imperial authority the fact that Virginia was separated from London by three thousand miles of ocean and three months of travel by ship, then Peter Jefferson's Goochland home must have seemed a rather long way from the metropolitan center of Augustan England.

London came a little closer to Peter Jefferson in the 1730s when he met and married Jane Randolph.[56] Her father, Isham, was the son of an Englishman, William Randolph, who had immigrated to Virginia from Ireland in the 1670s and proceeded to follow a rapidly developing Virginia tradition of marrying well and producing a brood of children. In Randolph's case he was exceptionally successful on both counts. His wife brought him a thousand of acres of land and gave him seven sons and two daughters, all of whom survived into adulthood, an almost unheard-of feat at the time.[57] Although born in Virginia, Isham Randolph was the captain of a merchant ship and spent most of his time in London, where he managed his business interests in transporting sweet-scented tobacco and enslaved Africans to markets across the Atlantic and dabbled in colonial affairs. It was in the Borough of Tower Hamlets, in a maritime neighborhood called Shadwell, that he met his wife, Jane Rogers. They were married in Whitechapel Parish in 1717 and lived in a home on "Shakespeare's Walk" in Shadwell for the next eighteen years. A daughter, Jane, was born there in 1720 and baptized around the corner as the offspring of "Jane and Isham Randolph, mariner."[58] In 1725 Randolph returned to Virginia with his English family and settled them at Dungeness, a property on the James River that he named for the familiar spit of land that marked for all ship captains the final turn from the Atlantic Ocean into the English Channel and the port of London.[59] Jane, then eighteen years old, married the thirty-one-year-old Peter Jefferson in October 1739.[60]

Together Jane and Peter moved to a two-hundred-acre plot of land that Peter bought from William Randolph, Jane's uncle, for the "biggest bowl of Arrack punch" at Henry Wetherburn's tavern in Williamsburg.[61] The move may have been a simple one, as Jane brought neither land nor servants nor slaves to the marriage. Her only dowry appears to have been two hundred pounds, which was noted in her father's will to be paid if there were sufficient funds left over after the satisfaction of his debts. There is no evidence that the payment was ever made.[62] More than fifty miles to the northwest of Goochland, in what became Albemarle County in 1744, Jane and Peter established a permanent reminder of her connection to London by calling their new home "Shadwell," which might well have had an ironic intention, because the bucolic, rather isolated Piedmont setting could not, for Jane, have been more strikingly different from her home in the poor, crowded maritime neighborhood on the Thames where she spent part of her childhood.[63]

During the middle decades of the eighteenth century, transatlantic economic and social processes dramatically transformed Albemarle County, along with the rest of Virginia. "Whereas seventeenth-century settlement had been mainly

English," one historian has found, "eighteenth-century emigration was emphatically British."[64] By 1750 Scots had come to dominate Virginia's commerce outside of the Tidewater and captured from their London competitors fifty percent of the tobacco trade.[65] Glasgow overtook London as the center of the tobacco trade in 1758.[66] Socially and culturally, the face of Virginia changed, too, as its white society swelled from a fairly homogenous English population of 55,163 in 1710 to an extraordinarily diverse British society of 199,156 in 1760.[67] At the middle of the century, Winchester, a village more than one hundred miles north of Shadwell, was "inhabited by a spurious race of mortals known as the Scotch-Irish."[68] The size of an average holding of property decreased, while the number of property owners rose by 66 percent between 1704 and 1750.[69] The most striking component of social and economic change, because of its relationship to the rapidity of the population's growth and the colony's cultural departure from English society, was the skyrocketing presence of enslaved Africans.[70] By 1760 one out of every three British Virginians was either African or of recent African descent, with many, if not most, of those Africans heading to the Jeffersons' Piedmont.[71]

At Shadwell, Jefferson could literally see that transformation of British Virginia. Hanging on the wall of his father's study was a massive "Map of the Most Inhabited Part of Virginia" that Peter Jefferson himself had helped draw, with his friend, Joshua Fry.[72] A 1721 report to the Board of Trade had noted only two towns in the entire colony; Jefferson and Fry demarcated twenty-five of them strung along Virginia's rivers and penetrating deep into its interior. The earlier map had outlined seventeen counties; Jefferson and Fry distinguished thirty-three. In fact by the time Fry and Jefferson's map was printed, British Virginians had created twenty-two new counties in thirty years and went on to establish ten more in the subsequent two decades.[73]

The names given to those counties suggested the severing of ties to English places and memories. Earlier maps clearly show the metropolitan attachment of Virginians as fourteen of the first twenty-five counties were named after English places, even Home Counties, such as Middlesex, Richmond, Surry, Norfolk, and Essex. In stark contrast, of the last thirty-four counties created in colonial Virginia, only one was named for an English location—Sussex. Instead names associated with German places and members of the royal household, such as Hanover, Brunswick, and Lunenberg, or with former governors of the province, such as Spotsylvania, Goochland, and Albemarle, dotted the landscape. Measuring a four feet long by two feet high, the map clearly illustrated to young Jefferson at Shadwell, and to the earl of Halifax, president of the Board of Trade at Whitehall, as few other mediums could, the growing extent and diversity of the Old Dominion.

What neither Jefferson nor Halifax could see, however, were the forces that drove Virginia's striking growth and that created the persuasions that eventually separated its peoples. Halifax in particular could not miss a cartouche depicting an idealized scene from Virginia life at midcentury, placed right above the dedication to him.[74] It depicts a group of men on a busy wharf. Several dark-skinned men, clearly African slaves, swathed in cloth, are engaged in the hard work of packing and rolling hogsheads of tobacco onto ships preparing to set sail. Another enslaved man can be seen delivering a goblet on a tray to a seated, fair-skinned gentleman, whose clay smoking pipe, finery, and air of effortlessness set him apart, even aloof, from the rest of the scene, even though other men, one in the garb of a merchant or a factor, the other dressed as a younger version of the gentleman, look to him for counsel or favor. In the background another man, maybe the captain of one of the ships or a tobacco inspector, stands with his back turned to the rest of the party; holding a tablet, he appears to be marking the weight of each hogshead before it is loaded. To young Jefferson, growing up at Shadwell in the 1750s and 1760s, the seated gentleman could have been any one of a number of provincial planters of his father's generation, men who were born in Virginia and had probably never traveled far beyond its borders. Their identification with Britishness came only from the books and newspapers they read; what they might have been taught at the College of William and Mary or by a private tutor; the occasional correspondence they shared with mercantile contacts or other Americans overseas; the symbolic presence of the Crown in material goods they possessed; the mythical presence of the king in official proceedings, in the person of the resident royal administrator (who may or may not have looked or acted the part); and, perhaps most telling of all, in the ways in which the particular transatlantic political economy of which they were part, and the differential British and provincial mercantile legislation, impacted their lives.

For Jefferson, as for his father and many other Piedmont tobacco planters from small to relatively large, the merchant figure in the map cartouche, who made much of the Virginians' material consumption and western expansion possible, was a Scottish factor—a local representative of a Scottish mercantile house. In the case of Peter and Thomas Jefferson, their factors were John Harvie, a close friend of Peter's and one of Thomas's guardians after his father's death, who worked for Alexander McCaul and the Glasgow firm of Kippen and Company, and Peter Davie, who ran a local store for another Glasgow tobacco firm, James and Robert Donald and Company.[75] By 1750 Scots "factors were established in every corner of the country," extending credit to planters on generous terms, made possible by the French tobacco monopoly, to guarantee full cargoes and a quick turnaround time for shipping to Scotland and from there to fulfill their commitments to European markets.[76] By the summer of 1769, one Virginia planter-merchant could accurately describe to an English partner that "ye Spirit of consigning is broke, & ye Scotch are become ye Engrossers."[77]

Cosmopolitan, especially Scottish, influences also played a prominent role in Jefferson's education. When he was nine, his first school experience was at the Latin School of the Reverend William Douglas. Upon first arriving in the colony from Scotland in the late 1740s, Douglas set himself up as a tutor to a family in

Westmoreland County. He soon chose to go to England and was successful in being ordained in the Anglican ministry. Douglas returned to Virginia and preached at Dover Church in Goochland, where Peter Jefferson was a vestryman.[78] Thomas remained a student under Douglas, learning the rudiments of Latin and Greek along with French, for five years, until Peter Jefferson's death in 1757.[79]

According to Jefferson's later recollections, the greatest influence on his learning came from another Scot, William Small, professor of natural philosophy at the College of William and Mary. Small was, according to Jefferson, the man who "probably fixed the destinies" of his life.[80] Less than ten years Jefferson's senior, Small was from the east coast of northern Scotland (not quite the Highlands), the small town of Carmyllie, just north of Dundee. He stayed nearby for his education, attending Marischal College in Aberdeen, the same school that Virginia's longtime senior cleric the Reverend James Blair had attended, from which he received an MA in 1755. Three years later, at the age of twenty-four, he took up the post at William and Mary and began a relationship with Jefferson that lasted the remainder of Small's short life. Jefferson spent less than two years at the college.[81] (Actually, when one considers the summer and Christmas holidays, and the three months in 1761 during which the school was shut down because of a smallpox scare, one wonders how much time Jefferson actually spent there.) During Jefferson's time in Williamsburg, Small introduced him to both George Wythe and Lt. Gov. Francis Fauquier. The four often dined together, and "to the habitual conversations on these occasions," Jefferson wrote, he owed much instruction.[82]

It must have been quite an unorthodox gathering, which raises the question of just what kind of instruction Jefferson gained at their table. Small was a young Scots intellectual at war with his college colleagues over reforms to the curriculum. Wythe was an esteemed lawyer but had received little formal education, had not been out of the colony in his more than forty years, and had earned the reputation among his more metropolitan acquaintances as a tiresome pedant, although one observer later said of him that "I have seldom known a man possess more modesty, or a more dove-like simplicity and gentleness of manner."[83] Fauquier, who arrived in Williamsburg at the same time as Small, was a Londoner who had served as a director of the South Sea Company and as a governor of the Foundling Hospital, and was a member of the Royal Society whose reputation as the ablest man who ever filled the governor's office may have rested mostly on his tendency to ignore instructions from his superiors. There was much to learn for the twenty-year-old Jefferson, who eagerly absorbed all the lessons this odd triumvirate had to teach. In any case the *petit salon* did not last. Small loathed Virginia and left for England after only four years in Williamsburg, leaving Jefferson in the care of Wythe as a law student.[84] Jefferson remained with Wythe for much of the next three years, returning to Shadwell and a new law practice in 1767. Fauquier's health steadily worsened as tensions between the colonies and Britain increased after the Stamp Act. He died in Virginia in 1768.

For the next several years, Jefferson lived at Shadwell, practiced law in Albemarle and nearby counties, and started to construct the house that later became Monticello. His only experience with anyone in the metropolis consisted of his occasional correspondence with his bookseller, Thomas Adams, who also happened to be a Virginian. Late in 1768 Albemarle voters elected Jefferson to the House of Burgesses, but his first session, the following May, ended after only nine days. Fauquier's successor, the mercurial Norborne Berkeley, Baron de Botetourt, dissolved the House for adopting resolutions disclaiming the right of Parliament to levy taxes in Virginia. The next day the former burgesses met and drafted an agreement to ban the importation of a number of British goods in protest of the Townshend Acts, after which Jefferson returned to Shadwell.

The next year, 1770, turned out to be something of a watershed in Jefferson's life. In February he and his family suffered a major blow. He reported to his friend John Page the "loss of my mother's house by fire, and . . . of every paper I had in the world, and almost every book . . . principally on my books of common law."[85] In March, British troops fired on a crowd of violent demonstrators in Boston. In June, Botetourt commissioned Jefferson "Lieutenant of the County of Albemarle and Chief Commander of all his Majesty's Militia, Horse and Foot."[86] Two weeks later Jefferson affixed his name to another nonimportation resolution that appointed county committees to enforce the previous measures. Shortly thereafter, on 27 June, he joined his fellow burgesses in a unanimous agreement to petition the king to end Parliament's pretension to tax Americans. Botetourt died, much lamented by provincials, in October 1770. In November, Jefferson "removed to the mountain," where he had "but one room, which, like the coblar's, serves me for parlour for kitchen and hall" and "for bedchamber and study, too."[87]

For all his provincialism, it is interesting to note that it seems that Jefferson fully intended to enter the Augustan world that defined Virginia culture. His father's rather idiosyncratic library included its secular scriptures—volumes of the *Spectator* and the *Guardian* that were, by the time Jefferson was born in 1743, almost thirty years old yet still in demand—which Jefferson recalled having read as a boy. More telling was his intention to follow the example of his cousins, many of whom had to gone to England for school, college, or the Inns of Court. Although none of his first cousins made the transatlantic trip (except for his mother's brother's family, who did not need to make the voyage because they actually lived in the English port city of Bristol), among his second cousins were John and Peyton Randolph, who had both gone to Middle Temple, and Ryland Randolph, who attended Trinity Hall, Cambridge, and Middle Temple. Among his more immediate contemporaries in his family, four—William Randolph, Beverley Randolph, John Randolph, and Philip Ludwell Grymes went to Eton in the 1760s; Theodorick Bland (who went on to medical school at the University of Edinburgh), Robert Bolling, and Robert Munford attended school at Wakefield in Yorkshire; and David and Richard Kidder Meade were at Harrow.[88] There they joined, in the 1750s and 1760s, a surprising number of their countrymen, such as Ralph Wormeley, Lewis and James Burwell, George Lee Mason Fitzhugh, Philip Ludwell, Arthur Lee, and Alexander and James Spotswood at Eton; John Carter, William Taylor, and Thomas Taylor Byrd at Tunbridge; Robert Beverley, Richard Henry Lee, Edward and John Ambler, John Banister, William Henry Fairfax, and Jack Power at Wakefield; Thomas Nelson at Hackney; John Baylor at Putney; Gawin Corbin at Grinstead; and John Brunskill at Appleby.[89] Although Grymes and Lewis Burwell both went on to Balliol College at Oxford, Cambridge appears to have been the school of choice for most of the Virginians who went to university in England, including Beverley (Trinity), John Ambler (Trinity), Baylor (Caius), Corbin (Queen's), Brunskill (Pembroke), Nelson (Christ's) and Wormeley (Trinity Hall). Furthermore many of them were simultaneously entered at the Inns of Court, although proof that they actually made the transatlantic trip and attended has been harder to come by (Henry Lee, for example, was entered at Middle Temple but never matriculated). That a decided majority of the Virginians who were educated in Britain became moderate Loyalists, in one form or another, was no coincidence. As Benjamin Rush later wrote, Thomas Nelson "informed me that he was the only person out of 9 or 10 Virginians that were sent with him to England for education that had taken a part in the American Revolution. The rest were all Tories"—a statement not far from the complete truth of the matter.[90]

And it is clear that Jefferson intended to join them. After finishing at William and Mary, he informed his friends of his plan to go to school in England. He explained to John Page in a letter from Shadwell in the summer of 1763 that his "resolution of going to Britain" was the main impediment to any idea to, in Page's words, "go immediately and lay siege in form" to his beloved "Belinda," Rebecca Burwell. To "begin an affair of that kind now, and carry it on so long a time in form is by no means a proper plan," he explained.[91] In any event any hint of the plan abruptly dropped from Jefferson's surviving correspondence, and there is no further mention of it after 1763. His Belinda went on to marry another, Jaquelin Ambler.[92]

Jefferson therefore remained a provincial. Most illustrative of his absence of transatlantic ties was, in 1770, the first—and what turned out to be the only—time to use whatever metropolitan influence he possessed to promote the interest of a friend. The episode proved woefully, even laughably, inadequate and serves as a reminder, on top of a largely meaningless militia commission, agreements to cut off British imports, and the other wrenching events of that year, of just how disconnected Jefferson and many of his fellow radicals were from their moderate counterparts.

James Ogilvie was a Highland Scot and Marischal College alumnus with whom Jefferson became friends in the 1760s when Ogilvie served as a tutor for a fellow planter's children. It became clear to Ogilvie, like many of his countrymen, that a living as an Anglican minister was better suited to his nature and his prospects for a wife than that of a lowly tutor. The power to ordain ministers for the colonies rested with the bishop of London, so Ogilvie went to the metropolis in 1769 in hopes of obtaining the bishop's approval. Because of a misunderstanding between Ogilvie and the Reverend James Horrocks, the bishop of London's representative in Virginia, over the limited extent of Ogilvie's grasp of Greek, the bishop claimed that it was beyond his power to ordain him in the face of Horrocks's opposition. Thus Ogilvie turned to Jefferson for help. From London in March 1770, he wrote Jefferson a plaintive letter applying "for your friendly offices" in obtaining letters of support for him from prominent Virginians or, in the alternative, convincing Horrocks to remove his opposition. He asked Jefferson to use his contacts in the colony to "procure a letter from [Lord] Fairfax [the proprietor of Virginia's entire northern region] requesting my ordination." A letter to James Abercromby, the colony's agent in London, also "may be of special service." And would Jefferson "procure another certificate signed by as many gentlemen of fortune and credit" as he could? "I have here prescribed you a severe trial of your friendship," Ogilvie admitted, but he thought that Jefferson would "not spare a little trouble to execute that on which the success of my future life depends."[93]

There was only one problem with Ogilvie's request. Neither Lord Fairfax nor James Abercromby had ever heard of Thomas Jefferson. Consequently any application from Jefferson to either of the men would have done Ogilvie very little good. Such impediments, however, did not stop Jefferson from enlisting the aid of his lone metropolitan connection: Thomas Adams, the Virginian bookseller. Jefferson explained to Adams the distressing situation in which Ogilvie, "this worthy representative of episcopal faith," found himself due to Horrocks's unreasonable argument that Ogilvie "did not possess a critical knowledge of the Greek." Ogilvie would have to remain in London, and the aspiring divine was financially unprepared for a long stay. Jefferson asked Adams to obtain credit for Ogilvie among the bookseller's "mercantile friends in London for any monies of which he may be in need, for the repayment of which I enter myself security." Financial assistance was the only thing Jefferson could do to help his friend in the metropolis. He clearly described to Adams the transatlantic political handicap under which he was laboring: "Having no connections or correspondence on that side of the water I apply to the single friendship from which I could hope effectual aid to any person there in whose welfare I am interested."[94]

The position of disaffection from the metropolis in which Jefferson so inconveniently found himself was representative of many other provincials who became radicals. Given the dominant shift of tobacco in the colony's economy from sweet-scented to oronoco and the dramatic patterns of British immigration to the Chesapeake in the eighteenth century, most connections had shifted to Scotland or were spread throughout the British Atlantic. These centrifugal historical processes appear to have been solely with political forces that may have done Virginia's interests more harm than good, comprised as they were of political agitators, such as John Wilkes, "political deviants whose position on the outermost fringes of politics exempted them to a large extent from many of the central imperatives of British political life."[95] A Massachusetts visitor to London confirmed as much when he informed John Hancock in early 1771 that "it would astonish any person to be inform'd of the misrepresentations which have been made for four or five years past to the Ministry by persons on your side of the Atlantic" but that he hoped, in vain as it turned out, "it will all come out in time."[96]

Nevertheless, in spite of the disconnection and miscommunication, many Virginians continued to have faith in the politics of moderation, constitutional sense, and reason—and the constitution they were intended to protect—well into the 1770s. Political actors such as Ralph Wormeley, John Randolph, Robert Beverley, and Robert Munford adhered to the Augustan style of political engagement and its definition of Britishness. A wise man, according to Wormeley in 1772, remained "not unreasonably attached to his own notions, delivering his opinions with coolness, and engaging the unheated approbation of rational men."[97] In the midst of the turmoil of 1775, John Randolph argued for "lenient Measures and moderate Expedients" that would "restore us to our former Tranquillity."[98]

In a striking turn from just a decade or two before, however, both were denounced with frightening ferocity as enemies to their country.[99] The political language their parents had spoken, a discourse characterized by its "Cool Reasoning," was replaced, almost overnight, it seemed, by the "harsh language of the most violent and intemperate."[100] Beverley, for one, was utterly astonished by the "strange Metamorphosis" that had come over Virginia. He could not understand how men who had been the closest of friends and relations could "no longer differ in political Opinions." No one, it seemed, was at all interested in "accommodating this Dispute," as if the constitutional argument was about something other than the means to secure an end to which all parties agreed: the liberty of the subject. Beverley certainly did "not esteem a Man a Jot the less for differing from me in Opinion" and would submit willingly to any argument "of sound Sense." But the "Temper of the Time," he admitted with no small measure of resignation, was "inflamed."[101] As far as they were concerned, constitutional sense had left the Chesapeake.

Robert Munford captured the encroaching revolutionary sensibility in his unproduced play, The Patriots, written in the mid-1770s.[102] Set "in times like these, of war and danger," Munford saw the Augustan moderates of old as the real Patriots. They were "mild, and secretly anxious for their country, but modest in expressions of zeal." False Patriots, on the other hand, did not know the meaning of the word moderation. They raised "the people's suspicions against all moderate men" and persecuted "innocent men, only because they differ in opinion."[103] Political debate was no longer a polite, reasonable conversation over different means to a common end; it had transformed into with-us-or-against-us combat over irreconcilable abstractions.

John Randolph was a particularly apt representative of the moderates who remained loyal to constitutional sense. It was not only part of his family history but also his personal experience. His father, Sir John Randolph, was educated for the law at Gray's Inn in London and called to the bar in 1717. He spent much of the next twenty years of his life shuttling between London and Virginia on various political missions for the colony, including the Excise Affair in the 1730s, and was one of only several native Virginians to have been knighted.[104] Both of his sons, John and Peyton, attended Middle Temple in London and were called to the bar, Peyton in 1744 and John in 1755.[105]

Randolph's experience in London must have profoundly shaped his moderation, every bit as much as Jefferson's provincialism shaped his radicalism. Just as Sir John first arrived in London in the midst of the flurry of patriotic Whiggish Loyalism in opposition to a Stuart threat, his son reached the metropolis in the midst of the citywide response to the Young Pretender's invasion, when "Loyalists" in the city reacted with blazing expressions of support for the Hanoverian monarch as the symbol of parliamentary sovereignty and, therefore, worthy of the commitment of "all true Patriots, all Lovers of Liberty." against Tory and Jacobite ideologues.[106] He was there when news arrived in April 1746 of the victory at Culloden. Horace Walpole described the remarkable scene in Randolph's London: "The town is all blazing around me, as I write, with fireworks and illuminations: I have some inclination to lap up half a dozen skyrockets to make you drink the Duke's health."[107] It was an illumination that, according to one newspaper, "seemed to change the night into day." The fashionable squares were aflame with flambeaux, the windows full of wax candles. From cellar to garret in house after house, all was an extraordinary sight—the sort of the thing that would likely be burned into the memory of any who saw it.[108]

This personal experience, especially when combined with that of his father, lends a great deal of meaning to Randolph's later statement that he "was nurtured in the mixed Principles of Obedience and Freedom, as they stand ingrafted in the English Constitution."[109] To be a Loyalist, therefore, in the parlance of the Augustan political culture in which both father and son were deeply immersed, was to remain loyal to the freedom secured by a sovereign parliament and symbolized by an appointed king—and, by definition, opposed to Tories and royalists wherever they might be found.[110]

Randolph's constitutional persuasion infused his *Considerations on the Present State of Virginia*, written in 1774 as an analysis of the developing constitutional crisis. "A more pleasing and natural Connection never subsisted between any different Bodies of Men than did of late," he wrote, "between Great Britain and her Colonies." British peoples on both sides of the Atlantic were "not only allied by Blood" but "still farther united, by the extensive Trade and Commerce carried on between us." Randolph saw their "Manners . . . Religion, and Language, the same." There was "no Diversity between the Laws of each Country but such as local Circumstance" required. Given such a congenial, multivalent relationship between the colonies and Great Britain, surely, Randolph argued, some practical accommodation could be reached between the two so long as men who possessed "a serene Mind, and sound Understanding" did not give way to "those who are running the Race of Popularity."[111]

In the 1770s moderates such as Randolph believed that *British America* was a term that was not only compatible but also complementary. The combination produced a relationship of far more strength and value than either could achieve separately. Moderates could hardly envision a world in which America's interests were not the same as Britain's, in which they did not continue to be part of the same ongoing English history that began in 1688. Yet, in August 1775, writing in his study at Monticello, Jefferson apologized to Randolph that "the situation of our country should render it not eligible to you to remain longer in it."[112] Randolph was no longer "eligible" to stay in Virginia because the predominant constitutional persuasion of the colony, and therefore its entire political culture, had indeed changed. Radical Patriots of revolutionary sensibility such as Jefferson could see a way to maintain the principles of the British constitution only by charting a new historical course. Randolph and many other Augustan Virginians could not accept that new course—and its violent repercussions—and chose to remain within the English history that their reason and experience proved was the only reliable way to protect freedom and liberty. "We both of us seem to be steering opposite Courses," Randolph observed to Jefferson. "The success of either lies in the Womb of Time."

Almost one thousand British Virginians whose connections with Great Britain were, in the end, only strong enough to help them leave America steered their course to the British army and navy and to England, including several members of the Virginia Governor's Council, former members of the House of Burgesses, and sons and daughters of some the most prominent families in the colony.[113] Among the Loyalists were names familiar to any student of the colonial Chesapeake, such as Randolph, Lee, Page, Byrd, Wormeley, Corbin, and Grymes. Dozens of them fought as officers in Loyalist regiments, including Jefferson's distant cousins, Beverley Robinson and John Randolph Grymes, who was wounded at Brandywine fighting against his friend and fellow Etonian John Spotswood. In doing so they often left behind every piece of property they owned, from their homes to the clothes in their wardrobes. Randolph, his wife, and his daughters, for example, left everything they had in Williamsburg—family, friends, and every belonging they could not easily carry with them. Every Loyalist who owned a slave had to make the choice between leaving for England or Scotland as the best means of staying British or remaining a slaveowner, because they could not be both.[114] In fact the two slaves of the only recorded Virginia Loyalist to make the attempt asserted their freedom the moment they stepped onto English soil in 1775—and they received it on the spot.[115]

Those moderate Virginians who could not leave were in many ways much less fortunate than those who had to leave everything behind. Members of the Council and House of Burgesses, such as Ralph Wormeley Jr. and John Tayloe Corbin, were arrested, sent away from their homes, and kept under guard for years. Wormeley was allowed to return to his house and family in 1778 only to find that all that he owned had been carried away by rogue bands of both Patriots and Loyalists.[116] William Byrd III, another councilor, faced a bleaker future. The owner of one of the most recognizable names in Virginia colonial history, he had spent much of his life in London and continued to own property there. One of his sons was an officer in the British army, and another had been a midshipman in the Royal Navy. The emotional stress caused by his desire to remain loyal and pressure to join the Patriot cause proved too much; Byrd committed suicide in 1777.[117]

Until his death in London in 1784, Randolph attempted to resolve the dispute. He looked for suitable employment through one of the only connections on which it seems that his family could always rely: the Walpoles. Sir Edward Walpole, Sir Robert's son and Horace's brother, succeeded in convincing Lord George Germain, the secretary of state for the colonies, to submit Randolph's name to the king for the position of chief justice of Quebec, should the position, as was expected, become open. Germain wrote to Walpole, "I shall do it with greater pleasure since I find you have so justly conceived a favourable opinion of that gentleman." The letter from Germain to Walpole also contains the only description of Randolph during his years of exile in London. Germain remarked that "I always look'd upon Mr. Randolph as an intelligent, well informed and well-affected man, and I have been ready upon all occasions to promote his interest as far as my power went." Randolph's value, however, as an informant on matters in the Chesapeake had clearly diminished in Germain's eyes. "He is particularly knowing in the affairs of Virginia," Germain wrote, "but whoever now forms his notions of America from the State that Country was in, a few years agoe will proceed upon very uncertain grounds, and Mr. Randolph well-knows that the Tempers of the people are either Changed, or fear so far operates upon them that they dare not avow any sentiments that are unfavorable to the present usurped Authority."[118]

If Randolph knew that the tempers of the people had changed, his last known political effort, and one of the last statements of constitutional sense in the Revolutionary era, did not show it. His "Plan of Accommodations" was a proposal he submitted to Germain in which he stressed his belief that the imperial relationship could be repaired if only the protagonists focused on the "Practice" of imperial politics instead of "good systems in Theory."[119] A successful remedy would use the lessons of historical experience to reproduce what had worked and jettison what had failed in the imperial constitution to reestablish the "political union with [Great] Britain." Ties of the "utmost Cordiality and affection" should "forever cement the two great Countries" and be the basis to settle "the important Subject of legislative authority." Much like his *Considerations on the Present State of Virginia*, Randolph's plan was an astute analysis of the practical constitutional problems that caused and further exacerbated the conflict between the colonies and Britain.

"Men link'd together by the same attachments and Circumstances," Randolph remembered, "wou'd never depart, from the political Interest of their Country."[120]

Shortly after sending off his plan to Germain, Randolph wrote one last letter to Jefferson. "Wou'd it not be prudent," Randolph rather unrealistically asked his friend and cousin, "to rescind your Declaration of Independence, be happily reunited to your ancient & natural Friend, & enjoy a Peace which I most religiously think w'd pass all Understanding?"[121] The letter was never sent. Randolph died in London in 1784.

When Randolph was in London in the 1740s, he bought a very special violin. In August 1775 Jefferson dissolved a curious legal arrangement with the purchase of that violin. Four years earlier he had entered into an agreement with Randolph that they believed would last the rest of their lives.[122] If Randolph were to die first, Jefferson would receive "the violin which the said John brought with him into Virginia" from England, "together with all his music composed for the violin," including, one presumes, William Boyce sonatas. If Randolph survived Jefferson, then "100 pounds sterling of the books of the said Thomas, to be chosen by the said John" would belong to Randolph. By 1775, however, another curious legal arrangement that many of their contemporaries thought would also last their lives—British America—had also dissolved. Recalling their agreement, but recognizing how problematic its terms had become, Randolph offered the prized instrument to Jefferson for thirteen pounds. On 17 August Jefferson bought the violin and recorded in his memorandum book: "This dissolves our bargain"—a statement that was as apt for relationship between Virginia and Britain as it was for the violin. It should be noted, however, that at Jefferson's death, long after he could no longer play a violin because of the wrist injury he had suffered in France, he still owned two of them, one of which he still called, more than fifty years after he bought it, the "Randolph violin."[123]

CHRISTOPHER F. MINTY

Reexamining Loyalist Identity during the American Revolution

In 1965 Brown University Press published Wallace Brown's *The King's Friends*.[1] It was a landmark achievement—the first large-scale prosopographical analysis of the Loyalists' compensation claims submitted after the Revolutionary War. In total Brown analyzed 2,908 claims. In reviewing the book for the *Virginia Magazine of History and Biography*, Robert M. Calhoon appreciated its significance. He reported that "*The King's Friends* succeeds magnificently in determining the *composition* of Loyalist claimants." More important, though, the "fragments of detail" Brown provided have proved useful to students and scholars since its publication.[2] It remains the standard quantitative interpretation of who the Loyalists were, providing the most thorough social history of those who, for whatever reason, stood with King George III.

The contribution of *The King's Friends* should not be underestimated. In the days before relational databases and spreadsheets, quantitative research was in its infancy. Methods in vogue in the mid-twentieth century would be passed over today. To determine Loyalists' occupations or wealth, for instance, Brown relied upon thousands of punch-holed index cards and pieces of string. But the outcome of his research, as well as Calhoon's, contributed to and in part drove the Loyalist studies renaissance of the 1960s and 1970s.[3]

Yet many criticized *The King's Friends*. Rather than appreciating the systematic nature of Brown's analysis and the book's major contribution in helping scholars move beyond the traditional view of Tory elites, reviewers could not, or perhaps would not, look beyond his sources. They argued that they were not reliable and that the Loyalist claimants were unique, atypical people who had both the financial and political wherewithal to go through the long, drawn-out process of submitting a claim as well as other Loyalists willing to submit supportive memorials or testimonies. In other words these people were not representative. But to the detriment of *The King's Friends*, Brown suggested they were. As Henry J. Young put it, he intimated that his claimants were "highly representative of American

Loyalism." Gordon S. Wood asserted that Brown never showed how this could be the case. Instead, Wood countered, he "merely assumes their representativeness."[4]

To this day, however, Brown's major findings—that most Loyalists were farmers and men of average wealth rather than the patrician elite—remain the standard interpretation of who the Loyalists were in the American Revolution. As Maya Jasanoff wrote in her prizewinning *Liberty's Exiles,* his "thorough analysis" showed that "Loyalism cut right across" the social spectrum. They were, she agreed, "every bit as 'American' as their Patriot fellow subjects." Recent doctoral dissertations have also relied on Brown's work. In 2008 Aaron Coleman argued that he did not consider Loyalists' social makeup because of the "persuasive published research" by the likes of Brown. And in 2014 Aaron Sullivan leaned upon his statistics when discussing Loyalism in Pennsylvania.[5]

But eighteenth-century participants in the American Revolution held a different view. Loyalists were not and did not equate to America's Patriots. The commander in chief of the British Army in North America for a large portion of the war, Gen. Sir Henry Clinton, described Loyalists thusly: "Their stations in life were above the level of a private solider, and their spirits are not such as will permit them to submit totally to military control. Stung with resentment at the ignominious treatment they have received, and urged by indigence to venture their lives for the supply of their wants, their wish was to gratify their double impulse, and to ravish from their oppressors the property which had often in fact been their own."[6]

For New York Loyalist Rev. Charles Inglis, equating Loyalists with Patriots was farcical: "The War is now properly a Presbyterian War." It was a religious war fought between Anglicans and Presbyterians, the latter of whom were Patriots and the former Loyalists. Mercy Otis Warren, one of the first historians of the Revolution, was less sympathetic, arguing that Loyalists "set their faces against the liberties of mankind" and worked against "the freedom of future generations." The renowned historian of England George Trevelyan was equally unkind. America's Loyalists, Trevelyan argued, articulated a sense of "superiority" and were notoriously "unreliable." The "handful" of Loyalists in the colonies did more to hurt that British war effort than help it.[7] Mudslinging aside, was Brown right to emphasize the numerical significance of farmers and others of modest stature?

This essay offers a modern interpretation of who the Loyalists—the people who, to use Calhoon's phrase, participated in this "Special Kind of Civil War"— were.[8] Focusing on 9,338 Loyalists from New York, who each signed a Loyalist declaration or took the oath of allegiance to King George III between April 1775 and November 1778, I analyze the social composition of these Loyalists and from it draw inferences as to the social characteristics of New York's Loyalist population.[9] I analyze these Loyalists' occupations, wealth, ages, and religions and, in so doing, offer an up-to-date profile of a large number of New York's Loyalists.[10]

It is important, however, to define the parameters of this essay. The subscribers of Loyalist declarations were entered into a relational database. Data concerning individuals' social characteristics was gathered from genealogical materials, newspapers, muster rolls, church records, probate records, inventories, and political subscriptions—sources that are more reliable and in many cases more detailed than the Loyalist compensation claims. Individual Loyalists have been cross-referenced to a diverse range of sources, matching people by name within the database wherever possible. The limitations of correlating common names and deciphering variant spellings are perennial problems with such an approach. So too is the absence of data, for which prosopography only partly compensates. It has not been possible to find information on every Loyalist. Colonists often made no conscious effort to preserve materials, and some records have been lost. Further, in spite of my best efforts, I was unable to locate comparable declarations or oaths in multiple New York counties: Albany, Charlotte, Cumberland, Dutchess, Gloucester, Richmond, Tryon, and Ulster.[11] Furthermore, tax lists are no longer extant for New York City or its surrounding counties for this period. Women are also absent from this analysis: none signed the declarations or took the oath of allegiance. Further, only eleven African Americans were identified, all of whom took the oath of allegiance in New York City in 1777. When Gov. William Tryon submitted the oath, their names were segregated under the category "Free Negroes."[12]

Nevertheless, in spite of these limitations, I have uncovered the lives of thousands of people, individuals whose lived experiences of the American Revolution have heretofore remained largely untold and underexplored.

Occupations

I identified occupations for 6,257 Loyalists, around 75 percent of the total pool and representing about 3 percent of the population of New York. Whereas Brown's study recorded the occupations of 1,071 New York claimants, he was able neither to correlate occupations with other variables nor to supplement quantitative analysis with thick description based on contemporary sources other than the Loyalist claimants.

In *The King's Friends,* Brown found that 75 percent of all claimants from New York were farmers. I also determined that farmers were the most common single occupation but found that they accounted for only 22 percent of all occupations. Correlating occupation with age, I found that that 46 percent of farmers and yeomen were fifteen years old or younger, indicating that families often signed lists together. They were also ethnically diverse. Jacques Cortelyou, for instance, was a Dutch Kings County farmer who signed a Loyalist document alongside two other members of his family, Peter and Isaac. The Cortelyou family was well established in New York. Their ancestor Jacques Cortelyou was surveyor general of New Amsterdam and was the first to produce a map of the city, known as the Castello Plan, in 1660. In contrast William Brown was a former British soldier who chose to remain in New York after fighting in the Seven Years' War. After settling on the "great Road from New York to Boston," Brown made small improvements on his homestead "until the unhappy Troubles broke out in America."[13] Gilbert Pugsley of Philipse Manor, Westchester County, was forced to sell his lease at an early point in the war because of his consistent refusals to acquiesce to Patriot rule. At the end of the war, he moved to New Brunswick.[14]

Unsurprisingly most farmers came from the rural counties of Westchester and Suffolk rather than the commercial areas of New York City or Kings County. For those who took the oath of allegiance in Suffolk County, occupations were identified for 2,212 Loyalists, representing 85 percent of the group whose occupation is known. Of those, farmers (1,255) and yeomen (1) made up 57 percent of the total. Of the 311 Loyalists in Westchester County, occupations were identified for 154, of which farmers (39) and yeomen (61) made up 65 percent of the group whose occupation is known. For Queens County, of the 1,269 Loyalists who signed a published declaration, occupations have been identified for 396, or 31 percent of the signatories. In this instance farmers (52) and yeomen (113) made up 42 percent of the group whose occupation is known. In Kings County, however, of 577 Loyalists who were administered the oath of allegiance, occupations were identified for 145 individuals. Of those, farmers (26) and yeomen (27) accounted for 37 percent of the group whose occupation is known.

Of the 3,394 Loyalists who were administered the oath of allegiance in New York City, farmers (170) and yeomen (319) made up 14 percent of the Loyalist population. The regional variation in New York represents the occupational diversity of the province, showing simply that farmers were more numerous in rural areas, such as Suffolk County, than in urban areas, such as New York City.

A second notable finding of this analysis, one that differs from Brown's, is the preponderance of artisans. Taken together from their individual trades, of which there were many, some 28 percent of Loyalist subscribers were artisans. They were found in each of the counties under examination and were most numerous in New York City—the most populous area under examination. In each of the counties under examination there were silversmiths, blacksmiths, chair- and shoemakers, and tailors. In New York City there was even a chocolate-maker and someone who identified himself as a "rum taster." Whereas Brown found only 9 percent of claimants were "artisans and craftsmen," different, more reliable sources suggest that Loyalism had considerable appeal to colonists of middling social status—people who made their living from a craft or skilled trade. Moreover, like New York's farmers, artisans represented a diverse group of people. For instance Isaac Heron, an Irish watchmaker who moved to New York City in the early 1760s, was a member of one of the city's preeminent political associations. Thomas and William Brownejohn, on the other hand, were druggists who placed regular newspaper advertisements for the "DRUGS & MEDICINES" they sold at their store in Hanover Square.[15]

In New York City, artisans were political actors in their own right, and they understood the political and military situation in which they were placed during the Revolution. In fact sometimes they even took advantage of it, using the war and the people around them to sustain themselves in a politically and economically shifting or dislocated society. Charles Oliver Bruff, a jeweler based in Maiden Lane, offers a suggestive insight into the mind-set of an artisan working in a society riven by war. In June 1775 he placed an advertisement in a newspaper detailing how he could prepare individual swords for Patriots to wield "in Defence of their LIBERTIES." These swords featured intricate designs that most certainly appealed to Patriots' republican sensibilities. "[M]ounted with beautiful grips," Bruff informed readers, broadswords could be affixed with "the Heads of Lord Chatham, and John Wilkes" and inscribed with various mottoes on their shells, including "*Magna Charta* and *Freedom*" and "*Wilkes* and *Liberty.*" A year later, he could now affix the heads of generals George Washington and Charles Lee and the mottoes "*Prosperity brave Washington, / For he Old England's Troops has made to run*" and "*Let the God of Hosts rule the Sway, / And make us Freemen in America.*" Bruff was aware of the people around him and recognized their political beliefs. For financial gain he tapped into their sympathies toward the likes of Washington and Wilkes and the cultural and political symbolism surrounding the Magna Carta. Yet Bruff was no Patriot. Following the reestablishment of British rule in September 1776, he signed Loyalist documents and directed his skills to "those gentlemen of the [British] navy and army." By 1778 he was engraving impressions of King George III, alleging that his was "the most elegant sword pattern that has ever made its appearance in America." Bruff also designed silver shoe buckles, "suitable for all Loyalists," with inscriptions of the British crown and an English rose. Loyalists and British forces could also get their blade inscribed with "*Success to the British arms.*" Farmers submitted to Patriot or British rule; so, too, did artisans. As Bruff's behavior illustrates, rather than acquiesce, some adjusted their allegiance to suit the demands of their particular marketplace, their particular customer base.[16]

The same quality of evidence is not available to retell the stories of the 209 laborers (3.34 percent of the total) who became Loyalists. That said, their names indicate that they came from a diverse social and ethnic background. There were Germans, such as Andrew DeHeister, Frederick Lidig and Joseph Lentz, alongside Dutchmen, such as Peter Van De Water; Scots, such as John McIntosh; and Englishmen, such as James and Matthew Rogers. In the end, like many in the artisanal trades, they represented the diversity of New York. Loyalism, in New York at least, was not just a working- or lower-class movement; it was far more broad-based.

Merchants also figure on the list of occupations (4.89 percent). New York City was a commercial hub, populated by merchants who lived on Broad, Wall, and Pearl Streets in the Dock and East Wards. These areas were closest to the port and had become the financial center of the province during the eighteenth century. Loyalism was strong in ports with connections to transatlantic commerce, including Boston; Charleston, South Carolina; Newport, Rhode Island; Norfolk, Virginia; and Philadelphia.[17] The figure for merchant occupations reported here is consistent with the overall estimate for the colonial population, especially since historians have shown how merchants were more numerous in market-driven economies, such as New York.[18] It is difficult to suggest just how many merchants there were in New York at this time, but the 306 merchants identified as having signed a Loyalist document suggest that a significant proportion of them chose to side with the Crown. They included men such as John Harris Cruger, a wealthy individual whose trade stretched across the Atlantic. Cruger was also chamberlain to New York City, and his brother, Henry, was a pro-American member of Parliament in Westminster. Equally prominent were Oliver DeLancey and John Watts. More than three decades of consistent trading had landed them among the city's wealthiest merchants and most prominent citizens. There were, however, merchants of lesser means. Evert Bancker Jr.'s, Charles Nicoll's, and Frederick Rhinelander's dealings were smaller than those of DeLancey and Watts. Bancker dealt mostly in basic, everyday items, while Nicoll sold wine and Rhinelander was an importer of crockery and earthenware.[19]

The main area of divergence between this study and *The King's Friends,* then, is in respect to the number of artisans. Brown claimed that they accounted for roughly 9 percent of New York's Loyalist population. I offer a different interpretation, suggesting that artisans were an integral component of Loyalism in New York. Theirs was the largest occupational category identified within this analysis, 6 percent more numerous than farmers and yeomen. These men were important members of their respective communities, and their services would have been highly sought after. Both before and during the Revolution, they relied upon popular business to make a living. Blacksmiths, for instance, would have produced their local town's grates and fences, while shoemakers would have made shoes for their townsfolk. They may have been underrepresented in Brown's sample because of their place within their respective communities. That is to say, artisans were so invested in the areas in which they lived that it may not have been financially viable for them to leave New York and travel to London or Nova Scotia to submit a claim. If immigrating to a new home was not traumatic enough, the cost of transporting tools would have been considerable. British offers of land grants in their new territories and settlements to self-exiled Loyalists might have appealed to farmers and yeomen, who may have secured larger plots of land than they had previously owned, but the underrepresentation of artisans in Brown's sample suggests that they felt differently. Land may have been valuable, but for a tailor, his studio may have been more valuable; for a blacksmith, it could be his workshop; and for a baker, his bakery may have kept him in New York. Furthermore, if artisans did not take their tools and start afresh, their post-Revolutionary startup costs would have been considerable. Hence, when the Revolution ended and Loyalists left New York, it is possible that a large proportion of artisans accepted the American victory and chose to stay, though further research is required to substantiate this.

Despite these variations, however, this study's findings do correlate to Brown's in several respects. Brown showed that around 190 Loyalists, about 18 percent, were involved in commerce; my analysis confirms Brown's findings: 1,113, or roughly 18 percent, of New York Loyalists were involved in commerce, either through transporting or selling goods. Similarly a majority of Brown's commercial claimants were from New York City; this study found that more than 75 percent of the commercial Loyalists identified were New York City inhabitants.

Wealth

In the absence of tax lists, probate records offer a more reliable estimate of personal wealth than the claims examined by Brown. Probate records provide an appraisal of the property of a deceased person for the purpose of proving a will and administering the personal estate. The recorded property values of bequests and moveable estate offer an indication of total personal wealth at death. These values are often expressed in different currencies, usually either British or New York sterling. Despite their usefulness, however, probates must be used with caution. They can sometimes be vague, missing vital information, or out of date. Thus each probate must be contextualized, if possible, against other sources to determine their reliability.[20]

With clear limitations and the appropriate cautions taken, I sampled a total of 227 probate records for Loyalists who died between 1775 and 1785. Around 168 contained information that was tabulated and analyzed. Brown adopted broad numerical categories and reported total wealth claimed, that is, a single estimate that included both real and personal wealth. My analysis incorporates a more nuanced approach. I have concentrated on reporting findings of personal wealth by allocating the data into one of ten categories, according to the distribution of results, and used statistical analysis to correlate the findings with occupations. The results provide a greater level of detail than Brown's profiling, revealing that 49 percent of sampled Loyalists from New York possessed personal wealth of two hundred pounds sterling or less, indicating that New York's Loyalists were not wealthy individuals.

This sample suggests instead that New York's Loyalist population were men of middling means, though there was considerable variation between them. Take, for instance, the probates of Benjamin Barker and Thomas Betts. Barker's personal wealth was worth five pounds sterling. Upon his death in 1782, he bequeathed his children varying sums of money, ranging from five shillings to five pounds, but included nothing else relating to personal property. Thomas Betts, a yeoman from Newtown, Queens County, bequeathed his nephew, Anthony, ten pounds, while his wife, Sarah, received one hundred pounds one year after his death. She also received the finest room in Betts's home as well as firewood and the privilege of keeping foals, geese, ducks, or turkeys.

My findings also illustrate the huge disparity in Loyalists' wealth, reinforcing the work of Gary B. Nash and Raymond A. Mohl.[21] Whereas some were poor and bequeathed very little, others were among the wealthiest men in New York. For example, when Abraham Furman died in early 1779, without any funds available for family members, he stipulated that his executors were to sell all his moveable estate "but the Grain on the Ground." In contrast, when Walter Franklin died, in 1780, his total estate was valued at more than £17,000, and he bequeathed numerous items to members of his family that indicated his elite status. Franklin's wife, Mary, received his "best Carriage or Chariot," two horses, all his household and kitchen utensils, and more than £1,000. His daughters, Maria and Sarah, both received over £2,250 as well as his mansion and four pieces of property. Overall seventeen Loyalists' estimated personal wealth was less than £22 sterling, and sixteen left more than £2,231 sterling. More important, the population of the ten categories used indicates that New York Loyalists were drawn from all levels of society.[22]

Age

No historian has previously examined the ages of American Loyalist populations with any degree of specificity. Of the 9,338 Loyalists identified here, dates of birth have been found for 3,263 of them. Their ages varied widely. Two Loyalists, Daniel Horsmanden and David Hains, were eighty-four years old at the start of the Revolution. Six others were also born in the seventeenth century. Elderly people, aged between sixty-three and eighty-four, account for 5.28 percent of New York's Loyalists. At the opposite end of the age spectrum, 81 Loyalists were twelve years old in 1775 (1.48 percent).[23]

The largest age group here, some 480 Loyalists, were aged between twelve and sixteen years old in 1775, accounting for around 15 percent of the Loyalist population. The second largest group covers those who were between seventeen and twenty-one years old in 1775, accounting for 14 percent of the Loyalist population (457). Loyalists at and under twenty-one years of age in 1775 account for about 29 percent of New York's Loyalist population. This may be an indicator of widespread father-son participation in Loyalist subscriptions, as already suggested. Moreover it suggests that their Loyalist "voluntarism" was encouraged by broad family networks.[24]

This contention can be supported by a second observation: more than 84 percent of New York Loyalists were aged fifty-two or under, individuals who were likely still working and contributing to their estate on a day-by-day basis. But it would be incorrect to assume that New York's Loyalists were middle-aged, as Massachusetts Loyalists tended to be.[25] Around 56 percent of New York's Loyalists were adult males aged between twenty-two and fifty-two. This can be broken down to reveal two groups: those between twenty-two and thirty-six years old (1,071), who account for about one-third of the complete total (31.83 percent), and those aged between thirty-seven and sixty-two (1,083), who account for another third (33.2 percent) of the total. The near-equitable distribution of frequencies among three age groups (29 percent under twenty-one years old, 33 percent between twenty-two and thirty-six, and 33 percent between thirty-seven and sixty-two) indicates that Loyalism was not a generational phenomenon.[26] For instance in Brookhaven, Suffolk County, the sixty-five-year-old Alexander Hawkins signed alongside his family members: thirty-two-year-old Simeon Hawkins, twenty-six-year-old Jonas Hawkins, twenty-three-year-old Benjamin Hawkins, and nineteen-year-old Thomas Hawkins.

Family networks were important outside Suffolk County, too. In New York City, Benjamin and Edward Buckbee took the oath of allegiance as well as Edward and William Laight and Frederick, William, William Jr., and Philip Rhinelander. In Kings County so too did members of the Hegeman, Ditmars, Suydam, Wyckoff, Stryker, Lefferts, and Lott families. In Westchester County twenty-eight members of the Purdy family signed the Westchester declaration. Family networks are apparent in Queens County, too, particularly with Dutch-speaking New Yorkers. There were more than five Brinkerhoffs, Rapaljes, Remsens, Schencks, Snedekers, Suydams, and Van Nostrandts. It is plausible to suggest, then, that fathers signed alongside their sons. It is probable that they too signed alongside other family members. Of course family networks were important in inward-looking counties such as Kings and Suffolk. The data confirms this, but it also shows that family was an important arbiter of political behavior in urban environments as well as other less inward-looking counties.

Thus when examining declarations and oaths, it is clear that colonists of all ages became Loyalists. And because a significant proportion of Loyalists were dependent or semidependent on their families—that is, those under twenty-one years of age—it is both probable and problematic that family allegiances were among the most influential factors when determining allegiance during the American Revolution. But can a child really be a Loyalist? Were they able to exercise free will in signing a document? For Maya Jasanoff, children should be included; but for Philip Ranlet, as he stated in a harsh review of Jasanoff's *Liberty's Exiles*, they should not.[27]

RELIGION

Historians have often made a correlation between Loyalism and Anglicanism in the American Revolution. In *The King's Friends*, Wallace Brown suggested that "there was an Anglican tinge to Loyalism" across the northern colonies. But Anglican Loyalists were not found only in the northern colonies; they were across the continent. In the colonies of Georgia, Maryland, and North Carolina as well as in Delaware, Connecticut, Massachusetts, New York, and Rhode Island, Anglicanism played a role in determining its adherents' allegiance. There is a consensus in the literature that Anglican Loyalists were more numerous in New York than in the other colonies. Ranlet argued that all New York Loyalists "were either Anglicans or those of other faiths who were influenced by an Anglican minister or some other staunch Tory," while Brown also suggested that the "bulk" of New York's Loyalist population were Anglican.[28]

Using sources that have heretofore been overlooked by historians, a micro-analysis of New York City's rank-and-file Loyalists shows that there were Anglicans, Quakers, Presbyterians, Moravians, Lutherans, German Reformists, and Dutch Reformists. But how many of each were there?[29] In New York City, Anglican Loyalists reinforced each other through marriage and pastoral relationships. Even though they were a minority in New York City, they constituted a majority of its Loyalist population. In total 850 Loyalists out of the 1,251 whose religion could be identified were Anglican. I identified 489 Anglicans who married in an Anglican Church between 1746 and 1785. Most of these individuals were married by the time of the American Revolution (59.68 percent). More often than not, they were married by an Anglican minister who went on to become a Loyalist (63.6 percent). The Revolutionary War, then, brought them together as their religion defined their allegiance. New York Loyalists who were Dutch Reformists, Presbyterians, Lutherans, German Reformists, and Moravians have been identified, as well. This study found 79 individuals who were Dutch Reformists, 67 Presbyterians, 41 Lutherans, 26 German Reformists, and 11 Moravians. Of the 1,231 Loyalists whose religious affiliations were identified, 69.04 percent were Anglican, 11.75 percent were Quakers, 6.41 were Dutch Reformists, 5.44 were Presbyterian, 3.33 were Lutherans, 1.11 were German Reformists, and 0.89 percent were Moravians.[30]

Baptismal records complement this analysis. Between 1775 and 1785, 442 Loyalists had children in New York that were baptized in an Anglican church. Most children were baptized in Trinity Church, but some were baptized in St. Paul's. Only one child was baptized in 1775; in 1776 and 1777, no children were baptized. Yet between 1778 and 1783, birth rates changed. Eighty-three percent of identified Anglican Loyalists had a child baptized. This may have been due, in part, to the security British control afforded them. Holly Brewer argues that colonists took a great deal of pride in baptizing their children and that it became a means to strengthen British imperialism. It demonstrated colonists' political commitment on an Atlantic scale. Baptism in British New York was more than a rite of admission to the Christian community. It was a demonstration of Loyalists' commitment to the rule of the king, both as head of state and head of the English Church.[31] On October 1, 1778, William Sutherland baptized his son Henry-Clinton Sutherland, seemingly naming him after the commander in chief of the British army. Another Loyalist whose allegiance was articulated through his child's name was David Buchanan. A Scotsman, Buchanan had his daughter baptized on February 21, 1781, as Anne Britannia Buchanan, naming her after the reigning monarch during the Act of Union, Queen Anne.[32]

Quakers were the second most numerous denomination identified. In total 157 Loyalists have been identified as belonging to the Society of Friends. This is significant because they were, as Joseph S. Tiedemann has written, "a tiny segment of the population." Roughly only 3 percent of New York City's inhabitants were Quakers, but about 13 percent of Loyalists whose religion can be identified were Quakers.

New York City Quakers' Loyalism can be explained through familial ties, their religious commitment to pacifism, and, as historians have argued, the fact that during this period the Society of Friends was undergoing a "spiritual revitalization" because of the religious polarization caused by the First Great Awakening.[33]

Quakers were not at the forefront of the revolutionary conflict between Britain and its American colonies. Instead they urged a path of moderation and conciliation. As Sydney James argued, Quakers' pacifism defined their responses to and behavior during moments of agitation. Their commitment to their religious principles was most important. As such pacifism was, wrote James, "the position to be held at all costs to preserve the good name of their church."[34] That is to say, the Friends were committed to pacifist principles and nonviolence, both of which were challenged by the Revolution.

What the high incidence of Quaker family members among New York's loyal population suggests, then, is that they viewed Loyalism as a political tool with which they could affect stability within their society. They associated their local circumstance under British rule with political security, stability, and, above all, their ability to rearticulate pacifism and nonviolence. New York Quakers' Loyalism became a form of political accommodation that enabled them to continue practicing their religion. As one post-Revolutionary report stated, though "a large number of Inhabitants . . . left their Homes" between 1775 and 1776, Quakers "generally kept their places." They "chose rather to hazard all than omit the attendance of their Religious Meetings." Elias Hicks, an inhabitant of Long Island, validated this view. Those "who stood faithful to their [religious] principles," wrote Hicks after the Revolution, "and did not meddle in the controversy, had, after a short period at first, considerable Favour allowed them."[35]

Although the number of Dutch Reformed members is low, it should be remembered that my analysis sampled only New York City; it was Kings County that was populated by Dutch-speaking inhabitants. If we assume that its Loyalists were, for the most part, Dutch Reformists, their numbers would significantly increase. Contemporaries also appreciated the number of Loyalists from the Dutch Church. As the Loyalist historian Thomas Jones remarked, it was "next in rank [to the Anglican Church], for its riches, its influence, and from the number of its wealthy, opulent, and reputable citizens," implying that Dutch Reformists were the second most numerous denomination among New York's Loyalists.[36]

The data concerning the other Protestant denominations is also significant. Given that Presbyterians were the second most politically influential religious group in New York City before the Revolution, their small numbers suggest that there was almost no correlation between Presbyterianism and Loyalism. In fact, given that New York Patriots William Livingston, Alexander McDougall, Rev. John Rogers, and John Morin Scott, among others, were prominent men who defended Presbyterianism throughout the imperial crisis and into the war itself, it could be inferred that most New York City Presbyterians were Patriots.[37]

By extension, then, the American Revolution was to some extent what J. C. D. Clark labeled a religious war.[38] Of the other dissenting religions identified, the Lutherans were the largest group, as the data confirms. The other religions present within New York City were on the numerical margins of society.[39]

Nancy L. Rhoden estimated that there were sixteen Anglican Loyalist ministers, two neutrals, and one Patriot. James Bell, however, contradicted Rhoden's findings, finding the allegiances of fourteen ministers out of a possible twenty. Bell argued that there were eleven Loyalist Anglican ministers. I have modified Bell's findings, finding that the labeling may have been insufficient and that he had no access to certain resources now available. In particular he labeled Benjamin Moore a Patriot, and he did not identify the allegiances of Joshua Bloomer and Leonard Cutting. All three ministers were Loyalists.[40] The proportional significance of Anglican ministers' Loyalism is therefore increased. Seventy-five percent became Loyalists (15). Of those whose allegiance could be determined, the only Anglican ministers to become Patriots in the province of New York were John Bowden and Samuel Provoost.[41]

What emerges are tentative correlations between Loyalism and religion in New York City. Despite the limited source base, the conclusions reinforce and, at times, extend historians' findings. When Ranlet argued that New York Loyalists were all Anglicans, he did not quantify his statement. He based his assumption on qualitative evidence. My analysis of Anglican records has taken the matter a step further; it quantifies his work. The strong association of Loyalism and Anglicanism in New York was distinct in Revolutionary America. Several historians have argued that there was no correlation between rank-and-file Loyalism and Anglicanism in Virginia, while Colin Nicolson put forward this same argument when examining Massachusetts. However, in New York City there is clear evidence of a strong correlation between Loyalism and Anglicanism. The link between Loyalism and Anglicanism also transcended the societal gap between the elite and the nonelite inhabitants of New York City. Alongside elite Anglican assemblymen such as Frederick Philipse and Jacob Walton were elite merchants such as William Bayard and Theophilact Bache; shopkeepers such as Christopher Blundell and Samuel Murgatroyd; a cordwainer, Isaac DeLaMater; a ship-chandler, Adam DeGrushee; and a tailor, Emmanuel Rinedollar. With these men was a breeches-maker, Cornelius Ryan, and a yeoman, Israel Underhill, among a range of other elite and nonelite Anglican Loyalists who represented the occupational diversity of New York City.[42]

To account for the overall importance of religion to these Anglicans' political persuasions is difficult, but some points can be made. Even though a small number of New York Anglican ministers became Patriots, prominent ministers within the city adhered to the ties they held with the Church of England, Great Britain, and George III. These men included Samuel Auchmuty, Charles Inglis, Benjamin Moore, and John Vardill, as well as other well-known Anglican ministers—Luke Babcock, Myles Cooper, Samuel Seabury, and Isaac Wilkins—and it is probable that they wielded influence over the political affiliations of their respective congregations. Indeed in 1778 Wilkins told Cooper that his "whole flock" were well.[43]

Other influences might also have affected Anglicans' behavior. They adhered to a long tradition of passive obedience and nonresistance to civil authorities. Loyalist pamphleteers argued that New York was stable under a hierarchical order upheld by British rule. In consequence a large number of New York Anglicans may have drawn upon the church's paternalism, the overall authority of George III and Parliament, and the cohesion that both the church and British rule provided when determining their political allegiances. Moreover it should not be forgotten that some Anglicans—all Loyalists, in fact—may have taken greater pride in their status as Britons, rather than as colonists, and used Protestantism as a foundation for their identity.

Wanted immediately,

A Lappedary, jeweller, silver smiths, sword cutlers, a blacksmith, three good hands at filing, and two chape filers: The highest wages will be given by

CHARLES OLIVER BRUFF,

And a quart of GROGG a day. The said Bruff is making the most elegant sword pattern that has ever made its appearance in America, his Majesty's likeness with a ornamented guard, letter'd all round, *Success to the British arms*; and a new-fashion'd De Artoise's pattern silver shoe buckle, suitable for all loyalists, letter'd round, *Success to the British arms*, and a crown at the four corners; over the joints is the Old English rose.

"Success to the British Arms," *New York Gazette and Weekly Mercury,*
August 17, 1778, Collection of the New-York Historical Society

There was no gray area between being a Loyalist and a Patriot for these Anglicans. It was this political Anglicanism that Loyalist ministers espoused on a regular basis. As Samuel Seabury wrote in *A View of the Controversy between Great Britain and Her Colonies* (1774), "the difference between a loyal subject and a rebel, is, that the one yields obedience to, and faithfully supports the supreme authority of the state, and the other endeavours to overthrow it." In Seabury's mind, as in other Anglicans', that was the "difference between a good and a bad subject." Similarly, as Charles Inglis argued, those who renounced their allegiance to George

III "risk[ed] their lives, liberties, and property." Loyalism, on the other hand, offered colonists a means to ensure "the security of their respective rights" as British
subjects. Anglicans' Loyalism maintained "every endearing connection" between
their sovereign and country.[44] Anglicans in New York may have looked upon certain leaders of the revolutionary movement and noted if they were Presbyterians,
correlating Dissenters with rebellion to reinforce their longstanding views. Many
individuals did this. Just as Inglis felt that the Revolution "originated from Dissenters" and was "a Presbyterian War" that was "chiefly supported by them," John
Wetherhead argued that "the Presbyterians of this Continent have sown the Seeds
of this Rebellion." In the end, as with all Loyalists, colonists gravitated toward
Loyalism for various reasons. Yet for Anglicans in New York City, religious affinity
was the most important. For them it was a "war of religion."[45]

Despite scholars' criticisms, *The King's Friends* shaped Loyalist studies for years.
Many historians and students relied on Brown's findings, with few offering revisions or substantiation. My analysis, however, has done just that—I have offered
some revisions and substantiated some of *The King's Friends'* findings. I have added
to Brown's work, too, showing how for some Loyalists religion was an important
influence upon their allegiance during the Revolutionary War. In almost every
demographical marker, New York's Loyalists represented the diversity of the colony in the years leading up to the American Revolution. *The King's Friends* showed
that a majority of Loyalists were men of middling means. This essay, undertaken
with the benefit of computer analysis, has presented something similar. Even
though Brown's work was completed more than fifty years ago, much of it, like
Robert Calhoon's, remains relevant today. Both Brown's and Calhoon's scholarship offer something that all scholars should appreciate: historians should not dis-
card something just because it is old, just as they should not welcome something
just because it is new.

In recent years historians have devoted considerable time defining Loyalism.
Edward Larkin has written on the topic, Philip Ranlet has discussed the possible
effects of not defining the term, and Maya Jasanoff included no definition in *Liberty's Exiles*.[46] But defining Loyalism might not offer the solution some appear to
seek. Any definition could neither represent all Loyalists nor please all scholars.
However broad or specific, a single definition would present too many questions
and not offer enough answers. Writers, historians, genealogists, and students
would not be able to examine the forest, because they would be too caught up
examining the trees.[47]

The future of Loyalist studies may instead lie in examining the people themselves, taking them for who they were and what they stood for. This essay, for instance, has used a reliable set of materials to examine around ten thousand people.
Its methods and approach offer a blueprint for analyzing other areas in the Revolutionary Atlantic, including those in mainland North America and the Caribbean.
This framework can also be used for a transatlantic study, comparing Loyalists

in Revolutionary America to Loyalists in other areas and at different times in the eighteenth century. British Loyalists during the 1790s and Irish Loyalists during the 1798 Rebellion, for example, offer other opportunities to determine who Loyalists were during the Age of Revolutions.

As Robert Calhoon wrote in 1973, America's Loyalists "were not fervent monarchists or partisans for an eighteenth-century vision of British imperialism." They were not "deviants," either. They were everyday eighteenth-century people: blacksmiths, cartmen, laborers, sailors, silversmiths, shopkeepers. There were clergymen, lawyers, merchants, and officeholders, too, of course. But they were a real minority. The American Revolution touched "every part of society," and, as Calhoon pointed out, America's Loyalists were caught up in it.[48]

Constructing Female Loyalism(s) in the Delaware Valley

Quaker Women Writers of the American Revolution

Loyalism has historically been defined by voting, fighting, legislating, or oath-taking. These androcentric metrics exclude a large group of people who were unable or refused to define themselves using these methods but were still categorized as Loyalists, despite their desire to be considered otherwise.[1] "Loyalty" is a particularly complicated concept where Quakers are concerned, since many Quakers considered themselves pacifists, neutralists, or disaffected, but rebels classified them as covert spies.[2]

Plenty of scholars have documented Quaker pacifism during the war, so I seek here not to argue that Quakers were treated as Loyalists but to describe how and where they resisted, defied, or embraced such categorization.[3] I am particularly interested in the ways in which women in the Society of Friends established loyalties for themselves, since they were not initially arrested with their male counterparts or forced to take loyalty oaths but were still punished for holding allegiances they could not affirm or deny in any official capacity. Most scholarship on war writing and rhetoric focuses on essays, pamphlets, and broadsides traditionally published by men, but I suggest interpreting manuscripts—letters and journals in particular—as the site of women's declarations and self-definitions, an approach that creates a theoretical shift in the way scholars read the medium of intimate political writing conducted in domestic spaces. These epistles were not only historical artifacts; they were also literary texts that writers used to construct the war's—and their own—narrative.

How Quakers Became Loyalists

Before I can explain how Quaker women writers defined "loyalty," I must first explain how pacifists became considered the "most dangerous enemy America knows."[4] As of June 18, 1776, at Congress's insistence, everyone in Pennsylvania had to take a loyalty oath, or "Test."[5] Quakers refused primarily because they believed these oaths would signify their support of the Revolution, and war violated the principle of the Inner Light, which says that if all people contain the light of God, then both lying and killing contaminate that light.[6] They also resented being asked to swear allegiance to the colonies, because the Sermon on the Mount instructed believers to "swear not at all."[7] Friends believed that all words, not just oaths, should be an "expression of Truth."[8]

Until 1777, when Gen. Sir William Howe landed at Head of Elk, Maryland, hoping to recruit Loyalists to defeat George Washington's army and capture Philadelphia, the Quakers' refusal to take the loyalty oath was grudgingly tolerated. Fearing that Howe was getting too close to his goal, however, Congress changed its mind about the Quakers and decided that their religious pacifism was actually latent Loyalism.[9] The discovery of what historians now know was a forged letter endorsed by the Spanktown Yearly Meeting (which did not exist) exacerbated those fears. The missive broached questions about Washington's army and claimed that Quakers were "the most Dangerous Enemies America knows" hiding behind "that Hypocritical Cloak of Religion."[10] After seeing the letter, the committee stated on August 28, 1777, that Quakers were inclined "to communicate Intelligence to the Enemy."[11] Committeemen searched the houses of suspected spies and, between September 1 and September 4, 1777, exiled twenty-two Friends to Winchester, Virginia, without trial.[12]

Some Quakers protested by petitioning for the prisoners' release, while others withdrew from their political positions as part of their refusal to support a corrupt government.[13] But the women I will be discussing here—Margaret Morris, Anna Rawle, and Sarah Logan Fisher—wrote letters and diaries that they circulated to friends, who shared their writings with others. These manuscripts map their fluctuating loyalties to the British monarchy, the Society of Friends, and the new nation. They suggest that some Quakers preferred a purposefully localized, interiorized identity and refused to look outward for definition. And they prove that these writers capitalized upon the fluidity of epistolary spaces to publicize (rather than publish) and circulate (rather than print) their rapidly fluctuating political ideologies.

This essay concerns three Quaker writers in the Delaware Valley—an area spread out across 130 miles along the Delaware River that included Philadelphia; Burlington, New Jersey; New Castle, Delaware; and Easton, Pennsylvania—because this geopolitical location serves as a useful microcosm for understanding the various gradients of loyalty during the American Revolution.[14] This region was home to some of the most influential and longstanding families of Friends. Although the rebels viewed anyone not for them as against them, such was not always the case. Disapproval over war in general or the rebel cause specifically did not always translate to Loyalist allegiance. Many of the women featured in this study loathed war because it brought violence and chaos, and their writings suggest that loyalty operated on a sliding scale.

The challenge in discussing Quaker loyalties is that some people actively assumed the Loyalist label and some had it affixed to them without their permission or intent. Political identity was not always voluntary. History has focused largely on what I call active Loyalists, who intentionally aligned themselves with the British. Philadelphia assemblyman Joseph Galloway used legislation to propose an American version of Parliament. James Rivington distributed Loyalist propaganda. Thomas Loveless acted as a spy. Other Loyalists, many of whom were Quakers, would have been categorized as passive Loyalists but likely would have self-identified as disaffected. External bodies (lawmakers, confiscation committees, and crowds, to name a few) determined these Loyalists by association, whom they convicted because of kinship, occupation, or religious affiliation.

There were, then, loyalisms, not Loyalism—loyalties, not Loyalty. The line demarcating an active from a passive Loyalist was often crossed and blurred. The distinction between Loyalism actively or passively assumed became a gray area when the Loyalist crossed from one category into the other or rejected them all, for any number of reasons. Much of this self-fashioning was constructed, for women, via manuscript writing—through letters and diaries, in particular.

THE LETTER-JOURNAL OF MARGARET MORRIS

On December 7, 1776, the Quaker Margaret Morris, who lived along the Delaware River, watched rebel troops arrive in Burlington, New Jersey. She recorded her observations of these troops in a series of letters that she penned in a diary addressed to her sister, Milcah Martha Moore, or "Patty." In that letter-diary she wrote that her two sons used a spyglass to watch the approaching soldiers. As Richard and John were watching, so they were being watched. The men they were observing quickly approached to ascertain the threat at the Morris house. The soldiers demanded that Morris deliver the "D—d tory . . . spy," meaning one of her sons.[15]

Neither John nor Richard were spies, but their mother was hiding one—a poet and minister named Jonathan Odell. Morris minced words when she said, "The Name of a Tory so near my *own door* seriously alarmd me, for a poor *refugee* [Odell], dignifyed by that Name, had claimd the shelter of my Roof & was at that very time conceald, like a thief in an Auger hole." Morris purchased her home, formerly William Franklin's mansion, with a "secret chamber" located at the end of a long hallway that was hidden behind a trick closet door. The chamber was only accessible to someone who knew how to dismantle the shelves and pry open the closet's back wall. This hiding place came equipped with an alarm bell triggered by a knob on the inside of the front door. If rung, the alarm could only be heard by the person hiding in the chamber—not by anyone outside of the house.[16] Instead of giving up Odell, Morris said that she "[rang] the bell violently, the Signal agreed on, if they came to Search" and bought time by stalling with her inquisitors. She then put on a "very simple look" & "cryd out, 'Bless me, I hope you are not Hessians—say, good Men, are you the Hessians?'" The men replied, "Do we look like Hessians?" to which Morris replied, "Indeed I don't know . . . but they are Men & you are Men."[17]

In this passage Morris capitalized upon her political fluidity. By insisting that she could not distinguish rebels from Loyalists because "they are Men & you are Men," she played upon the performative nature of political identity. She answered their questions with a question: Are you Hessians? The troops' smart retort—Do we look like Hessians?—suggested their frustration with her. Just as they were unable to identify her political affiliation, she refused to identify theirs. When she said that Hessians were "men," as the soldiers were, Morris reversed what the soldiers had done: she identified them by their sex rather than by their loyalties.

Morris's wordplay in her letter-journal highlights the way assumptions about women's apolitical status could work in their favor. On one level, her letter is a straightforward account of a woman who feared armed men would find a Tory in her house, which would have endangered everyone in it. But on another level, Morris was experimenting with the soldiers' political labels. Whereas they were looking for a "damned Tory spy," she said she knew no Tory—a pejorative term. To Morris, Odell was a refugee, a word that highlighted his victimization; to the local safety and confiscation committees, he was a traitor. And by extension Morris was too—her willingness to hide Odell would have made her a Loyalist to the rebels, regardless of how she classified herself. When the men asked if she was concealing a Tory, the answer stood before them, but they could not see it because Morris was female. They sought the man behind the closet, but they were looking for the woman in the doorway.

Morris's transparency was also to her detriment. Since she was a Quaker, her insistence on neutrality endangered her because rebels treated Friends as subversive Loyalists. The Quakers constructed, distributed, and read aloud letters at various regional meetings urging Friends to avoid fighting or lending aid.[18] Congress already suspected Quakers because they refused to take oaths, so Friends were not afforded the luxury of being neutral. Instead their neutrality acted like a blank page onto which the rebels could inscribe the loyalties they assumed the Quakers held. While external forces wanted people such as Morris to proclaim publicly their allegiances via oaths, many were uninterested in making such proclamations.[19]

Morris's letter-journal provided her a space to inscribe, explore, and test her loyalties for herself when few other spaces were safe or available. In many of her entries, she wrote about a desire to be left alone, rather than being forced to pick one side of the war or another. She longed for neutrality. In December 1776, just before the Battle of Trenton, she said that there was a "great deal of talk in the neighborhood about a neutral island" and that she "wish[ed] with great earnestness it may be allowed."[20] Other residents of Burlington felt the same way. One man "went . . . to the Count de Nope with a request that our town might be allowed to remain a neutral one," but the count refused.[21] "I . . . don't like the Count quite so well to-day as [I] did yesterday," she concluded.[22] Her encounter with the count underscored a problem that plagued many other Loyalist women as well: they could pen their loyalties, or lack of them, as much as they liked, but they were often reliant upon men in power to validate their claims. If those men decided to overwrite the women's declared ideologies, the disaffected had few options for resistance that would result in a change of status.

When a friend told Morris that her claims of neutrality could not save her from the Hessians, who would likely plunder her house, she responded by slightly shifting how she framed her identity. She protested the possibility that she could be a target and wrote, "I said they pillaged none but rebels, and we were not such; we had taken no part against them, &c. But that signified nothing; we should lose all."[23] In this passage Morris engaged in careful self-fashioning. She did not say that she was a Loyalist, and she did not say that she was a neutralist; rather she said that she was not a rebel. She surmised that being a gray-area Loyalist (in their estimation) or disaffected or neutralist (in her own) would perhaps cause the Hessians to pass her by. (Since Hessians plundered Loyalists and rebels indiscriminately, this was wishful thinking on her part.) Ultimately, however, she knew that how she wanted to self-identify "signified nothing" because the soldiers could construct their own definitions of and consequences for loyalty, so she could still lose everything. Morris's transparency aided and impaired her. Her fate depended largely on her luck, the soldiers' whims, and her performance's believability.

Morris's political body, and the letter-journal she used to define it, held contending loyalties, mirroring the geopolitical space in which Morris resided: the Delaware Valley. The river in front of Green Bank was full of soldiers from both sides. Accordingly, Morris's text forces the reader to struggle—I suggest purposefully— to determine the political affiliation of the key players in the narrative. Morris's language, like Morris herself, remained "neutral" throughout the book. Rather than identifying the men as rebels or Loyalists, she referred to them as "soldiers," "men with guns," or "gondola men."[24] As her diary demonstrated, claiming a political identity was a challenge in these tumultuous spaces. If she claimed the Crown while hiding Odell, she could be tried for treason. If she claimed the colonies while evading the Hessians, she could be robbed. If she claimed a side at all, the Society of Friends could disown her.[25] The letter-diary served as a space where she could map the fluid identities she assumed and discarded, rarely willing or able to adopt just one perspective on the war.

Morris abandoned (and simultaneously held onto) this neutrality on June 14, 1777, when she was asked to tend to a group of sick rebel soldiers. On this date the same men who had threatened to shoot her for harboring a spy began suffering an illness, so they sought out Morris, known for her medical expertise. She felt wary of the troops who approached her for aid, writing, "At first I thought they might have a design to put a trick on me, and get me aboard of their gondolas and then pillage my house, as they had done some others." But she soon realized that the fever's extent, not artifice, drove the rebels to seek her out. She remarked simply that she "treated them according to art, and they all got well."[26] A few days later, one of the recovered soldiers expressed his gratitude by delivering "a letter, a bushel of salt, a jug of molasses, a bag of rice, some tea, coffee, sugar, and some cloth for a coat for my poor boys—all sent by my kind sisters," which he had risked everything to deliver.[27]

That Morris copied this story of healing, kindness, and fidelity is interesting for a few reasons. The rebels, in general, were ungenerous to Quakers; these rebels, specifically, had threatened her family. And yet she told her sisters and any other readers of their kindness. She also admitted to helping a soldier in wartime, which the Society of Friends discouraged the Quakers from doing; if these men recovered, would they not continue to fight?[28] Morris reframed the decision to become involved in their plight as being the Christian thing to do, fashioning herself not as a Loyalist, neutralist, or rebel but as an agent of God (which is ultimately how the Society of Friends determined it would justify aiding injured citizens or soldiers). The rebels' provisions were not from the rebels themselves but from "our Heavenly Father. . . . May we never forget it." Comparing herself to Jesus when he fed a multitude of people with minimal provisions, she explained that the took the rebel provisions and "divided the bushel, and gave a pint to every poor person that came for it, and had a great plenty for our own use. Indeed it seemed as if our little store increased by distributing it, like the bread broken by our Saviour to the multitude, which, when he had blessed it, was so marvelously multiplied."[29] By framing herself as a disciple of Christ (or Christ himself) rather than a Loyalist or rebel, Morris sidestepped any charge that she was aiding the war effort. In this way she was a Christian doing God's work. She also completely removed the rebel who gave the supplies from her version of what happened. The discursive emphasis is on the sisters that sent the food, her own household that distributed it, the townspeople who received it, and the God that inspired her to share it. By dropping the soldier, Morris's role in healing him, and the provisions as repayment for that debt, she erased her involvement in the Revolution and replaced it with an act of faith.

Morris's discursive position in her diary allowed her to counter the competing narratives that threatened to force an external ideology upon her, while simultaneously providing her the space to move fluidly from one identity to the next, depending on what each situation she encountered demanded. This letter-journal suggests she was never wholly a pacifist, neutralist, disaffected, Loyalist, or rebel, but she was willing to adapt along with the changing landscape just beyond her front door. It served as a vehicle through which she could cross literal dividing lines—so that she could reach her relatives beyond Burlington—and metaphorical and generic ones as well.[30] Where she was not able to proclaim publicly her loyalties through oaths or via legislation, she was able to discover, track, and adapt her political identities on paper and send these thoughts across enemy lines, where she could affirm for her family and friends that she was remaining as close as she could to Quaker principles at a time when her ability to do so was tried and tested.

The Letter-Journal of Anna Rawle

Anna Rawle, also a Quaker, lived about twenty miles west of Margaret Morris in a house called Laurel Hill along the Schuylkill River. And while her experience constructing Loyalism overlapped in many ways with Morris's—particularly in that both were Quakers and both were targeted and harassed—the way that Rawle framed her political identity in her letter-journal differed because of her location and her family.

Rawle would likely have been considered suspicious at best, or a Loyalist by association at worst, because of her parents, Rebecca and Samuel Shoemaker.[31] Before the war began, Samuel served two terms in the Pennsylvania Assembly. In December 1777—just as troops were approaching Margaret Morris's house twenty miles away—he was appointed general of the police in Philadelphia, charged with squashing rebel dissent. The assembly then declared him guilty of treason on March 6, 1778, for siding with the king, and three months later he fled to New York with his son, William.[32] Rebecca joined him in March 1780 after the Supreme Executive Council exiled her after intercepting some of her letters that indicated she was helping Loyalists pass from rebel-occupied Philadelphia into New York.[33] If the assemblymen exiled the Shoemakers to New York because they were subversive Loyalist dissenters who needed to be contained, then they must have allowed Rawle and her sister, Peggy, to stay because they did not see these women as a threat.[34]

The family's separation meant that the letters between them had to travel past the boundaries of the Delaware Valley into New York and back again; this journey meant that both the letters and their authors encountered a variety of geopolitical terrains as the missives passed out of Quaker country into a Loyalist stronghold. In order to ensure that the letters reached their intended recipients, the authors had to enact various performances. Since the Pennsylvania Assembly had already intercepted Rebecca's letters, she had to adapt the genre she used to communicate with her children. She was being watched. So she began writing a letter-journal—a series of letters addressed to her children bound as a diary—perhaps because sending a group of letters once instead of many times decreased the opportunities for interception. Or perhaps she hoped that soldiers would not want to read a woman's diary as they would a letter. (She never says why.) To further evade detection, Anna Rawle employed Joseph Scott, an elderly man, to deliver her letter-journal to her mother in New York; she believed—rightly—that the soldiers would not molest him due to his age. Her mother also wrote her letters in code—substituting "S.S." for Samuel Shoemaker and "R.S." for herself, for example—and used pseudonyms for family members. Rebecca's son, William, became "Horatio"; her daughter Peggy, "Adelaide"; Anna's friend Sally, "Juliet"; and Anna, "Fanny."[35] Rawle was not very good at using her mother's coded system. When she tried to convince a family friend to deliver a letter to New York for her, assuring the friend that the letter was indecipherable, the deliverer laughed, saying Rawle's "S.S.'s are known thro' all Jersey."[36] Rawle tired quickly of this charade. "This public manner of writing restrains my pen and is very disagreable," she wrote to her mother, adding, "but I have no other way of assuring [you] of my duty and esteem."[37] As Rawle's letters to Shoemaker were passing from the Delaware Valley, a contested political space, into New York, a Loyalist safe haven, they were written so as to shift meaning along with the boundaries they had to cross. The coded names and undetectable deliveryman reflect the fear that information inside of the letters would brand Rawle (as it had already branded Shoemaker) a covert Loyalist. But Rawle's refusal to learn the coded system and her insistence upon continually traversing various disputed boundaries also indicates her defiance.

At times Rawle seems much less of a neutralist than her fellow Quaker Morris, even openly mocking the rebel cause. For example when she learned that General Cornwallis surrendered his army to General Washington at Yorktown, Virginia, in October 1781, she said she found the news "as surprizing as vexatious. People who are so stupidly regardless of their own interest"—meaning the British soldiers, whom she felt had given up—"are undeserving of compassion."[38] She then wrote that she and her family, like the other Quakers, refused to celebrate Cornwallis's defeat along with the rest of the town. Like Morris, Rawle usually stopped short of wholeheartedly endorsing one side or the other, but, unlike Morris, she expressed her so-called neutrality with open disdain for both sides. The British were fools for surrendering, but she did not endorse the Americans' win. So, like Morris, Rawle expressed herself not as a rebel, yet not as a Loyalist.

Rawle used not one but two "texts" to explore the slippage between being a neutralist, pacifist, and passive Loyalist; the first was her letter-journal, and the other was her house. Because distinguishing a Loyalist from a Patriot was often a difficult task, rebels demanded that townspeople who favored independence light a candle in the window to proclaim publicly their allegiances. Crowds passed lit windows and smashed dark ones. Rawle's was unlit. Her refusal to light the candle inscribed her loyalties—or lack of them—on the house itself. This darkness acted as a publication of a different sort. Like the eighteenth-century diary, the house (especially the window in question) was both a public and a private space. The occupants regulated the interior, but the crowd interpreted the exterior. And like a text, that darkened window's meaning passed out of the author's control once readers engaged with it.

In the letter-diary to her mother, the other textual space that she used to inscribe her loyalties, Rawle retaliated by fashioning the crowd as a bloodthirsty mob and her family as undeserving victims. This rhetoric countered the narrative that both the state and the crowd were telling about the Rawle/Shoemakers, which was that they were either covert Loyalists or spies (or both). Rawle wrote that a "mob . . . broke the shutters and the glass of the windows, and were coming in," though there were "none but forlorn women" inside. Her decision to name the group of people a "mob"—a word with a negative connotation—indicated judg-ment.[39] Rebels would have lauded this crowd action; Loyalists would have con-demned it. But she cloaked this condemnation in subtlety, concluding the sentence by framing herself not as a political figure with the luxury of choice but as an abandoned bystander surrounded by other victims of war.[40] Rawle's entry spent no time on why the crowd might have targeted her house. She elided her faith, her parents' exile, her mother's suspicious correspondence, and her own decision to leave her window dark. Instead she emphasized the violence—the result rather than the impetus for the attack, a discursive move that aligned her with neither the British nor the rebels but made her an object of pity to both.

In both the house and diary-as-text, men ultimately inscribed the public, po-litical meaning onto the Shoemaker family. Rawle emphasized that she never lit a candle, instead huddled inside of her home "in fear and trembling till, finding them grow more louder and violent, not knowing what to do, . . . ran into the yard." Two neighbors, Coburn and Bob Shewell, then snuck past the crowd to light candles for Rawle's family, which "pacified the mob, and after three huzzas they moved off."[41] Rawle avoided making any political statement by word or deed—either by lighting a candle or writing about whether or not she approved of her neighbor's actions. This lack of action would have been important to the Society of Friends, perhaps the best answer possible to the Quaker predicament. Lighting a blazing beacon of loyalty would have violated her pacifism; the Friends had already issued an epistle specifically forbidding lighting candles to claim an allegiance for one side or another.[42] Although laying low had been, to that point, advantageous for her, in this case it made her a target. By both refusing to light that candle and by writing about this incident as mob-driven, unprovoked, and undeserved, Rawle was able to criticize the rebels for their lack of control while simultaneously positioning herself as a hapless witness to, rather than a participant in, the war.

Of course the problem was that Rawle could write her version of what hap-pened all she wanted, but the crowd still destroyed her house. The passage in her letter-diary about her unlit window underscored the tension between active and passive Loyalism. Rawle may have meant for her dark window to symbolize her Loyalism, pacifism, neutrality, disaffection, or some combination, but the rebels read it as her unequivocal alignment with the British. The house-as-text was more difficult to control than the letter-diary (or perhaps not, since Rawle's letters were intercepted). The house's readers—in this case, the crowd—did not ask how Rawle desired to be interpreted; its analysis of her unlit window was the primary factor for deciding whether or not to spare her family.

If Rawle could not control how her house was inscribed, she could control the narrative about its destroyers. While the rebels fashioned themselves as Patri-ots celebrating a victory for freedom, she fashioned them as maniacal rapists run amuck. She wrote that she had to nail "boards up at the broken panels," since it "would not have been *safe* to have gone to bed" without patching the holes that the crowd left (emphasis added).[43] Her emphasis on safety had a sexual connotation. By stripping her house of its windows, the crowd stripped her of security. Anyone could and would come inside. Her neighbors were not safe, either. Rawle wrote that the men who broke into homes nearby found "all of the sons were out," so they "acted as they pleased"—another phrase that implies (though is perhaps deliberately unspecific about) sexual violence. Rebels targeted "Tory" women because raping them symbolized stripping them of their socioeconomic position.[44] If women were extensions of their Loyalist husbands via coverture, then raping those women meant harming the husbands too. During events such as the one Rawle described, it was not unusual for rebels to march a dirt-smudged woman and a hangman through the streets to suggest to onlookers that women who refused to support the rebels would be murdered or raped. The dirt implied that the women's political affiliations tainted their sexual virtue.[45] Rebel crowds believed that British affiliates had uncontrollable sexual appetites, which they (ironically) believed in taming by raping them. Rawle's decision to include this issue in her letter-journal to her family in New York makes a statement because, by discussing it, she denies the notion that the rebel leaders were noble men carrying out justice in the name of liberty. And because she discussed it, she could also condemn it—and the rebel perpetrators who carried it out. Does this condemnation, alone, make her a Loyalist? Rawle refused to commit. Instead of fashioning herself a Loyalist, she was a woman left behind. Whether because of the publicity of her correspondence, her status as a Quaker, or her perilous situation as a woman living alone, she did not explain why.

The Journal of Sarah Logan Fisher

Sarah Logan Fisher lived in Germantown, Pennsylvania, during the Revolution, about twenty miles away from Margaret Morris and five from Anna Rawle. Fisher, like Morris and Rawle, kept a journal that she used to track and publicize her loyalties. Her journal documented the arrest of Fisher's husband, Thomas (Tommy), and other men, all primarily Quakers, following Congress's search for spies in the Philadelphia area inspired by the forged Spanktown missive. The Supreme Executive Council refused to grant the prisoners a trial, arguing that the crisis required that it skip such formalities. George Bryan, president of the executive council, suggested instead that the prisoners be sent three hundred miles away to Virginia, where they sat for eight months until a decision could be made.[46] After Tommy was arrested, Fisher began addressing her journal to him, which he received while in exile. Fisher asked Tommy not to share what she had written with other inmates; that she had to make this request suggests that her journals' default setting was public unless she indicated otherwise, a fact that further attests to the muddy divide between intimate and private writing practices.[47]

While Rawle framed her political identity in opposition to crowd action, and Morris constructed hers by critiquing the troops, Fisher explored her loyalties by writing about her resistance to rebel demands for food, supplies, and shelter during her husband's absence. On May 2, 1776, the Supreme Executive Council authorized the requisition of four thousand blankets from Pennsylvania. Fisher refused to grant these requisitions, citing an epistle from the Meeting of Suffering "entreating Friends not to join in the present measures."[48] Rather than excusing them from these requests, this letter made Quakers a target. The council instructed its soldiers to single out Friends because they refused other means of support. "If [the rebels] carry [this wicked Resolve] into execution, it will be an act of violence almost too great to bear," Fisher wrote. She then went on to suggest that the soldiers charged with requisitions were unvirtuous, or "men of very little Principle, . . . so intolerably Dirty that even in the cleanest of their Houses, the stench . . . is great enough to cause an infection."[49] Allowing them inside of her house would infect it and everyone in it; by refusing access to entry, Fisher was keeping her house as neutral—and, in her words, clean—as possible. Her household was intact, the way she framed it, because she had not allowed other people's loyalties to taint it. In so doing she maintained her spiritual, political, and feminine virtue.

Eventually, though, Fisher encountered soldiers who did not ask; they took. When they demanded entry into her home, she said that they "had robd me of what was far dearer than any property I had in the World, . . . my Husband, & that I could by no means encourage War of any kind." But the soldiers ignored what she said and pushed past her, searching her home despite her protests. They asked to have "some person" (perhaps Fisher or a servant) accompany them to the bedrooms they wanted to search, and Fisher emphasized that she "positively refused." So the men went upstairs, and "tho there was a Carpet on every floor & a Blanket on every Bed, they came down & . . . told me they had had the pleasure of viewing my Rooms, but saw nothing that suited them." Fisher wrote that, when they finally left, the mercy was not the soldiers', but God's, "that Hand that had hitherto mercifully supported me."[50] Fisher had again (thinly) implied that the rebels were dishonorable people. They threatened to molest Fisher and her family, rummaged through her private chambers, and left only when they decided to do so. Because they held the weapons, they controlled Fisher's domestic space, but they did not control her letter-journal or its narrative. Instead of emphasizing that the soldiers temporarily controlled her space, Fisher highlighted for Tommy that they left empty-handed. These men could not seduce her. She compromised neither body nor faith.

Although Fisher claimed pacifism throughout her letter-journal, the difference in the way she wrote about the rebels and the Loyalists is striking. Though she did not favor the war, she clearly favored the British. She described the Americans as disorderly, destructive, barefoot, unhealthy, "dirty Creatures."[51] Upon reading George Washington's proclamation that all colonists should swear allegiance to America, she said Washington was a "great instance of a Heart deprav'd by Ambition."[52] "[P]erhaps infernals, would not be too harsh a name" for the Americans, she wrote, "for surely their Characters deserve to be stamped with the blackest eye, who wish to raise their own fortunes, by sacrificing thousands of Lives, & the total ruin of their Country."[53] But when the British occupied Philadelphia on September 26, 1777, she wrote that they arrived in "clean dress" with "their bright Sowrds [*sic*] glittering in the Sun." They looked "clean & healthy"—strikingly different from the diseased rebels she described earlier—but marched with "no wanton levity, or indecent mirth but a gravety [*sic*] well becoming the occasion." They took the city without "even firing a single Gun," she said, grateful for the civilized exchange of power.[54] Fisher described the rebel troops as filthy, disorganized, and riotous and the British troops as clean, shiny, and orderly. She constructed the rebels as greedy, duplicitous, and irreverent and the British as humble, grave, and earnest. While the Americans were attempting to script Fisher's loyalties for her, demanding supplies and lodging that, if given, would indicate her allegiances, she was writing her loyalties for herself. Her letter-journal acted as a semipublic, semiprivate space through which she could explore simultaneously her allegiances with the Quakers, her preference for the British, and her distrust of the Americans. Because of its conflicting and conflicted loyalties, this letter-journal's pages reflect the turmoil in the Delaware Valley. People were neutralists, pacifists, Loyalists, disaffected, and sometimes all four in this region because of the sociopolitical makeup of its residents, and the rhetoric in Fisher's journal reflects the tension that was present in that space.

The letter-diaries of Anna Rawle, Sarah Logan Fisher, and Margaret Morris both clarify and complicate our understanding of how Quakers constructed loyalty during the American Revolution. They affirm and enrich what early American scholars have suspected was true of eighteenth-century manuscrips: they were neither wholly public nor wholly private. Although the audience for these manuscripts was limited, they were shared with other people, making them a quasi-public proclamation of political identity. Rawle performed her loyalties for her mother and sister, Fisher for her husband and the other exiles, and Morris for her sister and her circle of friends. Then we must also consider that these writers were aware that their proclamations circulated to audiences beyond their control. Morris knew the Pennsylvania Assembly was monitoring Quaker correspondence. Rawle lamented that rebels stole her missives. Fisher resented that Tommy's letters might first pass rebel guards. And yet some of the writers attempted to control the public nature of their correspondence. Rawle gave her correspondents code names (though she used them inconsistently). Morris used only abbreviations and asked her sister to limit her audience to like-minded individuals. These manuscripts, like the writers themselves, moved fluidly between public and private spaces, which was both to the writers' advantage and to their detriment. Sometimes they could control the audience and sometimes not. Sometimes they could control reception but often not. But each writer felt compelled repeatedly to risk being discovered and to tell her story in her own way.

These letters and journals also remind us that, while the rebels may have had a "with us or against us" mentality, not all so-called Loyalists did. They suggest that gray-area Loyalists would identify as disaffected, neutralists, or pacifists, if given the opportunity, though sometimes they shifted their loyalties to fit their situations. Despite being pacifists, many of these writers were treated as if they had affiliations all their own, even before it was clear to the writer whether or not she did. Rawle's letters were monitored and her parents exiled. Fisher's house was attacked and her husband imprisoned. Morris's home was searched and her children threatened. When contemporary scholars talk about Quakers during the American Revolution, we must not extend the assumptions that the rebels made more than two hundred years ago. We should, instead, read these manuscripts as spaces of self-definition, even though men with authority could also override these declarations of political identity, rendering them ineffectual. Morris convinced the rebel soldiers that she was just a widow, and they left her unmolested. Rawle evaded exile with her parents. But Fisher claimed pacifism, and they took her husband and smashed her home. Evaluating what women wrote about themselves, rather than relying solely on other sources that attempted to define Loyalist women, is the key to developing a better understanding of the nuances of "loyalty" in war.

Loyalist Refugee Camp

A Reinterpretation of Occupied New York, 1776–83

In May 1776 Caleb Peck rented a farm from Sir John Johnson in Tryon County, New York. When his landlord raised the King's Royal Regiment, Peck enlisted. Over the next three years, Peck fought the king's enemies and by 1779 was safely garrisoned in Canada. His wife, Catherine, and their child had a harder time. By 1779 they had become refugees in British-occupied New York after being forced out of their home by vengeful revolutionaries. Fleeing with just what they could carry, they had become a pitiful sight.[1]

In December 1776 Richard Reading from Monmouth County, New Jersey, fled his farm to escape the retreating Continental Army. Richard was suspected of supporting the advancing British and decided to save his life by fleeing. He succeeded in getting as far as New York, but the Continentals caught his wife and two children. Over the next year, a drama played out as his family was held prisoner, their property was confiscated, and later they were banished from New Jersey as traitors. In late 1777 Richard's family were finally reunited in New York. They had also lost everything.[2]

In May 1777 Joseph Stacey Hastings of New Hampshire fled with this family to New York. He gave no clear reason. However, he had already joined the British garrison in Boston in 1776, suggesting he had Loyalist sympathies. The evidence shows that by the autumn of 1778 he was destitute and very ill. On 16 August he caught a fever that lasted three weeks. His wife then caught the same fever and spent six weeks in bed. At the end nobody in the Stacey family had the strength to work, and all were going hungry.[3]

On the eve of the Revolutionary War the families of Peck, Reading, and Stacey had never met. Over the next years, they all became struggling refugees in British New York. They did not share the same background, politics, or wartime experiences. All they shared was their new predicament. In this they were not alone. Between 1776 and 1782, thousands of colonists became refugees in British

New York, and they quickly changed the way the city worked. This essay explores what can be gained by thinking of Revolutionary New York as a distinctive type of Loyalist refugee camp, which the city had come to resemble physically. But more important, the refugees through negotiations with the British Army developed a distinctive Loyalist camp culture to rebuild their lives alongside the troops. Ultimately this essay suggests that approaching New York as a Loyalist refugee camp puts it at the center of the Revolutionary experience. More than just another wartime city, New York is the best place to study a fluid, contingent, and ultimately unpredictable wartime identity found throughout Revolutionary America.

All wars create refugees. The Revolutionary War was no exception. It certainly produced moments of profound political insight, but once the fighting started, it also created a flood of displaced people who were more concerned with food than freedom. These colonists were the casualties of battlefield politics. On a grand scale, the Revolutionary War was fought over independence. On a scale more recognizable to the participants, the it was fought over the allegiance of the civilian population. In every campaign British and American armies attempted to consolidate military victories by forcing local civilians to choose sides. Civilians had to declare their allegiances by staying or fleeing the victorious army. Faced with this dilemma, many abandoned their unpredictable old lives for the relative safety of British-occupied territory.

By far the largest number of refugees during the Revolution went to New York. The first refugees were displaced New Yorkers who had lost their homes in the fighting for the city in the summer of 1776. These numbered roughly five thousand.[4] They were soon joined by a steady flow of refugees from surrounding colonies as British offensives stalled and then went into retreat. "Great numbers of People are daily coming in," one officer wrote, "and the province of New York have petitioned the Commissioners [of Peace] to be Restored to the Kings favour."[5] In total studies have estimated a wartime refugee population of approximately twenty thousand.[6] What followed was a political experiment on the crowded city streets that created unprecedented refugee camp.

Historians have been drawn to New York as one of the strangest places in the Revolution. The reason is not hard to see. The city was an oddity. It was a British city in the middle of a collapsing empire. Other cities came under British military control but never for so long. The British occupation of Boston ended in May 1776. The occupation of Philadelphia lasted less than a year, from late September 1777 to June 1778. The occupation of Charleston managed to last for two years, from May 1780 to December 1782. The occupation of Savannah lasted a little longer, from late December 1778 to July 1782. Yet only New York was a British city for the entire Revolutionary War. The long British stay turned the city into a unique political experiment. New York evolved beyond a conquered city into occupied city and ultimately into a revolutionary city as redcoats and colonists rubbed shoulders and tried to make sense of each other. A tantalizing suggestion follows. New York must have something distinctive to tell about the British, and by extension Loyalist, experience of the Revolution.

Drawn to this complexity, generations of historians have turned New York into the protean city of Revolutionary historiography. Older studies were more interested in the significance of the city in a larger Revolutionary narrative. Early authors wanted their readers to understand that occupied New York was a distinctive place during the Revolution that could not to be understood in a few pages. It also inspired later historians. Some have focused on the British and discovered a "garrison city" as the British army turned it according to their military needs.[7] Others have followed the Loyalists and discovered a Loyalist citadel created by an elite few who linked their fate to British victory and heralded New York as an imperial city of the future.[8] A few have focused on the seemingly more apathetic inhabitants and conclude that New York was either an opportunist's paradise in which politics took second place to a murky world of self-interest or a trap for desperate colonists looking for refuge.[9] This approach is where Robert Calhoon made his intervention. In *Loyalists in Revolutionary America,* Calhoon argued that short-lived British victories early in the war lured Loyalist colonists to New York. However, when the British began losing, these late Loyalists found it impossible to go home and reluctantly spent the rest of the Revolution fighting to survive in their adopted home.[10] Today New York exists in historiography as a layered city. The key has become to explore the ways these different cities layered and interacted. Following the refugees and finding a refugee camp provides a way both to study a new layer and to resolve some of the contradictions offered by a city of naive and zealous followers and opportunists.

Refugees have complicated identities, and refugee camps are complicated places. Neither is simply a description. Instead both refugees and refugee camps must be approached as highly imagined constructs. The field of migration studies offers a guide to this world. Focusing on twentieth-century refugee camps in Africa and the Middle East, these studies have uncovered a distinctive political culture of necessity constructed by the refugees who need support and the authorities willing to help them. Governments or nongovernmental organizations attempt to define refugees through official policies, but refugees also attempt to define their own experiences. The underlying assumption of this study is that *refugee* is not a standard label to be applied from above but one created by displaced people as they create connections with sympathetic authority structures. A refugee camp is best thought of as a two-way negotiation about the qualities needed by refugees to get aid in which the most dynamic element comes from the refugees themselves.[11]

The work of Simon Turner on Hutu refugee camps in Tanzania is at the forefront of this literature. Turner set out to understand refugees in the massive Lukole Refugee Camp set up by the United Nations in the wake of Burundi's silent genocide in 1993.[12] Home to 120,000 Hutu exiles, Lukole was "like a city in the middle of nowhere" until 2008.[13] Turner spent a year in the camp in 1997–98 and uncovered a debate about refugee identity between the United Nations and the Hutu exiles. For the United Nations, the camp was a liminal spot outside of the normal political life of the citizen-subject. Genuine refugees were meant to be innocents. In reality the United Nations understood that all refugees had a more complicated past and therefore offered a way to become innocent by defining innocence as being passive. This redefinition became the key to understanding politics in the camp. Given the opportunity to reinvent their pasts, Turner found, Hutu refugees created a series of discourses to appeal to the UN's desire for innocence while keeping control of their own identity. In particular refugees acted out a narrative of a "catastrophic event" in 1993 that had abruptly changed everything about their past histories. Next they set about rebuilding their identities in the most advantageous way possible. Some emphasized their superiority by working closely with authorities. Some emphasized their vulnerability by focusing on personal suffering. All claimed to have a superior understanding compared to the camp bureaucracy. What emerged in Lukole was a debate between a prescriptive, top-down refugee identity and a creative, bottom-up one. Or, to summarize Turner's conclusion: the point where the homogenous bureaucracy of the camp and the heterogeneous population of the camp met is the key to understanding the operation of the camp. The exciting suggestion is that a refugee camp is more than just a place—a large number of displaced peoples administered by an authority. It is also a distinct political space defined by the reconstruction of refugee identities from above but most importantly from below.[14]

The insights from Turner's work offer a way to study the Loyalist political culture in British New York. Of course eighteenth-century New York was not the same as a late twentieth-century refugee camp. The differences are vast and should not be overlooked. Yet the theoretical model offers suggestive parallels of use to Revolutionary studies. The best recent work on the city has already shown that New York was a place of fluid identity and creative constructions similar to those in Turner's work. The standout study is Judith L. Van Buskirk's *Generous Enemies: Patriots and Loyalists in Revolutionary New York.* Van Buskirk argues that "occupied New York was never Fortress Britannica." Instead New York was the "most volatile of places whose fluid boundaries permitted a parade of Whigs, Loyalists, slaves, Hessians, and those of murky allegiances to interact throughout the war."[15] In particular Van Buskirk points to the networks of contacts that the refugees maintained in New York. Just because friends and families supported independence did not mean they should be forgotten, especially for those who were starving in New York. As such, Van Buskirk concludes, "ties of family and friendship often proved more important to Americans caught in the coils of revolution than did military or political differences."[16] Van Buskirk reveals the ways that Loyalism and self-interest clashed in the refugee population and prevented the creation of a coherent identity in the larger population. This essay builds upon the insight that Loyalism was fluid and attempts to explore the ways the British army and refugees turned Loyalism into a constructive strategy for surviving the war. Drawing on Turner's refugee camp model, I am interested in how the British army formulated a prescriptive Loyalism to control refugees through the distribution of supplies and how in turn the refugees used Loyalism as a self-conscious strategy to get the best deal they could. The result was an unintended consequence: talking about a Loyalist refugee camp gradually organized the chaos of New York into a Loyalist refugee camp.

The arrival of the British army turned New York into a burned-out ghost town. At the end of June 1776, residents around New York reported seeing ships massing on the horizon. Between July and September, the largest contingent of the British army sent to America during the Revolution conquered Staten Island, Long Island, and Manhattan Island and its prize of New York City. Quick victories did not immediately translate into support. When the British triumphantly marched into New York, only five thousand out of a prewar population of twenty-five thousand remained.[17] No sooner had the British secured the city than fire rampaged through the abandoned streets. The British blamed saboteurs hiding in the city, While the revolutionaries blamed looting redcoats.[18] And naturally everybody denied everything. Regardless of who started the fire, it destroyed a quarter of the city. Eyewitnesses estimated anywhere from 493 to more than 1,000 houses were destroyed in a broad swath down the West Side.[19] In the months after, the British went on to consolidate their victory, but in New York they faced the more immediate challenge of making sense of the empty and now devastated city.

The army commanders had no interest in rebuilding New York. The first priority of the commander in chief, Gen. Sir William Howe, was to turn the smoldering ruins into a garrison and staging ground for future campaigns. Immediately after the invasion, thirty thousand troops crowded the streets. Later a permanent garrison of three thousand soldiers and around twenty-five hundred dependents remained for the duration of the war.[20] To support this many men necessitated the complete takeover of every aspect of the city's life. Howe's deputies ignored the surviving royal government of New York and instead turned New York into an occupied city. The military commandeered much of the largely unscathed south of the city and, using local knowledge, confiscated rebel-owned housing for officers in what survived of the rest.[21] Churches and other public buildings were converted into barracks, infirmaries, and prisons. Orders were issued controlling the movement, storage, and sale of food, firewood, and the thousands of other things an army needs. New York became a paper-stuffed bureaucracy as the quartermaster's department recorded everything and issued passes for all exceptions. Anybody, soldier or civilian, caught breaking these rules would be judged before a court-martial.[22] Clearly the British army wanted to turn New York into an occupied city from which to fight the Revolution. This was not, however, the city they got.

As the British campaign continued, thousands of colonists slowly repopulated the city. The first people trickled in from the immediate hinterland carrying what they could. Others arrived after the British withdrew their protection from regions. The first and largest wave of refugees came in early 1777 from New Jersey. Members of this group often arrived with nothing more than the clothes on their backs. It was simply not easy to transport households during the war. Between 1777 and 1779, other waves came from Connecticut, Pennsylvania, Vermont, and Rhode Island. Between 1780 and 1782, refugees arrived from the southern colonies.[23] In total contemporary estimates and later studies suggest that there were as many as many as twelve thousand refugees by early 1777 and close to twenty thousand by 1782.[24] All of these colonists had different pasts but came to share a common present working out what their new lives would be in New York. One reality shaped this new identity: everyone who arrived in New York had to work out how to survive alongside the British army.

Occupied New York turned out to be a terrible city for refugees. With much of the infrastructure burned down and the rest full of British soldiers, the poverty-stricken refugees had to fight for their place. Shortages of everything were normal, and competition for what little was available was a fact of life. High and rising rents became inevitable as the stream of refugees all wanted accommodation. One study estimated that rents increased fourfold over the course of the war.[25] A contemporary witness wrote that there "was a constant increase in the article of Rents."[26] After paying rent, price gouging made food unaffordable. "This town," a visiting Englishmen complained, "is filled by a Set of Villains and Harpies, who are enriching themselves . . . having no kind of Conscience in the advance they put upon every Necessary of Life."[27] In April 1777 Gen. William Howe was forced to issue a proclamation fixing the prices of every staple within the city under punishment of court-martial.[28] At times some items, in particular firewood during the winters, became so scarce that nobody had enough money to afford them. "The King's Barracks indeed are full," one source explained, "but the citizens suffer."[29] And the barracks were only full because Howe threatened to seize all firewood hoarded around the city.[30] The refugees were not as intimidating and so got cold. "Many reputable people lay abed these days for want of fuel," wrote one shivering witness in January 1780.[31] Yet another noted that warm beds were not always enough: "We often hear of the deaths of the poor frozen in their Houses."[32] Add to these problems poor sanitation, widespread disease, and a growing crime epidemic, and refugees discovered that New York was a hellish place to live out the war. "Ditches and fortified places are full of stagnate water," one visiting Englishmen noted, pointing out the people smelled as bad. "Unwholesome smells," he continued, "are occasioned by such a number of people being crowded together in so small a compass almost like herrings in a barrel, most of them very dirty." He colorfully concluded that "if any author had an inclination to write a treatise upon stinks . . . , he never could meet with more subject matter than in New York."[33] It surprised no one when in 1779 both scarlet fever and smallpox epidemics broke out.[34] Mounting desperation made some turn to crime. One resident noted that by the end of the war New York was too dangerous "to walk the streets at night or be in a crowd in the day" and that scarcely a night passed without some crime being committed.[35] Clearly something had to be done to ensure the city's survival.

Refugees and British army officials increasingly debated how to make New York City function as both a refugee camp and an effective military garrison. What emerged was the mingling of a revolutionary politics of Loyalism and a New York politics of need. Essentially refugees had to be Loyalists to get aid from the British Army. However, given the chaos in New York, this was not a simple conversation. There were moments of conflict, but relatively few given the high-pressure environment.[36] Both sides tried to bargain for the best deal. The key issue became exactly who counted as a genuine refugee or, more accurately, what was Loyalist enough to impress the British. Three main discourses appeared.

Of course real power mattered, and the British army's being in charge defined the parameters of the debate. In 1776 the army had no model for what a refugee camp should look like. From the start it wanted only two types of Loyalists: soldiers to fight throughout America or loyal civilians to stay at home. Armed with the belief that Americans needed only encouragement to be loyal, General Howe and his brother, Adm. Richard Howe, in their secondary role as peace commissioners from King George III, issued unconditional pardons. They issued the first pardon by proclamation on October 21, 1776. The proclamations stated that "American born Subjects shall be permitted to enter into any of the provincial corps, or to return home as they shall think fit."[37] The soldiers would of course fight, but those at home could do nothing and wait for inevitable victory. As long as the British were winning, many colonists were willing to go along with this plan. Hundreds enlisted in new Loyalist regiments. Thousands more stayed at home. The Howe brothers could confidently write in November 1776 that "a very considerable number of persons who had been active in the rebellion . . . have already subscribed the declaration of allegiance."[38] However, as soon as the British began losing, in the last days of 1776, the policy fell apart. Now they only attracted refugees tainted with Loyalism and forced to leave their homes for the relative safety of New York. This was an unknown situation without a plan. The Howes issued a second pardon on March 15, 1777, but to little effect as more refugees appeared. The same problem occurred again when pardons were issued in 1778 and 1781. Instead of returning colonists to the king, they had turned them into displaced persons.

British commanders in New York quickly accepted the new reality of their situation and offered support to the refugees. It was not unusual for eighteenth-century armies to find themselves living with trailing camps of women and other dependents following the soldiers. From 1776 the army made a range of resources available to refugees through the office of military governor of New York, held for most of the war by James Robertson, who drew directly on army coffers or the quartermaster's department. The most basic support was an allowance calculated on the basis of number of men, women, and children in a family. The more dependents, the more money. The army assumed that refugees would supplement this basic handout with work. It in fact became one of the biggest employers, paying refugees to collect firewood, drive carts, and perform any number of menial tasks.[39] Refugees unable to work, such as the sick, old, or widowed, could receive additional support in the form of food or firewood allowance drawn from military stores. More occasionally the army provided subsidized or free housing confiscated from known traitors within the city.[40] These provisions were not designed to rebuild lives but to help refugees survive the immediate future.

This was not charity. The British could have simply continued the colonial poor laws. The literature on colonial poverty has shown how towns throughout eighteenth-century Americans developed a robust set of laws and institutions to tackle urban poverty.[41] New York was at the center of this transformation. In the years leading up the Revolution, the city authorities had increased the number of resources available to the poor. In 1771 the Society of the Hospital in the City of New York in America received a royal charter and began building a hospital. In 1772 the New York Assembly appropriated eight hundred pounds from excise duties on strong liquor sold in the city to fund the Hospital. In 1773 the assembly passed a new Act for the Settlement and Relief of the Poor that organized relief around the vestry system.[42] These examples of publicly funded relief were based on a traditional English classification of the deserving poor as local vagrants, unemployed, or helpless and not refugees. Yet as many of the officials with personal experience of this system returned to New York during the war, the army high command could have passed off the problem to civil authorities used to dealing with the poor.[43] Instead, however, the army created a new definition of the deserving poor based on current political needs.

The British army decided that only genuine refugees would be eligible for aid. But who counted as a genuine refugee? Clearly poverty was not enough, as this would involve far too large an expenditure. The British tried to differentiate Loyalists from opportunists and even spies. They simply did not trust colonists, and experience had taught most British soldiers that Americans were fickle—with refugees perhaps the worst of all. This stereotype dominated British thinking. One British officer made the point in a somewhat colorful letter home. "I should be very sorry to trust any one of them out of my sight," he explained. "They swallow the Oaths of Allegiance to the Kings, & Congress, Alternately, with as much ease as your Lordship does poached Eggs."[44] A colleague explained with more vitriol that the refugees were "poor simple country people" with "impudent, base, & hypocritical characters" and were poor "descendants of Britons."[45] With prescient resignation another official wrote: "We have a great many friends join us every day, but I believe they are such as we cannot depend upon as its supposed they only wait to go with the strongest."[46] Longer contact between the army and the refugees did not create a stronger relationship. If anything the tensions got worse. If the refugees wanted aid, they would first have to prove their Loyalism.

Ultimately the army approached the allocation of relief as a question of allegiance. To receive support all refugees had to pass a loyalty test. The policy to police allegiances emerged piecemeal alongside the aid in two key proclamations that created the bureaucracy for an authentic Loyalist city. The cornerstone policy came in January 1777 when James Robertson, a British officer and future civil governor or New York, mandated that all refugees must register with the army or be "disposed in some secure place or sent out of town."[47] Once registered, refugees had to convince the military government of their Loyalist credentials to receive aid. They would have to submit personal statements declaring their politics with whatever proof they could muster. This first policy was the opening move in creating a more coherent wartime refugee policy. In 1779 Robertson went further and created a special office led by an inspector for inquiring to investigate actively the loyalty of refugees entering the city before granting aid. All new appeals for aid had to be sent directly to this board for approval. At this point the cases were reviewed on an individual basis before being sent to the governor's office for final approval. With these two policies British officials had created—at least on paper— one of the most tightly controlled places in Revolutionary America and the official definition of a Loyalist refugee appeared.

With this loyalty test, the British wanted to impose a political innocence on the refugees and do away with any messy political realities that could interfere with the smooth running of the city. Instead of doubting the politics of the refugees, the army's policy was intended to make everyone who qualified equally Loyalists. No gradations appeared in the system to separate the passive from the active Loyalists. Interestingly the army did not require refugees to prove their Loyalism actively. For example they were not required to enlist in the Loyalist regiments formed in New York.[48] The army wanted refugees not to be revolutionaries and nothing more. This was a solution for New York with no suggestion of a wider applicability to British policy in America. With this final idea, the Army stopped and waited for the colonists to respond.

This potential to refashion was next seized by the ordinary refugees as they navigated the layers of city Loyalism. Refugees arriving in New York sooner or later had to ask how they could fit into this political structure. Supposedly to stay they had to all be Loyalists, pass the gatekeepers' test, and finally receive aid from the British. But what if their political history was more complex? As Christopher Minty has capably demonstrated in this volume, many of New York's most avowed Loyalists were in fact former Sons of Liberty. Such Loyalists were not unique. Few colonists could claim not to have changed their minds as the Revolution changed around them. The refugees represented every shade of politics possible. How could they rewrite their past overnight?

A small number believed they were already the archetypal Loyalist and did nothing but apply for aid. John Lovell of Boston, for example, believed his Loyalist credentials were beyond reproach. Lovell explained that "in support of the dignity of the King, his Representative and Laws of the Nations he has been compelled to suffer upwards of three years imprisonment." He had also spent upwards of five hundred pounds supporting his incarceration. Now he and his family were in distress and deserving of reimbursement and support. Anything further, he explained, was contained in a private letter he had already written to Roger Morris. With this authoritative dismissal, his memorial finished.[49] Lovell did not even include a referee to support his claim. The Bostonian assumed that three years in prison spoke for itself. Few people, however, had shared his partisan fate and could present such a clear-cut case.

Others who were not confident resting on their longstanding politics tried to sell their allegiance with an impressive tale or two of daring Loyalism. Samuel Jarvis regaled authorities with the account of his escape from Connecticut aboard a whaleboat. At midnight, Jarvis explained, a "mob of daring and unfeeling rebels" drove himself, his wife, three daughters, and "a little son" from their house in Stamford. Carrying just the clothes on their backs, the family was forced to the shore and into one of the whaleboats moored on the beach. After two hours they finally made it to New York, wading ashore in water almost up to their waists. In the cold and wet, his wife and two of his daughters became very sick. Jarvis made sure to point out that although his health was good, he was between sixty and seventy years of age at the time of the adventure. Now, in New York, his family had nothing and were "reduced . . . to the last extremity of real want."[50] The memorial contained no other proofs of Loyalism beyond the story of escape. Jarvis appeared to be gambling on the persuasiveness of a good yarn: why would he have to escape so dramatically in the dead of night if he was not a Loyalist?

The demand for a Loyalist pedigree or display of heroism created an almost impossible standard for the majority of refugees. The solution to the problem was elegant in its simplicity. Instead of proving their Loyalism to get material support, ordinary refugees used their need for material support as proof of their Loyalism. The review system put in place by the British gave them an opportunity to repackage their wartime experiences in this way. The certificates for British aid placed a lot of significance on a short, simple story that emphasized personal details. A common theme emerged: to present personal suffering as British suffering. The information was not fabricated, but it was an attempt to redefine Loyalism by their standards. The suffering could be material: the loss of land, for example. However, in the limited space available, refugees more often emphasized the tragedy of personal loss. What could be better proof of your commitment than losing a father, husband, or son for Britain? At least refugees gambled that by redefining the imperial crisis through personal suffering they could invoke a contractual relationship with the British. They hoped that the army commanders would feel responsible for the fate of the Loyalists they had, not the Loyalists of their military planning fantasies.

The majority of memorials made a basic connection between Loyalism and suffering. These memorials drew upon a formula of general distress endured by the whole family when the British army withdrew from territory. This was the most common refugee experience. They did not rely upon a specific example of Loyalism but a general assertion of being persecuted and forced into exile for an unspecified pro-British stance. Finally they left the reader with the vague implication of a future interrupted. Richard Reading from Monmouth County, New Jersey, wrote that he supported the British during their occupation in 1776–77 but was forced to flee, leaving "a considerable amount of Grain on the ground with many other necessaries for the support of his family."[51] Now they were destitute and needed help. Later that year, in upstate New York, the Winchester County Committee of Safety forced Griffen Cary to flee. He was safe in New York, Cary explained, but had no way to care for his six children.[52] Elizabeth Rogers from Norwalk, Connecticut, told a similar story. She was loyal, and her family lost everything when the British army raided the colony in 1779. For siding with the British—in an unspecified manner—she, her husband, and her two children were forced to flee to New York.[53] These memorials gained their power from their volume. Individually they proved little, but together they created a shared language of refugee Loyalism by repeatedly putting the same arguments before British eyes. The cumulative effect over time was to appropriate Loyalism and turn it into an allegiance refugees could use for their own advantage.

Colonists who could improve on this simple script did. While refugees were creating a common culture of suffering, there was no sense of unity beyond the text. Refugees understood that resources were limited. If you could show you had suffered more, then it stood to reason your case was more persuasive. Impressive examples of fortitude in the face of great suffering could then replace other more active forms of heroism. The key was to make the suffering dramatic and personal. This is where the most inventiveness appears, as refugees focused on moments of their Revolution that could be recast to make themselves appear Loyalist to the core.

Refugees who could prove suffering for specific acts of Loyalism wrote confident memorials. Hugh Munro from Albany had joined Gen. John Burgoyne's army at the Battle of Saratoga and was taken prisoner when the British surrendered. Suddenly his neighbors knew of his treachery and turned on his wife. Fearing for her life, she fled with their children to New York and now was desperate for help. Loyalism came to Samuel Watkins from Connecticut. He did not join the army but hid an "unfortunate Loyalist" who did. In the summer of 1780, the rebels discovered and executed the unnamed Loyalist, and Watkins's "own life was so endangered that he was obliged to come within the lines of for Protection."[54] At the same time, further south, another refugee had much greater success. In June 1780 Hannah Johnson was part of a Loyalist underground in in Bucks County, Pennsylvania. She had spent her war helping escaping British prisoners of war. She hid the soldiers for two or three weeks in her house before providing provisions for their next journey. Her husband would then lead them through the colony to New York. Using this system, Johnson explained, she had "assisted upwards of 100 British of War in making their escape into British lines." However the strain of living a double life for years had "reduced [them] to very low ebbs," and they decided to come to the safety of New York. Now the Johnsons wanted acknowledgement of their services. The petition finished with the assertion that many of the soldiers they helped escape—members of the Seventeenth Regiment of Foot—were in New York and could act as witnesses.[55] The combination of details and proof made Johnson's memorial very persuasive.

Other colonists emphasized personal hardship as a way to stand out from the crowd of refugees. The most common theme was illness. Colonists in good health turned to the suffering of their family as proof of their Loyalism by association. This was a particularly gendered argument dominated by wives trapped by their husbands' politics. Mrs. Percel, the wife of Abraham Percel, explained that "much upon the Account of her husbands Loyalty was Drove away by the Rebels with three Small Children." Now she had three children and "lost all they had bye the rebels after coming to this town" and had nothing left.[56] Mrs. Land was in a similar predicament. She explained her husband, Robert, joined a frontier expedition under Col. John Butler in 1778 but was "taken by the Rebels" and was still held in prison. She had been left with "three children and need[ed] provisions."[57] But it could have gotten worse. Susannah Wilkinson left Philadelphia with the British evacuation of the city, but tragedy struck her family. As they sailed from Philadelphia to New York, her husband drowned, leaving her with "a young child in a distressed and helpless condition."[58] Many wives explained that they had become refugees because of their husbands and had since been widowed with children. The suggestion clearly followed that the British army now had to assume the responsibility of their former husbands and support them.

Just as wives drew upon their husbands' suffering, parents emphasized the sacrifices of their children. Loyalism became multigenerational politics. Written with a mixture of pride and tragedy, parents explained how their older sons in particular were risking their lives for Britain. William Massay, "a Refugee, who has lately fled from a crueil and persecuting enemy to seek protection within his Majesty's lines," now had to cope with two sons fighting in a Loyalist corps, the New York–based "King's American Regiment." To prove the point, Massey secured the signature of the regimental commander, Colonel Fanning, and other officers.[59] Massay might have worried about losing the financial support of his sons but presented his worry about the fate of his sons as proof of his investment in the British cause. In turn he hoped that the British army would care for the worried parents of its newest recruits. Elizabeth McCrea from Virginia offered a similar presentation of her suffering through her son's service. "That being loyal herself," McCrea argued, "she brought her Children up in these principles." As the war started, she encouraged her two sons to join the "Kings Army." At the date of writing, 1779, one had died in Philadelphia, and the other was still fighting. While her sons fought and died for empire, she "been much persecuted, & brought to poverty by the rebels," and now needed aid.[60] The tragic death of one son made McCrea's appeal for aid even more persuasive, because it emphasized the McCreas fear for her remaining child. The message was clear: their son's willingness to fight for Britain entitled their parents to support. Each son, and each loss of life, made families' claims more persuasive.

Parents with younger children turned the focus onto the tragedy of infants who might never grow up to fight for Britain. Hannah Neil explained that her husband, John, had died serving in the First Battalion of Delancey's regiment and left her with two children. The only anecdotal detail came when she explained that one of her children is "but a few days old and in very poor circumstances." This was a blatant attempt to play on the sympathies of the British officer who finally decided on her appeal. What right-minded person could allow a newborn to suffer under the Union Jack? Mary Keating, the wife of another dead Loyalist soldier, tried to make the same point. She emphasized that she had three small children and that on their behalf hoped the commander in chief in would show "compassion, clemency and candour," which he had "so conspicuously shown on all occasion."[61] Deborah Cothell made an even more persuasive appeal. After her husband, Samuel, was taken prisoner, she was left with "five small children and nothing to support them" and desperately needed British aid.[62] While Neil had one newborn and Keating had three small children, Cothell sought to stand out with five small children. Such supplicants believed that emotional appeals could achieve the same result as a broken family or an enlisted son.

Grandparents could also be included in the "Loyalist" family. In a final twist, older refugees made an appeal to their own youthful obedience to the Crown to legitimize their appeal for British aid to ease their present suffering. Myndoert Viele explained that he was seventy-two and his wife sixty-two when they became refugees, and "both [are] unable to labour or do anything for their subsistence." Viele argued that he deserved aid not because of heroism during the Revolution but because of a lifetime of Loyalism that led to his persecution by the rebels. "That he has," Viele explained, "ever retained a faithful Allegiance to his Majesty and his Royal Predecessors—that on that Account he has been sent to this city [New York]."[63] He had been loyal to every Hanoverian king from George I to George III and now expected the British army to consider itself in his debt.

The inventiveness of refugee Loyalism should not be surprising. All of these petitions were successful. They exist only because they have survived among the British records from the occupation. On the back of each memorial, an unnamed British official wrote the name of the refugee and a short code for the number of men, women, and children receiving aid. Eventually these names were transcribed onto long rolls of refugees needing support. These were purely administrative documents breaking down the refugees into colony of origin.[64] The refugees had succeeded in finding a way to persuade the British army of their allegiance.

CONCLUSIONS

In 1777 one American prisoner of war, Lt. Jabez Fitch, witnessed a bizarre sight. It seemed to him that New York City was swarming with refugees desperately trying to be persuasive Loyalists. In his diary Fitch explained that POWs always had to be wary of the refugees' machinations. Revolutionary sympathizers gave the prisoners charity. The king's troops dismissed them as insolent rebels. The "malignant Torys" despised them as the enemy. But the most dangerous were the "worthless refugees and Vagrants" who "pretended to be friends of government."[65] Jabez was right. Refugees could very well look like "pretend" Loyalists. But he failed to understand why. The "worthless refugees and Vagrants" were participating in Loyalist refugee politics that would make little sense to an outsider. The tenuous nature of Loyalist status was life or death for many refugees, so they constructed that identity and defended it with vigor.

For as long as the British occupation lasted, the different discourses of refugee Loyalism worked alongside each other. Refugee Loyalism was a politics forged not around a common history but around a common present. Refugees had a personal story that brought them to New York. However they all found themselves trapped when they arrived. Only the richest could hope to survive without the support of the British army. From this starting point, refugees and the army manufactured a new type of refugee around competing definitions of the genuine Loyalist refugee. Taken together, they made up a distinctive political culture that defined British New York as a Loyalist refugee camp. In the longer term, refugee Loyalism because of its illusive foundations needed shoring up. Unable to leave New York for fear of persecution, refugees had unwittingly trapped themselves into a war of playing the role of the refugee Loyalist. This interpretation was only one facet of wartime New York, but it adds an important layer to the city. It is hard to ignore that daily life in Revolutionary New York was dominated by the refugee experience. Ultimately this essay argues that approaching New York City as a refugee camp puts it at the center of fluid, contingent, and ultimately unpredictable wartime political culture found throughout Revolutionary America.

Carole W. Troxler

Before and After Ramsour's Mill

Cornwallis's Complaints and Historical
Memory of Southern Backcountry Loyalists

Charles Lord Cornwallis, commanding British forces in the Southern Campaign, blamed backcountry Loyalists for ineffective recruiting. He said they were either too eager to join the British efforts or too reluctant, depending on the circumstances he was describing to his officers and superiors. The earl's assessments have all but frozen the historical memory of the region's Loyalist response. Cornwallis's statements dominated the references to Loyalists in the Southern Campaign, beginning with British civilian officials and the *Annual Register,* on which contemporary writers Charles Stedman, Banastre Tarleton, and others relied. Henry Dundas spoke from the inner circle of the prime minister in 1799 to resist British intervention on behalf of French revolutionaries. He argued, "I cannot forget the American war, where we were so miserably disappointed in the promised and expected co-operation."[1]

The perceptions of Cornwallis—and his displeasure—are understood readily and not to be disparaged. Shifting attention to the men who offered their services, however, and to the contexts in which they did so suggests that Cornwallis was speaking more from frustration than from reality. The recruiters examined here mobilized in southwestern North Carolina in June 1780. They were responding to pressures from local revolutionaries following the British seizure of Charleston, South Carolina, in May. On the heels of this mobilization, an engagement occurred on June 20, 1780, at Ramsour's Mill in present-day Lincoln County, North Carolina, near the uncertain border with South Carolina. On learning of the Loyalist defeat, Cornwallis blamed "premature" action of the recruiters and considered court-martialing those who held commissions. "The folly and imprudence of our friends are unpardonable," he swore.[2] Slightly more than three months later and less than thirty miles to the southwest, the decisive defeat of Carolina backcountry Loyalists took place at Kings Mountain. There most of the thousand or so Loyalists were killed, left to die of wounds, or taken prisoner. They came largely from the area that had turned out men for Ramsour's Mill.[3]

The June Loyalist mobilization demands analysis beyond its relationship with Kings Mountain, however. Cornwallis's castigation of the principal June recruiters brims with contradictions. Recognizing his inconsistencies does not invalidate his assessment of the immediate usefulness of the recruits. Rather Cornwallis accepted the advice of his potential militia leaders when they first approached him. He returned their request as an order to them. When revolutionary activity made compliance impossible, he lashed out against the Loyalists' disobedience. The general's written contradictions reveal that he well understood that the recruiters he rebuked had no choice. Yet blame them he did, memorably. Even more significant for understanding Loyalists in the Southern Campaign, historical memory has conflated the earl's response to the defeat at Ramsour's Mill with a string of comments about Loyalists he made during the period between the Kings Mountain defeat of October 7, 1780, and his Yorktown surrender on October 19, 1781. Cornwallis himself seems to have conflated his displeasure with Loyalists following Ramsour's Mill and during the year before Yorktown, when the Loyalist cause faced radically different circumstances.

Indeed Cornwallis's characterizations of Carolina backcountry Loyalists following the defeat at Ramsour's Mill became touchstones for assessing British losses throughout the entire Southern Campaign. This study does not suppose that southern backcountry Loyalists would have changed the course of the campaign—or even lived up to the expectations military planners held for them— if Cornwallis had comprehended their dilemmas in 1780 and had not disparaged them. The purpose for noting his inconsistencies and examining the recruiters and mobilizations is to extend the known landscapes across which much scholarly inquiry still peers from inside the commanders' tents. Blaming the recruiters served to exonerate Cornwallis for the British setback so soon after the Charleston triumph and only a fortnight after he took command. Moreover his explanations to superiors in New York and London and to his own officers drew on their shared, though unequal, social privilege. Disdain underlay the ease with which the earl blamed the backcountry recruiters for disrupting his expectations. In his culture the recruiters ranged in status from yeomen to a few gentlemen, and their recruits were yeomen and peasants. His easy barbs about them, left unfiltered, tightened their hold on historical memory. Examination of the circumstances and initiatives of six men who recruited other southern backcountry Loyalists for service prior to Ramsour's Mill can yield insights to supplement the earl's long-standing and much-quoted top-down assessments. This study focuses on Andrew Hamm, John Moore, Nicholas Welch, John Hamilton, Samuel Bryan, and James (or John) Boyd.

Part of the distortion of memory is the familiar framework for seeing the war in the southern colonies exclusively in terms of the Southern Campaign, and particularly in terms of engagements following the British taking of Charleston. The thrust of the war had begun its southward shift in the final days of 1778 when, following the French entry into the conflict, the British looked toward the Caribbean and the southern colonies and established a stronghold at Savannah, Georgia. In terms of the overall course of the war, the Southern Campaign was paramount during 1780–81, whether considered from the revolutionaries' loss of Savannah or of Charleston. Cornwallis took command of the British army in the South on June 5, 1780, less than a month after British forces took Charleston. When he turned inland to establish a secure post at Camden, South Carolina, it presented a new reality to the southern backcountry.

It was not a new war, however, for Loyalists who came forward from the western regions of South Carolina and North Carolina following the fall of their chief port. During the winter of 1775–76, revolutionaries had defeated and defused overt opposition in campaigns centering on a modest fortification at the village of Ninety Six in northwestern South Carolina and at Moore's Creek Bridge in eastern North Carolina. These early successes gave the emergent local authorities more than two years in which to function without imminent threat. During that time the Loyalist activists of 1775–76 were marked men. They followed a number of courses. Some took a state oath following capture and joined revolutionary militia, which did not yet require serving against British or Loyalists or even denouncing allegiance to the king. Individuals and groups hid in woods near their homes for months or went overland to East or West Florida, still under British control, or to western Pennsylvania. Others relinquished firearms and paid threefold or fourfold taxes to avoid militia service temporarily.[4] For these men their campaign started not so much with a British call to arms in 1780 as with earlier occasions when local revolutionaries used their institutions, particularly county courts and militia, to strengthen their hegemony. These efforts were under way in 1777–78.

Loyalist mobilization in western North Carolina before Maj. Patrick Ferguson began training militia at Ninety Six demonstrated "premature" aspects indeed from the perspective of Cornwallis's intentions to use local Loyalists. Conspicuously the British force that Loyalists had hoped for since 1776 was not yet present to coordinate them. Moreover men who had avoided militia service after showing their hands in 1775 and 1776 remained relatively untrained. A third illustration of "prematurity" was the impromptu nature of their leadership. The recruiters might have a commission from Cornwallis or another officer, but there was not yet a regional military establishment with a chain of command and direction. Some erstwhile revolutionary militia companies declared as a group for Loyalist service by electing captains known to oppose revolutionaries, a move that could not be secret. Other individuals and groups were ready to spring into action in the summer of 1780, having relatives who had been in East Florida for two years, avoiding the hated "black jack" oaths. (In 1777–78 both Carolinas had required militiamen to abjure allegiance to the Crown, a new provision.)[5]

Men who offered to recruit Loyalists in western North Carolina told Cornwallis forthrightly that they needed to wait until after harvest to embody them. Potential recruits needed time to gather and store their crops. The earl wrote that the North Carolinians who came into Charleston to offer their services in May and June 1780 told him they could bring him recruits after crops were gathered but not before. He sent them back into the interior with that understanding: keep your men still until British forces are in your area, which will be after harvest. They expected the wait to be mutually advantageous. The British force would want to live off the land, using food already harvested.[6] As it happened potential recruits did not have the luxury of anonymously waiting out the season. The revolutionaries were on them, not surprisingly, as soon as the British were settling into their first backcountry posts. Revolutionaries pressured suspected opponents and neutral men. Moreover Whig harassment of Tories throughout the area sharpened on the heels of Banastre Tarleton's success at the Waxhaws on May 29, 1780. Diarists in the Moravian towns in June passively recorded hearing of revolutionary militia harassing neutrals and Loyalists on the Yadkin River and Abbott's Creek, one of its large eastern tributaries.[7]

Andrew Hamm's Context

Andrew Hamm, a miller on Abbott's Creek, later referred to the harassment as "insults." In the 1750s and 1760s, the future Regulator spokesman Herman Husband had assisted Separate Baptists along Abbott's Creek to obtain land, and Moravian diarists had regarded the community as Regulators during the 1771 North Carolina Regulator crisis. In February 1776 revolutionaries captured twenty-one-year-old Hamm as he traveled toward the coast to join the expected British forces, and they "bound [him] over to remain quiet." Later he said he was not bothered again until the British took Charleston. Then his being drafted into the revolutionary militia precipitated a crisis; apparently this was when Hamm's "suffering" of "insults" occurred. Rather than serve with the revolutionaries, he and 111 other men organized themselves, probably at his mill. This was Hamm's setting for rising "prematurely," and it seems typical.[8] A Moravian church board in Salem recorded that throughout the first week in June, "soldiers [revolutionary militia] have been coming and going . . . asking sternly for deserters. . . . We also heard that some persons . . . [have made] a premature declaration in favor of the English, and have given them horses, and have even exchanged letters with them." Here as elsewhere revolutionaries were using militia to enforce the local political authority they claimed, now that the presence of British forces threatened it.[9]

Cornwallis did not record comprehension of this political dynamic. It lay beyond his purview, not only as a commander but also as part of the oligarchy governing Britain and its dependencies in the eighteenth century. Shared expectations among those whom the governor of East Florida called "the great Engines by which Government is upheld" rarely needed delineation among its network. That governor, Patrick Tonyn, made an exception in 1780, explaining to the secretary of state for America why southern Loyalists who had moved to East Florida were politically assertive there. "There prevails in America," Tonyn clarified, "a thirst for power, and a desire of consequence *unknown among the lower class of people in Europe.*"[10]

John Moore's Context

Meanwhile in the South Fork of the Catawba River, John Moore took the initiative for contacting potential recruits for a Loyalist militia. Unlike Hamm, Moore already was with British forces. In 1778 he had led a group of 250 men to East Florida. They had been among several groups who went there from the Carolina backcountry during 1777–78 to avoid "black jack" militia oaths. From East Florida, Moore and his men had been among the groups who went with the British to Savannah. Typically they began returning home as emissaries after lower Georgia was secured. Moore was with the British when they took Charleston and soon returned to his home area, where his family was influential.[11]

The extended family of John Moore had been Indian traders in western Pennsylvania prior to the Great War for Empire (a.k.a. the French and Indian War). John Moore's father, Moses Moore Sr., was among a number of settlers whom the Pennsylvania governor evicted for having encroached on Indian lands. A native of the Scottish-English Borders, Moses Moore sold other Pennsylvania land in the early 1750s, moved to the South Fork of the Catawba River, and bought land along Indian Creek. His siblings, children, and in-laws accompanied him. After the Revolution started, he continued to participate in the local county court through April 1780.[12]

Joseph Graham was in the general area and heard the talk of John Moore's return. Graham was a Mecklenburg County, North Carolina, revolutionary whose later memoirs form a valuable part of the corpus of firsthand or near-firsthand accounts of the war in the Carolina interior. One assumes that Graham absorbed the narrative regarding Moore's recruiting that was current at the time. Graham said Moore's first meeting was near Moore's home, six or seven miles from Ramsour's Mill, on June 10, only three days after Moore arrived from Charleston. According to Graham, Moore gathered about forty of his neighbors on Indian Creek and shared with them Cornwallis's admonition: stay quiet until after harvest, and be ready to join British forces when they arrive.[13]

Already, however, the revolutionary commander in southwestern North Carolina, Gen. Griffith Rutherford, knew of Moore's activities and directed local militia to break up whatever Moore was organizing. While the June 10 meeting was under way, news came that some Burke County revolutionaries were scouring the woods for men likely to join Moore. Next morning the Loyalists dispersed with the intention of catching the Burke County men, and they agreed to assemble at Ramsour's Mill three days later. About two hundred showed up. Maj. Nicholas Welch, a recruiter sent by John Hamilton, joined them. Hamilton was organizing a provincial corps of North Carolinians. By this time, according to Graham, "a number of Whigs" had come to the neighborhood "to harass the Tories."[14] This flushed out more Loyalists, perhaps numbering the thirteen hundred generally cited. The escalation came to a head with a general Whig-Tory melee at the mill on June 20, 1780. Afterward Moore reached the British at Camden with about thirty men. Their pay list, made in Charleston for the year ending June 14, 1781, gives twenty-two names, half of them German.[15]

When the wait-until-harvest-schedule was not kept and the Battle of Ramsour's Mill dampened further recruiting, Cornwallis was livid and remained so, coloring the experiences of Loyalist recruits in the South thereafter, whether as provincials or militia. He blamed the premature rising entirely on eager and impatient recruiters. First he distanced himself from John Moore. Writing Gen. Sir Henry Clinton at the end of June, Cornwallis delineated the "wait-until-after harvest" motif (which he had got from Loyalists and which Moore, according to Graham, had conveyed). Cornwallis said the misdirected Loyalists had been "encouraged and headed by a Col. Moore, *whom I knew nothing of.*"[16]

John Hamilton's Context

Perhaps blaming Moore, an "unknown" recruiter, was insufficient. The earl's heaviest blame fell on John Hamilton, organizer of the provincial corps eventually known as the Royal North Carolina Regiment. Hamilton was a Halifax, North Carolina, merchant. His family trading company linked the North Carolina piedmont with Tidewater Virginia and Glasgow. He had fled to New York in 1777 to avoid the state oath mandated by legislation that named him, and he took with him family members and some employees. At New York he had offered his services to generals Sir William Howe and Sir Henry Clinton. He participated in the attack on Savannah, at the head of about thirty other North Carolina refugees who had been in New York. The number of recruits he raised in the South would determine Hamilton's rank in the provincial corps, and he promptly set his network in action. North Carolina revolutionaries were on alert for Hamilton's Scottish recruits from the Upper Cape Fear Valley. Revolutionaries captured some of the Scots on their way to Georgia and detained them in prison ships, crude "Bull Pens," and revolutionary jails. Some escaped and reached the Georgia foothold.[17]

Hamilton and his corps accompanied the British forces throughout the Southern Campaign, from Savannah to Yorktown. In addition to men enrolled in the corps he headed, Hamilton usually was in charge of smaller groups of Loyalists. These included some militia and at least one group that considered itself a provincial corps but was treated as militia.[18] Charles Stedman served as Cornwallis's commissary throughout the campaign, and afterward he had high praise for "that valuable partizan, colonel Hamilton, of the North Carolina regiment." Stedman held that "the British nation owed more [to Hamilton] than to any other individual Loyalist in the British service."[19] After the war Cornwallis perfunctorily acknowledged Hamilton's military service, but during the campaign the earl regarded the stout, florid Scotsman as a "blockhead." Cornwallis put the blame for the premature rising and the defeat at Ramsour's Mill squarely on Hamilton. The premature

Loyalists, the earl said, had been "excited by the sanguine emissaries of the very sanguine and imprudent Lt. Col. Hamilton," and he threatened to "put [Hamilton's entire] regiment into garrison on Sullivan's Island."[20]

In addition the sartorial splendor and winning demeanor that attached to the memory of one of Hamilton's recruiters, Maj. Nicholas Welch, enhanced Graham's formative narrative. Apparently Welch's uniform was newer than Moore's was, and Welch had a recruiting purse. Graham noted such details. Later writers further dramatized them. Like Moore, Welch was a local man. He was German and had been part of the migration from western Pennsylvania in the 1750s.[21] After the war, giving an account of his services in a Loyalist claim for compensation of losses, Welch said Hamilton had sent him "to Ramseur's Mill to keep the Loyalists quiet until the proper time." Similarly Eli Branson, another of Hamilton's 1780 emissaries, later stated in his own claim that Hamilton had sent him to his home area, Chatham and Orange counties in central North Carolina, to "prevent Loyalists there from rising prematurely."[22] Conceivably the language used by Welch and Branson was influenced by Cornwallis's attack on Hamilton as the cause of the Ramsour's Mill losses. More likely their words reflect actual admonitions from Hamilton to remain quiet until British forces were in the area.

Samuel Bryan's Context

Once events were set in motion from Ramsour's Mill, the necessity to choose sides sharpened. This was when Samuel Bryan made his recruiting sweep from the Catawba River to the Yadkin River, gathering men who had refused to serve in revolutionary militia. The British could not avoid being impressed after Bryan ran a gamut of maneuvers directed by Rutherford and Col. William Davidson and delivered more than eight hundred men to the British forces in the South Carolina Cheraws on the lower Yadkin. Bryan's men were conspicuously unequipped to fight. At least one-third had no guns, and the others were poorly armed. Similarly a quarter of Moore's men had no firearms.[23] Why would so large a proportion of men, living where they did and routinely hunting, not have guns? Some may have been teenagers who shared a family weapon. Others may have turned in firearms as the price for nonservice or neutrality before the British took Charleston. One assumes that revolutionaries disarmed some of them in their homes, already a common practice.[24]

The proportion of Bryan's followers who had assembled at Ramsour's Mill and then escaped is unknown. What is clear is that men flocked to Bryan in the aftermath of Ramsour's Mill. Cornwallis's response to Bryan's efforts, although admiring, indicated that the earl still did not understand what the Loyalists' options had been when they left home. He told Clinton, "Col. Bryan, although he had promised to wait for my orders[,] lost all patience, and rose." In the same sentence, he acknowledged that Bryan's move was "in consequence" of revolutionary militia "persecuting our friends in the most cruel manner." Similarly Cornwallis wrote

Secretary of State for America Lord George Germain that Bryan's recruits said they had been "driven to" embody "by the most barbarous persecution."[25] Cornwallis's contradiction was clear: he blamed Bryan for leading the men out of danger but acknowledged that the men were "driven to" leave as a body. Did the earl think they should have remained and chosen between death and revolutionary service rather than burden him with their presence? Fighting had begun in the southern backcountry, whether Cornwallis was ready to work with its Loyalists or not.

Cornwallis was not eager for more men like Bryan's to join him; he took their support for granted and disdained them. Planning to move into North Carolina soon, he expected to "find friends enough in the next Province *of the same quality,*" he said, "and we must not undertake to supply too many *useless mouths.*"[26] The British forces would get a great deal of work from militia in addition to activities classed as "military" service. Routine tasks included digging and moving earth and harnessing themselves to wagons. During May and June 1780, Cornwallis reported progress in organizing Carolina militia,[27] but already he regarded militia recruits as useless burdens.

This is not the language the general would use nearly a year later in central North Carolina. Three weeks after his self-destructive victory at Guilford Courthouse in March 1781, he recalled that he had "marched to Bell's Mill on Deep River" days after the battle, "near part of the Country where the greatest number of our friends were supposed to reside. Many of the Inhabitants rode into Camp, shook me by the hand, said they were glad to see us, and to hear that we had beat Greene, and then rode home again."[28] This vignette served as a trope to dismiss Carolina backcountry Loyalists as "pretended or lukewarm friends" after its publication in 1783 made it low-hanging fruit for writers. They casually telescoped it back to connect it with Cornwallis's similarly colorful denunciation of "sanguine and imprudent" recruiters at the start of his Southern Campaign.

John Hamilton, incidentally, would have an answer for Cornwallis's disappointment with recruiting in central North Carolina following Guilford Courthouse. Hamilton's great grievance against Cornwallis was that recruits who came to join the British forces in North Carolina wanted to serve in a provincial corps, but Cornwallis required new enrollees to serve in militia. Hamilton, and other Scots, complained that Cornwallis offended many "gentlemen" in this way throughout 1781. It may not be too great a stretch to see a long shadow of Cornwallis's blaming Hamilton for the June 1780 "premature rising" still troubling their relationship—and Hamilton's circle of influence—throughout the war.[29]

Stedman, the commissary at Camden in 1780, thought Bryan and his recruits had left home in desperation because they had been "so harassed and oppressed," and he described the evidence of civil war they brought on their persons. "Never was a finer body of men collected," Stedman declared: "strong healthy, and accustomed to the severity of the climate; had they been properly disciplined, they might have rendered the most important services. Upon their marching into Camden they presented to our view the horrors of a civil war. Many of them had not seen their families for months, having lived in the woods to avoid the persecution of the Americans. Numbers of them were in rags, most of them men of property. There were men in Bryan's corps who possessed some hundred acres of land, farms highly cultivated, and well stocked; These, with families and friends, they abandoned."[30]

Indeed a 1750s settlement in the Forks of the Yadkin bore the name of Samuel Bryan's father, Morgan Bryan Sr. Already the elder Bryan and partners had settled hundreds of families in interior Pennsylvania and Virginia; their rolling migrations peopled sections of Kentucky in the late eighteenth century. Between 1748 and 1752, Bryan Sr. received grants totaling about three thousand acres on the Yadkin River and on its tributaries of Hogan's and Deep Creeks.[31] At the same time, sons John, Joseph, and William Bryan took additional tracts in the area. Further Morgan Bryan (Sr. or Jr.) took out warrants and obtained some surveys for at least three thousand additional acres along the Yadkin River, Dutchman's Creek, and Morgan's Creek in the following years. The expected grants had not ripened when Bryan Sr. died and the earl of Granville's proprietary land office closed, both in 1763. All these lands had been settled, however; ultimately it was revolutionaries who determined their ownership.

In 1778 the North Carolina legislature set up a land-granting procedure, authorizing its counties to take land entries. Whether the county-level land-granting officials would process entries made by the men who lived on certain tracts of land or by other men who were ready to move in on them was one of the local questions decided during the course of the Revolution. In some locales it was the pivotal issue.[32] Further the state's county courts and district superior courts resolved litigation over trespass and debt. Such cases commonly concerned land possession. Land tenure and its protection were tools to threaten men who held back from overt identification with the new government. Security of land tenure was a basic issue in Georgia and South Carolina also. Its importance increased as the war continued. In the South Carolina upcountry, the state legislature fulfilled the tacit promise to revolutionary supporters in 1783 by authorizing local militia commanders to list absent or dead Loyalists in their districts for confiscation of property, mainly land. In Georgia the issue of land security drove the war during its 1781–82 crisis, following a shift of legislative power to the backcountry.[33]

Nicholas Welch's Context

It has been noted that many who joined Loyalist recruiters at the time of Ramsour's Mill had turned out in February 1776 to meet the expected British force near Cape Fear, though not all had made it as far east as the intended rendezvous. Nicholas Welch left no evidence of having answered the royal governor's call in early 1776, but he responded to the British arrival in Georgia in the last days of 1778.

Welch later said that revolutionaries had first fined him for not serving in their militia and then jailed him twice for the same offense. He said he had spent more than £150 in lawyers' fees to avoid trial for treason. This may have occurred immediately after the British occupied Savannah and the surrounding area in December 1778. In February 1779 the North Carolina General Assembly directed the organization of light horse militia units throughout the backcountry, from Halifax at the Roanoke River's head of navigation through the western extent of the state. The move was in response to news that men who resisted revolutionary militia service were organizing in Tryon County, where Welch, Moore, and others were active.[34]

On February 6, 1779, a Tryon County revolutionary militia leader sent an alarm to the North Carolina General Assembly, then in session at Halifax. Writing from Crowder's Mountain in Tryon County, he said groups of men who had been hiding to avoid revolutionary militia service were traveling toward the British forces in Georgia at that moment. They were taking with them any men, horses, and equipment they could obtain quickly. He wrote:

> Those persons that formerly Stood out [refrained from militia service] are now embodying Themselves and Boast of their Great Numbers. This Day Timothy Riggs upon Oath declared that he, being abroad, was told by his Wife when he came home that During his absence there was to the number of one Hundred Tories well armed at his House, John Moore at the head of them, and Robbed him, the Said Riggs, of All his horses, Saddle and other things, taking two of his horses out of the plough. Likewise the said Riggs Saith upon Oath they Robbed Robert Mcman of his saddle and gun and other things. Another Deposition given In by Abraham Clark upon Oath Saith that Samuel Becker Staff told him, the Said Clark, that they were then three hundred Strong, and wanted him, the said Clark, to go with them, for at the Enoree [River] they would be two thousand Strong. John Watterson upon his Oath Correspond[s] Exactly with the Above mentioned. It is not yet known Whether they intend to make an attack there [on the Enoree] or whether they Intend to Join the English first, But Boast they will Be masters of the Country Soon.[35]

This February 1779 description naming John Moore as the organizer is a reminder that the western Carolinas sent men to join the British more than a year before Charleston fell. Moore in fact had gone to Georgia in 1778 and had returned for more recruits. Thus some hard lines were drawn, and some opponents of the revolutionaries were conspicuous, a full sixteen months before the "premature" risings Cornwallis and his readers linked with Ramsour's Mill.

Nicholas Welch's role in the February 1779 Loyalist mobilizations was to lead 270 North Carolinians toward Savannah to join Col. Archibald Campbell's forces. On the way they encountered revolutionary units at Kettle Creek and elsewhere in the watershed of the Savannah River. The result is that Welch reached the British forces with only 90 men. They joined Hamilton's provincial corps at Briar Creek, another Georgia tributary of the Savannah. Welch said he had lost the others in the encounters, chiefly Kettle Creek on February 14. He reported that "above fifty of the men [were] killed or wounded, some taken prisoners, and others declin[ed] the enterprise."[36]

The victors at Kettle Creek took their prisoners first to Augusta in the Georgia interior and then to Ninety Six. At the Augusta bull pen, more than one hundred other opponents of the revolutionaries joined the Kettle Creek prisoners. Intercepted on their way to join the British, they had accepted Brig. Gen. Andrew Williamson's offer to come into his camp and give bond to remain quiet so they could return to their homes without pursuit.[37] When these men finally reached home months after Williamson's entrapment, it cannot have been in a grateful or repentant manner. In September there were trials at Salisbury, North Carolina, for Rowan District men who had fought revolutionaries at Kettle Creek. Some of them had been tried at Ninety Six already. Only two were hanged at Salisbury, but their "long and cruel" imprisonment there, along with the trials themselves, sharpened the notoriety of the men during the following crises.[38]

Revolutionaries took at least 220 prisoners from Augusta to Ninety Six for trial. They sentenced about seventy to be hanged for sedition and prepared their graves but then moved the prisoners to a more secure blockhouse at Orangeburg and prolonged the experience. In April, heeding threats from the British in Georgia, the captors banished the remaining prisoners except for five they hanged. At the very least, as John Richard Alden noted in the 1950s, the aftershock from Kettle Creek foreshadowed the bitter partisan warfare that followed the British move into the backcountry in 1780.[39] Furthermore the groups that met defeat at Kettle Creek were active nearly a year and a half before the "premature" mobilizations (or remobilizations) that surprised Cornwallis in July 1780.

JOHN (OR JAMES) BOYD'S CONTEXT

The Loyalist leader at Kettle Creek was John or James Boyd. He has been thought to have accompanied Campbell from New York to Savannah, but he may have gone first through Georgia to the British installation at Saint Augustine in 1778. Soon after Campbell's forces took Savannah in December 1778, John (and/or James) Boyd headed for the backcountry, furnished with a commission, as Campbell said, "on account of his influence with the Back Woods men of North and South Carolina."[40] James Boyd and John Boyd lived near Raeburn Creek, a tributary of the Saluda River in present-day Laurens County, South Carolina, among a largely Quaker and Separate Baptist population that had moved to the area during the North Carolina Regulator upheaval of around 1765–71. James Lindley, one of the five Loyalists to be hanged together after Kettle Creek, was a justice of the peace in the Raeburn Creek settlement. In 1767 Lindley had led the migration from Orange County,

North Carolina, where he and his family held a high profile in Quaker circles. Concurrently some of his former neighbors had formed a largely Quaker settlement at Wrightsborough, slightly west of Augusta on the expanding Georgia frontier.[41] Both communities attracted people from the edges of white society. Robert S. Davis concluded that the Raeburn Creek residents and frequent visitors "lived as a political culture outside of the mainstream, and were a prime example of an insular colonial community that remained Loyalist." Boyd and others on their way to join the British in Georgia recruited at Raeburn Creek and Wrightsborough in late January 1779.[42] These newer and somewhat marginal neighborhoods that supplied recruits for Boyd contrast with the 1750s settlements where Welch, Bryan, and Moore drew from communities for which their families had been formative and where, by the 1770s, holdings of their extended families totaled hundreds or thousands of acres.

OBSERVATIONS

How can this study extend the southern Loyalist landscape further than Cornwallis's defensive pique early in the Southern Campaign? Patterns among the circumstances and experiences of the recruiters examined here are broad but not uniform.

The postwar experiences of the six men are outside the scope of this essay, but their denouements are relevant. Only Samuel Bryan continued his life in his home area. After his conviction for treason in March 1782, his deliverance from the Salisbury hangman followed high-level negotiations and occasioned deep debt. He died on his Rowan County farm in 1798. Nicholas Welch and his motherless children lived several years in East Florida and the Bahamas after the war. His brothers in Lincoln County, North Carolina, helped them return to the home area and then settle in the South Carolina upcountry. His brothers, having been captured while serving with Welch in Hamilton's corps, thereupon had joined a regiment of the North Carolina Continental Line; thereby they were well placed to assist him. Andrew Hamm and John Hamilton became permanent exiles, though Hamilton rejoined old acquaintances in Virginia and North Carolina as British consul at Norfolk from 1790 to 1812. He died in England four years later, still reputed in North Carolina as honorable, "well bred[,] and well fed." Hamm, having accompanied Cornwallis's withdrawal to Virginia in 1781, became a prisoner at Yorktown. Following exchange, he received land in New Brunswick and sent for his wife on Abbot's Creek. Their descendants continue in New Brunswick, where his name marks the landscape near Grand Bay. John (or James) Boyd seems to have died from a Kettle Creek wound. John Moore was reported to have been hanged by order of either Thomas Sumter or Wade Hampton. A family tradition survived at Moore's home, however, describing a letter he sent from England to his sister after the war. Meanwhile his father, Moses Moore Sr., was among a family group of twenty-four who went to Saint Augustine in the autumn of 1782 with British forces leaving the South. Five years later the family was living in Spanish territory on the Tombigbee River in present-day Alabama, where old Moses Moore still had a hand in the Indian trade.[43]

When the six recruiters undertook their investment in a British victory, their circumstances broadly reflected the rapid settlement of the southern backcountry during the previous twenty to thirty years, a development that accelerated and expanded after the Revolution. Boyd's recruiting area included offshoots of 1750s settlements that had undergone stresses of rapid immigration. Moore and Bryan were sons of men who had led large settlements of extended families and their associates from western Pennsylvania, the largest source of newcomers. Welch also had a high profile among former western Pennsylvanians on the southern frontier. Responding to the influx, the North Carolina colonial assembly had formed new counties in the 1750s and 1760s, and representatives of the Moore, Bryan, and Welch families had been among the earliest participants in their courts. They served alongside men of their economic and social standing who became revolutionary leaders in the 1770s. The 1776 state constitution was intended to take effect in 1777, but transitions of county courts from colonial to state authority were not uniform, some of them lagging until 1780. Varying in clarity and sometimes cryptic, minutes of the revolutionary-controlled county courts nevertheless can be coordinated with tax and militia records to delineate the minefields surrounding one's decision about allegiance.[44]

Moore, Hamilton, Welch, and Boyd displayed a second broad pattern. They and their followers were among groups who went to British-held areas prior to 1780 in response to actions of the new state governments. Most commonly they went to East Florida and Georgia and returned to their home areas in 1780. Generally they either joined loyal militia on their return or already had embodied as provincials under British supervision.[45]

The British seizure of Charleston and prompt move inland provoked a third and stronger enlistment pattern throughout the southern backcountry. Accommodations halted. Hamm typified many who had taken action in 1775–76. He had been allowed to "remain quiet" until his revolutionary neighbors demanded militia service following the fall of Charleston. Likewise revolutionaries did not harm Bryan until June 1780. The arrival of British forces altered options suddenly and starkly. Cornwallis either did not comprehend the options or dismissed them as irrelevant for his needs, as his statements regarding Bryan's and Moore's recruits expressed.

It can be supposed that the 1780 options facing people who could become useful to British efforts in the South were properly beneath the notice of military planners: "useless mouths." At least for the western Carolinas prior to Ferguson's energetic training, Cornwallis embodied this outlook. The stance extends to technical military history, which generally has dismissed Loyalist militia in the South on the grounds of its cumulative ineffectiveness. Matthew H. Spring's highly valuable treatment of the British army in the war for America includes one southern provincial regiment, Hamilton's, but not militia, observing, as others have, that the

British pursued a "southern strategy" only because they "erroneously believed that militant Loyalism was prevalent" there.[46]

Indeed British intelligence was obsolete in 1780, relying on reports and individual recall from 1776. An example that Cornwallis alluded to throughout the Southern Campaign is a description of the North Carolina backcountry written to a South Carolina Loyalist recruiter in Cornwallis's force as it began its entry to North Carolina in September 1780. The writer, John Cruden, was a Scottish merchant formerly based in Wilmington. He had been active as far west as Mecklenburg County prior to 1777. The merchant's outdated assessment of communities and individuals immediately gained Cornwallis's trust and an appointment for Cruden.[47] As British forces moved into the interior, they were unaware of (or uninterested in) local revolutionary hegemonies at varying stages of advancement and the fresh tensions they had aroused.

Was "militant Loyalism" ever "prevalent" in the southern backcountry? Answers to that question, like others requiring intense local examination, likely will vary with the times and places where researchers look. Records regarding office holding, land tenure, tax collection, legal disputes, estates, militia, and churches were produced unevenly and survive unevenly, but their depth is greater than the uses that have been made of them. Observable patterns may emerge from their study, whether framed chronologically, regionally, or otherwise. Then events inside and outside the commanders' tents can be rendered mutually germane. In the meantime it will be useful to stop reading backward from post–Kings Mountain events in the interior South and blaming their Loyalist shortcomings on mid-1780 "premature risings" of groups trying to reach British forces.

Pragmatism and Principle

Capt. Alexander Chesney and the Revolutionary War in South Carolina

Nineteen-year-old Pvt. Alexander Chesney of the Sixth South Carolina Provincial Regiment braced himself and crouched in the sand. He hoped to make himself as small a possible target for the redcoat artillerists across the channel on Long Island who had just showered his position with grapeshot. It was June 1776, and Chesney, with his Loyalist sentiments, longed to be in ranks with his present enemy instead of having to shoot at them. He was in the Patriot army, but he was no Patriot. Nor in his wildest imagination could he conceive that within a span of fifteen years he would have sons named in honor of two of the British officers across the way.[1]

The publication by Ohio State University in 1921 of Chesney's collected remembrances, journal, related documents, and additional notes chronicled the American Revolutionary War in the southern states from a previously unknown Loyalist perspective. Chesney's eyewitness account became one of the most important primary sources of the Revolution in South Carolina. Since that time his memoir has been extensively employed by historians to flesh out details in other works, but his story as a standalone narrative beyond the publication of his memoir has been neglected. Chesney, as it happened, evolved into an archetype of the southern Loyalists that were expected to rise en masse to help the British army destroy the rebels and reclaim their country. In the end the Loyalist situation in South Carolina was far more complicated and dangerous than anticipated. The British leadership was oftentimes badly disappointed by the number and fervor of Loyalists who rallied to the Union Jack, but they would not be disappointed by Chesney, who would prove himself, in the end, to be their staunch ally.[2]

Chesney's memoir raises several legitimate questions. He portrayed himself a faithful Loyalist from the very beginning, yet by his own admission he spent twice as much time in Patriot service as in service to the Crown. Did he employ selective recall to create a memory of himself as a pragmatic but resolute Loyalist? Or did he actually begin as a lukewarm or timid Loyalist who tried to walk the awkward middle road of community solidarity without outright treason until circumstances forced him into rebel military service? Did the strength of Patriot sentiment early in the war make overt Loyalism untenable in the moment?

Although a measure of skepticism over Chesney's early loyal sentiments may be warranted, in this brief treatment of his life his account will generally be accepted as credible. Instead of being written to bolster his claim of Loyalism in order to gain compensation from the British government for his losses sustained while serving the Crown in North America, it was composed six years after his claims were settled and is supported by his own sworn testimony, official documents, and the testimony of eyewitnesses to his Loyalism, including high-ranking British officers. At no point does he wax philosophic over politics, nor does he come across as self-promoting. Ultimately what Chesney was offers less insight for historians than what he later claimed to have been, which was a fervent Loyalist hidden amid the fires of rebellion. Chesney created a public memory that, he hoped, made sense of the constrained agency of Loyalist-leaning subjects in the recent Revolutionary past.[3]

Robert M. Calhoon characterized the Revolutionary War as a special kind of civil war, a struggle for national liberation in which Loyalists were integral participants. They were "hauled before committees of safety, vilified in [W]hig ideology, dispossessed, uprooted, and threatened with injury or death if they refused to acquiesce, and enrolled in large numbers in Loyalist military regiments." But he also pointed out that they were more than just eyewitnesses to the Revolution; they "were the most immediate victims of the upheaval." Nowhere than in South Carolina was Calhoon's description of the Loyalist dilemma more fitting, and perhaps no Loyalist better personified the elements of the Loyalist experience described by Calhoon than Alexander Chesney.[4]

What follows is the story of this young American who was sometimes forced by circumstances to act in ways that did not coincide with his political ideology as he navigated the treacherous waters of civil war. His trials and tribulations, seen mostly through his own eyes, provide insight into what it was like to be in the often untenable position of a backcountry South Carolina Loyalist.

A Pragmatic Loyalist in Rebel Service

Alexander Chesney was born into a middle-class farming family on September 12, 1756, in the small Dunclug community near the town of Ballymena in the county of Antrim, Ireland. His father, Robert Chesney (or McChesney), moved the family to America in 1772, following several previously emigrated Chesney relatives. Robert Chesney's family eventually settled on the north side of the Pacolet River near Grindal Shoals, about 12 miles from where it empties into the Broad River. This settlement was some 55 miles north by northeast of the village of Ninety Six and about 175 miles northwest of Charleston. Alexander subsequently obtained one hundred acres upon which he built a cabin and cleared the land, all mostly without assistance.[5]

Political tension between Great Britain and the North American colonies were coming to a head about the time the Chesney family made landfall and moved inland. Though miles distant from Charleston, backcountry settlers were becoming increasingly divided along political lines as well. Geographical and cultural isolation from the ruling lowcountry planter aristocracy caused those with loyal inclinations to become increasingly distrustful of the rebellion. A large proportion of backcountry Loyalists might have been content to sit out the conflict as neutrals but were so antagonized by the coercive tactics employed by those who sought independence from Great Britain that they eventually took up armed resistance. Irishmen, generally Scotch-Irish, made up about 25 percent of South Carolina Loyalists, and most of these in the backcountry were poor or moderately poor farmers. The Ninety Six District, where the Chesneys resided, held the largest concentration of such Loyalists outside of Charleston.[6]

The Chesney family had journeyed across the Atlantic from Ireland in the company of a congregation of Presbyterian Covenanters, virtually all of whom came to support independence. Alexander's Loyalism makes it highly unlikely that he was a member of this congregation. He never provided any information regarding his religious affiliation; however he was ultimately buried in a Presbyterian churchyard. Perhaps he bore true allegiance to the land of his birth and its monarch in gratitude for having received a land grant. Maybe it was family devotion, anger over recurrent Patriot depredations, or some combination of all of these factors. Loyalists (and Patriots for that matter) oftentimes acted more from solidarity with their family and local leaders than out of any deep ideological commitments. Whatever the motives, "only the unusual Tory thoughtlessly risked his property and life for Britain," as historian Jac Weller has noted. Mark James Gomsak pointed out that "men of this type were ruined, driven out of the country, or even killed," and indeed Chesney suffered severe consequences for his fealty to the Crown.[7]

Chesney's earliest recorded activity as a friend of the king was at a meeting near present-day Spartanburg during the summer of 1775. There he refused to sign the Articles of Association, an assent to support the rebel government presented by Charleston Presbyterian minister Rev. William Tennent. Moreover the young firebrand proposed a petition testifying to his neighbors' "abhorrence and detestation" of the rebellion and their resolution to support His Majesty's government. When a Patriot force led by Col. Richard Richardson and Lt. Col. William Thomson swept through the countryside pursuing and arresting prominent Loyalists (the "Snow Campaign" of November and December 1775), Chesney assisted the escape of a number of Loyalists and was undoubtedly personally acquainted with many of the local leaders taken prisoner, such as Col. Thomas Fletchall, Maj. Patrick Cunningham, and Capt. Richard Pearis.[8]

His father, Robert, was arrested and his house ransacked for harboring Loyalists. Not long after, Alexander was also arrested by a party of armed rebels under Col. James Stein. He was taken to Colonel Richardson's camp on the Reedy River (just west of present-day Greenville) and held there for a week or two before being released. However instead of being allowed to return home, he was retaken into custody and forced to choose between standing trial for aiding Loyalists or joining the Continental Army. If the Patriots intended to intimidate Chesney into submission, it worked. To save his own life and protect his family from ruin, he chose the latter course. On April 5, 1776, he enlisted as a private in the Sixth South Carolina Provincial Regiment of riflemen commanded by Lt. Col. Thomas Sumter, "the Gamecock."[9]

By June 1776 Sumter had brought the Sixth Regiment from the backcountry to Charleston in preparation for a British attack. Chesney's company was stationed at Bolton's Landing, a point on the mainland across from Long Island (now Isle of Palms), from where he was able to observe the camp of Maj. Gen. Henry Clinton's redcoats. One day while reconnoitering the British lines on Long Island, he came under fire from a cannon loaded with grapeshot, "one shot of which was within a few inches of killing me[,] having struck the sand close by where I had squatted down to avoid the discharge," he later wrote of the experience.[10]

Notwithstanding being fired upon by the British, he longed to join his present enemy. On at least one occasion, accompanied by brothers Charles and Christopher Brandon, Chesney attempted to desert to the British. Their scheme failed when the trio was unable to find a boat to carry them across the channel. They were unfortunate in that their movements were discovered, but fortunate that their purpose was unknown, and so they returned to camp. As a consequence Chesney was a spectator to General Clinton's abortive attempts to cross Breach Inlet from Long Island to the northern end of Sullivan's Island during the ill-fated June 28 Battle of Sullivan's Island, during which Cmdre. Sir Peter Parker's warships unsuccessfully battered Col. William Moultrie's palmetto-log fort.[11]

Meanwhile, with the encouragement of backcountry Loyalists, the Cherokees launched a series of brutal attacks on frontier settlements in western South Carolina. In July 1776 Maj. Andrew Williamson led a body of Patriot militiamen and provincials into Indian territory for what would be remembered as the Cherokee Campaign. The Sixth Regiment constituted a part of the provincial contingent. Over a three-month period, the Americans suffered several ambushes and fought numerous skirmishes but managed to ravage the countryside while sustaining only light casualties. Chesney nearly starved on the march on account of short rations but was more pleased to be on an expedition against someone other than redcoats despite a second brush with death.[12]

"In the course of the engagement five or six [Cherokees] concealed behind a log fired at me as I ascended the hill before the others, and one of their balls struck a saplin [sic] of about six inches diameter opposite my breast; fortunately the young tree broke the force of the ball and saved my life," he wrote of the incident. He certainly had no fondness for the Indians—by Chesney's count he helped destroy thirty-two Cherokee towns and was proud to have taken part in the July devastation.

One can only imagine his reaction in late August, while on this campaign, when he learned that the Continental Congress in Philadelphia had declared the independence of the United States of America—he left no comment on the matter.[13]

Following the Cherokee Campaign, the Sixth Regiment returned to the South Carolina lowcountry. In February 1777 the regiment was part of a force sent to Georgia to repel a British incursion from St. Augustine in East Florida. Chesney related being marched overland to Purysburg, a settlement about fifteen miles upstream from Savannah on the South Carolina side of the Savannah River, and then being transported downriver the rest of the way to Savannah. Aside from a total eclipse of the sun, this excursion was memorable to him mainly for his taking target practice on alligators that he and his mates saw partially submerged on the riverbank along the way. Chesney made sure to clarify that the Sixth Regiment never engaged the British directly, but he proudly remembered participating in several skirmishes with Creek war parties, noting in his memoir that he volunteered for these forays. He did not seem to care on whose side he was fighting when he was fighting Indians.[14]

Chesney's tenure in the Continental Army ran until June 1777. He was released from his obligatory service, returned home, purchased property on the Pacolet River, and resumed farming. It was good land—about half of the acreage was cleared and well fenced, a good house was on the site, and Chesney installed a flour mill and a sawmill. He also engaged in commerce, hauling agricultural produce by wagon to Charleston and returning with supplies needed by the backcountry settlers. Of his prosperous enterprise he later wrote, "I had success and realized a good deal, the profits being with care 300 per cent." Unfortunately this lucrative business came to an end in 1779 when the Americans impressed a wagon and team of horses and his other horses were stolen.[15]

Certainly there were still a good number of Loyalists in the backcountry, but they were generally quiet as the Patriots had the upper hand both militarily and politically. In March 1778 the South Carolina legislature passed a law that required free male inhabitants of the state aged sixteen and older to take an oath pledging allegiance to the state and promising to "faithfully support, maintain and defend the same against George the Third, King of Great Britain." Persons neglecting or refusing to comply would face harsh consequences. Chesney would serve in their army if compelled to do so, but he would not take such an oath. He joined with a party of men who intended to go to East Florida to avoid the compulsory vow, but they were not able to accomplish their flight.[16]

Chesney's stated intention, if testimony given in 1783 is to be believed, was that whenever he joined the Patriot militia it was with a view to desert to the British at the earliest opportunity. In early 1778 he mustered with Capt. Zachariah Bullock's company from the Ninety Six District and was elected by his loyal friends to the rank of lieutenant. Apparently there were others with him of similarly divided allegiances. Considering his elevation in rank, it is noteworthy that he never swore the state oath. (Chesney later maintained that it was never tendered to him.) The company marched to Earle's Ford on the North Pacolet River in North Carolina, about thirty-five miles from Grindal Shoals. The men spent a few months repairing and garrisoning a fort, where they remained until May 1778.[17]

Chesney again ventured into Georgia as a lieutenant in Capt. Alexander McWhorter's Patriot company under General Williamson's command, joining Brig. Gen. Robert Howe's amalgamation of Georgia and South Carolina Continentals and militiamen assembled at Fort Howe to repel a British incursion from East Florida. The British threat came to naught, but supplies were scarce, disease was rampant, and mortality among the troops was exceedingly high. After three months, during which Chesney suffered greatly with the "flux," an opportunity to desert never materialized. On one occasion he and his likeminded friends sent a man to reconnoiter the British, but the man never returned.[18]

The South Carolinians trekked north to Augusta, Georgia, and then back into South Carolina, where Williamson joined his force with that of Maj. Gen. Benjamin Lincoln, who commanded the Southern Department of the Continental Army. Lincoln's hurried march to Charleston forced Brig. Gen. Augustine Prévost to abandon his effort to capture the town and to withdraw his British army to James Island. Chesney eventually wound up with Lincoln west of the Ashley River near Charleston but missed the Battle of Stono Ferry on June 20, 1779, because he was sent home to enlist additional recruits for Patriot service. In light of his longtime Loyalist proclivity, it is ironic that Chesney was sent home to recruit. Whether he had given up the idea of defecting to the British or the overall strategic situation made desertion increasingly untenable is unknown, for he left no comments in his memoir to shed light on the matter.[19]

His activities at home cast an aura of doubt as to whether or not, at this point in the war, he remained the steadfast Loyalist that he characterized himself to be in his memoirs. He purchased land. He was trading with Charleston. And on January 3, 1780, twenty-four-year-old Alexander married his second cousin Margaret Hodge (born 1759), eldest daughter of Patriot William Hodge and his wife, Elizabeth Cook. As later events will show, he and his father-in-law seem to have maintained a harmonious relationship. Had Chesney accepted the current status quo? By the terms of his marriage contract, he received from Hodge two hundred acres on a Pacolet tributary, a tract on which were good houses and upward of thirty acres cleared and fenced. He subsequently gained an additional two hundred adjacent acres through which a valuable vein of copper ore ran, and he thus settled down to start a family. Within a few months, however, all hopes of domestic felicity for Alexander and Margaret Chesney were upended.[20]

A Resolute Loyalist in the Service of the King

Chesney stated in his narrative that at the beginning of 1780 he firmly believed that Charleston would eventually fall to the British. Two attempts had already been made—the failed attack on Sullivan's Island, of which Chesney was a by-stander in June 1776, and a halfhearted siege from the landward side in 1779 while he was marching with General Lincoln's army to relieve the city's beleaguered defenders. But in the spring of 1780, General Clinton returned to South Carolina, and this time he trapped Lincoln's army in Charleston, opened formal siege operations, and forced the surrender of the entire southern rebel army on May 12, 1780.[21]

Chesney formally "took protection" on June 27 and was among two hundred Loyalists from his local area who mustered in Ninety Six District. His prior Continental and Patriot militia service notwithstanding, his Loyalist comrades elected him to the rank of lieutenant, and he was given command of a company of Maj. Daniel Plummer's Regiment, Fair Forest Militia in Brig. Gen. Robert Cunningham's brigade of the Ninety Six District. Chesney was also appointed Plummer's adjutant. When they learned in mid-July that a body of rebels was coming against them, he was chosen to command a small contingent in an action at Bulloch's Creek (in present-day York County, South Carolina). The rebels who attempted to cross a ford were repulsed in a spirited engagement, of which Chesney wrote, "my father was present on this occasion and hearing the bullets whistle without seeing by whom they were fired, asked me where are they? I placed him near a tree until the affair was over, and resolved he should not be so exposed again."[22]

By this time Maj. Patrick Ferguson (1744–80), formerly of the Seventy-First Regiment of Foot (Highland Scots), had gravitated from service in regular army regiments to command Loyalist provincial and militia forces in the southern theater. Ferguson had witnessed the capriciousness of some of the backcountry South Carolina Loyalist militiamen, but in Chesney he found a man in whom he could entrust dangerous duty. After Chesney proved his reliability as a scout and courier, Ferguson offered him a handsome reward if he could locate a rebel camp at Cherokee Ford on the Broad River and ascertain the enemy's strength, composition (foot and horse), and movements. Chesney maintained in his memoir that he declined the reward outright, preferring to undertake the task solely for the good of His Majesty's service. He set off under the cover of darkness and reconnoitered the enemy position, but while making his way back to Ferguson, he was captured at Grindal Shoals. Fortunately his escape was as easy as his reconnaissance had been. Chesney's intelligence of five hundred enemy horsemen advancing toward Nicholas's Fort (west of present-day Spartanburg) on the Tyger River ultimately allowed Ferguson's corps to intercept the rebels at Wofford's Iron Works and salvage a tactical draw on August 8 at the Second Battle of Cedar Springs. Instead of a reward, Chesney accepted a promotion to captain as Ferguson's assistant adjutant general.[23]

A victorious skirmish against rebel militia on August 12 was sweetened when Chesney took prisoner his own recent captor. British arms were not always successful, however. Gen. Thomas Sumter's militia blocked Ferguson's battalion from joining Cornwallis in time to take part in the smashing triumph over Maj. Gen. Horatio Gates's Continental Army at Camden on August 16. Consequently Ferguson marched to the assistance of Loyalist militiamen and provincials under Col. Alexander Innes who were reeling from a lopsided defeat at the Battle of Musgrove Mill on August 19. Chesney commanded the rearguard after the main body crossed the Enoree River, and he successfully fended off a rebel attack on August 20. Encamped afterward in the vicinity of Fair Forest (within the limits of present-day Spartanburg), Chesney managed to slip home for a two-hour visit, during which he took opportunity to send "for those who had shamefully abandoned us some time ago to join us at the Iron-Works[,] in order to do three months' duty in or on the borders of North Carolina."[24]

During this time Chesney was busily occupied, as "scarcely a day passed without some fighting." One of these small, unnamed engagements was another skirmish near the Iron Works, during which, he claimed, his party defeated and dispersed men under Col. Thomas Brandon. It is possible that on the opposite side of the battlefield that day was his younger brother-in-law William Hodge (born 1762), who had been serving Patriot militia since 1778 but more recently in Colonel Brandon's Regiment since the fall of Charleston.[25]

At this point in his memoir, Chesney penned words critical of British policy, and it was the only time he took occasion to do so. After capturing Charleston in May 1780 but before departing for New York in June, General Clinton issued a handbill and a series of proclamations that, among other things, reestablished the loyal militia in South Carolina. Chesney reported dissatisfaction among the militiamen that men with three or fewer children, and every single man, were required to serve six months duty, even outside of the province if required. "This appeared like compulsion, instead of acting voluntarily as they conceived they were doing, and they were in consequence ready to give up the cause," Chesney said. He declared that it was owing only to the exertions of the officers, and he included himself, that "the tumult was happily appeased."[26]

In early September 1780, Ferguson marched his command into the western North Carolina backcountry, ostensibly to recruit more Loyalists but also to protect the left flank of Lord Cornwallis, who was marching the main part of the southern British army into North Carolina. Ferguson also received orders from Cornwallis instructing him to intercept Col. Elijah's Georgia Patriots, who were in flight toward refuge in North Carolina after abandoning an unsuccessful siege at Augusta. Chesney related his part in numerous unnamed small engagements that took place during this period, including one time when at the head of a division he took a prisoner who was the keeper of records from the Pacolet area. Chesney confiscated the records and sent them to his father's house for safekeeping.[27]

Little more than twenty miles from Chesney's home on the Pacolet River, Ferguson's Loyalists were attacked on October 7, 1780, by nine hundred Patriot militiamen at Kings Mountain. The terrain worked against them in a lopsided battle lasting less than an hour. "So rapid was their attack that I was in the act of dismounting to report that all was quiet and [that] the pickets [were] on the alert when we heard their firing about half a mile off," wrote Chesney, who immediately formed and deployed his men and junior officers. The Loyalists repelled several attempts by the frontiersmen to take the hill, and Chesney led one of these repulses, but they were eventually overwhelmed after Ferguson was cut down by rebel bullets.[28]

The battle ended in what Chesney described next as a combination of the chaos of battle, the fog of war, fear on the part of the vanquished, and a thirst for vengeance on the part of the victors: "Cap[t.] [Abraham] De Peyster succeeded to the command but soon after gave up and sent out a flag of truce, but as the Americans resumed their fire afterwards[,] ours was also renewed under the supposition that they would give no quarter; and a dreadful havoc took place until the flag was sent out a second time, then the work of destruction ceased; the Americans surrounded us with double lines, and we grounded arms with the loss of one third our numbers."[29]

The defeat and death of Ferguson at Kings Mountain crushed the Loyalist cause in the South Carolina backcountry and forced Cornwallis to retire from Charlotte and temporarily abandon his operations in North Carolina. Chesney's account of the battle is consistent with renditions provided by other participants, though when writing his memoir he clearly referred to published sources to refresh his memory. In any event the battle was lost, his friend and mentor Ferguson was dead along with a host of his loyal comrades, and he was wounded but lucky to be alive. "We passed the night on the spot where we surrendered amidst the dead and groans of the dying who had not surgical aid, or water to quench their thirst," he wrote.[30]

Early the next morning, he and the other prisoners were force-marched toward Gilbert Town between double lines of mounted rebels. The officers brought up the rear of the column, and the men were required to carry two muskets each, their flints having been first removed. Wounded and stripped of his shoes, Chesney trudged along with his mates in cold, damp weather without shelter or sustenance for two days until the captives received a single ear of Indian corn each.[31]

Upon reaching Gilbert Town, Chesney endured a drumhead court-martial that sentenced a number of Loyalists to death but executed only an unlucky few. The rumored approach of Lt. Col. Banastre Tarleton's dragoons prompted the rebels and their prisoners to march toward the Yadkin River, a movement during which the prisoners were savagely beaten along the way. Chesney claimed that Col. Benjamin Cleveland of the North Carolina Patriot militia offered him freedom on the condition that he would instruct his Patriot regiment in the military exercises taught to the Loyalist militia by Major Ferguson in camp at Fair Forest. Chesney summarily declined, and Cleveland swore that he would be executed as penalty for his refusal as soon as they reached Moravian Town (present-day Winston-Salem).[32]

Chesney made his escape early one evening (probably on October 15) before Cleveland could carry out his threat. He slept in the woods and lived off the land, eating black haws, fox grapes, and muscadines. A few days out he was almost recaptured when he nearly stumbled into a party of men "whom I knew to be Americans by white paper in their hats." It was a very close call. "I lay down and was so close to them that I could have touched one of their horses in passing; fortunately I was not observed." He was fortunate indeed—his former captors were executing prisoners who tried to escape but failed. Using his local knowledge of the Blue Ridge Mountains as his guide, he navigated home to Broad River. Along the way he came upon his brother-in-law John Heron, who had been with him at Kings Mountain. Heron and others had deserted early during the battle and escaped through the rebel lines by disguising themselves with a piece of paper in their hats, a strategy Chesney considered disgraceful (at least in retrospect).[33]

It took about two weeks for Chesney to cover the 120 miles home. When he arrived on October 31, he was greatly disheartened by what he found. The rebels had gained possession of the country, and Col. Thomas Brandon's men had stripped his place of nearly everything. His one consolation was seeing his newborn son, William, for the first time. Naming him, said Chesney, "was all the christening he had." Not knowing where to find British troops, he remained in the area for most of November but was forced to hide, concealing himself with two cousins in a cave dug in the branch of a creek under a hollow poplar. The space was so small and the roof so low that the three men were forced to lie flat, and except for victuals brought nightly by his cousin's wife, they might have starved. Only occasionally did he dare to venture out and stay with his father-in-law.[34]

When his cousin's wife brought the encouraging (but erroneous) news that Tarleton had defeated Sumter at Blackstock's Farm on November 20, Chesney assembled a company of loyal men, albeit with great difficulty, and took them to a rendezvous on the Enoree River. Unfortunately when he arrived, he found the spot firmly in the hands of rebels under the command of Maj. Benjamin Roebuck. Chesney and his contingent were immediately captured, disarmed, and marched off. After being captured twice before, and escaping and evading the enemy both times, he was a prisoner for a third time. Chesney and Roebuck were acquainted, and Roebuck subsequently paroled him to Ninety Six, where he was exchanged for Capt. John Clarke, son of Col. Elijah Clarke, who had been taken when the British captured Augusta.[35]

Exchange allowed him to resume active service. Chesney was promoted to captain in Plummer's regiment by British Lt. Col. Nisbet Balfour on December 1, 1780, and spent most of that month fortifying and garrisoning the jail at Ninety Six. When Lieutenant Colonel Tarleton arrived in search of Brig. Gen. Daniel Morgan's army of Continentals and rebel militia who were operating in the area, he sought guides familiar with the territory to search for Morgan. Chesney was just the man for the job, since Morgan's army was thought to be in the vicinity of

Chesney's home on the Pacolet. Rumors aside, he was unable to locate Morgan and rejoined Tarleton, who sent him out again, this time to work the local mills to grind much-needed flour for his army. When he reached the Pacolet, Chesney swam his horse across an unguarded ford, and by pure happenstance came upon on an empty camp between his and his father's houses. The deserted camp was so fresh that the campfires still smoldered, and at his father's place, he discovered that Morgan had passed only an hour before.[36]

Making a hurried visit to his wife, he was mortified to learn that Morgan's men had preceded him, destroying his crops and stripping his home of almost everything portable. The rebel marauders left Margaret and three-month-old William without even a blanket to shield them from the winter weather as they fled by night into the woods and the eventual safety of a nearby relative's house. Aside from Alexander's two horses and the clothes on their backs, the Chesneys were without possessions and virtually penniless. As for Margaret, "the terror she had gone through, and the exposure to the cold of a winter's night, gave a shock to her constitution from which she never recovered, and when her husband succeeded in tracing her out he found her utterly broken down."[37]

Undeterred by the plight of his family, Chesney beat it back to Tarleton, who was actively seeking to overtake and engage Morgan. Chesney caught up with the British column by 10 o'clock on the evening of January 16, 1781, near Hannah's Cowpens, a broad pasture lightly dotted with trees thirty miles west of Kings Mountain. It was there that Morgan's stratagem unfolded perfectly when he lured the brash Tarleton into making an impetuous sunrise attack on successive lines of American sharpshooters, militiamen, and Continental infantry. The British advanced against and overcame the first two lines, as anticipated by Morgan, but sustained heavy losses, particularly among the officers, and were entirely played out by the time they encountered veteran Continental infantry and cavalry. Tarleton committed his dragoons in a last desperate attempt to break Morgan's lines, but it was for naught—the British were decimated and put to flight.[38]

According to Chesney, "the rout was almost total. I was with Tarleton in the charge[,] who behaved bravely but imprudently[;] the consequence was his force dispersed in all directions the guns and many prisoners fell into the hands of the Americans . . . we suffered a total defeat by some dreadful bad management." Whether he was aware or not, Chesney's brother-in-law William Hodge was again across the battle lines, his regiment having joined Morgan at Cowpens. During the engagement Hodge was slightly injured and remained behind to take care of the other wounded.[39]

In the battle's aftermath, Chesney hurriedly gathered his wife and son and proceeded south to the Edisto River. Forced to abandon their home, relations, and friends, the refugee Chesney family was completely destitute. With few other options, Chesney took his family and deposited them in the relative security of a friend before heading to Charleston. His memoir reflected his acceptance of the consequences of his wartime military and political decisions and actions: "I have not been at Pacholet [*sic*] since," he later wrote, "nor am I likely to be."[40]

Since the fall of Charleston, when he was finally allowed to serve the side with which his ultimate loyalty lay, Chesney had witnessed little more than defeat, death, and loss—he was badly overdue for a change in his fortune. Contrary to all expectations, on the way to Charleston or perhaps when he arrived there, he fell in with two provincial officers who had fought at Kings Mountain and who were fully cognizant of the valuable services that he had provided. To help him get on his feet financially, they assisted him in getting paid for cattle and provisions that he had supplied to Ferguson's army.[41]

That certainly helped, but the officers were not yet satisfied with what they had accomplished on Chesney's behalf. They introduced him to Lieutenant Colonel Balfour, who in August 1780, during the backcountry muster of Loyalist militia, had been reassigned to the post of Charleston's commandant. Balfour ordered commissioner of sequestered estates John Cruden to allow the Chesney family to take up residence on one of the many sequestered lowcountry plantations. Chesney was subsequently given use of a house (and provisions and three slaves) about twenty-five miles west of Charleston near Jacksonboro in Colleton County. "Thus," he remembered, "was I at once introduced to a new set of Loyalists and I immediately removed my wife and child and [cousin] Charles Brandon with his family to [Thomas] Ferguson[']s Riverside plantation near Parker[']s ferry on Pond-Pond-river where I soon fixed myself very comfortably having purchased in Charles-town some bedding &c to set up house-keeping a second time. . . . I joined the negroes allowed me for my family with others on the Plantation and began to make a crop of Indian corn and rice."[42]

The moment put in sharp relief Chesney's commitment to the British Empire. His was not a critique of Patriot hypocrisy or dismay with coastal elites. This was not a man with qualms about how his society worked, unlike some of his contemporaries such as Alexander Hewatt. Planted nicely as a Colleton County gentleman, Chesney was satisfied with South Carolina life as it existed before the Revolution and at war with those who had disrupted his pursuit of it.

Chesney's plantation quietude was short-lived. During the spring of 1781, Patriot militias became increasingly active in the South Carolina lowcountry, led by Brig. Gen. Francis Marion, Col. William Harden, and Col. Isaac Hayne, who was from the vicinity of where Chesney had taken residence. Like Ferguson had done, Balfour first used Chesney as a messenger. Later, at Balfour's request, he raised a body of cavalry, for which Balfour gave him a commission on April 20, 1781, as lieutenant of independent scouts in Capt. John Fanning's Independent Troop, South Carolina Volunteer Horse. He and his men were posted to Dorchester, and he moved Margaret and William there for safety's sake. From Dorchester he operated against the resurgent Patriot militias. "There were daily skirmishes at this period, the Americans constantly contracting our posts in every direction," he noted in his memoir, and during one of these engagements in June, he received his second wound. He and his troop had crossed the Edisto at Parker's Ferry by night; "the boats having been removed to impede our march[,] I swam my horse over accompanied by others and procured feather-beds to transport those who could not swim across the River." While driving the enemy in the early morning light, he leapt his horse over a sunken fence and was stabbed in the thigh by a concealed rebel partisan armed with a spear, who he immediately took prisoner.[43]

In June 1781 Chesney took part in Lt. Col. Francis Lord Rawdon's march from Charleston to the relief of Lt. Col. John Harris Cruger's besieged garrison at Ninety Six. When halted at Orangeburg on the return, Rawdon asked if Chesney knew of anyone who was familiar with the roads to Charleston. The Americans had crossed Broad and Santee Rivers in force, and he needed a rider to carry a request to Balfour for reinforcement. "As all the expresses sent hitherto had either been killed or taken prisoners; being perfectly acquainted with the whole of the neighboring country I immediately went and offered my services to his Lordship; which were readily accepted; I was offered any horse in the camp I might think better than my own, but I thought myself the best mounted officer there and found[,] before many minutes[,] use for every muscle of the good animal that carried me."[44]

Chesney immediately departed Orangeburg for Charleston and was scarcely past the sentries when he was spotted and chased by a party of four or five rebel horsemen, two of whom kept up the chase for nearly twenty miles through the woods. Eluding his pursuers and avoiding enemy pickets "who must inevitably have taken or killed me, had I not by good fortune missed the common path, which they were carefully guarding," he reached Dorchester, there seeing his wife just long enough for a fresh horse to be saddled. By the time he reached Charleston and delivered the dispatch to Balfour, he had covered the seventy-five miles from Orangeburg in twelve hours. Balfour wasted no time sending help to Rawdon, who was able to force his way through the enemy toward Charleston.[45]

Chesney returned to Dorchester, where he was grieved to learn that in his brief absence a rebel raiding party had absconded from a nearby pasture with three hundred horses, including his own. In fact the Americans had gained control of most of the country except the immediate environs of Charleston, including the Quarter House tavern, on the road to Dorchester about five miles north of town, where he was posted.[46]

As lieutenant in a corps charged with the defense of sequestered estates, he had yet another near-death experience during an excursion up the Cooper River to secure a cachet of rice. The schooner on which he was aboard capsized, drowning twelve men. Many of the drowned were his men, and he escaped with his life only because he was on deck at the time and was able to swim ashore. He described the heartrending scene when the schooner turned keel-up, "and not being quite filled with water immediately, the men could exist for a little time; we heard them crying for assistance and did all we could to afford it but unfortunately only one man could be got out in time to save his life and this was effected by cutting a hole in the vessels bottom. I lost my watch, sword and several other things."[47]

During the winter of 1781–1782, the primacy of American forces compelled the British to withdraw down the Charleston Neck. Wood was required for fuel, warmth, and cooking, and Chesney was employed as inspector of woodcutters. His orders stipulated that "no wood Cutt by any person will be paid for unless the Cutter produces a receipt sign'd by Cap[t.] Chesney—he will also take care that the wood is cute [sic] as near as possible to the best Landing & that the Cords are full measure." His work required a vast number of axe men, and in assuming this leadership role, he used the opportunity to help his less-fortunate brethren. "I chose a number of Loyalists," he said, "whom I found within the lines in a destitute condition; and this gave them immediate relief; preventing numbers by that means from starving."[48]

Matters continued to spiral in a downward direction, not just for the British in Charleston but personally for Chesney. He was practically undone when Margaret succumbed to the flux on November 28, 1781. He attributed her death to the lingering effects from being thrown out of the family home and forced to spend several days outside during the winter of 1780. She was buried on James Island. Chesney's health was also broken; hard work and constant exposure had taken their toll.[49]

In January 1782 physical illness and despair caused him to give up the firewood detail that gave him so much satisfaction. He sent eighteen-month-old William to live with his grandmother and grandfather on the Pacolet and yielded to the urgings of his friends to go home to Ireland. The surrender of Cornwallis at Yorktown virtually assured the independence of the United States, and Chesney's work protecting sequestered estates put him in a perilous situation with the Patriots, who bitterly resented those associated with administering or profiting from their estates. In his twenty-sixth year, Chesney booked passage on the transport *Lady Susan* and sailed from Charleston on April 5, 1782. After a pleasant passage, the *Lady Susan* landed in Ireland on May 20, 1782, ending an eventful decade-long sojourn in America, a place to which he never returned.[50]

Chesney intended to have his son sent to him in Ireland but later claimed that he "found that it would be very difficult . . . to arrange." He never again saw William, and communication between them was nonexistent until 1818, when, according to family lore, "[William] heard accidentally that his father was alive, and wrote him a dutiful letter stating that he was himself the father of a family, and could not leave the country of his adoption."[51]

The details of his life after such an adventurous decade in North America could easily fill another essay in this collection. For a number of years, he was an important and successful advocate for Loyalists in Britain seeking compensation for their losses during the American war, a role that brought him into contact with Cornwallis, Rawdon, Tarleton, and Balfour. Chesney remarried, added to his family, and entered upon a thirty-five-year career with the Irish Board of Customs. While a coast officer, he thwarted smugglers and survived their assassination attempt. As a commissioned officer in his local militia, his prior military experience proved invaluable as he played a role in putting down the Irish Rebellion of 1798. He died at Kilkeel, County Down, on January 12, 1845, at the age of eighty-eight and was laid to rest in the churchyard of Mourne Presbyterian Church.[52]

In all Alexander Chesney spent four years of reluctant service in the army of those in open rebellion against his king. Nonetheless there is solid testimony from his Loyalist contemporaries that despite his service in the American army, he never gave up his Loyalist inclination. Col. John Phillips later affirmed that "his motives were his attachment to Britain" and that he firmly believed Chesney was "in his mind a determined Loyalist from the beginning tho' he was obliged to carry Arms for the Rebels. . . . During the time he . . . was prisoner in Gen['l.] Williamson[']s Army [Chesney] communicated to him his intentions to make his Escape from that Army." Phillips praised Chesney as a most zealous and active partisan and affirmed that he had been of particularly good service to Lt. Col. Banastre Tarleton and Maj. Patrick Ferguson, adding that he "ran risques w'ch nothing would have tempted [me] to have done." Col. Zacharias Gibbs concurred and added that when Ferguson sought "a faithful Man who [would] go into the Enemy's Camp then at Cherokee Ford & count the number of their Men and bring Intelligence of their Movements," it was Chesney, the intrepid scout, who went out and returned with the desired information.[53]

He also received high praise from the British army officers under whom he served. John Cruden wrote that "in justice to him I can not but acknowledge that he gave proof of Zeal & Spirit as well as activity & Enterprise, which I hope will recommend him to the Notice of all those attach[']d to His Majesty[']s Government." Nisbet Balfour testified that Chesney was "a very determin'd Loyalist, & that he has render'd many Services to His Majesty's Government ever since the present Rebellion—That he always has done his Duty as an Officer, & has ever faithfully accomplished every matter that has been entrusted to him." Francis Rawdon readily granted that "he behaved with exemplary zeal & fidelity." Cornwallis called him "a deserving Man, and an active and zealous Loyalist."[54]

These testimonials to Chesney's Loyalism were given in support of his application to the British government for compensation for his own losses sustained during the American war. Chesney himself declared, "I also flattered myself with the hopes that, from my uncommon exertions in the *field as an officer,* and from the many very essential *secret services* I rendered Govt. during the late War . . . to be classed with the most meritorious, and deserving men. And to have received some compensation with them, to enable me to support my family . . . I have ever placed an unlimited confidence on the faith of Goverm['t]. and sacrificed my *all* for its support."[55]

"New Hope" in Shelburne, Nova Scotia

Loyalist Dreams in the Journal of British Engineer William Booth, 1780s–90s

Loyalist Jane Holderness; her Yorkshire husband, William; and their six children were part of the Loyalist migration to Shelburne at the conclusion of the American Revolution. The family began their North American adventure as British immigrants, who had the misfortune of arriving in Boston as the Revolution was unfolding. As a result they joined the Loyalist exodus out of the city to Halifax and then to New York City, where they operated a mercery and millinery shop until the final Loyalist exodus in 1783. In Shelburne, William bought a schooner appropriately christened *New Hope* and began trading in the West Indies, while Jane took in boarders for additional income.[1] The Holdernesses' experience is significant for several reasons. First it is a reminder that Loyalist identity is best understood from a "microhistorical perspective," for, as Edward Gray notes, it has "multiple, contested, and contradictory meanings in various contexts."[2] One of the contexts that must be interrogated is "exile," or in this case, the "communities of exile" formed by Loyalists in such places as British North America, West Africa, and England. In his classic essay "The Loyalist Perception," Robert M. Calhoon argues that it is important for historians to "explore as analytically as possible the Loyalists' perception of reality, the structure of their values, and the pattern of their rational and emotional responses within each of the historical contexts from which they operated." Exile is an evocative historical context, for this is where, in Calhoon's words, a "new sense of Loyalist identity emerged."[3] In 1994 the collection titled *Loyalists and Community in North America*, edited by Calhoon, Timothy M. Barnes, and George Rawlyk, took up this task and examined Loyalists in the context of various colonial communities, including Upper Canada, New Brunswick, and Nova Scotia. This essay contributes to the historiography of Loyalist communities by exploring in more detail the negotiation of Loyalist identity in an even more localized context: the community of Shelburne, Nova Scotia, where the Holderness family settled.

Historians know of Jane Holderness and her kin from the personal journal of Capt. William Booth, a British military engineer who was posted to Shelburne in the late 1780s. His journal, titled *Remarks and Rough Memorandums,* has been described as one of the "most substantial and important but least known and least consulted documents of Loyalist Nova Scotia."[4] Although Booth himself was not a Loyalist, most of his friends and acquaintances in Shelburne were loyal refugees. They set the emotional tone of Shelburne, and Booth's journal catches the spirit of his times. He shares migrants' stories of disappointment and dispossession but also gives a sense of their "Loyalist dreams" and "new hopes."[5]

One of the most oft-cited Loyalist dreams in British North America is articulated by Ann Gorman Condon in her book *The Envy of the American States: The Loyalist Dream for New Brunswick.* In this version of the dream, elite Loyalists hoped to create in New Brunswick the "most gentlemanlike [society] on earth," which would be the envy and the antithesis of the nation that expelled them.[6] This "gentlemanlike" society would take the form of a landed gentry. Although some Loyalists did establish large rural estates, their vision of a hierarchical British social order proved unsustainable due to a shortage of labor to work the estates and insufficient funds to sustain their genteel lifestyles. Although social historians have illustrated the diversity of the Loyalists who migrated north, it is still this dream of the gentry that has monopolized all others in the popular imagination in Canada. This is because it has acquired the power of myth, propounding the message that the Loyalists who arrived in British North America were the cream of the crop of the American colonies.[7] While a few genteel Loyalists who settled in Shelburne may have articulated a similar dream, most of those who gravitated to the colonial outport were modest shopkeepers and artisans or free black Loyalists and slaves. What were their Loyalist dreams? And what can Booth's journal reveal about them?

The Tarnishing of White Loyalist Dreams in Shelburne

William Booth was posted to Nova Scotia in 1785, where he served as acting commander of engineers in Halifax for a year and then made his way to Shelburne, on the colony's southwest coast. Booth did not enjoy his time in Shelburne, where he frequently squabbled with local military authorities and members of the ordnance establishment. In December 1789 he obtained leave to return home, having lost his thirty-nine-year old wife, Hannah (née Proudfoot), to a severe illness.[8] Nonetheless, while in Shelburne he befriended a number of local civilians who aided in his recovery from ill health upon the death of his wife.[9]

Booth's acquaintances in Shelburne were modest Loyalists. An examination of the roster of the Port Roseway Associates (an emigration society formed in New York City to organize the migration to Shelburne) shows that most of the associates were "town-bred men" from the middling strata.[10] They hoped that migration would lead to social mobility. Loyalist dreams quickly took physical form as settlers built large homes and held a regular round of balls and assemblies in local parlors and taverns. Historians and contemporaries have criticized Shelburne's Loyalists for spending too much of their time and capital on conspicuous consumption instead of the serious tasks involved in making a living. Booth himself noted that his Loyalist friends were known for "build[ing] larger houses than was afterward found necessary." He noted that Jane Holderness's residence, although unfinished, was the "second or third best house in town"; she also had the "best Garden in the Place."[11] John Atkins, Booth's first landlord, and a blockman from Philadelphia with a family and two servants, spent most of his income on a large residence. This propensity to build impressive dwellings may have been irresponsible, but it is also understandable as a manifestation of "middling gentility."[12] A "revolution of manners"[13] was under way in the Atlantic world in the eighteenth century. As the requirements for genteel status broadened, the middling sort began to establish their own forms of gentility. In this context Booth's Loyalist friends invented a politics of acquired consumer respectability well suited to their aspirations of social mobility. This desire to acquire middling gentility was magnified in the pioneer context of Shelburne, where "old forms and standards meant little and status was in a state of flux."[14]

Middling dreams soon tarnished, however, as did Shelburne's economy. Jasanoff refers to Shelburne as a "shock city,"[15] an urban community experiencing infrastructure challenges related to rapid growth and, in Shelburne's case, an even faster decline. This remote outport became one of the largest settlements on the Eastern Seaboard by 1784, boasting somewhere in the vicinity of eight thousand to twelve thousand people, but the dream fell apart almost immediately. The town's decline has been attributed to various factors: the lack of foresight exhibited by various levels of government in planning for the Loyalist influx, the inability of the economy to support the burgeoning population, and the Loyalists' lack of strong leadership and their unrealistic expectations and inability to adjust to the frontier. This economic malaise precipitated an exodus out of Shelburne to places such as Halifax, Upper Canada, the United States, and the West Indies. By 1786, 710 rate payers were on the assessment rolls; ten years later, only 125. By 1827, 2,623 were residing in the vicinity of Shelburne.[16]

Many of those who stayed in Shelburne lost their life savings, most notably the investments in their homes. Booth notes on February 5, 1789, that "house rent very reasonable from their [sic] being so many vacant." Alexander Leckie, a Shelburne judge, asked for approximately sixty pounds per annum to rent his house but had to settle for ten. A few days later, Booth commented once again that "Houses and Rent wonderfully cheap at this Time." His former neighbor, merchant John Minshull, was letting his townhouse for twelve pounds per annum. A year and a half earlier, "this house . . . would not have been let for 100£ pr: annum." This loss of rental income must have cost Minshull dearly, for according to Booth, he paid fifteen hundred pounds to build the house.[17] Booth himself paid twenty-two pounds per annum for lodging in John Atkins's house, and "Atkins ask'd me 36 £ rent for the whole house in 1787." By September 1789 Atkins was reduced to renting it for five pounds per year. Booth records that a small home was sold at auction in March 1789 for sixteen pounds, including the lot, which had initially cost fifty pounds. As Booth concluded: "All the rents are lowered in the same way, and many People are glad to get Tenants for any Trifle."[18]

It is not surprising then, that Loyalist identity in Shelburne was grounded in a sense of hardship and betrayal. According to Calhoon, Loyalists' perception of their situation in exile was informed by an "ironic discovery that they were victims of both American aggression and British incompetence."[19] Local tradition holds that many residents in the shock city were displeased by the renaming of their town from Port Roseway to Shelburne, for many blamed the Second Earl of Shelburne, the British prime minister at the end the Revolution, for betraying them at the treaty table.[20] The lyrics to "A Shelburne Song," which Booth transcribed from the newspaper into his journal, epitomize this sense of martyrdom. The second verse begins:

> On Scotia's barren rocky shore,
> Consign'd to labour and be poor;
> For what the King in bounty gave,
> Half serv'd to poor; half kept by knave.
> Our province taxes next to pay,
> Our duties high and must obey;
> D[i]vested of our Country's laws,
> To represent our civil cause.[21]

This verse embodies the Loyalists' utter disappointment with their situation in Nova Scotia, but also a belief that they had been cheated of their dream of upward mobility and economic independence by an inefficient distribution of the king's bounty and the imposition of high taxes. As a result they were "consign'd to labour and be poor," clearly not what they had anticipated in their new home.

The incompetence and corruption of local officials also aggravated the loyal refugees of Shelburne. Under the subtitle "An Instance of Unfair Usage," Booth relayed Jane Holderness's story of mistreatment by surveyor Benjamin Marston: "Mrs. H— said . . . they had been obliged to purchase what land they possess, and at one time they had paid 50 Guineas for 50 feet of ground to build a store on, the next door is the house they now live in, and when some water lots were to have been drawn and which Mr. Holderness had given in his name as one. . . . Mr. Marsden [sic] struck his name out saying he had land enough. . . . This was certainly acting unfair, for supposing his circumstances had enabled him to have sold. He was not to be deprived of his rights as a settler in Shelburne. Many who got land sold it almost immediately and set off with the cash in hand. None but those who tipp'd Mr. Marsden were allowed to the chance of ground. Mr. Holderness would not do this, as it was not included in the treaty, and therefore was thrown out."[22] Calhoon accepts that Loyalists such as Holderness felt mistreated but argues that they transformed this frustration into a "tough, realistic, and implacable determination to surmount the difficulties of rebuilding their lives and constructing a new political social order in British North America."[23] Loyalists in exile did evince pluck and determination in the long term, but in the late 1780s in this boom and bust community, Loyalist perception was characterized by despair and vexation. This is expressed in verses six and seven of "A New Song to an Old Tune," transcribed by Booth in his entry for December 13, 1787:

> Being vex'd and fatigued at those frequent humbugs
> Poor Yankee, frost bitten, his Shoulder then shrugs
> He collects his few chattels that Remain'd on the ground
> And sets off with a copper for every pound—
> Derrydown
> When arrived at New York his friends gather Round
> Expecting to find him worth ten thousand Pounds
> But no sooner is Yankee set down in the house
> Then he relates his sad story of not worth a louse.
> Derrydown (an old English tune).[24]

Loyalist identity is often defined as political and ideological. Poor Yankee's main concerns, however, were economic. His "sad story" was that he that he left Nova Scotia with "few chattels" and a "copper for every pound." When he arrived in New York City, his friends expected to find him "worth ten thousand Pounds." Their assumption embodied the dream of economic advancement held by many white Loyalists in exile.

The Loyalists' disappointment and despondency in Shelburne was married to a sense of uprootedness and impermanence. Like many of the Loyalists profiled in Jasanoff's *Liberty's Exiles,* Booth's friends experienced multiple displacements. Dr. George Drummond, Booth's best friend in Shelburne, was forced to leave his work as a surveyor and teacher in Philadelphia and take on a position in New York City as an "assistant surgeon" at the New York General Hospital. Then he migrated to Shelburne as a Loyalist in May 1783. Atkins, Booth's aforementioned landlord, who had essentially lost everything in Shelburne, acquired a reference and loan from Booth to get him as far as New Providence, where Booth heard that he was seeking work as a plantation overseer.[25] Loyalists such as Holderness existed in a state of precariousness. The family's schooner did not provide the "new hope" that they were anticipating, and their Loyalist dream of economic independence was fading. She told Booth that she did not think they would stay in the town: "She says her Family must be thought of having 6 young Children and no Trade stirring here."[26]

Contested Dreams: Black Loyalists in Birchtown

Shelburne's white Loyalist newcomers were accompanied by 1,500–2,000 free African Americans, who had served behind British lines during the Revolution. Many of these so-called black Loyalists settled in a "parallel Loyalist community"[27] located on the northwest arm of Shelburne Harbour called Birchtown, named after Brig. Gen. Samuel Birch, who had provided them with certificates of freedom in New York City. At its height Birchtown was one of the largest communities of free blacks in North America at that time.[28] By January 8, 1784, there were 1,485 black men on the victualler's list; by late fall that number had increased to 1,531.[29] There is a debate over whether these residents of Birchtown should be labeled as Loyalists. Barry Cahill argues that they were primarily fugitive slaves who ran away from slavery rather than toward the British lines. James St. G. Walker, however, uses petitions to show that these runaways viewed themselves as Loyalists. In a petition to Governor Carleton of New Brunswick, William Fisher describes himself as "a Black Man" and a "poor indegent [*sic*] Loyalist hopeing [*sic*] your Excellency will take into consideration and will grant me the same as is granted to all other Loyalists." Thomas Peters, a sergeant in the Black Pioneers, presented two petitions directly to the British Cabinet in 1790: he introduced the first "on Behalf of himself and others, the Black Pioneers and loyal Black Refugees"; for the second he explained that he had been "deputed by his Fellow Soldiers and by other Free Negroes and People of Colour Refugees."[30] It is clear that these petitioners viewed themselves as loyal refugees and soldiers who felt entitled to their own Loyalist dreams.

Booth was introduced to Birchtown via community leader Stephen Blucke. In his journal Booth described Blucke as "a man of surprising address, being perfectly polite, and, I believe he has had superior Education.—If he had not been so fortunate, he has certainly made good use of his time—he don't appear to exceed eight and twenty—his wife is a Negro Woman—as is his mother. They are People from Barbados—."[31] Very little is known about Blucke, his mother, or his wife, Margaret. Unlike most of the other residents of Birchtown, who had fled as runaway slaves to the British lines, he was born free in the Barbados, while his wife had bought her freedom as a teenager in New York. Both appeared to be educated, well-mannered, and fairly well off. *The Book of Negroes* describes Stephen as "stout" and thirty-one years old and Margaret as a forty-year old "stout wench." They arrived in Shelburne on the ship *L'Abondence* in August 1783, bringing with them "a likely girl," twenty-year old Isabella Gibbons, who had been purchased and freed by Margaret.[32] Booth described Blucke as a "Mulatto," as did many other accounts, although Cahill argues that there is little evidence that he was "anything other than a full-blooded West Indian of African descent." He also suggests that Blucke has been labeled a mulatto because white Loyalist society found it easier to explain his gentility and leadership qualities if he were "at least a racial half-breed."[33] In any case Blucke was made superintendent of the black Loyalist companies during the evacuation and, in this capacity, brought six companies (approximately five hundred individuals) to Shelburne.[34]

Shortly after his arrival, surveyor Benjamin Marston accompanied Blucke to the "North West Arm . . . to show him the ground allotted for his people. They are well satisfied with it." Two days later Marston recorded "laying out lands for . . . Bluck's gentry." Despite this promising start, the residents of Birchtown encountered obstacles in receiving their land. All Loyalists in Shelburne County were promised a town lot and fifty acres of farm land. Of the 649 black Loyalists at Birchtown, only 184 (approximately one-third) received any farm lots at all, and those lots were often straddled with boulders and located in remote areas. They also had to wait until the white Loyalists' demands were met. In the meantime Blucke used his power and influence to acquire a two-hundred-acre lot in April 1786 but did not submit a petition on behalf of other residents until 1788. When these grants were finalized, the black Loyalists averaged only thirty-four acres, compared to the white settlers near Birchtown, who averaged seventy-four acres.[35]

Blucke's sizable land grant suggests that he had genteel aspirations. His honorific status was elevated in 1784, when Gov. John Parr commissioned him as lieutenant colonel of the black militia in the Shelburne District. Three years later he became schoolmaster of an Anglican charity school for black children run by the Associates of Dr. Bray, which initially had thirty-six students and operated for almost ten years. Blucke was also the only African American resident to rent a pew in the Anglican church for twenty shillings a year (rentals ranged from fifteen to forty-five shillings per year).[36] These dreams of upward mobility led one commentator to refer to him as a "white negro."[37] Indeed Booth saw Blucke's experience as little different from that of the other white Loyalists in Shelburne: "this Poor man, like many others in Shelburne Settlements—set off on the great Scale, with his expectations much too far excited." Like the middling white refugees, "he began by Building a spacious house, and laying out an excellent Garden, the Garden he has attended to the latter, but the Building he has been obliged to stop the progress of; having only, as far as I could see, completed his Kitchen, with a small Room—His neighbours, who, were at first 800 or thereabouts, are now reduced to a third of that number; very poorly lodged indeed."[38]

By matching Booth's description of Blucke's lodging to other "tantalizing clues," archaeologists in 1998 excavated a site (called AkDi-23) that many believe to have been Blucke's dwelling. The artifacts uncovered at AkDi-23, now on display at the Black Loyalist Heritage Centre in Birchtown Nova Scotia, are "exceptional" on a number of levels. The ceramics (creamware and pearlware) and clothing items stand in "stark contrast" to the modest wares uncovered elsewhere in Birchtown. The shoe-buckle frames would have been "very striking, especially in Birchtown where it would have been an exceptional possession." An iron spur is perhaps the most "unusual find." As project archaeologist Laird Niven put it: "The sight of someone riding through the poverty of Birchtown with spurs on their boots, would have been something to behold." This led the Birchtown excavation team to conclude that the community was a "much more vivid and varied [place] than has previously been acknowledged."[39]

Blucke's Loyalist dream was upscale, consumer oriented, and based on respectability politics. In that sense he shared much in common with Shelburne's white Loyalists who engaged in sociability and built nice houses. Most black Loyalists in Birchtown, however, had much simpler aspirations: freedom, a piece of land, and the reestablishment of their faith community. Black Loyalists in Birchtown initially looked to both secular and religious leaders for guidance. The captains of the black companies, as well as superintendent Blucke himself, helped community members arrange land grants, submit petitions, and find employment opportunities. Thomas Peters submitted multiple land petitions on behalf of himself and many black settlers in Nova Scotia and New Brunswick. However these secular leaders were soon overwhelmed by the arrival of evangelical preachers. Virtually overnight Birchtown became "home to some of the major leaders of the African-American religious community in North America."[40] Methodist minister Moses Wilkinson, or "Daddy Wilkinson," brought a following with him to Nova Scotia, including George Washington's fugitive slave Harry Washington. Wilkinson was a very charismatic preacher, despite being crippled and blind, probably as a result of contracting smallpox when he deserted to Lord Dunmore's flotilla in Virginia. Runaway slave David George, who became the "best known of the religious figures in Birchtown," also formed a Baptist congregation in the vicinity. His meetinghouse, which was the first Baptist church to be established in Nova Scotia, was also "a lineal descendant of the congregation [George] formed a decade earlier in the backcountry at Silver Bluff [South Carolina]." Another minister, the Reverend John Marrant, also labored in Birchtown on behalf of the Countess of Huntingdon's Connexion.[41]

The church plays a prominent role in black Loyalist historiography, as evangelical Christianity reached a large number of slaves and free blacks in the eighteenth century. The black preachers of Birchtown, according to one scholar, made up the "heart" of the First Great Awakening, which swept through America from the 1790s to the 1830s. Methodists and Baptists welcomed converts regardless of race. Nathan O. Hatch has noted: "The forms of Christianity that prospered among African Americans were not accepting of the status quo. They supported a moral revulsion of slavery and promised eventual deliverance, putting God on the side of change and freedom."[42] During the first winter at Birchtown, Boston King recalled, "the work of religion began to revive among us, and many were convinced of the sinfulness of sin, and turned from the error of their ways."[43]

This emphasis on the influence of black preachers has, however, obscured the reality that there was more than one black Loyalist identity. Blucke embodied an identity grounded in gentility, consumption, and education. Indeed the establishment of the charity school for black children "helped to create a separate black identity."[44] Because Blucke was an Anglican (and thus acceptable to the Associates of Dr. Bray) and the "best educated man" in the community, it was "logical that he should be selected as the school's first master."[45] The chief magistrate for the district of Shelburne, Isaac Wilkins, inspected the school and was impressed with the progress of Blucke's thirty-six pupils, as well as the "conduct and efficient management of Birchtown's education."[46] When Bishop Charles Inglis visited in 1790, Blucke had forty-four students, which led the bishop to reflect that Birchtown's black settlers were "better served" than the five hundred white children whose parents could not afford tuition at Shelburne's white schools.[47]

This alternate version of the Loyalist dream has been downplayed in Loyalist historiography.[48] In Jasanoff's overview of the Loyalist diaspora, no mention is made of Blucke in the context of Nova Scotia. David George, on the other hand, is included in her "cast of characters," while Boston King and Daddy Wilkinson are "supporting figures."[49]

She also effuses that "if the devil was among the white Loyalists of Shelburne, God glowed over the blacks and Birchtown."[50] It may be argued that the latter approach to black Loyalist identity, with its focus on community and Christian empowerment, is more attractive, for it "facilitate[es] social levelling, retrospectively breaking down class barriers among black people." This approach to black Loyalist history is also more attuned to "modern cultural sensibilities" generated by the civil rights movement.[51] A focus on community and Christianity also allows the historian to cover a wider swath of the population, who were too impoverished to embrace seriously the notions of gentility or consumerism.

Another reason for the prominence of the evangelical narrative is its connection to the Back-to-Africa movement. Recruiters for the Sierra Leone Company attempted to convince settlers of African heritage in Nova Scotia and New Brunswick to begin a new life overseas by helping to colonize West Africa. On October 26, 1791, three hundred to four hundred prospective settlers attended a meeting at Moses Wilkinson's Methodist church to listen to the proposals of the Sierra Leone Company, as articulated by military officer and abolitionist John Clarkson. Within three days five hundred black Loyalists had signed up. By the end of the recruitment period, approximately twelve hundred people had given their names. [52] This was considerably more interest than the abolitionists had anticipated.

Why did the recruiters find such a receptive audience among the black Loyalists of Birchtown? The Sierra Leone Company offered to African Americans the same dream that Britain had offered them in Nova Scotia: the opportunity to own land and attain economic independence. The handbill informing black Loyalists of the terms they would receive in Africa noted that "every Free Black . . . shall have a Grant of not less than Twenty Acres of Land for himself, Ten for his wife, and five for every child." The free blacks in Shelburne and elsewhere were also attracted by the promise that they would not be treated as second-class citizens by virtue of the color of their skin: "That for all stores, provisions, or, supplies from the Company's

Warehouse, the company shall receive an equitable compensation, according to fixed rules, extending to blacks and whites indeterminately." Also "the civil, military, personal, and commercial rights and duties of Blacks and Whites, shall be the same, and secured in the same manner." And of course the former slaves were attracted by the "full assurance" that they would receive "personal protection from slavery." The company declared that it would not "deal or traffic in the buying or selling of Slaves" or "have, hold, appropriate, or employ any person or persons in a state of slavery."[53]

Religious leaders also mobilized migrants by drawing on one of the central narratives of their faith: the story of Exodus, which related how God freed his chosen people and sent them on a "pilgrimage through the wilderness" to a land of milk and honey.[54] The black Loyalists, like the ancient Israelites, had fled as slaves through the wilderness to Nova Scotia. Perhaps another pilgrimage over the ocean would finally bring them to their promised land. Most of the aforementioned evangelical leaders left Birchtown for Sierra Leone, taking their congregations with them. Moreover individual black Loyalists were motivated to leave by their desire to spread Christianity to the indigenous population in Africa. Boston King noted in his memoir: "Recollecting the concern I had felt in years past, for the conversion of the Africans, I resolved to embrace the opportunity of visiting that country; and therefore went to one of the Agents employed in this business, and acquainted him with my intention. The gentleman informed Mr. Clarkson, that I was under no necessity of leaving Nova Scotia, because I was comfortably provided for: But when I told them, that it was not for the sake of the advantages I hope to reap in Africa, which induced me to undertake the voyage, but from a desire that had long possessed my mind, of contributing to the best of my poor ability, in spreading the knowledge of Christianity in that country."[55]

This reminds that, although black Loyalists wished to exert "black sovereignty" in Africa, they were also an "advance guard of British colonization in a region dominated by indigenous powers."[56] Although forty-seven members of the Birchtown community who had signed up for Sierra Leone had been abducted as children and thus found themselves "returning to the land of their birth,"[57] most had experienced multiple displacements over the course of their lives and had created fluid and syncretic identities. They were not "Africans" per se but "cultural creoles" in Ira Berlin's sense of the term: "by their experiences and sometimes by their persons, they had become part of the three worlds [Africa, Europe, and America] that came together along the Atlantic littoral. . . . fluent in the new languages, and intimate with its trade and cultures [including religion], they were cosmopolitan in the fullest sense."[58]

Historians such as Jasanoff, Cassandra Pybus, and Simon Schama have been attracted to the black Loyalists because of their "global quest for liberty."[59] Their epic journey from one side of the world to the other has also been fictionalized in Lawrence Hill's 2007 award-winning novel *The Book of Negroes,* which chronicles the story of Aminata Diallo, who is captured in West Africa, works as a plantation slave in South Carolina and as a domestic servant in New York City, deserts to the British lines during the American Revolution, joins the exodus of Loyalists for Nova Scotia, and from Birchtown returns to Sierra Leone.[60] While the transatlantic experience of the black Loyalists is significant, one must remember that not everyone in Birchtown left for Africa. Blucke, who initially acted as a local liaison with the Sierra Leone Company acquiring information for the residents and appearing occasionally in John Clarkson's journal,[61] ultimately stayed behind in Birchtown. Blucke and fifty-two heads of household submitted a petition to Gov. John Parr, dated November 1, 1791, opposing the colonization scheme, arguing that "members of our brethren, are so infatuated as to embrace the proposals of the Sierra Leone Company which (with all due Submission) we conceive will be utter annihilation." Since the British monarch was prepared to assume part of the cost of the exodus to West Africa, the petitioners asked for their share of "royal bounty" in the form of a grant "as may enable us to purchase a Cow and two Sheep, which (if obtained) will make us comfortable on our little farms." It has been suggested that Blucke succumbed to pressures from white residents, who opposed the exodus because of the loss of cheap labor. It must be remembered, however, that Blucke was an educated man and no doubt had his own reasons for deciding to stay, as did the other families who signed the memorial. According to historian James St. G. Walker, this memorial is the "only piece of documentary evidence to show that a group of blacks who were free to leave deliberately chose the alternative to remain in Nova Scotia."[62] It is interesting to note that all of the black Loyalists who decided to stay were landowners and nonevangelicals. They did not fit the profile of the transatlantic migrants, but they should nonetheless be recognized as representing an alternative Loyalist identity with a dream grounded in local aspirations. To their credit, the interpreters at the new Black Loyalist Heritage Centre in Birchtown encourage visitors to follow the diverse trajectories of individual refugees and their families, thus illustrating the multiplicity of Loyalist dreams and experiences.

Neither dream had a happy ending. In Sierra Leone new arrivals struggled with the indigenous populations, nearby slavers, and the paternalistic governance of the Sierra Leone Company. By 1800 black Loyalists from Nova Scotia were embroiled in a coup.[63] On the other side of the Atlantic, Blucke's dream remained as unfinished as his house. His reputation as a community leader undoubtedly suffered when he bore a child with his young charge Isabella. This is probably why his wife, Margaret, returned to New York City in 1789. Shortly after Margaret wrote to the Reverend John Marrant, her "dear respected friend," to find out what he knew about "Mr. Blucke," for "I cannot find out what he is doing." She seemed more concerned about Isabella: "my mind and heart is filled with concern and trouble on account of that poor unhappy girl Isabella, in the manner she lives."[64] This unfortunate situation reflects the social and personal upheaval created by the American Revolution. Black Loyalist kin were often separated during the act of mass desertion, through familial discord or re-enslavement, as was the case for Mary Postell, who was sold from her children in Shelburne.[65] Family separation was not just a black Loyalist problem, however. White Loyalist husbands and fathers often left their families to serve in the British army or in a Loyalist regiment. Hannah Ingraham, of Concord, New York, was only four years old when her father joined the King's American Regiment in 1776. She did not see him again until 1783, when family left for St Anne's Point (Fredericton).[66]

By 1792 Blucke's star was falling. His name appeared on a list of the "poorest and most distressed sufferers" of the fires that ravaged Shelburne. Probably the most significant blow to his standing in the community was the closing of the school in 1795. In his last report to the Associates of Dr. Bray, Blucke claimed to have thirty-six children during the previous eighteen months, while the Associates' records show that only fourteen children remained, many having left for Sierra Leone. This discrepancy led the Associates to "doubt the Legality of Mr Bluck's Claim," and they refused to pay his salary. Blucke swore an oath before magistrate Gideon White that he spoke the truth, and the Associates eventually paid him. To make matters worse, he was accused of doctoring the "schoolmaster's accounts." As an ambitious black man looking to make his way up the ladder, he was an easy target for embezzlement charges. Blucke was eventually cleared, but suspicions lingered. By 1796 "Blucke disappear[ed] from history." It likely that he left Birchtown, as did so many others before and after him.[67] It must be remembered, however, that although Blucke left, those who did remain formed the basis of the present-day black Nova Scotian population of Shelburne County.

To return to William Booth, he was clearly sympathetic to the plight of the black Loyalists in Birchtown. Life had not been easy for them since their arrival. Farming was difficult. Booth reasoned that this was because they knew little about subsistence farming: "[Blucke's] neighbours . . . have given no proof of their judgement in Farming about this spot, having in My opinion, neglected this *that* which would have, in the end, turned out to the most advantage: 'Tis a valley with much stones, and a little swampy; but to appearance easily drained and sewered." He elaborated that "they are no Farmers, and but very indifferent Gardeners; The farmers, who are the men and most desirable in every young Country; are off— or at least very few remaining—."[68] Black Loyalists failed at farming for multiple reasons, including inexperience, the poor quality of the soil (which was thin and acidic), and lack of access to land and capital. Many were ultimately forced into forms of "exploitive sharecropping."[69]

Booth argued that the free blacks should have been given priority in choice of land grants: "These men (if I may be allowed to say it), should have been the first People, both wth respect to choice, and situation; even (I may wth advantage assert) had their inclinations been to settle on that Part where the Town now stands; I don't mention this from opinion of the Land there, being better, because I know otherwise; I only say it, in consideration of the great necessity there was; to court and indulge those most valuable People to so Young, and difficult a Country; for turning to any use, or advantage. If *they* were disappointed in their hopes, on viewing what was destined to them, should they attempt to sacrifice their last shilling, before they could wth any cheerfulness view a small appearance of any Harvest; How much more difficult must it to for those, who are totally ignorant of the industrious Farmer's *Plough* and *Harrow!*—"[70]

Why was Booth willing to give his African American neighbors the benefit of the doubt? He described them as a "most valuable People" and a "Poor, but really spirited People." In other words they were industrious, unlike many white Loyalists, who seemed to complain about everything. In Booth's eyes such a workforce was necessary to develop "so Young and difficult a Country." But ironically the free blacks' reputation as a diligent (and cheap) labor force also explains why white merchants such as Stephen Skinner opposed their exodus. Booth also sympathized with the black Loyalists because they were poor, for he had witnessed escalating poverty during Shelburne's decline. Moreover, as an officer and a gentleman, he abided by the tenets of polite society, which instructed him to have "compassion for suffering" and to "treat all persons with respect, the rich as well as the poor."[71]

Booth was not alone in his assessment of the challenges faced by the black Loyalists. British commander in chief Sir Guy Carleton's handling of Gen. George Washington after the war ensured that many fugitive slaves who had served the British were able to join the Loyalist exodus out of New York City to resettle in communities such as Birchtown. Carleton was by no means an abolitionist but acted partly out of a sense of personal honor: "Promises had been made, promises must be kept." He also reflected an emergent sense of "national honor . . . and the paternalistic government's responsibility to uphold it . . . that would rapidly gain momentum among the rulers of the postwar British Empire."[72]

As deputy surveyor in Shelburne, Benjamin Marston also thought that the free blacks had been treated shabbily during the process of land allocation. As soon as he began to lay out land lots in Birchtown, he recorded in his journal that "the People of Shelburne" proceeded to appoint their own rival surveyor, who laid out fifty-acre lots and began to sell them to white Loyalists "on ye Black men's ground" without "even a shadow of a license." It has been suggested that white Loyalists, in the context of a contested land allocation process, resented "the sight of former slaves receiving the same kinds of concessions they themselves were struggling to realize." This tension over land as well as cheap labor precipitated the first race riot in British North America in late July 1784, as disbanded soldiers tore down the houses of about twenty free blacks, including that belonging to David George.[73] Marston soon discovered that he too was being "threatened by the Rioters" for a couple of reasons: for allegations of favoritism during the land lottery and for being too sympathetic to the black Loyalists. He fled Shelburne, pursued as far as Point Carleton by unhappy Shelburnians, who threatened to "hang him on sight."[74]

Booth continued to express interest in the subsistence of the black Loyalists. He contended in his journal that fishing was their "chief and most profitable employment." Blucke reported to the Associates of Dr. Bray that he had built a fishing vessel: "we have no prospect of a livelihood here without adventuring on the fishing boats." In the excavation of the site believed to have been Blucke's residence, archaeologists found a fishing net, which suggests the significance of fishing as a way to contribute to the family economy. The year that Boston King had been hired for a "summer's fishing" at Bay Chaleur had been the "best winter I ever saw in Birchtown."[75] But, as Booth realized, it was difficult to begin an operation without capital: "it must be known, that even a Fisherman requires a little Yellow and white earth [cash] to commence his business." He further explained that "those that cannot get into this Employ [fishing], Work as Labourers; clearing Land, by the Acre, which they do for 8 dollars, cutting cordwood for fires, and hunting in the Season."[76] In his entry for April 15, 1789, Booth recorded meeting a woodcutter: "A Black Man brought Pickets for Mrs. H's Garden—I asked him what he sold them at? Said 3 coppers a Bundle, how many in the bundle? He said 5, of eight ft in length—The above is the rate of 5 shillings per hundred—The man cuts them and brings them to the house for this price—."[77] It is probably this man who provided the inspiration for Booth's watercolor of a "black woodcutter," one of the only contemporary likenesses of a black Loyalist in the Loyalist diaspora . Six months later Booth recorded buying two ducks from a "Black Woman from Birchtown." He asked her "how many Inhabitants were in Birch Town, says about 400 besides children."[78] Besides forming a large source of cheap labor for Shelburne's white employers, black Loyalists also sold themselves into indentured servitude as artisans or domestics, which meant that they "simply continued to do the work they had performed as slaves."[79] The black Loyalists' predicament was made worse by a famine that hit the area in the late 1780s. As a result many were reduced to hardscrabble, inescapable poverty.[80] For many black Loyalists, they could not do worse than remain in Nova Scotia. One traumatized individual said to John Clarkson regarding the hard work required to colonize Sierra Leone: 'Mr. Massa, me no hear, nor no mind, me work like slave, cannot do worse, Massa. . . . If me die, me die, had rather die in me own country than this cold place."[81]

Black Loyalists experienced other obstacles in their journey to full and meaningful freedom. Most disadvantaged were those who were re-enslaved in exile, the most well-known being Mary Postell of Shelburne. Postell had run away from a South Carolina planter during the Revolution, claiming freedom behind British lines, although her certificate of freedom had been taken from her by a white official who claimed he wanted to see her papers. When she and her husband migrated to Saint Augustine, Florida, as part of the Loyalist migration, they worked as servants for Jesse Gray. In Postell's own words, Gray used "grievous threatenings and other enormous abuses [to] compel terrify and oblige [us] to serve, Work, and Labour." Gray claimed Postell was legally his slave and sold her to his brother Samuel. After Postell bore her first child, Jesse Gray bought her back and immigrated to Shelburne. In Shelburne, Postell and her children were compelled to "Work and Labour . . . as the Slave and Slaves" of Gray. Eventually Gray sold Postell (for "one hundred bushels of potatoes") and her daughter Flora, keeping daughter Nell as his own property. In 1791 Postell launched an indictment against Gray "for taking away her children." Gray was eventually declared not guilty, as Postell "had not proven that she had been a free person." Her life course reflects the fluidity and impermanence of Loyalist Shelburne, but in a much more tragic sense, as the stakes were higher: either freedom or bondage. Nonetheless Postell's re-enslavement should not "obscure for historians the fact that she pressed the case as far as possible" in the courts of Shelburne.[82]

SLAVERY AS PART OF THE LOYALIST DREAM

Free blacks from Birchtown were not the only people of African descent that Booth encountered in daily life. He also owned a couple of domestic slaves, Nancy and Betty Anna, who had belonged to his wife and had probably originated from her brothers' plantation in Grenada in 1786.[83] In owning these domestics, Booth reflected the widespread pattern of slave ownership in Shelburne. Jane Holderness had a black maid; Atkins had also come to town with two servants. Slavery was an important component of the white Loyalist dream in Nova Scotia. White settlers believed that they needed slaves to ensure economic independence. Catherine M.A. Cottreau-Robins argues in this volume that slave owners such as Timothy Ruggles created a "landscape of slavery" in the colony by building his plantations. He represents the efforts of elite Loyalists to re-create their former lifestyles, which ultimately guaranteed the continuation of slavery in exile.[84] This emphasis on slavery is an important shift in Loyalist historiography, for slavery has not been a "significant part of the narrative of Canada." Although slavery had been present in the Maritime colonies since the early seventeenth century, the Loyalist migration led to an intensification and expansion of slavery in the region. It is estimated that between fifteen hundred and two thousand slaves arrived in Nova Scotia and New Brunswick as part of this migration. Like the Loyalists themselves, most slaves emanated from New England and the Middle Colonies, but a significant minority also came from the southern colonies. Slaves contributed to a mixed economy: they worked as domestics, farmhands, sailors, dockworkers, artisans, and general laborers. In many ways slaves helped to build Nova Scotia's infrastructure by "cutting settlements out of the fearsome timber and rock that greeted them on their arrival."[85]

In a return prepared by British officials in 1783, "nearly 15% of those who went to Shelburne (1,312 of 8,896) remained in some form of servitude or slavery." It is unclear whether these individuals were indentured or waged servants (white or black) or black slaves. This problem of identification created an institution that was "widespread" but "highly contested" and unstable. Slavery was recognized under British Common Law as a form of private property in Nova Scotia, but it was "legally insecure" in the sense that it had no statutory basis. Historians do know that slaves were owned by a broad cross-section of inhabitants in Nova Scotia. In a study of forty-five slave-owning households in Shelburne, based on the 1786 and 1787 tax assessments, 42 percent were "involved in the service or maritime industries, or were skilled workers." While wealthy merchants and gentlemen "made up a substantial proportion" of the slaveholders in Shelburne, they were "part of a much wider system of slaveholding that extended throughout the various classes."[86]

The dreams and expectations of slaves are difficult to determine. But it is clear from their constant efforts to run away and to contest their status in the local courts that they desperately sought freedom from bondage. Scholars have also identified a multitude of ways in which slaves in Nova Scotia resisted their dehumanization, as they did throughout the Atlantic World. In Shelburne fifty handbills were issued in 1785 that banned "Negro Frolicks." These frolics were dances that "embodied deeply held religious and spiritual values, and were an expression of African aesthetics." It is important to note that efforts to clamp down on African American frolics in Shelburne were ultimately ineffective, for they were still being held a year later. This shows a fierce determination among slaves and free blacks to maintain their culture in Shelburne. Slaves in Nova Scotia also "challenged their masters on a personal level through interactions within households."[87] Nancy and Betty Anna, Booth's domestic slaves, regularly engaged in small acts of defiance. On February 11, 1789, Booth recorded that they would not eat their dinners. He gave Nancy "a little lecture for this," noting that she had "behaved very disrespectful for some time pass'd—."[88] After Booth moved into Holderness's house as a boarder, the "Black Girls" began to sleep in the kitchen by the hearth despite his order to sleep in a garret over his chamber. This created some friction with landlady Holderness, who did not approve of the girls sleeping in her kitchen. Booth eventually came to an agreement regarding room and board for his domestics, who were to dine with her slave, and gave Holderness's maid a small sum for "shewing my Black Servants to do things in the Kitchen &c."[89]

Booth also struggled with the behavior of his Irish Loyalist manservant, Thomas Graves. One example of this occurred when he suffered from digestive issues after eating a poorly cooked steak. Booth remonstrated in his journal that "I am inclined to think that my Sancho did this on purpose, for soon after dinner he came up to ask me how I liked the Beef Steak, saying he dressed it himself—I replied it was a bad steak, and that he should cook no more for me—." This illustrates that the fluidity between servitude and slavery that characterized Shelburne society also existed in Booth's household. Booth believed that both his manservant and black female domestics engaged in this type of behavior "for a sake of a piece of their own wit—they will often spoil the best things—for having been obliged to live on the same thing."[90] He painted his servant and slaves with the same brush again after hearing male and female voices singing in the cellar immediately under his room. He suspected that the man's voice was Graves, "which I look'd on as a mark of some contempt and disrespect to the afflicted situation I am in at the moment, in the loss of my best mistress [the death of his wife Hannah]—." Nancy and Betty Anna accused Holderness's maid of singing: "This, in her, I could not prevent, though I cannot help remarking it as an instance of their unfeeling disposition—."[91] If Graves had been singing with the maid, which is probable even though he denied it, his behavior does illustrate that servants and slaves associated with each other, again stressing the fluidity between them.

Booth eventually presented Graves with an ultimatum, that "if he and the girls did not do as I order'd I would get rid of them all immediately, let the consequence be what it would—."[92] Despite numerous threats to fire him, Graves continued in Booth's employ. One of the female slaves, however, was eventually discharged. Booth sent the "elder and less manageable of the pair," Betty Anna, back to his brother-in-law's plantation in Grenada via the Bahamas. Booth wrote to his brother-in-law, Samuel Proudfoot: "I have one still with me who turns out well [Nancy], the other [Betty Anna] was clever but somewhat inclined to be a Teefee, Teefee according to their own language, however, she is young and to be easily reformed."[93] This practice of sending slaves to the Caribbean was followed by other Loyalist slave owners in Shelburne. In his journal Booth recorded conversing with Anglican rector Rev. John Hamilton Rowland, whose female slave had recently been sold for thirty pounds in New Providence Island, Bahamas. Captain Wheeler, to whom Booth had entrusted his slave, told him that the governor of the Bahamas, Lord Dunmore, had allowed him two guineas [£2.2.0] for each slave carried from Nova Scotia to the Bahamas for sale in the Nassau slave market.[94]

Slavery was clearly part of the Loyalist dream for white Loyalists of all classes in Shelburne. Slave owners entered exile with their slaves and servants in tow. But these slaves brought with them their own cultural practices, as well as a desire to resist bondage, a trait that they shared with poor white servants such as Thomas Graves. This reflects the fluid nature of slavery and servitude in Nova Scotia, as articulated by Amani Whitfield. Whitfield also argues that by the 1810s–20s, "several groups of white immigrants were also doing poorly and could not have survived without government rations." I would argue that poor white Loyalists such as Graves also suffered from economic inequality. Nonetheless they did not experience "the same level of discrimination as people of African descent."[95] Although Booth threatened to sack Graves several times, it was Betty Anna who paid the ultimate price and was sent to the West Indies, like many other slaves in Shelburne.

Conclusion

William Booth's manuscript journal illustrates that Loyalist identity in Shelburne was variable, mutable, and highly contested in the late 1780s. Booth's entries provide insight into the aspirations of white nonelite refugees in Nova Scotia, such as Dr. George Drummond, Jane Holderness, and John Atkins, and respectable black Loyalists such as Stephen Blucke, who flocked to Shelburne in search of upward mobility. These refugees of the American Revolution aspired to middling gentility, as they built large houses, wore nice clothes, and participated in dinner parties. Most loyal refugees in Birchtown hoped for more basic freedoms, such as a life without bondage, a piece of land on which to raise their families, and the ability to practice their faith. They had entered into exile to escape the peculiar institution (excluding African Americans such as Blucke who were born free), but unfortunately many were pulled back again into bondage, by becoming re-enslaved or entering a state of enforced servitude. As one scholar has noted, "when the Black Loyalists arrived in the Maritimes to settle, a new beginning was signaled for many. For others, the history of subjugation that accompanied them continued and left an imprint and a legacy in the developing northeast British colonies."[96] Regardless of the nature of their Loyalist dreams, most fell apart in the flux, as Shelburne entered a downward spiral. Loyalist identity in this community of exile became marked by a sense of loss and uncertainty. Eventually Loyalists were able to reshape their Loyalist dreams in new ways in other locations throughout the Loyalist diaspora. Some caught "Niagara fever" and trekked to Upper Canada. Others went back to the United States to reunite with family. Approximately one third of the black Loyalists sought a new promised land in West Africa, although they continued to face many of the same challenges. For the slaves who ended up in Shelburne, unless they escaped or found ways to resist, they must have felt like they were caught up in the same recurring nightmare.

CATHERINE M. A. COTTREAU-ROBINS

Exploring the Landscape of Slavery in Loyalist Era Nova Scotia

When the American Revolution came to an end, thousands of American Loyalists were forced into exile. Most of the Loyalists relocated in British North America, particularly the eastern provinces known as Maritime Canada. As demonstrated by many historians, the impact was significant and enduring.[1] This essay describes a study of the Loyalists in this region using both documentary and archaeological evidence.[2] The focus is on two Loyalist families and their enslaved people who journeyed from Massachusetts and New York to Nova Scotia.

It is the story of the enslaved black Loyalists[3] and their place in Nova Scotia's colonial history that separates this study from others. This story, given the challenges with the eighteenth-century archival record particular to marginalized populations, has been addressed by fostering a holistic perspective that considers a single geography—the plantation. The holistic perspective was developed through an interdisciplinary methodology that combines Atlantic world history, historical archaeology, and cultural geography and is informed by the people, places, and culture that shaped the Loyalist plantation.[4] The concept that emerged with this method was one that put into place the structure and organization of a Loyalist plantation in the late eighteenth century. When mapped, the interdisciplinary data provided clues to a landscape of slavery in Nova Scotia's Loyalist era, one directly linked to Loyalist efforts for continuity.[5]

SEARCHING FOR THE ENSLAVED

Until recently the standard Canadian historical narrative on slavery was that Canadians embraced freedom by receiving enslaved people fleeing American slavery and guaranteeing their freedom.[6] Increasingly Canadians are becoming aware of their country's slave-holding past, and research and public exhibitions have amplified this understanding.

Owing to the limited documentary resources and dialogue on the subject, reaching the story of the enslaved is rife with challenges. In Nova Scotia one primary document has become key to charting a path and is often scoured for clues. *The Book of Negroes* is a ledger created by the British during the evacuation of New York in 1783. It holds the names and descriptions of three thousand enslaved and free black refugees, the ships that carried them northward and abroad, and their destinations in Maritime Canada, as well as information concerning the slaveholders.[7]

The Book of Negroes provided a Loyalist case study, pursued in this essay, of Brig. Gen. Timothy Ruggles. The ledger holds evidence of slaves noted as "the General's Property." Specifically an entry for April 23–27, 1783, lists the brig *Ranger* bound for Annapolis Royal, Nova Scotia. The vessel had aboard Hester Ruggles, age seven, "fine wench," the property of General Ruggles; Jeffery Ruggles, age six, "fine boy" and the property of General Ruggles; Prince, age nineteen, "stout B[lack]," for the general's son Richard Ruggles of Annapolis; Robert Williams, age twenty-three, "stout, B," listed as with General Ruggles, was described as free born at Shrewsbury, New Jersey; John Coslin, age twenty-five, "stout, M[ullatto]," also noted as with General Ruggles, was described as free born at North Hampshire, Virginia, of free parents.[8]

HISTORY RESEARCH STREAM

An analysis of historical texts surrounding Ruggles gleans a rich depiction of Nova Scotia's slavery period. Ruggles is a conduit—a way to the enslaved. He was familiar with slave-holding in both Massachusetts and Nova Scotia, and through the historical record about him, which was extensive especially in Massachusetts, his place in the "gentry clique,"[9] his Loyalist ideology and vision for an Anglo-American empire, and his deep connection to the land and the need to improve it are made clear.

Timothy Ruggles was well educated, affluent, and well connected. He graduated from Harvard in 1732 at the age of twenty-one and practiced law. His hometown was Rochester, Massachusetts, and around 1740 he moved to Sandwich. While in Sandwich he met and married Bathsheba Newcomb, a widow and accomplished tavern owner. He advanced his reputation as a lawyer for thirteen years in Sandwich and in 1753–54 moved to Hardwick, Massachusetts, in present-day Worcester County.

When Ruggles and his family settled in Hardwick, he had accumulated a healthy fortune. With his wealth he began to develop a county seat suitable to a gentleman of his social standing and legal influence. In time the estate became the most noteworthy in the area, with sizable agricultural holdings, a mansion house, riding park, thirty horse stables, and deer park complete with hounds. With slaves[10] in the household and working the estate, he entertained frequently and in grand style. Experimental or scientific gardening, particularly with apples, and the breeding of thoroughbred horses and cattle were other noted pursuits.[11]

Ruggles was appointed judge of the Court of Common Pleas in 1756, and from 1762 until the American Revolution he was chief justice of that court. Not long after moving to Hardwick, as the Seven Years' War developed, he turned to military matters. For his service he was made brigadier general as well as surveyor general of the woods. In 1762 his leadership role in Massachusetts expanded when he was chosen Speaker of the House of Representatives.

Ruggles's lengthy leadership role in the Seven Years' War informed his resolve as a Loyalist.[12] The period represented the social apogee of his career: as a litigator, military man, judge, legislator, Speaker of the House, man of property, and agriculturalist. He continued in his various positions and worked to develop his estate and position. Yet his vision of a true Anglo-America splintered as tests to social and political cohesion intensified and discontent escalated with the tightening of the imperial grip. A critical episode occurred in October 1765 during the Stamp Act Crisis, which affirmed Ruggles's loyalty to the king and Parliament nearly a decade before the Revolution officially began.[13] Ruggles had been elected president of this First Colonial Congress. To the astonishment of many, he refused to sign the declaration. To explain himself, he took to the press in the *Boston Post Boy and Advertiser* (May 5, 1766).[14] His resolve for king and Parliament positioned Ruggles early on among Loyalists who envisioned an Anglo-American empire in which the mother country and its colonies would work together to improve economically, politically, and culturally.

Ruggles remained highly active in the affairs of his colony in the Revolutionary period and continued to confront challenges to unity and stability.[15] Ann Gorman Condon summed up Ruggles's position well in her study of the Loyalists in pre-Revolutionary America. Why enter into conflict with Great Britain when "a quality of life that was safer, richer, more stable—and even freer—than any they could hope to provide for themselves in the foreseeable future" was at hand?[16]

In 1774, following his appointment as mandamus councillor, Ruggles was forced from his estate in Hardwick.[17] Similar to other Loyalists fleeing rural townships, Ruggles escaped to the nearby city of Boston with his sons Richard and John and servants shortly before war officially broke out. A notice published in the Massachusetts Spy, or, American Oracle of Liberty dated October 29, 1778, listed Ruggles and his sons as enemies of the state and therefore part of an act to prevent their return.[18] He then did not appear in official records until 1783, at which time he had migrated to Annapolis County, Nova Scotia. Now in his early seventies, he was then at Annapolis Royal and/or Granville with his sons and at least eight servants/slaves.[19] He made application for a land grant, submitted his memorial for compensation from the British government, and began settling in.[20]

Ruggles worked the thousand-acre lot with his sons, hired hands, slaves, house servants, and possibly indentured servants. North Mountain in Wilmot Township, the location of his farmstead, was forested when he arrived. In the decade he was on the mountain, the group shaped the land in recollection of his Hardwick estate. Near the top of North Mountain, in the community known today as Spa Springs, on a spot commanding a spectacular view, Ruggles built his house. He planted the first apple orchard in the county using seedlings imported from his Hardwick farms. On the steep slope east of the main house, in a vaulted natural hothouse, Ruggles experimented with other varieties of trees and shrubs, expanding the skills as a scientific gardener he was noted for in Worcester County.[21]

According to historian Leone Cousins, Ruggles's new home soon became the model farm of the district.[22] Ruggles died at Wilmot in 1795 at the age of eighty-four. His obituary, printed in the *Royal Gazette,* was written by Rev. John Wiswall, the first rector of Wilmot Parish and a friend and North Mountain neighbor.[23]

From his obituary a portrait of the man emerges. Ruggles's most active and prominent years were those of the Seven Years' War, though his zealous efforts to improve and reform did not cease with its conclusion. According to Wiswall's obituary, he framed himself a student of the Enlightenment, an agricultural innovator, and an improver comparable to Landon Carter or even Thomas Jefferson of Virginia. All three were dedicated to agricultural improvement, all three were students of reason, all three were active legislators, all three had position, influence and wealth, and all three had slaves. The fundamental difference is Ruggles's fealty to the Crown. Ruggles may or may not have been a typical Loyalist, but he was a prototypical member of the American planter elite who set about rebuilding his American fortunes in Canada.

Paul Revere, "A Warm Place in Hell," 1768. Courtesy American Antiquarian Society

ARCHAEOLOGY RESEARCH STREAM

The historical record tells much, but archaeological fieldwork allows this study to peer past textuality and view the Ruggles plantation and all its inhabitants in greater detail. The fieldwork ranged from pedestrian survey of the land grants in Hardwick and Wilmot, noting features and areas of archaeological potential, to excavation that resulted in recorded artifact collections, architectural remains, and landscape features. The archaeology stream worked in tandem with the documentary record to amplify the narrative of the Ruggles group particularly regarding his settlement approach and his relationship with the pioneers shaping a home and plantation for him. Often slaves, servants, and laborers are only recorded briefly as notations in estate ledgers or probate inventories, as bequests in wills, or as numbers in the columns of tax valuations. Archaeology, a record of physical evidence, therefore becomes essential to developing the narrative.

A main goal of this study was to find a place on Ruggles's land in Nova Scotia where slaves had lived and to excavate that place in order to gain insight into their daily lives. One of the archaeology sites recorded on the North Mountain land grant contained the remains of a rudimentary shelter close to the Ruggles Road,[24] with a dry-laid stone foundation, interior hearth, and a collection of basic domestic and architectural material culture consistent with the late eighteenth century. Particular focus was shifted to this small hut or cabin given its potential eighteenth-century connection and shared characteristics with other recorded slave quarters of the Revolutionary War period: the dry-laid stone foundation, earthen floor, clapboard construction, sparse window glass, small size, and location close to the fields and visible from the main house. Artifacts and architectural features did not exhibit Africanisms as documented by researchers in the United States, nor did they exhibit a recognizable process of creolization—a fusing of African and British or European traditions—or even a representation of two distinct groups (slave and slaveholder or enslaved and free).[25] Undoubtedly, though, this was a place where people of lower economic status lived, probably workers or laborers. They were likely black Loyalists, given the artifact patterns observed and recalling that Ruggles and his sons were slaveholders.[26]

Through the archaeology it was learned that Ruggles constructed a significant house on North Mountain. Behind the house there was a barn and a walled pasture. Remnant apple orchards surround the Ruggles site as well as early roadways no longer in use. East from Ruggles's house, across the Ruggles Road and in a naturally heated gully, is the vaulted garden area. Remnant dry-laid stone walls mark the place as well as old stands of fruit trees. On the Ruggles Road, south of the mansion house but viewable from the main elevation, is the site of two residences: a mid-nineteenth-century home and a late eighteenth-century to early nineteenth-century rudimentary hut designated a laborers' or slaves' quarters.

It is this site, situated near the fields and adjacent the road, with its indications of enslaved occupants, that is the most intriguing. A clear differentiation in socioeconomic status can be seen between the hut and the later nineteenth-century residence next door as well as the mansion house up the road. At the cabin there is little material culture and structural evidence. The home was small and simple and separate from the main house; however, given removal of trees, it was in clear view. Excavation revealed a standard of living considerably lower than others on the land grant. The shelter that was constructed of wood with a clapboard finish contained a small stone hearth and perhaps a small window.

On North Mountain, under Timothy Ruggles, the Anglo-American influence affected the built environment, and this influence was consistent with the artifacts collected. Could the slave-holding Anglo-American/Loyalist framework active on North Mountain mask a culturally defined black Loyalist presence? Was such a living quarter typical for the enslaved in Loyalist Nova Scotia? As of this publication, fieldwork is ongoing.[27]

Excavating in the laborer's hut area on the Ruggles Road, North Mountain, Annapolis County, Nova Scotia. Courtesy of the author

LANDSCAPE RESEARCH STREAM

The cultural geography or landscape stream emphasized the study of two eighteenth-century plantation landscapes: Timothy Ruggles's estate in Hardwick and his farmstead on North Mountain. Both were examined and recorded in detail for similarities and differences, historical features, arrangement, modification, and use.

The landscape stream connects the historical and archaeological information with the geographical places shaped by Ruggles and those who lived on his plantations. The landscape framework is an opportunity to explore why Ruggles did as he did in the places where he lived and links Ruggles's culture—Anglo-American Loyalist elite—to his physical spaces. I argue that these two homesteads can be understood as symbolic places. His plantations represented his values as a gentleman and a well-informed leader with status, wealth, education, and British favor. Ruggles held his core values so firmly that even when faced with forced migration, war, and personal loss, he desired to represent them again in a very tangible way on his Nova Scotia land grant. It was possible to "trace relations in power" (as in the master-slave or planter-laborer relationship) and the "conditions of labour" (as evidenced by the remains of the hut) in Ruggles's landscapes.[28] After all the landscapes themselves are the largest historical artifact. "This suggests that landscapes are products of human values, meanings and symbols, and of the, usually, dominant culture within society; they are cultural products."[29]

The argument for Loyalist continuity mainly stems from the landscape portion of the research. Ruggles spent a decade stamping on North Mountain the New England landscape he dominated in Hardwick. Essentially he continued a formula in Nova Scotia that had been very successful in Massachusetts, one that resulted in a highly regarded, productive, and developing plantation supported, most essentially, by laborers of all modes from house servants to field-workers. The result of his efforts in Nova Scotia, after a decade on North Mountain, was regarded as "very fine and commanding a most extensive prospect with excellent soil."[30]

Information gleaned from documentary sources and field observations illustrated Ruggles's efforts as he turned land to landscape. The list of similarities between the two plantations in Hardwick and North Mountain was evidence of a continued approach to development and management of a plantation.[31] Layered in this argument were questions about Ruggles's ideology, his relationship to power and wealth, and what he considered to be the natural order of things. His landscapes were cultural products that were meaningful to him and symbolized his ideas, his values regarding improvement and prosperity, and a hierarchal framework rooted in the Enlightenment agenda. Also contributing to these cultural products was Ruggles's Loyalism. Being a Loyalist was an integral part of his identity. He was a true Anglo-American and was in favor of a solution that would see Britain and America as collaborators for the improvement and stability of America rather than adversaries.[32] In essence at both estates Ruggles worked to develop country seats, with an impressive house and productive agricultural enterprises, ensuring a domestic landmark visible for miles, constantly improving, and dominated by his presence and context. His view of himself as American gentry, with the full benefit of a tried and trusted British framework that he imprinted on the land, precluded a vision of himself as an American revolutionary.

With the evidence and artifacts accumulated, interplay between the three streams demonstrates that the story of the enslaved and their place in Nova Scotia's eighteenth-century historical narrative can been deepened and enriched.[33] It has been learned that a legacy of slave holding migrated north with the Loyalist refugees. Ruggles was comfortable with the system of forced labor prevalent in the day and supported by a contemporary ideology of natural hierarchy among men and under God. Massachusetts records indicated a history of slave holding in the Ruggles family. Ruggles's Loyalist memorial documents note servants in Hardwick.[34] When forced to Nova Scotia to start over, he brought with him the resources he felt he needed. Within a decade Ruggles and his servants and slaves had contributed to the transformation of the North Mountain land grant into a recognizable and admired plantation. Ideologically, materially, and spatially, American plantation slavery imported seamlessly into eighteenth-century Nova Scotia.

The Ruggles narrative confirms that in Loyalist-era Nova Scotia there was an active slave-holding policy carried out and maintained by the Loyalist colonial elite. Established in other mainland British colonies through parliamentary rule, this slave-holding policy arrived en masse to Nova Scotia, with the Loyalists ushering in Nova Scotia's age of slavery. Forced labor was used to settle, rebuild, and prosper on a scale previously not experienced in the province. Slavery was supported by the government, and the institution retained its place among the thousands of newly arrived British subjects as they started over.

Influenced by an inability to maximize economies of scale, however, slavery among the Loyalists in Nova Scotia differed from the American colonies. There were fewer enslaved people in the province, and many parts of the colony were undeveloped and unsettled. The Loyalists did not land in a place where well-established industries thrived, urban centers bustled, or vast plantations produced harvests over lengthy growing seasons requiring substantial labor forces. For the Loyalists, black and white, the primary activity was basic pioneering. Daily life consisted of clearing land, building shelters, and planting crops. Records for colonial America note that enslaved workers labored side by side with the slave owner during the initial pioneering phase of settlement. Similar activity likely occurred on North Mountain. Nothing in the record supports the notion that, because of Anglo-American origins, Nova Scotia's late eighteenth-century slave system was more benevolent than other slave systems.[35] It may have been a less structured form of slavery than other post-Revolutionary systems because tasks were shared out of necessity as a plantation landscape was carved out of the forest.

The landscape review supports a theme of continuity in cultural geography across time and space, but what is the deeper meaning behind the concerted effort by Ruggles to maintain continuity and develop his spaces as symbols of who he was, what he represented, and what he believed? Ruggles saw himself as part of the long-established colonial gentry stemming from his family prominence in Massachusetts since the early seventeenth century. As he worked to establish plantations on the highest point of land, he was signaling the power and status of the ruling class and communicating messages that separated him from the dispersed, small landholding, working majority around him, as well as his workers and slaves. Ruggles's colonial encounter with the land was to continue a Loyalist framework as manifested in the shaping of his country estates. His plantation landscapes represented his ideology in action.

In Nova Scotia the focus for Ruggles was on starting over and creating the plantation. There was no ideological revolution, no assault on the patriarchal structure, and no challenge to the king's rule. He was content to work with the land and refrain from public and military life. Such uncontested order would maintain his place under God but above what he governed: the land, the family who joined him, and his servants, hired hands, and slaves.

Finally Ruggles's plantations shed light on the Loyalist period as Nova Scotia's age of slavery. Never before had Nova Scotia experienced this scale of African American migration. The archaeological and landscape records provide insights concerning how that took shape on the ground, specifically the planter-laborer dynamic, the mansion house on the hill, and the workers' cabin near the fields but in view. Thousands of slave owners were receiving free grants of land to start over, and many used enslaved labor to do the physical work. Many like Ruggles sought a re-creation of their lost colonial ideals by remaking the land of Nova Scotia in the image of American slavery.

As the data from the three research areas coalesced, a map began to develop over the historic Wilmot township. Across the individual land grants on North Mountain, Ruggles, his family members, and close associates linked to enslaved individuals appeared nearby. Additionally eight more neighbors of Ruggles, comparable to him in many ways and most likely engaged in slavery in Nova Scotia or colonial America, were pinpointed not far away. Lastly, moving into the larger Wilmot township, five more grants held by peers of Ruggles with shared backgrounds and practices and likely connected to slavery are identifiable.[36]

As the data streams came together, clues to a wider and deeper landscape of slavery in the Loyalist period became evident. The enslaved were not sporadically placed and therefore largely invisible on Nova Scotia's historic landscape, as has been the standard narrative.[37] There was a stronger presence. The next step was to test this concept in another part of the province. A new Loyalist family and their settlement on Nova Scotia's Avon River presented an ideal framework.

Capt. John Grant of New York and Summerville

Capt. John Robert Grant, unlike Ruggles, was not born to a prominent American family with a lengthy history in the New England colonies.[38] He was born in Scotland in 1729 and at a young age began his military career as part of the Forty-Second Highlanders, also known as the "Black Watch." By 1743 Grant was a lieutenant and gaining experience in battle. The Seven Years' War found him on the American frontier against the French at Ticonderoga and under the command of Gen. James Abercrombie.[39] Grant advanced to the rank of captain, and by 1759 he was recorded as serving with his regiment in Quebec under General Wolfe.[40] In that same year he left his regiment to court his future wife, Sarah Bergen of the Bergens of Brooklyn, Long Island. Their home was a farm of 150 acres on the south side of Jamaica in Queens County, Long Island. Grant soon resumed his military career and by 1762, as captain in the New York Regiment of Foot, had seen battle on the Mohawk River. It is in this period that he sustained injuries that plagued him from this period onward.[41]

Headstone for Captain Grant's eldest son,
Michael Bergen Grant, dated 1817. Courtesy of the author

As the Revolutionary period approached, Grant received increasing pressure from his in-laws to join the Whigs. His Loyalism was steadfast. Eventually harassment and exile dictated the uprooting of his family. Like Ruggles his farmhouse was wrecked and property confiscated.

The Revolutionary period was filled with turmoil and illness for Grant. His family experienced substantial losses estimated by Grant at five thousand pounds.[42] They remained in Jamaica, Long Island, with the British until the evacuation of New York by the king's troops.[43] In October 1783 his family left without him on the transport *Stafford* and arrived in Halifax, Nova Scotia, ten days later. Grant had accepted a land grant of three thousand acres in the township of Newport (now the community of Summerville). Situated along the Avon River, the property was mostly forested.[44] The journey was difficult, with Captain Grant seriously ill and unable to make it to the Newport township property, to be known as Loyal Hill, until May 1784. Together the Loyal Hill group consisted of Grant; his wife, Sarah; and six of their seven children. Nine slaves are noted, but only eight names listed: Sam (thirty-two), Nance (twenty-eight), Pompy (twenty-two), Fillis (thirteen), Tom (eleven), Maso (nine), Harry (seven), and Betsy (two).[45] Family history notes that a separate house was constructed for the "servants" when enough land had been cleared. When they died they were buried on the western slope within the Grant private burial ground.

The search of the documentary record thus far provides clues about how the landscape took shape once the Grants settled in. Preliminary archaeological field-work has confirmed the location of the initial family home and son Michael's more substantial house higher up on the slope. Another smaller dwelling foundation closer to the river may be the slave house.

The historic family cemetery still exists southeast of the main farmhouse. Though in fragile condition, a few headstones remain, including that of son Michael, who died suddenly in 1817.[46] A more detailed examination of the cemetery will delineate its size and capture remnant markers such as those of the enslaved on the western edge noted by descendants.[47]

Already similarities and differences between the Grant and Ruggles plantations are evident. Both had significant farms in America and both were granted sizable tracts of land in Nova Scotia. It was important to Ruggles and to Grant to have the principal houses constructed overlooking the most prominent vistas, and enslaved labor was integral to the development of those statements. Country seats visible for a considerable distance were necessary to both.

The migration to Nova Scotia was more of a struggle for Grant. Though he arrived with a larger complement of help and was granted a larger parcel directly adjacent an active waterway, illness left him unable to participate on the level that Ruggles did. Ruggles had exceptional health for his age and the benefit of hands-on agricultural expertise particularly when it came to orcharding, bees, and horses. Grant's abilities are unknown, and he was largely unable to engage. Regarding the enslaved, by accounts reviewed thus far, a separate dwelling was constructed. Was the quarter for all or for field-workers only? What was the division of labor and the standard of living under the Grants as compared to Ruggles?[48]

To conclude, the documentary and field investigation of the Grants is in its early stages. Already similarities between Ruggles and Grant and their plantations have emerged. A key difference, Loyal Hill's location directly adjacent the majestic Avon River, will generate new insights regarding movement, transportation, development of industry, and ultimately the daily life of the slaves working to make the enterprise a success for the Grants.

Loyalist planters, like the two prominent slaveholders presented here, could easily be found across Nova Scotia. It is the enslaved individuals who were essential to their continuity, however, that need concentrated effort to rediscover. Their stories in the history of Maritime Canada are just beginning to be told. Assuredly, as Loyal Hill is uncovered and what lies below is examined, the theme of Loyalist continuity—that Loyalist framework stamped across the province—will be confirmed and accentuated through the historical reality of Nova Scotia's slavery landscape.

PART II

Moderation

SALLY E. HADDEN

Lawyering for Loyalists in the Post–Revolutionary War Period

In the wake of the American Revolution, recovering property that had been lost, confiscated, or wrongfully withheld became nearly a full-time job for some lawyers.[1] Loyalists, scattered around the Atlantic littoral, took advantage of peace to begin the process of reclaiming what had been theirs before the Revolution began. Their efforts gave attorneys such as Harrison Gray Otis and Christopher Gore, of Massachusetts, a new type of client: one who typically lived overseas, either in London, Halifax, or the Caribbean—a client a lawyer might never lay eyes upon. Otis and Gore, like a few other lawyers living in larger cities of the new nation, became adept at working with displaced Loyalists located in many parts of the Atlantic, assisting them in efforts to retrieve their shattered fortunes. In some cases lawyers such as these were successful for their clients, but in other instances no amount of legal maneuvering could restore what had been lost. Whether winning or losing, however, attorneys such as Otis and Gore could still claim their fees for work done—making the legal profession a peculiar beneficiary of the Revolutionary War's asset-reclamation project that so many Loyalists undertook.

Reclaiming lost Loyalist property, through one means or another, was familiar labor for lawyers working in this period. It represented only a slight modification of the routine toil most attorneys of the eighteenth century engaged in, for they often spent more than half their time collecting debts on behalf of clients, in or out of court. Recovering lost debts, land, horses, slaves, and even ships was such a part of everyday life for eighteenth-century lawyers that most kept stock letters and preprinted documents on hand for just such purposes, ready for the moment when a client came calling. The wheels of justice turned slowly, and lawyers tried to counsel clients to adopt a patience that many found hard to accept. Harrison Gray Otis, working on behalf of one London client in the 1780s, reminded him how difficult collection was, a result of the appeals process in lawsuits and the lack of hard money. "You know," he reminded his client, Loyalist Robert Hallowell, that "in our country" all collections were a "very slow and gradual process."[2] Patience was sometimes in short supply, and tempers could fray easily at what seemed like endless appeals; even as clients chafed at delays, lawyers were accustomed to the slow but steady rhythm of lawsuits. This lawyerly patience also arose from the irregular pattern that prevailed in getting clients, whose presence (or absence) fluctuated with weather, planting and harvesting seasons, and even whether a lawyer had an office across from the courthouse door.

Loyalist clients, however, generally did not come calling at a lawyer's door, as others did. Quite a few appear to have been known to their attorneys only via correspondence. Lawyers who did not have the opportunity to meet with their clients face to face typically generated more correspondence, for they had to request documents, ask questions, propose legal strategies, and explain court proceedings to people distant from both office and courthouse. That they did so created a treasure trove for historians to mine: these bundles of correspondence document how lawyers and Loyalists worked together to reclaim property that the Revolution parted from its owners.

Why would a lawyer work for a client at a distance, and worse, a Loyalist client whose politics might well run counter to prevailing political sentiments in a town such as Boston? After all, in the pre-Revolutionary period, being known as a "friend of government" routinely led, for lawyers, to a loss of clients among the increasingly Patriotic communities that made up early America. Thomas Hutchinson, Massachusetts governor in 1770, said as much when writing to his English superiors about Samuel Fitch, the Crown attorney responsible for prosecuting violations in the court of admiralty. According to Hutchinson, Fitch claimed that "his fees Since his appointment have not equaled what he has lost by his clients leaving him because he belongs to the admiralty & if nothing is allowed as salary he will give it up." Hutchinson grumbled, "You know how much we stand in need of good Crown Lawyers."[3] In the postwar period, such animosities toward pro-British individuals must have lingered, so one might wonder what overcame the potential negative associations of working on behalf of avowed British supporters.

Two reasons persuaded lawyers to agree to handle the work of Loyalist clients. First, there might have been preexisting ties that bound lawyer and client together, as was the case with Boston lawyer Otis and his Loyalist grandfather, whose story unfolds below. Family ties need not be the only ones, however; businesses that needed American debt collectors operated before and after the Revolution, and some retained the same counselors at law after the war as those they used before it commenced. Second, not a few attorneys worked purely for profit and expected to be paid handsomely. Lawyers, then as now, rarely worked for free. Every debt recovered came with the equivalent of a finder's fee, a commission paid to the attorney for the time and labor, paper and ink that had gone into the court proceedings necessary to win legal rights to the debt and then hound and harass the debtor until the full sum was paid. In the wake of the Revolution, a few lawyers seemed to attract Loyalist clients whose land and property remained beyond their grasp—either because a debtor refused to pay or because the state had (in the midst of the Revolution) taken steps to confiscate the property.

Otis was a young attorney, newly minted and recently entered into practice in Boston, when family ties brought him work to do on behalf of absent relatives. He was educated at Harvard and intended to study law with his uncle, but James Otis's gradual decline into illness prevented him from doing so. A family friend, John Lowell, took young Otis into his office to complete his training. Lowell, a politically savvy man, trimmed his way through the tumultuous 1770s by cultivating friendships on both sides, Tory and Patriot. Moreover he recognized that the departure of numerous Boston lawyers with the British fleet in 1776 represented a major business opportunity: Lowell relocated his law offices from Newburyport to Boston in March of that year. He became the most popular criminal lawyer in the state and amassed a huge client roster during the war's early years. He was also, according to his biographer, a favorite of many Loyalists, including Isaac Royall and William Vassall.[4] Toward the end of the war, Lowell began to divest himself of his courtroom duties so he could spend more time on politics. He passed his clients on to men he had trained, such as Rufus Amory, Christopher Gore, and Otis. Getting clients in the immediate aftermath of the Revolution was not easy; the financial climate was uncertain, and by 1786, when Otis was admitted to the Massachusetts bar, the state was politically unsettled due to Shays's Rebellion.[5] With his father bankrupt and his mother's relatives fled to England as Loyalists, Otis had even been compelled to take out a loan to purchase his own law books and open his first law office.[6] Making one's way as an untried attorney was hard work, and Otis was undoubtedly grateful for the clients his former teacher Lowell directed to him.

In addition to Lowell's patronage, Otis benefited as a young lawyer from an extensive kin network who came to his rescue, steering legal business his way so that he could attain financial solvency as soon as possible. Giving a young lawyer new yet routine business matters to handle was commonplace for eighteenth-century families: older relations expected young lawyers not only to draw up their wills, but also to oversee estate administration after their deaths, providing a steady flow of funds into a lawyer's office that could prop up a new practice with an infusion of cash. Otis's family tree was divided between Patriot and Loyalist: his paternal grandfather, Patriot to the core, had accepted continental money at face value during the Revolution when it had depreciated significantly, sometimes more than 80 percent. His actions contributed to the bankruptcy of his son, Otis's father. Meanwhile Otis's maternal grandfather, Harrison Gray (his namesake), fled Boston as part of the Loyalist refugee movement, eventually retiring to London with a number of Otis's other relatives. Gray lost three houses in Boston and much land scattered in many townships, which he hoped his grandson could recover.[7] Over the next twenty years, Gray maintained a correspondence with his lawyer grandson, who in the postwar years built up a healthy practice attempting to retrieve the broken and scattered fortunes of dispersed Loyalists such as his grandfather.[8]

Gray could only wait and learn from afar what happened to his estate as the Patriots took charge. In May 1775 his estate was confiscated by the Massachusetts Patriot government, and all personal belongings he had left behind were taken for sale. His daughter Elizabeth (Otis's mother) wrote mournfully, "Wish you had carried more of your Effects with you, hope and pray you may be well provided for."[9] Her prescience on this point was well taken. Gray's grandson, Otis, was charged with trying to recover whatever he could of his grandfather's lost property, a difficult challenge given Gray's decision to flee Massachusetts as a Loyalist. Otis's interest might be considered self-serving in that his mother stood to benefit from any monies he could recover on his grandfather's behalf. But given how expensive life in London was proving to be, it seems unlikely that much would be left behind for Elizabeth Otis to inherit should she outlive her father.

Otis's Patriot credentials allowed him to stay in contact with exiles in England while working in Boston. His father's family, the Otises, were deeply engaged in the Patriot cause, through his Aunt Mercy's writings, his Uncle James's fiery oratory, and his Uncle Joseph's military activities as general. Otis himself served for two years in an artillery regiment for Massachusetts before studying law full-time. His family connections to both sides of the conflict positioned him well to serve both Patriots and Loyalists as legal business resumed with full force in the postwar period.[10] His usual method of recovering debts for Loyalists was to have their debts signed over to him, making Otis the creditor, so that the jury could not be swayed to dismiss the suit on the ground that the creditor was a Loyalist in exile whose debt should not be paid.[11] Otis's Patriotic service and Otis kin made this legal strategy highly effective.

In the case of his grandfather's debts, however, even this method might not prove to be enough. His grandfather Gray had served as a mandamus councillor for the British after the revocation of the Massachusetts charter in 1774. Before May 1774 councillors (who sat as the upper house of the colonial legislature) were nominated by the lower house and confirmed by the governor; once the charter was revoked, all councillors were chosen exclusively by the governor, Gen. Thomas Gage, under the new Coercive Acts. This method of selection insured the councillors' absolute loyalty to the Crown and likewise made them immediately suspect in the eyes of Patriots. Public pressure caused more than half the mandamus councillors to resign, but those who held onto their appointments—such as Gray—invariably fled when the war began or the British evacuated. The taint of serving as British placemen in 1774–75 was simply too strong. Further, every mandamus councillor who had not resigned became a target for wartime property confiscation and worse. Gray was banished by law in October 1778, and in April 1779, of all Massachusetts men named in the Massachusetts act of confiscation, he was listed fourth as a "notorious conspirator"—a signal distinction indicating that his stance on the Revolution was particularly odious.[12] Although other confiscated property was returned to a few Loyalists following the peace treaty that ended the Revolution, the twenty-nine men named as notorious conspirators in the 1779 law were deliberately exempted; their property remained beyond the peace treaty and was not to be returned—a singular distinction, suggestive of the level of hatred directed at them even after the war's conclusion because of the ways in which their prewar actions as "friends of government" had alienated many Patriots.[13]

Otis's connection to such a well-known Tory would work against him in this instance, in the eyes of jurymen who had so much influence upon debt recovery. When Gray wrote to his grandson, asking why he was not making more headway in recovering the confiscated property, Otis responded a little tartly: "You seem to intimate that all laws in force against the refugees must be repeald [*sic*], and the Priviledge of citizens allowed them." Gray must be aware that he was not just any refugee. "With regard to those who in this State are distinguished in the Conspirator Act [as Gray was], I must confess I do not think they will ever be enabled to retrieve their property here, as the confiscation of it is considered as perfect and completed before the peace."[14]

Despite Otis's method of posing as the creditor in lawsuits, American juries disliked paying Tory creditors and preferred to shield Patriot debtors out of spite. As a result many debt collectors, like Otis, worked outside of the legal system through informal means of persuasion. Their reasons for doing so are not hard to understand: powerful individuals, such as John Hancock, could use their influence to sway juries against Loyalist creditors and likewise could make life difficult in other ways for creditors who pressed too hard attempting to recover a debt. To a young man such as Otis, individuals such as Hancock appeared to have all the advantages.

For more than four years, Otis attempted to collect nearly one thousand pounds that Hancock owed his grandfather without going to court, where he was certain he would lose against an eminent man such as Hancock. The debt was one justly owed: Otis's grandfather, when treasurer of the colony, had paid Hancock an advance on his salary at the time when the legislature of Massachusetts had no money in its treasury—taxes having gone unpaid for nearly two years at the time Gray gave Hancock the money out of his own pocket, expecting the legislature (eventually) to repay him. When Gray fled the colony at the war's outset, the debt remained unpaid. His grandson spent four years writing endless letters, sitting in Hancock's anteroom, setting up appointments that might then be delayed, and never had any satisfaction. He never pressed Hancock too hard, for as Otis wrote to his grandfather, "it is the part of prudence in a young man to refrain from provoking aversion," and he was of the opinion that while Hancock would never pay the debt if pressed to do so in court, he might be willing to do so privately, as if it were a favor he conferred.[15] Otis urged his grandfather to assign the Hancock debt to him—one of the few Gray did not assign—so that Otis could use sentiment against Hancock in recovering the debt. Otis wrote his grandfather about the strategy he intended to employ: he would present himself as a relatively impoverished young man whose poor current fortunes were due to the fact that he did not have the rich prospects in life he had once had when his family was wealthier—and Hancock could redress this fact.[16] Playing on Hancock's sympathies in this fashion was a weapon that his grandfather would not permit, however. Gray was unwilling to engage in this legal subterfuge with Hancock, perhaps because of the Patriot's eminence and wealth—the debt was justly owed, and he may have considered that Hancock's delaying tactics verged on dishonorable for a man of his social standing. That young Otis was doing all he could on his grandfather's behalf was not lost on the elderly gentleman, though he was an ocean away: in 1792 he wrote his grandson that, through third parties, he had heard much about the efforts made to get Hancock to pay up, and "no one could exert himself to serve me in this respect more than you have done, for which you have my thanks."[17]

In the end Hancock successfully evaded Otis's pleas about repayment until his death in 1793. Only after his death, and the subsequent planned remarriage of his widow to a ship captain, was Otis able to recover part of the debt. Otis knew that going to law against the widow of a leading Patriot was unlikely to win any jury sympathies, so he resorted to subterfuge. He discovered that Widow Hancock's intended second husband, a Captain Scott, planned to settle his bride in England. Otis let a rumor circulate that he would prosecute the debt in England, where Patriot sentiment could have no sway over a local jury (indeed quite the opposite effect was likely—Otis might collect the debt in full plus interest). The newly married couple presented themselves to Otis in 1795 and repaid a portion of the money still owed.[18] This final triumph of debt collection could not bring joy to Otis's grandfather, for he had died in 1794, one year after his adversary, Hancock.[19] Otis reported the arrival of funds to his father: of the nearly one thousand pounds originally owed by Hancock, now worth twelve hundred pounds with interest, Otis had recovered approximately six hundred.

Success with one Loyalist client could bring others to a young lawyer's doorstep. Having begun to make some headway in clearing up his grandfather's debts brought Otis to the attention of Susannah Boutineau, widow of another mandamus councillor and banished Tory, James Boutineau. The Boutineaus fled to England when the British left Boston in 1776. Otis's work on behalf of Susannah Boutineau in turn brought him another Loyalist client, former mandamus councillor Robert Hallowell.[20] Boutineau and Hallowell certainly knew Otis's grandfather and were probably given his recommendation to try their luck recouping debts in America using his Patriot grandson. Another Tory relation, Elizabeth Brown, also contacted Otis about recovering her confiscated property.[21] These and other individuals provided Otis with a steady stream of Loyalist customers who put money in his pocket at a time in his career when he needed clients. They had little left to lose and the possibility of recovering some or all of their wealth. Young Otis, a former soldier of the Continental Army, might successfully play upon his own reputation and persuade a Boston jury to look beyond the acts of banishment or confiscation. Clients may have also been drawn to him because his efforts yielded real dividends. He reported to his father in 1795 that he "had sav'd more from the ruins of [his] Grandfather's fortune than all the agents of all the proscribed Absentees together, excepting the instance of Mrs. Boutineau, for whom I likewise acted."[22]

Otis worked to recover assets in New Hampshire and Vermont as well as Massachusetts on behalf of his overseas clients. Legal restrictions were not the same everywhere, and lawyer Otis bent his efforts toward getting property returned no matter where it was. He had little success recovering Vermont real estate belonging to his grandfather, however: the man who had sold the Vermont land to his grandfather had sold it a second time, taken the money, and spent it, while the second purchaser had registered his deed, which Gray never did—in the end the land in Vermont could not be regained. Meanwhile the state of New Hampshire passed no general confiscation act, which meant his grandfather's prospects for legal success seemed greater. Leaders of Peterborough, where his grandfather's land lay, had violated state law to sell it at an improperly convened auction, failing to stipulate the precise time of the auction in notices they distributed, and selling the property at bargain basement prices. Such underhanded dealings offered a glimmer of hope for the property's recovery. Gray gave his deed to the New Hampshire property to his grandson and urged him to make the best of the matter, for Gray seemed to think the land could never be reclaimed once the state had sold it. Despite Otis's best efforts, his grandfather was right.[23]

Fortunately for Gray, while property sold via confiscation was more often than not lost completely, private indebtedness still remained subject to court proceedings, and Otis worked in the courts assiduously on behalf of his older relation. Still attempting to collect his grandfather's debts in the late 1780s, he warned that private debts, though being repaid slowly, might be cut off completely if the state passed a sequestration act—effectively embargoing the repayment of debts to absent Tories, even if they had signed over those debts to local residents such as Otis. In February 1789 Otis pessimistically informed Gray that "affairs in this country are gradually returning to good order" but that if a sequestration act went from possibility to reality, "the whole will be irretrievably sunk," and his private debts might disappear as completely as his confiscated property.[24] This type of act was threatened again and again in the Massachusetts assembly and, as relations with England deteriorated in the early 1790s, became ever more likely, but never came to pass.

In many respects the legal career of Christopher Gore paralleled that of Otis. Both men studied at Harvard, completed their legal training with John Lowell, and advanced their fledgling legal careers by assisting Loyalists recovering their property. Eventually the two men managed to rise to posts of significant political responsibility in the 1790s through opportunism and good fortune. As shall become clearer below, Gore's financial juggling relied upon money collected on behalf of his English clients, which gave him enough ready cash to purchase state and national government bonds when they reached their nadir, before they were repaid at full value. This permitted him to rise financially to supreme heights within Boston society—and subsequently flourish in a series of positions both within Massachusetts and in the new national government. Gore, like Otis, was one of the attorneys who made a new kind of legal career from the wreckage left in the wake of the American Revolution.

Like Otis's, Gore's upbringing positioned him to serve both Loyalists and Patriots in the years after the Revolution concluded. His father, John Gore, chose the king's side, departing with the English fleet on March 17, 1776, when they evacuated Boston. The senior Gore had been a merchant and painter, whose principal line of work—concocting coats of arms and painting them on carriages—drew him into close relationships with most of Boston's governing elite in the 1750s, '60s, and '70s.[25] Though he had celebrated with the Sons of Liberty on the anniversary of the stamp officers' resignation in 1769, John Gore was careful to trim his political sails to follow the prevailing winds.[26] In 1774 Gore was a loyal addressor to both Gov. Thomas Hutchinson and Gen. Thomas Gage, indicating his affiliation with the royalist cause as the war drew nearer, or perhaps he just favored law and order as they did; his connections to the leading figures in Boston gained him a commission in the elite Ancient and Honourable Artillery Company of Massachusetts.[27] He helped police the city of Boston while it was under British control in 1775, before taking ship with other departing Loyalists.[28] These actions undoubtedly were the primary reasons why Gore was threatened with arrest and deportation if he returned to Boston.[29] Later his property was confiscated by the state, and an allowance was paid from its proceeds to the family who remained behind.[30] While in London, Gore filed a memorial with the Loyalist claims commission, listing property and notes of hand that he considered debts forfeited on behalf of his loyalty to the Crown.[31]

Although Gore fled to England, the Gore family was divided in its loyalties. Christopher Gore's mother and siblings remained in Massachusetts, where his brother Samuel was reputedly a "Mohawk" in the Tea Party of 1773 and an active Son of Liberty.[32] Following Christopher's graduation from Harvard College in 1776, he briefly joined an artillery regiment, serving as its clerk until 1778. The activities did not consume all his time; following graduation he also began to study law with John Lowell, the same Boston practitioner who helped Otis commence his legal career.[33]

With the departure of so many Loyalist lawyers and judges, Gore was admitted to the Suffolk County bar in July 1778 after only two years of study rather than the usual three, allowing him to practice law while the Revolution was under way. He needed to, for during his father's absence he was the primary breadwinner for his mother and three unmarried sisters.[34] One of his first actions was to petition the state legislature for the release of funds related to their father's confiscated property; John Gore's property had been administered as if he were dead, placing it under the care of the judge of probate. The younger Gores needed the funds still in the hands of the probate judge—in Christopher's case he began to receive rent from a building his father had owned, and this undoubtedly helped him settle various outstanding debts related to his legal training. The judge released funds to Christopher, his brother Samuel, and their sisters in 1779.[35]

When the war was over, John Gore returned to Boston, where he lived the remainder of his days; in 1787 he filed a petition with the state assembly asking for an "act of Naturalization" to regularize his status.[36] The petition was in all likelihood drawn up by his lawyer son. With Patriots such as James Bowdoin and Thomas Dawes vouching for him, Gore was officially pardoned by the Massachusetts legislature, and eventually he died in Boston in 1796.[37] No doubt the patriotic service and support of the other Gore family members helped overcome the stigma attached to his original departure with the English fleet. Naturalization was a legal process that many former Loyalists willingly submitted to in order to rejoin family or regain property. Otis wrote from Boston to his grandfather that any Loyalists still overseas could return "to this country" to be "naturalized without difficulty, and also . . . those whose estates were not absolutely confiscated may recover their debts." Only those men listed by name in confiscation acts, like his grandfather, could not hope to recover their property, Otis thought.[38]

The process of reclaiming a family's property and regularizing the status of a Loyalist was one that young Christopher Gore therefore understood well, having practiced in the case of his father and obtained a successful outcome. He probably already was well established doing this as early as 1784, using every means possible to regain lost goods on behalf of clients and attempting to restore to them legally what they had had before. Gore was not the only Boston-based lawyer to do so: his mentor John Lowell, Lowell's son (also named John), and esteemed attorney William Tudor likewise built up thriving practices working on behalf of overseas dispossessed Loyalists.[39] Known Loyalists hired a number of Patriot lawyers to retrieve their lost fortunes, such as James Bowdoin, Perez Morton, and Theodore Sedgwick.[40] The departure of many Loyalist lawyers gave younger men such as Gore and Otis a slight advantage in gaining a larger share of business than they might otherwise have had as novice practitioners.[41]

In the 1780s Gore used a leather account book to record all the financial transactions related to his overseas clients living in Nova Scotia, France, London, Edinburgh, and the Caribbean. He worked for numerous clients living at a distance but most frequently for commercial houses: Gore routinely appeared in court for London merchants Joy and Hopkins, Winthrop and Tod of South Carolina, Bredell and Ward of London, Hugh Mossman of Edinburgh, and Blanchard and Lewis, another large London trading company.[42] One of his longest-lasting attorney-client relationships was with Champion and Dickason, the trading firm based in

London. For the years in which Gore created composite account lists, noting his total profits from all transactions (as he did in 1785 and 1786), it becomes clear that his business was skyrocketing with assistance from overseas clients such as Alexander Champion and Thomas Dickason. In 1785 Gore received in cash more than £2,500 owed to his overseas clients; in 1786 the figure was closer to £4,500. This did not represent a net profit but rather cash flowing through his hands from debtors of clients from whom he collected after winning in court or finalizing a settlement; his percentage of those collected funds, plus his fees, was less but still significant. In 1785, from work on behalf of only two overseas clients, Gore earned more than £350. His income was effectively a function of how well he could do on his clients' behalf: if they won, he won. And overseas clients paid handsomely, if he could win for them. In 1785 alone, of the £2,571, 9 shillings, and 4 ½ pence that he collected on behalf of all his clients, revenues derived from his work for Champion and Dickason—suing their American-based debtors in a Boston court—netted nearly £2,000, or almost 80 percent of the total. Clearly Gore's ability to collect and remit funds to his clients gained him both their goodwill and their continued business in the years to come. As a newly married man, he wished to thrive for his family's sake (he married the daughter of one of the leading maritime insurance agents, Edward Payne, in 1785), and as circumstances would turn out, his legal work flourished with aplomb. At the start of the 1780s, Gore wrote his friend Daniel Newcomb (in the somewhat peculiar third person) that "C. G. has more business than he had reason to expect. He has maintained himself very comfortably, has argu'd several causes at the bar, and has been much flatter'd."[43] Nearly ten years later, in 1789, he wrote his Harvard classmate Rufus King that "my clients are generally of the class which is able to pay, and I think I can say, without vanity, that my conduct is not dissatisfactory to them."[44]

Gore charged his clients based on what he did on their behalf. Appearances in court started at forty shillings a suit and rapidly escalated, depending upon the complexity of the suit. In November 1785 he recorded his work arguing on behalf of numerous clients in several suits against opposing counsel Greenleaf, Parkman, Adams, Frazier and Geyer, charging forty shillings to debate four of the suits but six pounds for the suit against Greenleaf. He charged for horse hire, certificates, taking depositions, payments to the sheriff to summon witnesses, and writing up deeds—any effort that he made was charged to the client. When he collected payments from defeated opponents, he typically received bills of exchange, often drawn on London. For negotiating those he likewise charged a commission, which might range from 1.25 to 5 percent each time.[45]

Success as a lawyer led to high profits and a desire to invest the proceeds. Gore could have become a silent partner in insurance underwriting with the help of his father-in-law or bankrolled long-distance trading voyages to China, which was becoming more common among Bostonians with money in this period. Instead he chose the slightly more conservative route of purchasing property and the somewhat more speculative route of investing in government paper. Gore bought land and houses throughout Boston, Waltham, and other nearby towns, but he sought other opportunities as well. Like Abigail Adams he recognized that bonds had the potential of a great return, if the government honored them at face value.[46] In the "mid-eighties Christopher Gore bought [Massachusetts] government securities for $3,743 that carried a face value of $25,000" and that paid annual interest of close to $450. When the Massachusetts assembly determined to pay its bondholders at face value (during the contentious period leading up to Shays's rebellion), Gore realized a profit of nearly 800 percent on his investment.[47] He was encouraged to speculate further in government securities by his associate Andrew Craigie, who profited handsomely from his insider knowledge about state debt and the likelihood that the national government would eventually repay it in full.[48] In 1788 he and Craigie set a goal of capturing $100,000 in continental bonds and certificates, which they managed to do with about £7,000, which at 6 shillings to the dollar represented an investment of about $3,000. For some of the purchases, Gore paid only 4 or 5 shillings in the pound. Some of the money came from Gore's wife's marriage portion, which was upward of $5,000. Regardless of where he got the money from, when Alexander Hamilton proposed repayment of the national and state debts at par, in 1790, the value of Gore's investments again soared.[49] Small wonder that John Adams commented to his son, fledgling attorney John Quincy Adams, that "Mr Tudor, Gore, Dawes, and Some others are ingenious Men" when he pointed out the leaders of the Boston bar.[50] Adams was inferring their ingenuity was due to more than just their skill in the courtroom in this letter, for after some further comments, he admonished his son not to show the letter to anyone and to keep the contents to himself. A few days later, John Quincy replied with an equally secretive assessment that Gore's "family connections have . . . been extremely serviceable to him, and it is said that he has made an independent Fortune, by speculation in the public funds. I have heard it asserted that he is the richest lawyer in the Commonwealth." Young Adams described the somewhat questionable method that Gore, Tudor, and others had employed to advance themselves financially. "These gentlemen I am told have played at that hazardous game with monies deposited in their hands; and have been enabled by the temporary possession of property belonging to foreigners, to become masters of sums to an equal amount before they have been called upon for payment."[51] Gore's access to thousands of pounds, on behalf of his wife and overseas clients such as Champion and Dickason, as well as many others, permitted him to speculate in what could have become a dangerous game of using Peter's money to gamble with Paul.

By 1788 Gore had amassed enough wealth that he could enter public service, first in the state legislature and then, in 1789, as US district attorney for the Massachusetts District. That appointment was due in no small measure to his wealth and position at the bar, where he had acquired a reputation as a leading commercial lawyer.[52] That same year Gore purchased a three-story house on Bowdoin Square and hired servants to work there; the home was appraised for taxes at a value of twenty thousand dollars.[53] Not bad for a man who had entered legal practice barely a decade earlier. Gore was known for his dedication to his clients; one biographer noted that "it was his uniform practice, from the commencement of his professional labors to their close, and during the whole of his political life, either to sit up very late, or to rise very early in the morning, that he might fully prepare himself for the business of the following day. The company of friends, domestic society, and personal indulgence, were all sacrificed to duty."[54] In a little more than ten years after entering private practice, Gore could afford to leave private practice for government work, which almost assuredly meant taking a cut in salary; most men of this time regarded the post of attorney general as one that brought less remuneration than remaining in the private sector. His wealth spread like tendrils across city and region: his success as a lawyer and bond speculator allowed him to purchase more than twenty different parcels of land in Boston, with additional property in Rutland, Cambridge, and Waltham.[55] Seven years later Gore became a diplomat, helping to negotiate Jay's Treaty with England—accepting a post abroad that, again, paid him relatively little.[56] His skill as an attorney, for negotiation as well as confrontation, no doubt also gained him prestige, or as his anonymous eulogist phrased it, "his powers of eloquence, rendered him a favorite and successful member of the bar."[57]

Like Gore, Otis also rose to positions of political responsibility. He was elected to Congress as a Federalist in the late 1790s and was thereafter the United States district attorney for Massachusetts in 1796, following Gore's resignation from that post. In Massachusetts he served many years in the state house and senate, and eventually Otis returned to Washington in 1817 as a US senator. His many years of public service, at the state and national level, were heavily financed by his earlier legal work, which Otis parlayed into a small fortune through investments in Boston real estate, particularly Beacon Hill. Otis and his wife always had homes in the most stylish neighborhoods, and they lived in three successive homes designed by the eminent architect Charles Bulfinch.[58] In rather unlikely ways, the legal work Gore and Otis did on behalf of their overseas clients after the Revolutionary War later allowed these same lawyers to enjoy lives of affluence while undertaking relatively low-paying political work in the early Republic.

The lost fortunes of so many Loyalists are a standard trope in the Revolution's literature, a given fact that masks the postwar despair and reduced living standards of many Loyalist men and women accustomed to easier, better lives. Those living in poorer circumstances who had known happier, richer days could hardly be faulted for bitterness toward their American debtors, as well as the inadequate response of Parliament in handling Loyalist claims. Mandamus councillors such as Harrison Gray, who had sacrificed all on the altar of loyalty and devotion to the Crown, expected better treatment and seemed destined to disappointment. However, lawyers such as Harrison Gray Otis, Christopher Gore, John Lowell, William

Tudor, and others worked assiduously to retrieve some shattered Loyalist fortunes after the Revolution. This is the overlooked story: that some Loyalists managed to retrieve a portion of their lands, debts, and goods via the judicial process in America after the war and thus reclaim a measure of the losses Parliament did not repay. Those who did so often had the best documentation, the best connections, and not a little luck on their side (as with Otis and Widow Hancock).

That lawyers worked diligently to secure these Loyalist debts is without doubt: if they succeeded they stood to profit even more than the basic fees charged to clients. But their payment consisted of more than just money. What irony: Loyalist funds recovered via persuasion and lawsuit advanced the American political careers of opportunistic lawyers to posts of high government trust. Gore and Otis started their legal careers with relatively little, died rich, and in between enjoyed many political successes. Fees made by winning suits on behalf of Loyalists (and investing those Loyalist funds in US government bonds in Gore's case) helped to catapult these attorneys to wealth and positions such as US attorney, judge, senator, even governor. Although there were many financial losers among the Loyalists, the few winners who recouped their losses in American courts helped underwrite American political careers—a novel postwar twist to the Patriot and Loyalist story.

Gregory T. Knouff

"That Abundant Infamous Roach"

Breed and Ruth Batcheller, Moderate Loyalism, Language, and Domestic Power in Revolutionary New Hampshire

On March 19, 1784, Breed Batcheller, "late of Packersfield in the Province of New Hampshire now resident in Annapolis Royal in the Province of Nova Scotia," submitted his Loyalist claim to the British government. It contained all the hallmarks of postwar constructions of exiled Loyalist identity. Batcheller identified himself as a "loyal faithful subject to his Majesty and uniformly attached to the British Government." He recalled that "at the call of his Sovereign British Army commanded by General Burgoyne," he "recruited a Company of Loyal Americans, which he had the honor of commanding in several engagements against the Rebels, in one of which he was seriously wounded." After Gen. John Burgoyne's "unfortunate defeat" at Saratoga, Batcheller went to occupied New York for the rest of the war, where he was "always ready and willing to risk his life in support of His Majesty's Government." The Revolutionary New Hampshire government "confiscated and sold his estate," valued at £3,321, and he was "banished [from] his native Country."[1] His portrayal of himself as unambiguously loyal to Britain raises questions common in many Loyalist claims. Batcheller left his revolutionary community more than two years after the outbreak of the conflict. In this period, he shifted from being disaffected by the Revolution to taking up arms against it. His initial strategy to remain at home and do nothing would indicate he was an active supporter of the rebellion, while taking no overt actions against the revolutionaries. As someone who did not accept the legitimacy of the new government while living in a region under its authority, he was a "moderate Loyalist" who hoped to ride out the war without fighting on either side. His experience revealed that he was pushed out of Packersfield by his local enemies rather than heeding the "call of his sovereign." As he rued his banishment from his "native country," Batcheller exhibited another later development in Loyalist identity, the dual sense of being both American and a British subject banished from home.[2] Moreover his family never joined him in exile. His wife, Ruth, and their children remained in Packersfield. Ruth had already sought use of some of the family's confiscated lands from the Revolutionary New

Hampshire government and never indicated a desire to leave. When he "unfortunately drowned in the basin of Annapolis," Batcheller died alone without the Loyalist Claims Commission ever acting on his claim.[3]

Batcheller was an example of the many North Americans who were disaffected moderate Loyalists seeking some accommodation to the new regime, which initially allowed little middle ground.[4] In New Hampshire the rapid collapse of the formerly functional royal government led to a jarring redefinition of domestic authority that quickly marginalized dissenters.[5] Unlike most other revolutionary states, New Hampshire was mercifully spared significant combat operations on its soil. The British never invaded, and the only option for Loyalists willing to fight was to leave for British lines. As a result civil conflict largely focused on controlling dissenting speech.[6] This issue was a concern in all the revolutionary states, but in the absence of internal civil war, it was central in New Hampshire.[7] In particular the New Hampshire Loyalist experience was shaped by a long-standing metaphor of politics that reflected the fusion of household and public authority. It focused on questions of fidelity to the state, the nature of patriarchal power, and notions of duty in marriage. One image emphasized obedience to authority while suggesting that the leadership of the opposition comprised dangerous, self-aggrandizing seducers of the masses. This "seduction" usually took the form of dissenting political speech. Another metaphor suggested contractual notions of domestic authority inherent in mutually beneficial, if not egalitarian, marriages and families. This argument implied that those in an inferior power relation in the family, that is, children and wives, had natural rights. If these rights were violated, subordinated family members had a legitimate right to separate from that authority. This essay argues that Batcheller's being forced to resort to active Loyalism can be explained in this context by his refusal or inability to control his dissenting speech. Thus revolutionaries came to see him as an intolerably dangerous, seditious seducer of his neighbors. Others in the region who also utilized a strategy of moderate Loyalism managed to remain in their communities despite harassment by local revolutionary committees of safety that policed dissent. This was largely due to their ability to moderate their speech or recant it at the appropriate time. An examination of Batcheller's experience of the seditious seducer metaphor demonstrates the importance of language to perceptions of power. Furthermore it underscores the close links between household and gendered authority and politics in Revolutionary America. Once larger questions were raised about the absolute authority of husbands over their wives in political metaphors, marital power relations were destabilized and sometimes politicized. In this context Ruth Batcheller's decision not to join her husband is significant and shows her ability to do what her husband could not: remain in Packersfield and protect the family. Her success in retaining some familial lands during and after the Revolution can be attributed to her shrewder understanding of political speech and her ability to assert her duty to the state over that to her husband.[8]

Breed Batcheller (born 1740) and Ruth Davis (born 1746) were both from relatively prominent Massachusetts families.[9] Batcheller enlisted in imperial forces during the French and Indian War from 1756 through 1759. He later recounted "that in the last war with France, I had the honor of serving his majesty as a subaltern officer."[10] After the war he practiced surveying and made a sizeable land purchase in southwestern New Hampshire from the Masonian Proprietors in Monadnock Number Six. In 1766 he became the town's first permanent resident and married Ruth. They started a family, and Breed thrived as a landowner, speculator, merchant, innkeeper, and surveyor. In 1768 he completed a survey of the town for the proprietors and soon was appointed by the town to be the proprietor's clerk.[11] Batcheller was, however, controversial among some of his neighbors. When the town applied for incorporation in 1773 as Packersfield, accusations emerged against him that he failed in his duties as clerk and surveyor to meet the proprietors' terms and "deluded" the governor.[12] In the same period, Batcheller sued Oliver Wright for libel. Wright purportedly called him "a knave, a devilish rogue, and a cheating fellow," who kept "a false book" in his mercantile accounts.[13] This imagery would have important political implications because during the crisis over Parliament's right to tax the colonies, an important metaphor of domestic politics was the danger of verbal seduction. A representative New Hampshire essay from the Stamp Act period warned that "at a time when the torrent runs high, and the state is unsettled, self-designing men will push themselves forward at all adventures, hoping for nothing more than self-promotion, tho' at the ruin of the public."[14] Such rhetoric echoed the didactic elements of seduction novels of the period, which emphasized the destruction of virtuous women led astray by rakes. Another account cautioned that the "loquacious or talkative man" did not care about the public good but rather "his passion, when the least opportunity offers, must be gratified: A too fond CREDULITY furnishes him with matter, and a volubility of tongue with delivering his sentiments; By this the ears of others are inflam'd, and a report by him so nourish'd prevails. Thus the public is deluded."[15]

The controversy over incorporation of Packersfield and Batcheller's reputation occurred at the same time as royal government in the province was under siege. Royal governor John Wentworth, nephew of the previous governor, was the scion of the colony's most powerful family. The Wentworths, who were well-connected Portsmouth Anglican merchants, created a mighty network of political patronage within the colony and in Britain. Governor Wentworth was able to weather earlier storms, but the crisis over the Coercive Acts finally rendered the province ungovernable as popular resistance and support for the Continental Congress grew. After Wentworth dissolved the colonial assembly in June 1774, towns elected extralegal provincial congresses to sit at Exeter; these congresses became the de facto revolutionary government. On August 24, 1775, Wentworth fled the province.[16] By the beginning of 1775, Packersfield turned its attention to the directives of the Continental Congress and the New Hampshire Provincial Congress. In terms of his imperial politics, it appears that Batcheller was typical of the moderate Whigs who were critical of parliamentary policy before resistance turned to rebellion. At Batcheller's later trial in 1777, Dr. Nathaniel Breed testified that "before Lexington fight . . . Batchelor was in favour of the country."[17] Another witness explained Batcheller's initial caution in embracing the Continental Association, noting that "when the non-importation agreement" was discussed, "Batchelor objected to it. [He said it] should [be] considered longer."[18] However he remained active in the town's politics. On January 20, 1775, Batcheller was elected to a committee of correspondence.[19] He was able to do this without affirming the Continental Association because Packersfield lagged behind other New Hampshire towns in establishing a committee of safety for its enforcement, which they finally created on April 12, 1775.[20] When news of the Battles of Lexington and Concord reached the region days later, the local militia regiment in which Batcheller was a major mustered and prepared to march. Batcheller was cautious and skeptical. Rather than march immediately with his men from Packersfield, he stated that "he did not believe anything about" the news of "regulars coming out." So he went to Keene for confirmation. He arrived at Cambridge, where his men were, a few days afterward, and as the Packersfield Committee of Safety reported, "He carried no sort of weapon and refused to have anything to do with his company." They also stated that his explanation for his delay in joining the troops was suspicious and pointed to his reputation for deception. They explained, "He was asked why he did not come down before he answered and said he was at Keene a writing and sending posts over the country but we do not believe any such thing."[21] He may well have been seeking confirmation of the outbreak of war and corresponding with others in the region since he was on a committee of correspondence. But it was clear that Batcheller had decided in Cambridge to end his military service against the British army.

When Governor Wentworth and many of his Loyalist allies fled the province in August 1775, it was unclear what those who remained skeptical of the new authorities should do. Meshech Weare, president of the New Hampshire Provincial Congress, explained that New Hampshire was governed by the Provincial Congress "and the committees of the respective towns" and that "those that do not join with us are silent, and dare not openly attempt to obstruct our measures."[22] These revolutionary polities expected full obedience from their subjects. The few that did speak out were dealt with through committee hearings. William Start, for example, was arrested and taken to Exeter, "expecting some person to appear and charge him with some crime committed against somebody, he knows not who or what, but no one appeared." Start testified that "he neither said nor meant any thing by any means inimical to his country." He was nonetheless ordered to move fifteen miles from his family's home in Portsmouth in an effort to keep him away from his neighbors, whom he might influence.[23] Samuel Hale, a Portsmouth lawyer, was forced to leave his home in 1775 because his "moderate conduct rendered this memorialist uncommonly obnoxious, it subjected him to so many personal insults, and he was so much harassed by their committees, that his personal safety became extremely problematical."[24] The revolutionaries were making a clear statement that dissenters could be banned from their communities if they would not recant.

Batcheller wished to remain at home. He adopted a strategy of moderate Loyalism in this period, often citing his adherence to "Gage's Proclamation," which offered to pardon all those who took up arms against the regulars after Lexington and Concord if they would peaceably go and remain at home.[25] He intended to sit out the war quietly without recognizing the legitimacy of the new regime in hope of a swift British victory, but again his activities as a merchant attracted attention. In December 1775 the Packersfield Committee of Safety confronted him with the damning evidence that "he has made much disturbance in the country by buying a large quantity of East India tea and peddling it out through the country."[26] Batcheller not only refused to adhere to the Continental Association, but he was profiting from his resale of the tea. The Fitzwilliam Committee of Safety also complained that Batcheller had "a large quantity of India tea and [was] freely offering it for sale."[27] While his motives appeared more economic than ideological, the committees viewed it as Batcheller's seducing the people from their duty through the allures of his goods. The Packersfield committee "tried to have him sign a covenant with us but he refuses making a mere mock of such method saying that it was against the law and by asking if we did not know that Gage had proclaimed" against it. When the committee tried to bring him for a hearing, Batcheller denigrated its authority: "he refused to come saying that we were prejudiced persons and said that we shall not come in to his house but we might come to his door and talk and stand over with his hogs." Such public disrespect for the committee was a major threat to its power. Batcheller demanded that the committee not imprison him and said he would only be examined by "five men choosing them out several towns and we might choose two of them he would choose two of them and we might agree upon the chairman."[28] Of course the committee could not agree to this, because it undermined their authority. Batcheller indicated that local matters that had nothing to do with political allegiance might influence his treatment. One committee member, Eleazer Twitchell, was a petitioner against Batcheller in the incorporation complaint. Vexed as they were, the committee felt it did not yet have the authority to detain him.

The creation of an independent New Hampshire state government offered such authority to take action against people such as Batcheller. On January 5, 1776, New Hampshire created the first effective government independent of Britain in the rebellious colonies. The new constitution rendered the Fifth Provincial Congress into a House of Representatives. With no governor the state committee of safety would fulfill executive functions when the legislature was not in session.[29] This was a radical step toward independence that would require some persuasion and justification.

The most influential case for independence was made in Thomas Paine's *Common Sense*, published in January 1776. Paine made many arguments through analogies, including the pervasive parent-child metaphor. Another one alluded to matrimony and separation. In July 1775 he published an earlier essay, "Reflections on Unhappy Marriages." It criticized European traditions of marriage based either on initial passion or financial calculation. It extolled ideal Native American marriages based on "mutual affection" and spouses' knowledge that they have "liberty to separate."[30] While Paine attributed this freedom to Indian culture, colonists practiced what Clare A. Lyons has characterized as "self-divorce" in which one or the other aggrieved parties posted an advertisement in a paper announcing the "elopement" or desertion of marriage of the other.[31] In *Common Sense* Paine called for dissolving ties to Britain through marital analogy. He evoked the abandonment of the wedding vows: "Bring the doctrine of reconciliation to the touchstone of nature, and then tell me, whether you can hereafter love, honour, and faithfully serve the power that hath carried fire and sword into your land."[32] Most strikingly Paine characterized America as a wronged wife with a family that she should support on her own: "It matters very little now, what the King of England either says or does; he hath wickedly broken through every moral and human obligation. . . . It is now the interest of America to provide for herself. She hath already a large and young family, whom it is more her duty to take care of. . . . If ye wish to preserve your native country uncontaminated by European corruption, ye must in secret wish a separation."[33]

As Paine implied marriage as a political metaphor, he suggested a companionate ideal in which both spouses had rights. He ridiculed blind obedience to cruel patriarchal power and asserted that when governments violated natural rights, "tis time to part."[34] Such arguments spoke to the fusion of household and state power and could raise questions about wives' obligations, even under coverture.

In contrast the New Hampshire state government emphasized the need for all its subjects to obey its authority. They were not attacking patriarchal authority but reconstituting it in a new form. A public broadside announcing the creation of the new government in 1776 contained the warning that "when our enemies are watching all opportunities to ensnare and divide us, everyone would strive to prevent, and if possible, to quell all appearance of party spirit."[35] The state and town committees of safety now had official status in policing dissenters, and the first step was to identify them. In April 1776 the state of New Hampshire ordered one of the most aggressive association tests in Revolutionary America. It required adult men, "lunatics, idiots, and Negroes excepted," to swear to oppose the British "with arms." Local committees reported the names of all 773 men who refused the oath.[36] In the small town of Packersfield, only Batcheller refused, but in the larger neighboring town of Keene, 13 did not sign.[37] The oath put Batcheller in a difficult position. If he took it, he violated Gage's original proclamation. If he did not, the state and local committees could eventually restrict his freedoms. It made his strategy of moderate Loyalism increasingly tenuous if he wished to remain in his community while making no public commitment to the Revolution. The situation grew worse as the Northern Continental Army was retreating out of Canada and British general John Burgoyne launched his invasion of the Lake Champlain–Hudson River Corridor. The trope of the Tory or moderate Whig as artful deceiver of the masses began to appear in revolutionary essays published in the papers. For example on June 29, 1776, an essay by "a Watchman" declared that there is no "more ridiculous character than that of a *tory* or a *pretended* moderate man." The essayist urged readers to "emancipate yourselves from the delusions of such artful men."[38] Revolutionaries continued to evoke the images of seditious Tory seducers of the people over the entire war. Essays appearing in 1780 in the *New Hampshire Gazette* titled "New Hampshire Crisis" argued that leniency toward suspected Tories would threaten the state and warned: "Our open and avowed enemies who have been indulged to speak and act agreeable to their infernal principles, have cooled or brought over to the side of opposition, all those whose minds were not proof against the deceitful wiles of those unpardonable Traitors."[39] By 1781 the state revised its treason law to stipulate that any person who "shall seduce or persuade any inhabitant or inhabitants of this state, to renounce his or their allegiance to this state and government thereof . . . shall be adjudged guilty of high treason against this state and be put to death."[40]

In June 1777, while Burgoyne's army was operating close to New Hampshire, the state government passed an act to allow the state committee of safety to imprison anyone whom they "shall deem the safety of the commonwealth requires should be restrained of his personal liberty." Such prisoners were to be held "without bail" until released by state authority. The committees of safety had sweeping powers to arrest, examine, and detain suspicious persons for an indefinite period based on hearsay evidence.[41] Should a committee confine a prisoner to jail, they might suffer indefinite confinement. Jeremiah Clough wrote to his father in August 1777: "I can't find as there is any evidence against me unless some unguarded words that I should have spoke. . . . I am held here close confined without trial or bail which I can't live so no longer."[42] Batcheller, as evidenced by his 1775 interaction with the Packersfield committee, particularly feared imprisonment. In part his defiant demeanor was probably a crass strategy to get them to leave him alone. However the longer he remained in the community, the more the committee feared he might be secretly discouraging enlistments in the Continental Army or trying to persuade people to his views. By early 1777 the committee had arrested and lodged him in the Keene jail. He remained there until Meshech Weare, the chair of the state committee of safety, came to hear evidence against him and several other suspected Loyalists. Abner Sanger noted Weare arrived on February 1, 1777, when "Major Batchelder of Packersfield, Sam [Oliver] Parker of Stoddard, and Robert Gilmore of Keene are in prison by the rebels."[43] On March 20 the New Hampshire General Court ruled that all three could post five-hundred-pound bonds, remain confined to their hometowns, and promise to behave as "a good true subject of this State."[44] Moderate elements of the New Hampshire state government, advised by Weare, were seeking pragmatic accommodation with people such as Batcheller who they deemed not to be a major threat.[45] Some Patriot moderates believed that the persecution of peaceable dissenters was a waste of time. For example New Hampshire state representative John Langdon stated that members of government needed to "do the necessary business of the colony, instead of hearing Tory matters."[46]

The local committees, however, were outraged at the state's actions. The committee of the neighboring town of Surry immediately wrote to Weare, criticizing his decision to grant bail. They called Batcheller an "abundant infamous roach" who was too dangerous "to be liberated to go at large." More ominously they said that he "threatened to give the small pox or stick it in to people as he phrased it."[47] This was precisely during a time when smallpox was taking its toll on the Continental Army, and a rumor was circulating that a secret group of Tories in New Hampshire who were already counterfeiting state currency were planning "this Spring to spread the small pox through the country."[48] The Packersfield committee echoed these concerns: "Major Breed Batchellor though put under bonds continues to insult and abuse selectmen and Committee of this town by threatening and abusive language he has threatened to give the small pox to those that come in this way all without any just provocation and we suspect he is concerned in the counterfeit paper money. The town people are uneasy and afraid of him and insist on his being closely confined and brought to condign punishment and expect [if] something is [not] soon done we fear he will be executed by common rabble."[49]

On June 12, 1777, Batcheller was present at a special court session at Keene that heard evidence in his case. None of the witnesses implicated him in counterfeiting, but a few said he threatened the local committees with smallpox or other violence in order to prevent his apprehension.[50] Some of the testimony was contradictory, but the general pattern confirmed Batcheller's moderate Loyalism. It was clear that he refused to be drafted for revolutionary military service, hire a substitute, or pay taxes to support the military. Yet unlike other local Loyalists on trial, he never indicated any intention to fight for Britain.[51] While many testified that he was "always against independency," almost everyone confirmed his desire not be involved in military service or violence on any side. As his neighbor John Farwell framed it, Batcheller assured him that "he would not fight on either side but would stay at home and raise potatoes." Numerous witnesses testified that he had asserted a variant of a statement that he "would give all he had in the world except his wife and children if this matter might be settled without blood." It also became apparent that Batcheller's primary problem with authority was with that of the local committees, not what he saw as the comparatively moderate New Hampshire state government seated at Exeter. Joseph Collins reported: "He was willing to be tried by impartial men but not by Committee. He had been abused by a mob. [Committee member, Benjamin] Nurse said he would kill Bachellor. He understood [from] him that Committee and men under arms were a mob. He wished the cause might be settled on honourable terms." Henry Bemer testified that Batcheller said "he would be tried at Exeter, but not by the mob."[52]

Ultimately Batcheller was viewed as dangerous primarily because of what he said rather than what he did. And while sometimes his speech was threatening or insulting, he still evinced a proclivity to make persuasive political arguments to his neighbors that made him appear moderate and reasonable. Thus he continued to fit the seditious seducer Loyalist stereotype in New Hampshire at exactly the time when British forces were in closest proximity to his town. James Philips, for example, testified that Batcheller "was sorry so much blood should be shed. The merchants was the cause of it all. Heard him drink a health to the subject and subjects to America." Here Batcheller appeared to be friendly to "the country," while evoking what might have been a growing war weariness after two years. His reference to "the merchants" was meant to speak to class resentment toward the powerful seacoast merchants of both the Wentworth oligarchy and the others who opposed them who now were prominent in New Hampshire revolutionary politics. He also appealed to other popular prejudices to indicate his desire to protect the town, stating that "he would not fight the regulars but would the Indians for he hated them." Abijah Brown explained how sometimes Batcheller appeared to support rebellion, noting: "he said he could not believe the regulars were come out of Concord, but then appeared friendly to the country. Afterwards says we shall drive the regulars by and by."[53] Thus he was able to offer a moderate Whig identity in order ultimately to critique revolutionary authorities. The major problem that Batcheller appeared to have in his moderate Loyalist strategy was his own inability not to dissent at crucial times. Of course he was not the only one whose speech was ungovernable. At Samuel Smith's June 1777 trial in Cheshire County, John Butrick testified that he tried to warn Smith, "if you cannot think as other people do you had better not speak."[54]

On June 12 the New Hampshire government took action to jail and bring to trial the growing number of the disaffected viewed as too dangerous to remain in their communities. The state committee of safety would preside and make final determinations.[55] Among those sentenced to jail and later trial in Exeter was Batcheller. According to him, in a letter to Col. Isaac Wyman, "I understand there is a warrant out for me and that the officer is ordered to . . . carry me to Exeter Gaol where I might lie for trial till September Court, which is a great hardship under the situation of my family." Batcheller stated that he was willing to be tried in Exeter but requested to either remain at home under bonds or at least be given the liberty of the town of Exeter "exclusive of the gaol till court." He further denounced the influence of his local enemies, stating: "The treatment I received is hard though undeserved and the evidence taken on but one side, who were prejudiced persons chiefly. Could the court be rightly informed of the provocations and insults I have received from those my enemies, and the evidence heard on the other side, they would not pay any regard to the evidence against me, as there would be vastly more in my favor than against me. And as to the inadvertent expressions I must acknowledge they are right—but however to be insulted and threatened to be shot. My fences cut away, cattle turned into my grass and hay carried off and destroyed would provoke any human being or say cause and angel to sin if possible." He concluded that if anyone did try to imprison him, "I shall live in the wilderness rather than the gaol till September Court for trial."[56] Batcheller made good on this promise and lived in a nearby cave while the local committee sought to arrest him. He was clandestinely supplied by his wife and some neighbors until he finally decided he had to flee to the British army. With local revolutionaries in hot pursuit in the woods, he left southwestern New Hampshire.[57]

Batcheller joined Burgoyne's army in July 1777 and was commissioned as a captain in Lieutenant Colonel Peters's Queen's Loyal Rangers. He explained that he abandoned his "habitation and family" after "receiving such insults, imprisonment, and abuse, etc. as are common for Royalists to receive among Rebels." It must have been in this period of late July and early August that Batcheller recruited his company as he states in his Loyalist claim. He was in combat at the Battle of Bennington on August 16, 1777, where he was wounded. Batcheller stated that his wound is "very troublesome, as the ball is lodged among the bones of the shoulder and is not yet extracted." Following Burgoyne's surrender at Saratoga on October 17, 1777, the wounded and invalid Batcheller was part of the convention and evacuated to Quebec. In Canada he continued to receive only the pay of a lieutenant and was unable to support himself, let alone his family, in exile.[58] Disabled at age thirty-seven during service to the empire, Batcheller was never again able to work his own land. In 1778 he was transferred to occupied New York.[59] He continued to receive "subsistence" pay from the British army and worked occasionally as a guide for Col. Beverly Robinson's troops. In addition to his disabling wound, he was in ill health in the period 1781–83, and he requested "one quarter subsistence more" to pay his board and medical bills.[60]

Meanwhile Batcheller left his family behind to deal with the wrath of the revolutionaries. Since he joined the British military, he would be treated as a traitor. On November 19, 1778, the New Hampshire government passed a proscription law forbidding him and others who had joined the British from returning to the state. On November 28 New Hampshire passed a confiscation act, which also named Batcheller.[61] Batcheller's exasperated shift in strategy to fight with the British was a financial catastrophe for him and his family. Ruth Batcheller, typical of many wives of Loyalists, was separated from her husband and left behind as the de facto head of her household.[62] Local officials inventoried the estate before the confiscation act went into effect. The selectmen of Packersfield, Hollis, and Marlborough (the towns where Batcheller owned property) seized his holdings between May and October 1778.[63] Ruth Batcheller's ability to provide subsistence for her family was sorely tested. Some of her neighbors treated her cruelly. Abner Sanger noted in his journal on April 25, 1778: "This day is a vendue of Major Batchelder's cattle and poultry at Packersfield by the rebels of said town. They rob his wife of her potatoes."[64]

Batcheller, unlike many New Hampshire Loyalists' wives, made no attempt to join her husband in any of his various exiles. For example on October 23, 1778, Mary Ann Bourn requested permission to join her husband, Patrick, in occupied New York "with her family (consisting of only two children) and also with the few moveables she has."[65] Three days after Bourn submitted her petition, Ruth Batcheller offered a very different petition. She committed to remaining in Packersfield and protecting her family as well as she could. Although it was difficult, she managed to do so. Part of the reason for her success was that Ruth was far more adept at finessing language in a way that was nominally respectful of revolutionary authority. She pointed out that since Breed joined the British in 1777, "leaving your petitioner with five small children," the Packersfield selectmen rented out his estate "allowing your petitioner very little of the profits of it for the support of herself and children." She requested that she have a portion of the corn grown on Breed's confiscated lands in Marlborough to be able to feed the family. She alluded to the concern of becoming a burden to the community, but she also indicated that she had a support network. She stated, "if it had not been for the assistance of friends they must have suffered." Most striking was her renunciation of her husband's joining the British. Ruth asked the state government not to be "involved in misery and ruin [of] the helpless and innocent for the crimes of him who ought to have been their support."[66] She acknowledged Breed's treason and maintained the family's innocence. They had all remained faithful to the state, even if the patriarch of the family had not. Furthermore she indicated his failure in his patriarchal duty to "support" the family. Ruth took up the role of provider in the wake of her husband's abrogation of his familial responsibilities. Thus she fit the model of Paine's wronged wife who needed to separate for the ultimate good of the family. The state government did not immediately take up her petition, as they were focused on passing the state proscription and confiscation acts in this period.[67] However, an accommodation was reached eventually, as Ruth revealed in a subsequent petition that "by the indulgence of the honorable judge of probates, has been for some years past, indulged with the improvement of the home farm."[68] Although it was very different from their earlier affluence, Ruth was able to secure a living for the family in Packersfield. She also shrewdly implied her fidelity to New Hampshire over her duty to her husband's will. As Linda Kerber pointed out, in court cases in which wives of Loyalists argued their obedience to the state over the obligations under coverture, the revolutionaries usually "chose coverture."[69] In some cases, however, wives were able to exploit the rhetoric of women's rights in marriage that could be violated to the extent that they might seek independent settlement. In the competing claims of patriarchal authority, Ruth was able to present herself as a dutiful subject of New Hampshire, "innocent" of her husband's crime.

Other wives of Loyalists used strategies to maintain some control over their property that contrasted with Ruth Batcheller's. Prudence Baxter, for example, described her husband, Simon, as having "gone over to the enemy." She too sought to "save a small part of land when the extra expenses and all demands are paid [on the confiscated estate] for some of her rising posterity to labor upon that with the sweat of their brow." However, she was more equivocal in describing the nature of civil discord in the state, referring to it as when "those difficulties first arose respecting Tory and Whig."[70] Rather than call her husband a criminal, as did Batcheller, she alluded to political disagreements. In a subsequent petition, however, Baxter altered her rhetoric, as she feared her captured husband was in danger of being executed for "high treason." She asked for mercy for her husband, citing his earlier service to the province and humane treatment of revolutionary prisoners. She requested that his citizenship be restored and that he be allowed to take the oath of allegiance. Prudence noted that "the glory of a merciful deed is in proportion to the crime for which the deed of mercy was extended."[71] Unlike Breed Batcheller, however, Simon Baxter petitioned New Hampshire in 1781 to allow his wife and family to join him in exile, citing "certain feelings which must forever strongly attach a man to the wife of his bosom and to his children."[72]

Jane Holland, the wife of the notorious Londonderry, New Hampshire, Loyalist Stephen Holland, exhibited a strong political consciousness, but one that was in accord with her husband. After Stephen escaped jail and fled to the British in 1778, Jane petitioned to retain control over some of the family's property and claimed that some of it "was formerly her own; and which neither she nor her present family have by any means forfeited." She attributed her family's economic catastrophe not to her husband's actions but rather to an act of "the wise disposer of all human events."[73] Further, according to the selectmen of Londonderry who tried to confiscate Holland's estate, Jane showed greater fidelity to British rather than US authority. The selectmen complained that she "ridiculed and despised the authority and law of this or any of the United States and tells us to let her see the man or number of men that dare touch her property. She says she has friends that know what is law and that can and will defend her and concludes with this that Colonel Holland will return in a few weeks in greater honor and glory than ever and tread on the neck of his enemies, etc."[74]

Jane Holland exhibited the characteristics of the seditious seducer figure herself and appeared increasingly dangerous to revolutionary authorities. Not surprisingly, as reported in Holland's Loyalist claim, in May 1779 she and her children were banished from New Hampshire.[75]

Meanwhile, as Breed Batcheller spent the rest of the war in occupied New York, Ruth and the children remained at home and did not join or visit him. Unlike Prudence Baxter, she never pled to the state of New Hampshire to forgive her husband's treason. Nor did she threaten neighbors with lawsuits or the return of her husband, as did Jane Holland. Her careful moderation coupled with a public break with her husband was working. As the war ended, Breed Batcheller was scheduled to be evacuated from New York with other Loyalists to Nova Scotia in 1783. Many Loyalists began making the move to Nova Scotia in 1782, and those who remained in New York began planning for what appeared to be a permanent move. Evidence shows Breed and Ruth exchanged letters in this period. It is likely that the future of the family and its residence was a major topic, especially since Breed was forbidden from returning to New Hampshire. In a cryptic journal entry on November 29, 1782, Abner Sanger recounted that "Mrs. Batchelder come towards night and committed her letters to me to write an answer to her husband."[76] These letters have not survived, but the topic of whether the rest of the family should follow Batcheller to Nova Scotia was probably addressed. Curiously it appeared that Ruth asked Sanger to write her final reply to her husband. This may have been due to the fact that although Sanger was a laborer, he was well-read, well-versed in politics, and a moderate Loyalist who had himself been imprisoned briefly during the war but remained in the community. Furthermore his twin brother, Eleazer, joined British forces and was proscribed as was Batcheller.[77] He and Ruth had firsthand experience with how the war had sundered families. Her refusal to make a "final reply" to her husband and delegation of the task to Sanger may have reflected Ruth's recognition of a formal separation in the marriage.

As difficult as the situation was for Ruth and the children, it was dire for Batcheller. In a petition to General Sir Guy Carleton requesting additional subsistence rations because of his illness and disability, he explained his bleak prospects for life in Nova Scotia. He wrote that "being immediately to remove to Nova Scotia, having a wife and five children am entirely unable to provide himself with necessaries for the voyage or to carry one schilling to assist him in a new country."[78] He implied that he was still trying to help support his family, but his economic and physical states were grim. He arrived alone at Digby, Nova Scotia, in 1783, recorded as "Brude Bachelor."[79] Batcheller filed his Loyalist claim on March 19, 1784, in the hopes of being reimbursed for his confiscated property. In it he did not mention his need to support his family and only stated in regard to them, "from a sense of duty to the government he was born under, he left his family and estate."[80] Upon his death in 1785, before receiving compensation for his claim, his probated estate in Nova Scotia underscored his late poverty. Most of his property was clothing. In addition he had some dishes, utensils, a sword, a trunk, "some dried apples," and "a French grammar and pocket books."[81] Batcheller died alone in a liminal state. Cast out of his native country and exiled to an unfamiliar province, he awaited the compensation from British government for which he sacrificed much. It came neither to him nor to his heirs. Batcheller's life experience embodied a theme that Philip Gould has found as central in Loyalist literature. Rather than being caught between the two worlds of being American and being British, Loyalists exhibited "the more unsettling crisis of being alone and nowhere."[82] He had sacrificed his livelihood and connections to family for the greater good of an empire in which he remained an isolated, exiled refugee. Taken in context, this service was not rendered through purely volitional patriotism to the king but rather as a result of the revolutionaries' rejection of his presence. If, as he often stated, protecting his family and property was his first priority, his joining the British war effort was an unmitigated disaster. He might well have waited out a term of imprisonment or even avoided it had he been more circumspect with his speech. Sanger had done so even as everyone in Keene knew his Loyalist sympathies. Batcheller's verbally aggressive demeanor with both friends and foes had unwittingly made him appear to be an intolerably dangerous, seditious seducer of the people in his community.

Ruth was no longer a separated wife but a widow, which provided new opportunities to reacquire some of the family's property. Her husband's death rendered moot any claim he could have to property that she might hold. On June 2, 1789, she petitioned the New Hampshire government to expand upon the probate judge's arrangement in which she and her family lived on the family farm in Packersfield and give the "home farm to your petitioner and her children and to their heirs forever." She again framed their difficulties as the fault of her husband in language that recognized the legitimacy of the United States. She stated that Batcheller "was dissatisfied with the measures the states adopted, in order to obtain their liberties, and delivering themselves from the hands of the Britons, and therefore left his wife, children and estate, and went to the British army."[83] In particular she wanted permission to make improvements to the farm and its lands in order to augment its "profits" to support her family. The state government allowed Ruth to "have the improvement of the within mentioned farm until the estate of Breed Batchelor is settled free from all rents."[84] Although it was nowhere near the estimated total value of his estate as documented in Breed's Loyalist claim, Ruth was able to attain her primary goal. The family would be able to apply "all their labor and industry" for a "comfortable support."[85] As Paine imagined, the abandoned, wronged wife could become independent and provide for her children and heirs. The 1790 US Census listed Ruth as the head of household on her Packersfield farm in a household with two men and two women.[86] In contrast to the experience of those Loyalist wives who migrated with their husbands and lived in postwar communities that emphasized obedience and patriarchal subordination of wives, Ruth was a respected member of the community in her own right.[87]

The family did not, however, give up pursuing Batcheller's Loyalist claim. His eldest son, Thomas Packer Batcheller, gathered evidence showing the value of the family's confiscated estate and travelled to England in 1791 to pursue the claim. It is not clear whether he coordinated his plans with his mother. The awarding of the Loyalist claim would have complicated her attempts to hold onto the family farm. However the value of the confiscated estate would reestablish the family's affluence. It was a familial Atlantic strategy. Ruth was the head of the Batcheller family in the United States. Thomas presented himself as heir to his father's estate and the family's representative in England. However the Lords of Treasury had no desire to take up dormant claims that they considered closed. In 1792 the government offered Thomas Batcheller seven hundred acres of land in Upper Canada and £48, which he declined in order to pursue his father's claim. Thomas became impoverished and in 1793 was forced to take a job as a district surveyor on a canal in Yorkshire.[88] His descriptions of his father's actions initially reproduced the language of his father's and many other Loyalist claims. He noted Batcheller was "a loyal subject to his Majesty, and was firmly attached to British government, openly opposing at all times, the seditious practices which brought on the unhappy dissensions in America, by which conduct he rendered himself so obnoxious as made it necessary for him to leave his family and estate."[89]

Unlike his mother's plea to the New Hampshire government, in which she blamed Batcheller for the situation of the family, unsurprisingly Thomas blamed the rebels and stated that his father's fidelity to the empire trumped his responsibility to stay with his family. Over time, however, Thomas's bitterness toward Britain grew. Seeking a donation from the Commissioners for Relieving French Emigrants, he stated that he hoped "his father's loyalty to the British King" might entitle his family to "a share of the public munificence at your disposal, as much as if his loyalty had been manifested to the King of the French."[90] On August 24, 1798, Batcheller wrote of his desire to leave London and "return to his mother and family, after an absence of more than seven years." He made one final plea for his father's claim, calling him "a faithful and loyal parent, who ruined himself and family by his integrity to the House of Hanover, and to British government."[91] The shift in tone from earlier petitions suggested that Thomas blamed the government for his family's ruin by not living up its obligations to Loyalists. One week later he was notified that the government would not act on his claim and "that nothing would be done by way of compensation, except a gratuity of forty eight pounds and a passage to America."[92] The New Hampshire government had been more humanitarian in their treatment of the Batcheller family than had the British.

Meanwhile, thanks to Ruth's efforts, the family continued to be reintegrated into the community. The Batcheller's eldest child, Betsey, married Stephen Chase, a member of a prominent Keene family in 1787.[93] Thomas returned to the area and married Anna Baker in 1805. He became, like his father, "a real estate speculator" and died in Keene in 1828.[94] Eventually the farm did pass back to Ruth, her children, and heirs. She and her son John remained in the Packersfield farm well into the nineteenth century. Thomas and Betsy subsequently sold their interests in the estate to their brother John. On August 12, 1809, John sold his claims to his mother, leaving her the sole owner. She remained at her home until 1828, when she sold the farm to her grandson, John's son, Breed. Ruth lived with Betsy in Keene until her death at age ninety-four in 1840.[95] She never remarried in her long life after outliving her husband by fifty-five years and being separated for eight years before his death. Her obituary in the *New Hampshire Sentinel* still listed her as the "widow of Major Breed Batcheller."[96]

The American Revolution led to a change in government that was facilitated by deployment of various metaphors of household authority that variously challenged and affirmed notions of patriarchal power. Breed Batcheller lost his authority in his community in part because of how he fit the image of the dangerous, clandestine Loyalist seducer of the people. Ruth was able to utilize political discourse about unions as contractual compacts in which even subordinated members had rights to her family's advantage. The Batchellers' stories illustrated the complex interaction of the language of political tropes with Loyalist families' experiences. Unable to accept new sources of authority manifested in local committees, Breed's verbal dissent was the primary means of his failure to maintain his moderate Loyalist stance without violence or loss of property. As T. H. Breen has shown, the local committees of safety were indeed insurgent "schools of revolution" that politicized the people.[97] Their successful regulation of language and dissent created a Manichean world where the disaffected or moderate Loyalists had little choice but compliance or complete silence. The Batchellers' experience was unique in many ways, and they were not representative of New Hampshire Loyalists or even moderate Loyalists. Rather it suggests that a fuller consideration of struggles over controlling dissenting speech reveals a broad range of opposition to the Revolution and varied results. It also underscores the importance of examining Loyalism's effects on families.[98] Given the close connection between household and political authority, varieties of disaffection and familial situations mutually affected each other. Moreover conventional notions of gendered power in Revolutionary America were challenged and reconstructed. This essay has suggested the importance of how various understandings of marital union were used to explain subject relations to the state. Like the more well-known parent-child metaphors, they further politicized the household while rendering the state recognizable as a household. Ruth Batcheller was able to make her case for fidelity to the state over that to her husband in a way that did not appear to be threatening to the social order. Jan Lewis has shown how this imagery of marriage as political metaphor persisted in important ways well into the early Republic. The concern then was with the "vile seducer" and how the figure might use power to undermine fidelity in a virtuous republican union.[99] This imagery grew in part out of those generated by Loyalists and revolutionaries in the decades before. Concerns over ideal union and seduction provide a specific historical context in which the outcome of Batchellers' travails can be understood as a meeting of republican domestic theory with the experiences of moderate Loyalist spouses.

BRETT PALFREYMAN

The Nonjuror Problem in Pennsylvania

During the American Revolution, contemporary observers estimated that Pennsylvania's rebel government disenfranchised somewhere between 40 and 50 percent of the eligible voters in its jurisdiction for refusing to swear an oath declaring allegiance to the independent state and abjuring the king of Great Britain.[1] The so-called nonjurors were permitted to reside in Pennsylvania and subjected to taxation but denied the right to vote, to hold public office, to serve on juries, to travel without restriction, to establish schools, to possess firearms, and other basic freedoms. The spectrum of the disqualified included a variety of former colonists who had declined to take the oath for a variety of reasons. There were true royalists who believed that Pennsylvania was still the rightful dominion of the king. There were pacifists and conscientious objectors—Quakers, Moravians, and others who opposed war, violence, or even the very act of oath taking on moral and religious grounds. There were probably some Pennsylvanians who never knew that an oath was required or were unable to appear before a justice of the peace within the allotted time because of poor health, other business, or plain distance. And the rest must have fit in somewhere along the middle of the continuum between declared Patriots and active Tories, simply preferring to wait and see how the conflict would play out rather than taking sides so early. But whatever their particular combinations of motivations, Pennsylvania's wartime government viewed all non–oath takers as fundamentally suspect and placed them firmly outside of the boundaries of "the people."

Within seven years after the end of the war, however, the status of the nonjurors changed dramatically. In 1786 the state government reopened the window for potential citizens to swear the oath they had failed to take during the fighting. In 1787 legislators relaxed the terms of the pledge so that more people might feel comfortable taking it. In 1789 they did away with the oath system entirely.[2] By the end of the 1780s, all of the nonjurors—all the vacillators, moral objectors, slight leaners, late deciders, side switchers, and truly uncommitted who had made up the spectrum of non–oath takers—enjoyed the same civil and political rights as other Pennsylvanians. In real terms they would have the same access to the revolutionary ideals of life, liberty, and property as other Americans.

Historians have long sought to explain this precipitous transformation in the standing of the nonjurors, but not for the sake of the disqualified individuals themselves. Rather scholars of the early Republic have been more concerned with the consequences for Pennsylvania in general—not just *that* nonjurors rejoined the political community, but *how* they affected the direction of state politics once they did. At the end of the Revolution, two loose political factions vied for control of Pennsylvania's independent government.[3] The Constitutionalist Party, dominant through most of the war years, built its platform around the support and maintenance of the innovative state constitution of 1776, with its powerful unicameral legislature and weak executive branch. The Constitutionalists were opposed by the Republicans, a rough coalition of politicians and voters dedicated to modifying the revolutionary state constitution and setting some limits on the power of the popularly elected legislature. These two parties were relatively evenly balanced in postwar Pennsylvania, trading small victories and control of the assembly back and forth throughout most of the 1780s.[4]

This is where the reenfranchisement of the nonjurors usually enters the story. The basic outline of the existing narrative is relatively straightforward: (1) Republicans won the political battle to reintegrate the nonjurors in the years after the war; (2) Given the franchise, nonjurors overwhelmingly threw their votes back to the party that had supported them; and (3) The sudden infusion of so many new voters gave the Republican Party the electoral strength to dominate state politics throughout the remainder of the 1780s. In the words of Pauline Maier, this sudden "swing of previously disfranchised voters" gave the Republican Party a stable "popular majority" going into the late 1780s. Owen Ireland agrees that the "reenfranchisement of substantial numbers of [nonjurors] . . . dramatically changed the political orientation" of the electorate.[5]

But while historians seem to agree about the consequences of the reincorporation of the nonjurors, there has been little consensus regarding its causes. Why did Republicans invest so much time, energy, and political capital on behalf of these potential political suspects? Why did Constitutionalists work equally hard to exclude them? Progressive scholars such as Robert Brunhouse, Jackson Turner Main, and Terry Bouton have suggested that Republicans and nonjurors had a natural affinity based on shared social status, as the members of both groups tended to be wealthier, more urban, more commercially oriented, and more predominant in Philadelphia and the eastern part of the state. Their Constitutionalist opponents, on the other hand, tended to be more rural and more agrarian-minded, owned smaller amounts of land, and drew their strength from the western counties.[6]

Historian Owen Ireland has since challenged the fundamental economic and sectional divisions underlying the progressive interpretation, arguing that the "most persistent and predictable component[s] of political partisanship" in state politics were not class or location but ethnicity and religion. The Republican Party and the nonjurors tended to be Quakers and Anglicans with English roots, Lutherans, and various other German sectarians. The Constitutionalist Party, meanwhile, drew their bulk of their support from Scotch-Irish Presbyterians and ethnic German Calvinists. Thus, for Ireland, when Republicans reached out to nonjurors, they did so as fellow Quakers, Anglicans, and Lutherans; and when Constitutionalists opposed reintegration, they did so as competing religious groups. Here again Republicans and nonjurors seem to have shared what Ireland calls a "consciousness-of-kind"—a common identity and set of shared interests that united the two groups and separated both from the Constitutionalists.[7]

These historical interpretations stress identity politics as the central explanatory force underlying the battle over the reintegration of nonjurors in postwar Pennsylvania. While the progressives and Ireland disagree about the most salient elements of that identity, both are convinced that Pennsylvanians argued for or against reintegration based on who the nonjurors were. Yet in focusing on economic and sectional differences, as the progressives do, or on religion and ethnicity, as Ireland does, these historians tend to underemphasize another fundamental identity attached to the nonjurors—their status as suspected Loyalists and potential enemies of the Revolution. When Pennsylvanians wrote or spoke about the nonjurors in public debates, newspaper editorials, or on the floor of the assembly, they argued about a much more visceral and immediate question: the problem of dealing with a substantial population of possible political dissidents in the wake of a long and violent civil war. They discussed the demands of public security in a fragile, still untested political community; they considered whether inclusion or exclusion was the wisest policy for handling individuals and groups who might prove politically unreliable. Most of all they argued about the meaning and legacy of the Revolution—about exactly what they had won and who they had won it for. In other words Pennsylvanians talked about the status of the nonjurors in the same ways that Americans in other states talked about the problem of managing the population of real and suspected Loyalists who lingered in the states after the Revolution.

In this sense the experience of the nonjurors in Pennsylvania is part of a larger story about the fate of former Loyalists who chose to stay in the Republic after 1783. Some sixty thousand supporters of the king fled the United States during the war and after, headed to Canada, England, the Caribbean, Africa, India, and even Australia.[8] Convinced they had no future in independent America, these refugees left behind family, friends, homes, and businesses in order to immigrate to territories still belonging to the empire. But many more—perhaps several hundred thousand—lacked the resources, the opportunity, or the motivation to uproot their lives and begin anew in far-flung corners of the world. These Loyalists settled for a different kind of risk—one closer to home, perhaps, but certainly no less unsettling.

They decided to stay in the States and submit to the authority of people and governments who had been their deadly enemies for nearly a decade of civil war.

Of course not all of the nonjurors in Pennsylvania were bona fide "Loyalists" by any traditional definition. Many did not oppose the Revolution, even if they declined to support it actively by swearing allegiance to the rebels. But by refusing to make this public commitment, all non–oath takers became suspect in the eyes of the wartime government. Whatever each individual's particular motivations—whatever his or her true position on the great question of independence—Pennsylvania viewed them, at best, as self-serving "trimmers" too cowardly to take a stand or, at worst, as closeted enemies of the state. As skeptical legislators wrote in 1784, "what the motives of these men were for refusing [to take the test oath], they have not told us." But since nonjurors failed to swear allegiance, and did so knowing the consequences of their silence, lawmakers felt "naturally constrained to believe that they were . . . professed British subjects, or enemies to liberty and the rights of mankind, or cowards that meanly skulked to skreen [*sic*] themselves and their property in the hour of difficulty and danger."[9] Identity politics—the nonjurors' status as economic actors and as members of religious and ethnic groups—surely mattered after the war. But before any sort of reconciliation or reintegration could take place, Pennsylvanians had to come to terms with non–oath takers as potential enemies of the Revolution. In this sense the reenfranchisement of this population—and all the electoral and political repercussions that flowed from it—was part of a larger process of peacemaking that occurred throughout post-Revolutionary America between victorious Patriots, on the one side, and Loyalists, trimmers, neutrals, equivocators, late deciders, and a variety of other political suspects on the other.[10]

Over the course of the Revolution, Pennsylvania's independent government adopted a range of strategies for dealing with suspected political dissidents. As in other states, rebel leaders targeted several hundred of the state's most notorious, influential, and wealthy Tories with legislative and executive proclamations of attainder that confiscated property and banished individuals.[11] But what about the rest of the population? How could the state separate the faithful citizens within its borders from the equivocators, the calculating opportunists, the half-hearted Whigs, the secret royalists, and everyone else? Some Pennsylvanians, as state legislators noted in 1777, had openly committed themselves to the cause of independence and risked their lives and fortunes in the service of the Revolution. But others had yet to make their intentions known; they had "with[e]ld their service and allegiance" from the new polity and remained at least outwardly neutral. The problem for the state's leaders, then, since "both those sorts of persons . . . [are] mixed, and in some measure undistinguished from each other," was telling the true friends of the independence movement from the enemies. Pennsylvania responded with a series of Test Acts, laws requiring that all free white male inhabitants over the age of eighteen swear an oath declaring their allegiance to the new state and abjuring the king of Great Britain. Anyone who refused or neglected to take the pledge would forfeit the rights and privileges of citizenship and be pushed decisively outside the limits of "the people."[12]

The wartime Test Acts were designed to force Pennsylvanians to make a clear, public decision on the great question of independence: either openly declare fidelity to the state or knowingly acknowledge opposition by silence. The new laws also mandated that potential citizens make the choice within a specified period of time—to pick a side while the outcome of the war was uncertain, to commit while it cost something to commit—rather than playing the middle and waiting to see how the conflict would unfold. Wartime legislators declared Loyalism to be the default position in Pennsylvania; they assumed that inaction indicated a preference for the status quo. They placed the burden of acquiring citizenship on individuals, requiring that genuine Patriots prove their attachment to Revolution by some positive, overt, and, importantly, measurable step. The oath effectively took neutrality off the table; it moved all non–oath takers into the column of the disaffected and made the Revolution a "with us or against us" proposition in Pennsylvania. For the authors of the Test Laws, political citizenship was a privilege to be earned by sacrifice and struggle, not a natural right freely granted to all, regardless of behavior. "Allegiance and protection are reciprocal," they wrote, "and those who will not bear the former, are not . . . intitled to the benefits of the latter."[13]

The status of the nonjurors was perhaps the most important unresolved question surrounding the end of the Revolution in Pennsylvania.[14] Virtually everyone involved in the debate over whether the Test Laws ought to be maintained after the war was, as legislators reported in 1784, "impressed with a deep sense of the important consequences of the present measures." For the nonjurors themselves, the outcome of the controversy meant the difference between citizenship and what they described as a "state of vassalage"—their real access to life, liberty, and property in independent America.[15] For political partisans on both sides, the disenfranchised represented an enormous pool of untapped voters that, if suddenly unleashed into the electorate, could drastically alter the state's delicate political equilibrium. As one particularly astute assemblyman observed in 1785, the nonjurors, if abruptly reinstated, would be "able to send a large body into [the] legislature" at any moment.[16] And for Pennsylvania at large, the resolution of the nonjuror problem would help define the boundaries of citizenship, the relationship between state security and individual freedom, and the ultimate meaning of the Revolution. Physician and statesmen Benjamin Rush may have indulged in a bit of self-important exaggeration when he suggested that the "fate and liberty of the world, perhaps, are now suspended by our example." But Rush was not the only Pennsylvanian who recognized that the settlement of the Revolution—the way the war ended—could be just as meaningful as the fight itself. The real legacy of the grand struggle for independence, he argued, lay not in the old government that

Pennsylvanians had cast off but in the nature of the new society they meant to create. "The next seven years, more than the last seven years," Rush wrote at the end of the war, would demonstrate to the rest of the world whether a republic of the people could long endure.[17]

When Constitutionalists and Republicans discussed the nonjuror problem in postwar Pennsylvania, they generally argued about two things: the proper balance between security and liberty in a purportedly free society and the meaning and character of the revolutionary struggle. On the issue of public safety, the heart of the controversy stemmed from a few fundamental questions: Who were the nonjurors? Why had they refused to take the oath? Were they really dangerous political dissidents or merely a motley collection of pacifists, neutrals, pragmatists, and various others too noncommittal to represent any real threat? Was any particular individual's wartime record a reliable predictor of his potential for peaceful reintegration and republican citizenship? Constitutionalists affirmed that the oath system had served its purpose admirably—it had effectively separated, as well as any single legal mechanism could, the friends of the Revolution from the enemies. "We have no other way to judge men, but by their actions," wrote an editorialist in Carlisle. By their actions during the war (or, more properly, by their lack of action), nonjurors had proven themselves "men void of conscience, virtue, and integrity, pests to mankind, [who] of course would be pestilential to the commonwealth." Among the disqualified, reported state representative John Smilie, "those who . . . entertained sentiments in favour of Britain" were still "pretty numerous." The "revolution had not effected [a] universal change of opinion in the state." There was, Smilie continued, "a vast body of people here, who abhorred a republican form of government. These were dangerous."[18]

Like other opponents of Loyalist reintegration throughout the Union, Constitutionalists in Pennsylvania insisted that the state's primary obligation to protect its legitimate citizens outweighed the claimed rights and liberties of potential political suspects. When rejecting a petition from nonjurors seeking political reinstatement in 1785, Constitutionalists in the assembly announced that it would be "impolitic and dangerous" to admit "inimical" persons to a "common participation in the government so soon after the war." Assemblyman Robert Whitehill reminded the House that those colonists who declined to pick a side during the fighting had stood ready to ingratiate themselves with either afterward. "These people lay by the whole course of the war," Whitehill charged. "Had Britain conquered, and America been subdued, they would then be declared the friends of the former. But the war being closed, and the event contrary to their expectations, they now turn their views a different way."[19] No political community—let alone a fragile, unfinished one such as Pennsylvania—could survive for long with a substantial population of internal dissenters lurking within its borders. The new state needed sturdy, reliable friends of independence, not irresolute self-servers who lacked the necessary fortitude to stick out their necks when the cards were down.

Constitutionalists maintained that any sort of amnesty for non–oath takers after the war would only jeopardize the state's dearly bought independence and invite further violence. Indeed exclusionists in the legislature claimed that nonjurors were so ubiquitous in some districts that "elections might reasonably be expected to be carried in favour of men who . . . still cherish the hope of a subordinate reunion with Great Britain." Should Tories regain control of the commonwealth, Constitutionalists threatened, indignant Whigs would surely be roused to "open new scenes of blood: For it seems impossible that the free spirited sons of Pennsylvania, after establishing her independence with their swords, should ever submit to be governed by traitors, trimmers, or time-serving whigs." Even though a peace treaty had been signed far across the sea, Constitutionalists feared that the danger of recurring civil violence at home in Pennsylvania had not yet passed. "THEY who have gained a victory over the instruments of oppression in the field of battle," warned an editorialist in Philadelphia, "have but half completed the defence of their liberty. Peace cannot extinguish those animosities which war has been fomenting." Your "present security," he reminded readers, "without great precaution, may be only a fatal repose." With the mighty British army still hovering along the western frontier, treacherous Indians still rampaging across the countryside, and independence as yet unsecured, Constitutionalists insisted that reins of government could only be entrusted to proven friends of the Revolution.[20]

Republicans responded forcefully on the question of public security. The best way to protect a fledgling political society and bring peace to a war-ravaged population, they claimed, was to assimilate and absorb potential opponents, rather than pushing them away. Certainly nonjurors had failed to take open steps in favor of the rebellion, but that did not mean that they were inherently dangerous or incapable of becoming useful members of the new Republic. "It is a wretched principle," wrote a newspaper contributor, "to think that all who differ from us in either politics or religion are bad men, destitute of virtue and conscience. . . . I am persuaded that many of those, who could not see their way clear to join the American cause, are men of integrity and worth." Republicans asserted that failing to take the oath was not necessarily evidence of disloyalty—or at least disloyalty enough to merit such a drastic punishment. Pennsylvania gained nothing by denying citizenship to men who "at worst, could only be charged with having been neutrals."[21] Advocates for the nonjurors offered a narrower definition of criminal disaffection, extending only to active enemies of the state, and suggested a correspondingly inclusive understanding of citizenship that would bring most non–oath takers back into the fold. According to Assemblyman Robert Morris, the true royalists and other enemies of the Revolution—"those who relied on Great-Britain"—were already "gone away" to Canada, England, and other distant corners of the British Empire. "Those nonjurors who remain[ed]" after 1783, he continued, "are such, as from fears, doubts, or religious scruples, refused to join us." Quakers, Moravians, and other conscientious objectors could be just as "firm friends to liberty and the rights of mankind, and as zealous defenders of American freedom, as any in the country." They had only been "stiled [*sic*] enemies to their country and Tories" because they "did not see the necessity of taking up arms" and "declined engaging in hostile preparations." Can "any guilt or odium fall upon those persons," asked another supportive legislator, "whom conscientious scruples would not permit to bear arms?"[22]

Advocates of reintegration suggested that the end of the war had transformed the political reality on the ground in Pennsylvania. Perhaps extraordinary measures may have been necessary at the height of the fighting, but now the war was over and a peace treaty had been signed. "When we were in the heat of battle," admitted one Republican writer—"when our passions were raised by scenes of bloodshed and desolation . . . [and] the important contest hung doubtful"—it was "not very surprising" that Pennsylvanians were, at times, "transported beyond the bounds of human right and sound policy." Even if the Test Laws had been somewhat more heavy-handed and repressive than a free people might prefer, such exigencies were probably unavoidable in time of war. During those dark days, agreed a group of sympathetic petitioners in Philadelphia, there were "existing necessities to justify the disfranchising, for a time, [of] all persons who would not give a solemn declaration of their fidelity to a state actually invaded by an hostile army." But now, in 1785, "such necessities, by the happy termination of the war, are altogether removed." The fighting was over; the last British warships had sailed in defeat over the eastern horizon. With peace and independence secured, there remained "no reasons" that could "justify the longer keeping so numerous a body of people . . . under so odious a description."[23]

Besides, Republicans argued, as Pennsylvanians looked forward to a new era of peace and independence, they ought to focus their attention on cultivating new alliances rather than resurrecting old resentments. The oath of allegiance no longer served to protect Pennsylvania from its internal enemies; rather ongoing discrimination merely created enemies out of people who might otherwise be valuable citizens. The nonjurors "form a large body of the inhabitants of the state," claimed Robert Morris, and "debarred from the rights and privileges of citizens, they cannot but be disaffected to it." If non–oath takers had been reluctant to commit themselves to the state during the war, then surely continuing persecution and segregation afterward would only drive them further away. When Pennsylvania disqualified potential subjects for wartime choices, advised an author in the *Carlisle Gazette*, "we force them to continue to be our enemies." Retaining a substantial population under such conditions—allowed to remain in the state but given every reason to resist the new government—would be "madness in the extreme."[24] Honest people, Republicans insisted, were certainly capable of changing their political commitments over time. By maintaining the extreme "with or against us" mentality of the war years, Pennsylvania's independent government was only de-priving itself of the services and support of individuals who might become useful citizens. It was hardly "a matter of consequence," another editorialist concluded, what "political opinions the nonjurors held nine or ten years ago." If Pennsylvanians were truly concerned about security and harmony in the future, they ought to turn their attention to "what opinions [the nonjurors] now hold" and "consider by what means they may be most useful to the community."[25]

For Republicans, then, the wisest and safest strategy going forward was an approach that involved reconciliation and reintegration for all but the most egregious enemies of the Revolution. According to Robert Morris, genuine security and stability was best achieved not by excluding every possible political suspect from the life of the state but by transforming those potential adversaries into allies. It "is less dangerous to have those people our friends," he announced on the floor of the assembly, "than to continue them our enemies, by retaining them in a state of vassalage." Representative Robert Loller agreed that the reincorporation of the nonjurors on relatively generous terms was simply "good policy." Given a fair opportunity to join the new political community, most of the disqualified would probably become friends to the independent government. And "every wise government," Loller finished, "will make as many friends as possible."[26]

At the same time, Constitutionalists and Republicans also viewed the fate of the nonjurors as a powerful and highly visible metric of the meaning of the Revolution—of what they had accomplished and who had earned the right to share in the benefits. Both sides agreed that the grand struggle for independence was more than a common political coup, simply replacing one set of foreign rulers with another set of domestic ones. Both wanted to believe that a more fundamental transformation had taken place—an elemental change in the relationship between the government and the governed and the structure and purpose of political society. They disagreed, however, on exactly what that change would look like in ordinary Pennsylvanians' lives and to whom it ought to extend.

Constitutionalists maintained that the privileges of victory and nationhood belonged exclusively to those who had paid their fair share of the cost. While the rebellion may have begun as an independence war meant to liberate the states from a foreign king, they argued, it had become a civil war between different segments within the colonial population and ultimately ended with the conquest of one over the other.[27] The disaffected had worked to "reduce and to enslave" the rebel states or sat idly by, offering no help or support to their rightful country "during the season of [its] trial and distress." And they had lost. Now, as conquerors, American Patriots had won the unquestionable right to decide who would share in the fruits of their Revolution and the uncontestable power to dictate the terms of peace to the conquered.[28]

Constitutionalists asserted that existing measures to penalize the nonjurors in postwar Pennsylvania were nothing more than the natural and righteous consequences of the outcome of the fighting. According to Assemblyman John Smilie, the "war was a lottery." Those colonists "who took the oaths of allegiance and abjuration during the contest" had "staked everything" and thereby earned the right to claim the full privileges of membership in the new commonwealth. But now, Smilie complained, the nonjurors—"those who staked nothing"—"come forward, and ask a share of the prize." "It is enough," shouted unsympathetic residents in Bucks County, that such persons "should be suffered to live under the benign influence of a free government." But mere residence was all they ought to expect—they "can have no claim to a participation of its administration." It was only natural that "those who declined to participate in the toils, the sacrifices, and the hazard of the late revolution should not enjoy all the benefit and advantage arising from that inestimable blessing."[29]

Like opponents of Loyalist reintegration in other states, Constitutionalists regarded lingering non-oath takers as an ongoing threat to the fragile political and social reforms of the Revolution. Government by the people required citizens with virtue, selflessness, civic disinterestedness, and scrupulous faithfulness. Nonjurors lacked these qualities—indeed they had become nonjurors precisely because they failed to demonstrate fidelity when their beleaguered country needed them most. Genuine American Patriots had sacrificed blood and treasure to win their rights and liberties on the battlefield. Why would the states experiment with any policy, however humane or magnanimous it might seem, that would jeopardize those precious achievements afterward? "If suffered to come among us," promised a public committee of concerned citizens, the disaffected would "sap the first principles of the revolution"—they would seek to restore old hierarchies, check the spread of democratic reforms, or even conspire to deliver Pennsylvania back into the hands of the king. "We may judge what men will do by what they have done," echoed an editorialist in the *Carlisle Gazette*. If the nonjurors continued to be capricious and unreliable, the dearly bought fruits of the independence movement in Pennsylvania would surely be at risk. "What else must we expect," the anonymous author asked, "if we admit those to a right of suffrage, or an equal share in our government, who have exerted their utmost power and influence to bind down tyranny and despotism on us, by aiding and abetting our enemies?"[30]

Put simply, Constitutionalists feared that the nonjurors were (and would continue to be) a discrete and autonomous bloc within the new commonwealth—a powerful faction in Pennsylvania but not of Pennsylvania. The grand struggle for independence had not made some colonists into bona fide Patriots and others into equivocators, shirkers, and secret enemies; rather the cauldron of revolution had only revealed deep-seated political predilections that were already lurking beneath the surface. Nonjurors, it now seemed clear, were intrinsically weak, submissive, and unwilling to carry their fair share of the burdens of republican citizenship. Their critical failure on the great question of 1776 was but one manifestation of a congenitally defective political character. It was only a matter of time before more such breaches of trust would inevitably follow. Put simply, opponents of reintegration were convinced that nonjurors would always be nonjurors—that they would remain faithless, fickle, and ruled by self-interest, even after the conflict that had first exposed these flaws was over.

Republicans, on the other hand, built their case for reintegration around very different visions of what the Revolution had been about and who ought to be included. Americans had sacrificed so much, they argued, not to deny rights and liberties to whole segments of the population but to guarantee those rights and liberties for all (or at least for all otherwise-eligible free white male adults). If any policy could undermine the true purpose and meaning of the independence movement, it was a system that demanded taxes from inhabitants while denying them access to representation. When we "tax a number of men whom we exclude from a representation in the assembly," wrote a Republican in York County, "we are guilty of tyranny; that very tyranny against which we drew the American sword." If Americans used their newfound political authority to commit the very injustices they had fought to escape, then how much had the Revolution really accomplished? "The liberty for which the American soldiers fought," wrote a newspaper contributor under the pseudonym "Mentor," was not "the liberty of tyrannizing over near one half of the citizens, but it was the liberty of the whole."[31]

For Republicans, then, the problem with the Test Laws was not the idea of excluding true enemies of the state. Even the most passionate advocates for the nonjurors disavowed any intention to help attainted Loyalists, restore confiscated property, or worst of all, reinstall elements of the old colonial proprietary government.[32] The real root of the problem was procedural—the way the state identified the criminally disaffected and distributed penalties. The existing oath system simply cast too wide and indiscriminating a net. Colonists might have said the words (or not said the words) for any number of reasons that had nothing to do with political ideology, republicanism, or the sacred rights of the people. Conscientious objections, family ties, business obligations, cautious pragmatism, or pure ignorance—all could affect individual Pennsylvanians' decisions on the great question of independence. According to Rush, the assumption that any particular colonist was wholly attached to the Revolution simply because he had a "certificate of an oath" was just as "absurd" as it would be for a "man to plead his title to the kingdom of Heaven, by producing at the Supreme Tribunal nothing but a register of his baptism."[33]

The only proper procedure for depriving otherwise-eligible citizens of essential rights, Republicans insisted, was indictment for some crime declared by antecedent law, trial by jury, and conviction. Indeed the Revolution itself had been fought to preserve the notion that individuals ought to be presumed innocent until they were proven guilty. "If any person has committed treason or any other crime" and is "liable to punishment," argued a Republican editorialist, "let him, after a fair trial, upon legal conviction, be punished accordingly. But let no man . . . be deemed other than innocent, until by proper evidence, he be proved guilty." The Test Laws deprived whole categories of Pennsylvanians of the most crucial freedoms without any substantive legal process to distinguish the real criminals and enemies of the state from the rest. State Representative Robert Loller's assessment of the problem was particularly frank: "Among the non-jurors, as among all other bodies of people," he announced before the assembly, "there are good and bad. . . . Could we devise any measure to exclude the bad, I should readily go into it." But the oath system cast good and bad together—it punished the innocent alongside the guilty, drew in conscientious objectors, left no space for good-faith conversions, and effectively criminalized neutrality. Since there was no practical way to isolate and ostracize the true enemies of the Revolution—and only the true enemies of the Revolution—Loller preferred to err on the side of inclusion.[34] In this sense Republicans saw the reintegration of all the nonjurors—even those who may have questioned independence—as the best means of fulfilling the true meaning of the revolutionary movement.

With these arguments about immediate policy and long-term legacy largely in place at the end of the war, the legislative fortunes of the Test Laws rose and fell with the relative balance of power in the legislature and the shrewdness of each side's political maneuvering. Republicans captured their first majority in the Eighth Session of the General Assembly in 1783 and 1784 as the Constitutionalist coalition that had carried Pennsylvania through the war began to fragment and splinter. Republican legislators quickly focused their newfound political clout on the problem of the nonjurors, successfully drafting a bill to moderate the Test Laws and pushing it through committee. But when the measure came to the assembly floor for an up-or-down vote, nineteen Constitutionalists stood up and walked out of the chamber, denying Republicans quorum and leaving the bill effectively dead on arrival. Constitutionalists regained control of the assembly the following session and rejected with enthusiasm petitions from individual nonjurors seeking accommodations, promising that colonists who had taken no part in the establishment of independence could never expect to share in its benefits.[35]

Despite these early successes in the first battles over the Test Laws, however, Constitutionalists soon found themselves losing the war. Republicans won another majority in the Tenth Session of the General Assembly in 1785 and 1786 and once again began the process of dismantling the oath system. In March 1786, at the urging of Benjamin Franklin, new president of the executive council, Republicans passed a bill reopening the oath period and allowing all nonjurors who had failed to swear allegiance early in the war a second chance to join the polity. Since "the independence of America is established, and a general peace concluded," legislators wrote, it was time to afford nonjurors "another opportunity of testifying their allegiance and fidelity." In March 1787 Republicans acted again to relax the language of the pledge, abandoning the section about abjuration of the British Crown and requiring only that Pennsylvanians swear a simple oath declaring fidelity to the state. The long and bitter struggle over the Test Laws finally ended in 1789 when Republicans in the assembly officially repealed any and all laws connecting the rights of citizenship to an oath of allegiance.[36] By the end of the decade, the vast majority of former nonjurors enjoyed the same civil and political rights as other Pennsylvanians.

Historians have yet to understand fully the process of reintegration that transformed nonjurors from suspected enemies of the Revolution into citizens in postwar Pennsylvania. Surely identity politics and self-interest help explain why Republicans struggled to emancipate the nonjurors, why nonjurors decided to throw their support back to the Republican Party, and why Constitutionalists fought to obstruct the whole process. The sudden infusion of so many new voters did in fact dramatically alter the delicate political balance in postwar Pennsylvania, giving the Republican Party the electoral clout to implement its political agenda—be it, as progressive historians theorize, a campaign by socioeconomic elites to consolidate political power, or, as Owen Ireland suggests, an effort by one religious and ethnic coalition to dominate another. But when Pennsylvanians actually wrote or spoke about the fate of nonjurors after the war, they argued about much more immediate and practical questions: the problem of managing a large population of suspected political dissidents in the wake of a long, violent, and only delicately settled civil war. Before Pennsylvanians could reckon with nonjurors as prospective social, economic, religious, or ethnic actors, they had to come to terms with them as nonjurors—that is, as people who had refused or neglected to commit wholly to the very making of the independent state itself.

In this sense the reincorporation of the nonjurors in Pennsylvania was part of a Union-wide debate about the status of Loyalists, neutrals, pacifists, equivocators, side switchers, and a great variety of other political suspects who remained in the United States after the war. In Pennsylvania, as in other states, victorious Patriots had to decide what to do with the losers of the Revolution. The continuing presence of large populations of defeated people forced Americans to confront crucial questions about the boundaries of citizenship, the proper balance between the security of the state and the rights of individuals, and the ultimate legacy of the struggle for independence. And in Pennsylvania, as in other states, the vast majority of lingering political suspects ultimately managed to rejoin new political societies. The ironic result was that the debate about nonjurors—Pennsylvanians who were never sure they wanted a Revolution—played a critical role in determining what that Revolution would mean.

Aaron Nathan Coleman

Justice and Moderation?

The Reintegration of the American Loyalists as an Episode of Transitional Justice

The American Revolution was a civil war. Not only did it pit England against its own colonies over questions of who would govern, but it also divided communities and whole colonies as well as neighbors and families. A consequence of this intracolonial division was a conflict that, at times, spawned intense violence and brutality. Nor did these animosities end with the war. Most Americans, flushed with victory, used the immediate postwar period as an opportunity to exact legal and extralegal retribution against those Loyalists who remained in the United States. Not all Americans accepted this postwar treatment of Loyalists, however. Some advocated that the Loyalists' conscious decision to restart their lives in a republican America afforded them with the same legal rights and liberties cherished by victorious Americans. In essence, then, contest over the reintegration of the Loyalists represents a moment of transitional justice, of when Americans, emerging from the aftermath of a civil war, wrestled with the idea of accepting former enemies as equal citizens. Situating the reintegration of the Loyalists as an episode of transitional justice can help clarify how Americans understood the Revolution.[1]

Originating in the fields of law and political science, transitional justice focuses on the political and legal aftermaths of violent civil wars. It provides a theoretical framework for how the victors in a conflict can transition to a peaceful democratic political order while also ensuring that the rights of the defeated are restored and respected.[2] Developing as it did in the late twentieth and early twenty-first century, transitional justice studies have focused primarily on Cold War Europe, South Africa's transition from apartheid, and instability in third world countries such as Iraq. With few notable exceptions, historians have been excluded from the field of transitional justice. This is unfortunate, especially since the foundations of transitional justice are rooted in history and historical events. Any effort to address past wrongs is inherently an exercise of history. Ronen Steinberg has ably revealed how historians, with their special concern for the contextual complexities of the past, can provide transitional justice studies with a level of contextual analysis often missing in those works.[3] Not only this, and despite the claim of one of the leading scholars of transitional justice, history is full of moments of transitional justice, such as the reintegration of the Loyalists after the American Revolution, where victors in a civil war had to address what was to become of the losing side.[4] Transitional justice scholars, therefore, can learn from the past how certain people, operating within their contextual time and place, transformed their recent strife into a lasting reconciliation. By studying how historians can reveal the contextual complexities of the past and the various choices and reasons behind a historical peoples' decisions, transitional justice scholars can gain an appreciation for how historical reality can reveal the practical limitations of theory. History can also provide real examples of how a society overcame the difficulties in transitioning from a civil war to a universal respect for liberty and the rule of law. At the same time, historians must be careful when borrowing theoretical frameworks from political and social sciences. They must resist the temptation to make theory fit into the complexity of the past. Historical events do not unfold in any theoretical fashion or mold. When used properly, however, scholars of transitional justice and historians can learn from one another how one postwar society sought justice through admixtures that were part ideology and part improvisation.

Lustration of the Loyalists

As transitional justice studies reveal, lustration efforts, the attempt to purge undesirables from the new political order, are among the more common features of any civil war and its immediate aftermath. These purges occur in the belief that those who supported the previous regime are undeserving to participate in the new civil society.[5] The Revolution had this type of lustration as Loyalist officials, such as Thomas Hutchinson, voluntarily abandoned their positions and fled the colonies.[6] Yet the forcible removal of Loyalists from positions of authority represented only a minor part of the overall effort to purge Loyalists through legal and extralegal means. The American Patriots supported the punishment of Loyalists not only because they remained committed to the British Crown, but also, more important, because their presence threatened the political ideas of a virtuous citizenry that Americans considered fundamental for republican government.

Most accounts of the Revolution fail to appreciate the speed with which Patriots seized control of the disintegrated colonial government, which allowed them to move against their foes before the Loyalists could react. Interestingly the first legal punishments against Loyalists came with the Continental Association of 1774. Enacted by the First Continental Congress in October of 1774, the association, while concerned principally with establishing nonimportation of British goods, nevertheless recommended that local communities observe "the conduct of all persons touching upon this Association," which, in a practical sense, meant everyone. If a majority of the members of local committees were satisfied that a violation had occurred, the violator was to be branded a "fo[e] to the rights of British-Americans . . . universally contemned as the enem[y] of American liberty . . . [with] all dealings" ceased.[7]

Upon declaring independence, and taking their cue from the Congress, the states enacted a series of antiloyalist measures. Generally state legislatures passed seven forms of legislation against Loyalists. Those forms included Test Acts, which forced Loyalists upon pain of punishment to swear allegiance to the American cause; acts limiting the political speech and action of particular individuals; acts disenfranchising Loyalists or removing them from any public office; acts quarantining, banishing, or otherwise expelling Tories from the state; acts making it a crime to adhere to Great Britain; and acts taxing, amercing (i.e., fining), or confiscating Loyalists' land. Finally a number of states enacted a number of Bills of Attainder that accused and convicted, without a trial or jury, a suspected Loyalist of treason. Pennsylvania, for example, attained for treason and sentenced to death 490 people. Some of these laws came at the behest and recommendation of the Second Continental Congress—such as the Test Acts and those related to the confiscation of property—while the rest derived from the states themselves.[8] Overall, and with no exceptions, the Patriot government practiced legal lustration on a wide basis.

The most common forms of violence visited upon the Loyalists were extralegal and retributive actions designed to punish Loyalists for not supporting the American cause. A particular favorite form of violence among Patriot forces was the riding of a rail, known as "Grand Toory Rides." The procedure included forcing a narrow rail between the (always male) Loyalist's legs. Patriot groups would then lift the rail and carry the Loyalist along, all the while bobbing the rail and forcing the Loyalists to bounce along it, thereby causing obvious and great pain. Such was the fate of Dr. Joseph Clarke of Reading, Massachusetts. While in Hartford, Connecticut, a group seized Clarke because of his "firm Attachment to the King and Constitution" and forced him to ride a rail. Due to the pain, "he several times fainted," and his injuries were in such a "Manner as unfit for description in a News-Paper." Peter Elting commented on how Patriot groups in New York City forced a number of Loyalists to ride rails. As he wrote Richard Varick, "We had some Grand Toory Rides in this City. . . . Several of them were handled verry Roughly Being Carried through the streets on Rails, there Cloaths Tore from there [sic] backs and there Bodies pretty well mingled with the dust."[9]

The legislative and extralegal efforts against the Loyalists were typical of most civil wars where supporters on either side sought to punish their opponents. What makes the American Revolution unique, however, was the overarching belief among most Patriots that they were already a free people. The revolutionary effort to establish republican self-government, therefore, represented the attempt to conserve liberties from a despotic mother country. The difference, however, rested in the American belief that Loyalists lacked the republican virtue necessary to preserve liberty. Hence Americans viewed the legal and extralegal lustrations as a morally necessary to defend and purify their body politic.

Throughout the Revolution Patriots condemned Loyalists in general terms that revealed the influence of republican ideology upon their actions. As "An Inhabitant" argued in New York, supporters of England were guilty of being "some of the basest villains that ever disgraced any society."[10] Nathaniel Whittaker dedicated an entire sermon to the idea that since the Loyalists lacked republican virtue by placing their own self-interest above that of the community, they forfeited the protection of civil society and deserved punishment. He criticized Loyalists for being the "free-born sons of *America,* so lost to all sense of honor, Liberty, and every noble feeling, as to join the cry, and press for submission."[11] Nor was Whittaker alone in his ideological condemnation of the Loyalists. In *The American Crisis* Thomas Paine asked his readers, "And what is a Tory? Good God! What is he? . . . Every Tory is a coward, for a servile, slavish, self-interested fear is the foundation of Toryism; and a man under such influence, though he may be cruel, never can be brave."[12] Members of the Continental Congress, as well as their constituents, shared these sentiments. William Whipple confessed that he wished some states would adopt programs banishing Loyalists because they were "wretches" who would "ever . . . be curses to Society."[13] Legislative enactments directed at Loyalists often stated how their depravity necessitated the measure. Pennsylvania's Test Act of 1777 noted that "sordid and mercenary motives" forced the state to enact the law delineating between a virtuous Patriot and unnatural Loyalists. Maryland's "Act to Punish Certain Crimes and Misdemeanors, and to Prevent the Growth of Toryism" was even more explicit of the baseness of Loyalists when it stated that its clemency policy had failed to reclaim Tories "from their evil Practices," leaving them "still pursuing their dark and criminal designs of enslaving America." Delaware's "Act of Free Pardon," issued in the summer of 1778, acknowledged some Americans were influenced by the "deluded or wicked" into joining the British cause. Their pardon—like those issued by other states during the Revolution—allowed Americans to regain a virtue seduced away by Loyalists.[14] The Continental Congress made perhaps the boldest claims of Loyalist wickedness. In its January 1776 resolution, known as the "Tory Act," Congress noted that "and with respect to all such unworthy Americans, as regardless of their duty to their creator, their country, and their posterity, have taken part with our oppressors, and influenced by the hope or possession of ignominious rewards, strive to recommend themselves to the bounty of administration by misrepresenting and traducing the conduct and principles of the friends of American liberty, and opposing every measure formed for its preservation and security."[15]

Successful Loyalist reintegration would have to overcome these purges. Americans would have to accept Loyalists as equal members of their republican societies and possessing the same liberties as themselves. The immediate aftermath of the war, however, suggested a difficult reconciliation. Most Americans, seeing the defeat of the British as a vindication of their republican and constitutional beliefs, refused to accept those whose presence represented direct threats to the Revolution's foundations. As a result, in the immediate aftermath of the War for Independence, new and intensified rounds of lustration commenced.

From across the Confederation, numerous petitions from various local bodies and further antiloyalist legislation passed by several states all show the intense American desire to expel the Loyalists. Each of these actions, much like their wartime precursors, employed republican ideas in their salvos against returning or keeping Loyalists. A June 1783 proceeding of Freemen in Philadelphia held that Loyalists should not be readmitted into the City of Brotherly Love because Loyalists were "lost to all decency, virtue, and public spirit." Not only were they deprived of decency and virtue, but also their wickedness led Loyalists to feast "with a malevolent satisfaction" at Patriot sufferings. The Freemen informed the Pennsylvania legislature that they would take it upon themselves to measure the character of all entering strangers to determine whether they met the requirement necessary to be considered Patriot citizens. In Saratoga, New York, the site of the Continental Army's most stunning victory, another committee resolved that Loyalists should not be permitted to participate in the community. Using harsher language than most of these resolutions, the Saratoga committee argued that the Loyalists were a "species of villainy" that, if they could have worked their will, would have made slaves of Americans. The committee asserted that any Loyalist attempting to return to the area would be "treated with the severity due to his crimes and infamous defection." In the anonymously authored "Observer no. X", the author warned that the malice of the Loyalists would "sap the foundation of our great superstructure of independence" and would, if permitted to reside in Massachusetts, "intoxicate our youth" with vice. The only remedy was removing the Loyalists.[16]

These resolutions and writings condemned Loyalists on the assumption that they lacked the republican virtue required to put the community's interest above their own. These resolutions also belied a Patriot fear that should Loyalists be peacefully readmitted, they would infiltrate both society and government and fetter the populace with the tyranny just overthrown. Nathaniel Whittaker best exemplified this position. In his postwar sermon titled "The Reward of Toryism," the Massachusetts minister damned the Loyalists in ways that few others did. Whittaker charged Loyalists with a "savage barbarity" that celebrated the "torture and blood" of Americans. He claimed that anyone calling for the forgiveness of Loyalists' sins "must be very ignorant of the nature of a forgiving spirit, and of Christ's command too, who suppose that executing public justice on felons and murderers, is inconsistent therewith. Should this be admitted, we must resign all the good and happiness of society into the hands of thieves, robbers, and assassins. Love, forgiveness of enemies, and compassion, are most amiable virtues; but they degenerate into criminal weakness, as they spring from a vitiated heart, when they are employed to discharge criminals from consigned punishment." Whittaker did not deny the necessity of Christian forgiveness, but "God and reason teach that they who endanger the safety of the community should be removed from it; for the happiness of many is of more value than of a few: therefore, *we are bound to seek the good of the state, in preference to that of individuals.*"[17] The connection to Loyalists' lustration and republican ideology could not be clearer.

Forgiveness, Justice, and Reconciliation

Transitional justice studies note that among the more important elements of any post-civil-war conflict is the ability of the society to reconcile, to put away past animosities, and offer both legitimate justice and, if possible, forgiveness. Thus any successful reintegration required Americans to soften the radical appeals to virtue and focus instead on the more moderate strands of republican thought that stressed the rule of law and toleration. That reintegration did occur at all can be attributed to the efforts of a group of Americans who connected the idea of reconciliation to this moderate republicanism. By linking these two ideas, they convinced their fellow Patriots that the Revolution's success hinged on the forgiveness, justice, and reconciliation between former enemies.

Among the most important steps in the postwar reconciliation between Patriot and Loyalists emerged from Article 6 of the Treaty of Paris. Perhaps the most striking example of transitional justice in the entire American Revolution, the provision indemnified the wartime actions of both Patriots and Loyalists and prohibited any future persecution of Loyalists. In essence Article 6 called for the forgiveness that is fundamental for any post-civil-war context. It sought to end American persecution of Loyalists and start the process of rehabilitation, reconciliation, and reunification of the former antagonists. At the same time, by ending legal persecution of Loyalists, it provided for the possibility that Americans would personally forgive their Loyalist neighbors and allow the resumption of their lives as equal members of the community.

As idyllic as these notions seemed, the American peace negotiators were under no illusions about their immediate success. They realized that most Americans would be loath to forgive some Loyalists for their wartime actions. John Jay, the lead American negotiator on this issue, distinguished between two types of Loyalists. One group, he suggested, would never receive American forgiveness due to their actions during the war. Jay bluntly told British negotiator Richard Oswald that Americans would never "suffer them to live in their" country, "even although we had lands to set them down upon, nor would those Persons be sure of their Lives there." Yet this group "[was] not of any great Number." Jay's discussion of the second group, the "less obnoxious" Loyalists, which were those who remained loyal to the Crown but took little part in the war, demonstrated how the treaty would affect Loyalist rehabilitation. "The Clause of Amnesty," opined the former president of the Continental Congress, "would make all such of them as were not under Judgment, or Prosecution, perfectly easy in their several Stations; and he made no doubt but, after a Peace the several States would treat them with as much lenity as their Case would admit of. And the bulk of these being besides of low rank, they would successively fall into the Sundry Occupations of the Country, and so Government would be saved the Expense of transporting and subsisting them."[18]

Although the peace commissioners worried they may have "yielded too much in favor of the royalists," they believed the measures formulated "justice and good policy."[19] As it soon became clear, most Americans disagreed with the negotiators' conclusions. While Americans celebrated the ending of the war and the generous boundaries of the United States, Article 6 angered them greatly. In episodes that echoed wartime actions, state legislatures and other groups visited retributive legal and physical violence upon Loyalists in hopes of purging them from the community. A Boston town meeting also passed a resolution forbidding the return of any Loyalist, and it instructed the town's committee of correspondence to "oppose every Enemy . . . and declared Traitors to their Country." Loyalists throughout New York, and particularly in New York City, met a violent fate as New Yorkers tarred, feathered, and "whipped in the most inhumane manner" any openly avowed Loyalists. Dutchess County, New York, banished a known Loyalist who had resided peacefully in the country throughout the course of the Revolution. South Carolina witnessed perhaps the worst treaty-inspired violence. Throughout July 1783 Charleston, which the British evacuated less than a year earlier, was plagued with a series of violent mob riots, one of which burned a wharf owned by Christopher Gadsden, a supporter of the treaty, because it contained Loyalist goods. Another mob "pumped" several Loyalists who it believed were "obnoxious to the state." This mob also imprisoned Dr. William Wells, a Loyalist who had returned to the city to collect debts. When the mob action in Charleston calmed later in the month, a large town gathering numbering in the thousands met and resolved against allowing the return of any person who supported the British cause.[20]

While Loyalists faced extralegal action from local communities, state legislatures also reacted negatively toward the treaty's attempts to ensure Loyalist reconciliation. The Virginia legislature defeated a citizenship bill because the measure excluded from citizenship only those Loyalists who openly fought against Virginia and the United States. Earlier in that same legislative session, Patrick Henry suffered a rare legislative defeat when the Virginia legislature tabled his bill to lower barriers against immigration. His measure was in response to the governor's proclamation that barred the return of any Loyalist.[21] North Carolina joined its neighbor in denying citizenship to former Loyalists, as well as watering down an amnesty bill to render it ineffective and pointless. The state also enacted a measure that indemnified its citizens from lawsuits brought about by Loyalists. New Jersey, despite permitting Tories a generally peaceful reentry to the state, nonetheless enacted a measure that would render any Loyalist or otherwise suspected Tory "incapable forever" the holding of any public office. Massachusetts and South Carolina continued to sell off confiscated Loyalist property. In May 1783 New York passed its infamous Trespass Act, which allowed New York City Patriots who had fled when the British occupied the city to collect damages from Loyalists use of their property. New York added to the Trespass Act and joined Massachusetts in enacting legislation to continue the sale of confiscated Loyalist property. The Bay State also passed a measure titled "An Act for Asserting the Right of This Free and Sovereign Commonwealth to Expel Such Alien as May Be Dangerous," which declared that any person who voluntarily fled the state between October 1774 and 1780 had forfeited their rights to citizenship and property.[22]

All across the Confederation, local communities enacted resolutions or published instructions to their representatives urging state legislatures to hold the line against returning Loyalists. To a large degree, republican ideology drove the opposition to returning Loyalists. Allowing former enemies to live as equals would be "the worst of policy and the greatest injustice to the interest of the zealous supporters of our liberty."[23] These emotions derived from the fears of local residents—no matter how real or imagined—of the influence Loyalists might have upon the political and social character of their area. A meeting of the Worcester, Massachusetts, Freemen exemplified this attitude. "The sentiments of the absentees [i.e., returning Loyalists], their principles, their languages, and their feelings" are "fixedly opposed to those rights, and to that freedom" Patriot Americans shed blood for. As a result the town, as did so many across the country, voted not to accept any returning Tories, believing that the chance of former Loyalists becoming "good subjects" was "groundless and fallacious."[24]

At the same time as these new antiloyalist actions were occurring, a growing group of Americans began advocating for the end of the postwar violence and called for a peaceful assimilation of Loyalists. Although these protreaty and prore-integration Americans were never an organized group, they nevertheless offered similar arguments. They connected the failure to fulfill Articles 4, 5, and 6 of the treaty and allow the peaceful return of Loyalists to the legitimacy of United States and of the Revolution. If the guiding ideas of the Revolution rested upon the republican emphasis of self-government, liberty, and the rule of law instead of the purity of virtue, then failure to comply with the treaty, and the intensity of the antiloyalist violence that accompanied its reception, made those ideas seem hollow. In the vernacular of eighteenth-century America, at stake was the "character," or reputation, of the Revolution. As North Carolina jurist James Iredell reported to his wife, the violation of the treaty meant that "the national character [was] disgraced" and made the new country a place not fit to live. Thomas Jefferson echoed these sentiments, arguing that "proceeding in direct contradiction to" the treaty was "neither consistent with the faith of an honest individual nor favorable to the character of a nation which has that character to establish . . . or retrieve." It was Jay who best explained the problem. The "irregular and violent popular Proceedings and Resolutions against the Tories hurt us in Europe," he argued, because it validated the leading European belief that republican self-government was impossible. Thus by not carrying out the "good faith and sound policy" offered by treaty and taking the necessary steps in putting the war behind them, Americans were accountable for the potential failure of Revolution and its ideas of the rule of law and republican self-government.[25]

No American explained the connection of Loyalist reintegration and the objectives of the Revolution better than Alexander Hamilton. In early 1784 Hamilton published two lengthy newspaper essays (later published as a pamphlet) under the pseudonym of "Phocion."[26] The choice of the name was not accidental, and American readers, steeped as they were in classical history, would have realized immediately the author's intent. Phocion was the Athenian general who called for a peaceful coexistence with Macedonia.[27] By calling himself Phocion, Hamilton signaled to his readers that Patriots needed to accept their former enemies. Furthermore Hamilton's essays are among the most important writings of his life, ranking behind only by his contributions to *The Federalist* and his famous state papers as secretary of the treasury. Making these essays all the more remarkable was how they dealt with issues now commonly associated with transitional justice.

Like other proreintegration Americans, Hamilton tied the peaceful reintegration of the Loyalists and enforcement of the treaty to the success of the Revolution. Hamilton opened by noting that a stirring of "passions" was common during war, but with the war now over, New Yorkers—and by extension all Americans—had to replace them with policies of "equity and prudence" and the end of the "indiscriminate guilt" assigned to Loyalists.[28] He admitted that achieving these goals was difficult, since some "heated and inconsiderate spirits" continued espousing "inflammatory and pernicious doctrines" against the Loyalists. Although these castigators claimed that their attacks upon the Loyalists defended the Revolution's principles, Phocion advised his readers to ignore these "pretend" appeals. They came from "zealots . . . ignorant of the advantages of a spirit of toleration," who sought justification for "revenge, cruelty, persecution, and perfidy." Instead Hamilton appealed to what he called the real "spirit of Whiggism," which was "generous, humane, beneficent, and just." It "cherishes legal liberty, holds the rights of every individual sacred, condemns or punishes no man without regular trial and conviction of some crime declared by antecedent laws, reprobates equally the punishment of the citizen by arbitrary acts of laws as by the lawless combination of unauthorized individuals."[29]

Hamilton warned that ignoring the indemnification provision of Article 6 and further persecution of the Loyalists established a "dangerous precedent" for self-government. Indemnifying Loyalist actions represented a "dictate of natural justice, and a fundamental principle of law and liberty." To violate it willingly and deny those former Loyalists the equal rights that Americans possess violated the "eternally true" principles of the Revolution and presented ominous signs that self-government was devolving into arbitrary tyranny. To Hamilton "no middle line" existed between republican liberty and tyranny. Liberty in "its true sense must be the enjoyment of the common privileges of subjects under the same government." Thus a peaceful and fair reintegration of the Loyalists meant extending this definition to them. To have former Loyalists living as perpetual "enemies to the government" was "mischievous and absurd."[30] If Americans wished to "govern well," which was the only method to "perpetuate our liberties," then the "single interest of the community" was to follow the "dictates of moderation" rather than the radicalism associated with antiloyalist violence. "Justice and moderation," he assured readers, guaranteed the "surest supports of every government."[31]

Hamilton argued that following the policies of liberty, justice, and moderation meant that peace and reconciliation between Patriots and Loyalists could be achieved. With New York "affording them not only protection but participation in its privileges," these former Loyalists "will undoubtedly become its friends."[32] Failure to follow these policies, however, meant nothing short of the failure of the Revolution. Summing up his argument, he maintained that "if we set out with justice, moderation, liberality, and a scrupulous regard to the constitution, the government will acquire a spirit and tone, productive of permanent blessings to the community. If, on the contrary, the public   councils are guided by humor, passion, and prejudice; if from resentment to individuals, or a dread of partial inconveniences, the constitution is slighted or explained away, upon every frivolous pretext, the future spirit of government will be feeble, distracted, and arbitrary. The rights of the subject will be the sport of every party vicissitude. There will be no settled rule of conduct, but everything will fluctuate with the alternate prevalancy [sic] of contending factions."[33]

Hamilton, despite not having the vocabulary or legal equipment now commonly associated with transitional justice, nevertheless made the transitional justice case for why Loyalists should be reintegrated. His appeal to move past the wartime violence against the Loyalists and embrace policies of acceptance and toleration are the hallmarks of transitional justice. Nor was he alone. The South Carolina judge Aedanus Burke echoed Hamilton's call for reconciliation. Burke was intimately familiar with antiloyalist sentiment. In 1784 South Carolina charged Matthew Love with crimes committed during war. Troubled by the use of legal proceedings seemingly designed to punish Love for his wartime Loyalism, Burke annulled the charges. Upon learning of the decision, a mob formed and extracted its own justice by lynching the recently released Loyalist.[34] This firsthand experience fueled Burke's call for a restoration of peace and justice in South Carolina. He took particular aim at the state's antiloyalist legislation and a recent proclamation by the governor, John Rutledge, that denied suffrage rights to those who fled to Charleston after the British took control of the city during the war. Burke devoted an entire pamphlet to attacking the immoderate nature of the measures and the threat they posed to peaceful reconciliation.

Writing under the name of Cassius, one of Caesar's conspirators and the attempted saviors of republican Rome, Burke, like other proreintegration supporters, worried that the extreme antiloyalist sentiment in his state threatened the Revolution and the rule of law. He could not imagine why a "free country upon the earth" would engage in such radical behavior as to cause "such ruin on so many families" and "political mischief."[35] He admitted that most civil wars led to "miseries" on each side. These wartime miseries, however, should not extend to postwar peace. In fact a "reinstatement in the participation of their rights and privileges" should be one of the first actions once those troubles passed and normalcy returned. The governor's proclamation and the antiloyalist laws, however, threatened the "future peace and liberty" of the people.[36]

Burke reminded his readers how the rights of both Americans and Loyalists "were founded upon something other than parchment" and could not be tossed aside out of hatred, passion, or the "usurpations of a few."[37] They were permanent and applied universally, even to former enemies. The antiloyalist legislation, he warned, was not just "impolitic" but ranked among the "most serious proscriptions of which we have any account of in all history."[38] If his state did not repeal those measures and offered no reconciliation to Loyalists, history would remember only the immoderate radicalism of the Revolution.

Making this situation even worse, Burke contended, was how the law targeted those who fled to Charleston after the collapse of the Patriot government. Since the "sovereign power was in a state of temporary death," those who took refuge with the conquering power were innocent of treason; they had no other recourse. In fact those who sought safety in Charleston ranked among the strongest zealots for the American cause. It was these citizens, Burke implored, that "helped pave the way for reconciliation." South Carolina repaid that devotion by not only forgetting their efforts but also making them endure fear and abuse "as if they were convicts, and are now little better than vassals in their own city" forced to be "ruled and taxed without their consent."[39] Such actions, Burke maintained, mocked the Revolution, liberty, and the republican virtue displayed by these citizens.

South Carolina could rectify this problem by returning to the magnanimous principles of Revolution and passing an act of oblivion. Such a measure was "absolutely necessary to restore tranquility." Without "burying in oblivion past transactions," the civil war would continue "under the shape of justice, which is most oppressive, and of all other injustice, excites the great destination, and the most violent factions and division." It allowed the violent passions of civil war to persist unabated.[40] If this fear of perpetual civil war and false justice were not enough, Burke concluded by offering a prophecy. "God Almighty," he asserted, "has so ordered the affairs of men in this world, that a mischievous legislature, any more than mischievous individual, can never succeed in oppression and injustice without drawing down a curse and misfortune on itself. And should the legislature of South Carolina and Georgia persist in the fearful measure lately pursued, I make no ceremony to foretell, that we and they shall remain a conscious example with posterity, to prove, that people are incapable of governing themselves. Tyranny will be furnished from our history with another new example to establish her favorite principle, "'that mankind were destined by nature for slavery, and to be hewers of wood and drawers of water for one or a few.'"[41]

By linking peace, justice, and reconciliation with their former enemies to the larger ideas of the American Revolution, Hamilton and Burke influenced and shaped American thinking and policy toward reintegrating Loyalists. By 1787 practically every state had enacted some form of Burke's act of oblivion, which effectively forgave those Loyalists who stayed in the United States for their wartime allegiances. With these measures these former Loyalists resumed their lives and pursued their rights to liberty and happiness. At the same time, however, not all credit goes to Hamilton or Burke. There remained a final issue, one of historical accident and circumstance and unpredictable by theory, which helped cement a successful reintegration. That is the issue of time. By 1787 former Loyalists had had the time necessary to demonstrate that they would be peaceful and productive republican citizens. These displays of peaceful coexistence proved wrong the arguments of antireintegration forces and confirmed the transitional justice arguments of Hamilton and Burke. As Americans saw firsthand how former Loyalists adapted and embraced the new political realities, there remained little reason to maintain past antagonisms.

Historians and transitional justice theorists can learn from one another. From the wartime efforts at lustration to the reintegration arguments advocating justice, reconciliation, and peace, transitional justice studies can offer historians a framework to understand better and clarify the relationship between Patriots and Loyalists. Yet historians should be careful when using modern theoretical frameworks to explain historical events. Theory and reality are not the same thing. Transitional justice cannot explain why Patriots sought a lustration of the Loyalists, the underpinning ideas or motivations behind the Revolution, or why Hamilton and Burke believed Loyalist reintegration important for the Revolution's success. All it can offer is a methodology in which to better comprehend those events. The historian still has to offer contextual reasons as to why events unfolded the way they did. At the same time, and more important, transitional justice studies must acknowledge a space for historical context in the application of social and legal theories. The ideas underpinning transitional justice do not operate in a vacuum; they are applied to real people bound by contextual time and place. This human element must always be taken into account. For how a people and societies implement the ideas of transitional justice are contingent, in part, on their historical backgrounds. Transitional justice scholars cannot and should not expect reality to operate exactly as their theories explain. If the study of the past teaches anything, it is that events never unfold in a predictable or scientific ways. There are always human and societal explanations for the success or failure of transitional justice theory that history can assist in providing and clarifying. Put another way, any successful reintegration and transition always occurs in a contextual fashion. Transitional justice might be able to explain how a society can potentially overcome wartime evils, but understanding and appreciating historical contexts and contingencies can explain why the society surmounted them. Students of transitional justice can learn much from an appreciation for the contextual complexities of the past. Knowledge of history, then, can assist transitional justice scholars in understanding how conditions and circumstances shape the success of transitional justice.

Rebecca Brannon

America's Revolutionary Experience with Transitional Justice

Transitional justice is not an easy fit with the historical discipline. Most of the work in the field has been done by political scientists and law professors and tends to have a proscriptive tone—do x to avoid the terrible and destabilizing results of unbridled revenge. The field does not easily trade in doubt or (with a few notable exceptions) the idea that varied local circumstances effect what kinds of methods lead to successful transitions. Further the field of transitional justice as an approach only emerged in the 1990s and therefore has been born in and developed in a globalized world. Almost all examples of transitional justice depend on international organizations that supersede or work around nation-states. Since functional and powerful international, globalized organizations such as the United Nations NGOs are a recent invention, the theoretical apparatus of the field does not work easily for historical examples. Transitional justice has been most simply defined by field leader Jon Elster as "the process of trials, purges, and reparations that take place after the transition from one political regime to another."[1] While the theory does not technically require that either the old or new political regime be a democratic one, in practice the scholars using the theory do imagine it taking place in a democratic context and therefore see the successful practice of transitional justice as part of democratizing in the wake of the end of empire.

Perhaps most important, the field (with the exception of Elster) rejects history as a useful guide. Ruti Teitel, a leader in the field, begins her survey of transitional justice with the Nuremberg trials, and others also begin with this mid-twentieth-century example.[2] Elster is the rare transitional justice scholar who uses historical examples, and although he also works in the intensely theoretical language of many political scientists, when he works with historical examples he pays attention to the cultural differences in each example and even flags these differences for his readers. His more historically sensitive approach, in which he refuses to slap one model on all situations, has not become the leading one.

And yet historians keep trying to tell transitional justice scholars this is a mistake. Transitional justice may be the term and theory currently in vogue, but conflicts are as old as time, and many societies, even premodern ones, have devised ways to bring about both a successful political transition and buy-in from people who felt that they had been heard and justice was served. Ronen Steinberg (in French Revolutionary history) and Aaron N. Coleman (in this volume) have each tried to show how historical examples of transitional justice can refine the field.[3] I wish them luck, but I am not convinced historians can get transitional justice scholars to listen. Instead I wish to consider how we historians can take the methods of analysis and language of transitional justice and use it to understand the strategies and approaches that allowed Americans to reconcile after the brutal civil war of the American Revolution. Perhaps this approach can show an underlying order to what seems a veritable smorgasbord of laws and approaches enacted in thirteen separate states at different times. Further I suggest to transitional justice scholars that this is an interesting corrective to the blindness inherent in an approach to ending conflict that exclusively relies on empowered international organizations in an age of globalization. Our current era of transitional justice is really underwritten by and created by the end of empire, which gave rise to a vigorous international infrastructure capable of intervening around the globe in the democratically inclined detritus left by the collapse of empire. At a moment at the end of the eighteenth century when the disgorgement of empire and the rise of independent democratic nation-states had just begun, how did approaches to transitional justice shape the rise of such democratic nation-states?

The Coordination of Wartime Transitional Justice

Part of what is maddening as a scholar of Loyalist reintegration and American experiences with transitional justice, but is very telling about the way the new United States worked, is that while purges (lustration) of the Loyalists were coordinated by national policy during the War for Independence, after the war the issue of transitioning to reintegrating former Loyalists was handed back to the states and often devolved to local control. There was no genuine national policy for or against either reconciliation itself or any particular approach to bringing about a successful reintegration. Instead successive congresses stepped aside while offering vague bromides. Public intellectuals in the states offered individual appeals in state newspapers but did remarkably little coordinating with each other. Each state formulated its own response to the pressing issue of instituting transitional justice. While advocates of different approaches to the problem of transition certainly read newspaper accounts of other state's efforts to deal with "the Loyalist problem" and used favorable examples at times to make their case, there was remarkably little coordination across states. Yet this determined resistance to a national attempt at transitional justice (and Loyalist reintegration) obscures the reality that there was a national movement toward increasing leniency toward many former Loyalists and a commitment to integrating them within the new democratic nation.

The infant United States had a coordinated national policy toward the Loyalists even before the shooting began in 1775 and certainly before the words of the Declaration of Independence strove to make the Revolution a war for a lofty vision of human liberty. While policies were legally enacted by the individual states, as befitted the vision of maintaining power at the state level encapsulated in the Articles of Confederation, the battery of Test Acts and treason legislation passed by each state was actually instigated by Congress, which specifically enjoined such legislation on the states. The national policy was coordinated less out of a vision of transitional justice, however, than a desire to discourage opposition to the new Patriot government in the midst of a civil war.

On March 4, 1776, on the eve of the beginning of the second year of active campaigning in the Revolutionary War, the Continental Congress pressed all states to disarm all those who were "notoriously disaffected." The effort to control Loyalists was therefore born from military necessity—the problem of waging civil war and a war against an external enemy at the same time. Congress found it vital to the war effort to dissuade the wavering disaffected from siding with and aiding the British army—so much so they encouraged all states to make harassment of Loyalists their legal position. The few committed Loyalists, especially in states without war on their doorstep, would leave for British-occupied stronghold cities, while the larger number of moderate and disaffected people would be effectively neutralized by the threat of losing their property. In response all of the states quickly passed Test Acts by 1778. Massachusetts passed the first Test Act in barely three months after the congressional mandate. Pennsylvania followed in June 1777. Every other state passed a Test Act, even those that were otherwise sympathetic to the disaffected and Loyalists in their midst, such as Rhode Island.[4] These were largely meant to pressure wavering disaffected men into taking the oath, thereby separating a few diehard Loyalists from the rest of the pack.

Test Acts required all adult males to take an oath of loyalty and military support for the new, democratic Patriot regime and to have that oath publicly recorded. In practice men also had to keep the piece of paper recording their oath and be prepared to produce it in case their loyalty was later questioned. The Test Act "proof" therefore came to function as a mandatory Revolutionary-era form of identification. Penalties for refusing the oath differed from state to state but included disenfranchisement from the vote, inability to hold office, and of course extralegal punishments such as public humiliation and constant fear of physical harm. Such incapacitations are typical of transitional justice regimes around the world today, but these drew on imaginative uses of traditional common-law restrictions. The incapacitations struck at both economic independence and civil belonging. Rhode Island offered the least restrictive incapacitations, merely making non–oath takers unable to bring suit in court. The vast majority of states drew up more comprehensive legal incapacitations striking at citizenship, drawing salaries from the public coffers, and even buying and selling real estate without encumbrances.[5]

Most states also supplemented the initial Test Acts with later, harsher legislation titled treason acts and/or confiscation acts. These drew up specific lists of individuals who faced legal purge from the states. These acts confiscated all property (real and moveable), denied citizenship and revoked all accompanying rights and protections, and enforced both with the threat of levying the traditional punishment for treason—death—if named Loyalists did not heed the law and leave the state. Most of these harsh laws protected legal dependents, such as aged parents, minor children, and wives, although South Carolina was notable for deliberately stripping families of property rights along with male Loyalists. Other states at least guaranteed the historic dower right of one-third of the estate for wives (and through them minor children's support).[6] While only a fraction of the total Loyalist population were specifically identified in these treason and confiscation acts, the idea was to expel the most "obnoxious" Loyalists (those who had served the British as army officers or high-ranking civil officials, often in charge of expropriating profits from Patriot estates during the war) and expropriate their property. The wartime purges and incapacitations were a deliberate national policy of transitional justice in a nation struggling to make any workable national policy at all. Loyalist policy was one of the few things Patriot Americans agreed with one another about.

Peace treaty negotiations opened up the issue of transitional justice as a national concern. Individual states were continuing to both reconsider and refine their individual approaches to transitional justice, but the decisions the nation would make in negotiating the treaty would have implications for the entire project of transitional justice. The status and fate of the American Loyalists was a central point of the negotiations. The American negotiators for the final peace treaty were resistant to any enforceable agreement to ameliorate the condition of the Loyalists, but they were eager to secure a treaty that guaranteed American independence, including of all the major American cities that were occupied by the British as the peace treaty was signed. The Americans had never managed to dislodge the British from these cities, despite many attempts, and a treaty could potentially mean the British just stayed in all the territory they held. Americans became insistent later in the negotiation process that they keep fishing rights in British Canada.[7] In order to achieve these other aims, American negotiators were willing to do something in response to consistent British pressure to allow Loyalists to return and reclaim their property after the conclusion of the war. The British negotiators naturally argued that Loyalist reintegration and complete restoration of property and citizenship was necessary in order to effect justice, but their real (and obvious) motivation was to limit the need for the British to offer financial redress and ongoing support to the Loyalists. On the other hand, the

British negotiators represented a government eager to end the war and also every bit as eager as the Americans to resume trade (as the British Caribbean planters badly wanted to continue their trade with the new United States, which, Ruma Chopra points out in her essay for this volume, had other consequences), and so they were also under pressure to sell out the interests of the Loyalists if necessary.

The eventual provisional and final peace treaty contained three provisions touching on the issue of Loyalist integration. Article 4 guaranteed all debts contracted before the Revolution and was fairly uncontroversial at the national level, although many southerners were resistant to paying back their prewar debts to British merchants. Article 6 barred any state from additional confiscations after the treaty date, closing the door on any additional efforts to punish former Loyalists through economic means. Statutes of limitation are customary in current transitional justice efforts and may in fact be absolutely necessary in order to guarantee a stable reconciliation. While there was some comment at the town level against this provision, for the most part people accepted the idea of a statute of limitations moving forward. States had already purged many Loyalists and enforced incapacitations on others, and so barring additional new confiscations was unlikely to change anything.

The most controversial section was Article 5, which called on Congress to "earnestly recommend it to the legislatures of the respective states to provide for the restitution of all estates." The language of the treaty made it clear that unsold estates were supposed to be returned to the original owner, and estates that had already been disposed of were to be fairly recompensed by the state. Further it guaranteed all former Loyalists one year of free, unfettered ability to live in and travel around the United States. Ostensibly this was to allow them to reclaim their property and to collect any debts. But in practice it also offered an open door to Loyalists determined to reoccupy their property and reestablish vital social relations in order to launch a full-scale effort at full redemption. Courts were enjoined to allow people who had legal claims to previously confiscated estates to pursue the "prosecution of their just rights."[8]

At the time absolutely no one was happy with the terms of the peace treaty. Parliament was horrified by the settlement terms for former Loyalists, in several cases terming them "dishonorable." Two British negotiators resigned from the peace commission over what they correctly identified as weak protections for American Loyalists. On the other hand, many Americans were enraged when the peace treaty provisions regarding Loyalists were read aloud in American towns and cities, and in some places they rioted and turned to public humiliation against a handful of especially disliked Loyalists. Americans did not seem to notice that all provisions for the protection of the Loyalists were in fact cynical. John Adams laughed to his fellow negotiator Henry Laurens that "our countrymen love Buck Skins Beaver Skins, Tom Cod & Pine Trees too well, to hang their Ministers for accepting them, or even for purchasing them by a little too much 'Reciprocity' to the Tories." As Adams noted, securing the rights of trade was more important than denying Loyalist restoration on principle.[9]

The Loyalists themselves felt slapped in the face. Loyalist refugees in England complained vociferously about being so poorly treated. One angrily called it an "Irish peace" designed by "old coblers" who were blinded by age and by implication had lost their mental capacities as well. Thomas Hutchinson Jr., a descendant of a wealthy and powerful Massachusetts family, termed himself a "beggar" in the wake of the treaty.[10] The Loyalists in England at the time of the peace treaty were right to be outraged—because they were right to understand that their interests were central to nobody and that neither the British nor the American Patriots would uniformly offer them full economic and social restoration just because the treaty "recommended" it.

The reality was that the controversial Article 5 had merely "recommended" an end to confiscation and purges, and negotiators on both sides had deliberately designed language that carried no real weight. Laurens, one of the American negotiators, wrote his relative James Laurens that the treaty called for "Congress to recommend to the several States restitution of Estates which had been confiscated" but reassured him that he should "observe tis to be a *recommendation*" (emphasis added). The language making it a recommendation only meant that the individual states could feel free to ignore any instructions to ameliorate the legal condition of the purged Loyalists. American negotiators made it clear in an official joint letter home a month before the treaty took effect that all of the language in the treaty was intended as a loophole requiring nothing. "The Words for restoring the Property of *Real British Subjects* were well understood and explained between us not to mean or comprehend American Refugees. . . . This mode of Expression was preferr'd by [the British negotiators] as a more delicate Mode of excluding those Refugees." American negotiators made it clear in their individual and official joint communications home that the problematic Article 5 of the treaty was specifically intended to pacify the Loyalist refugees in London, so that the British did not have to deal with them. It did not require any American state to readmit them or restore their property. Further Americans in power made it clear to the British, even to British commanders before withdrawal, that the national government could not "make the least interference" in the "civil Laws within the several States." No one in any official position ever expected that the peace treaty would require, or even encourage, movement in reintegrating Loyalists.[11]

Transitional justice would have to come from within American society itself. This is a lesson to the contemporary field of transitional justice studies. American society proved to be able to effect transitional justice ultimately leading to the reintegration of many former Loyalists and bringing about reconciliation—and did it from inside, rather than being strong-armed by an international organization. The only international obligation was the peace treaty, and it did not require transitional justice or final reintegration. The work of healing would come from within.

Retribution Culture and the Importance of Incapacitations

Transitional justice regimes commonly use purges of undesirables, public trials of symbolic figures of clear public interest, reparations to those who were victimized under the previous regime, and incapacitations and gradations of punishments for many of the accused victimizers. As Elster has pointed out, these do not always map perfectly onto the conditions in the wake of a civil war such as the American Revolution.[12] Yet it turns out that during the war, and in the years thereafter, Americans did in fact clarify their wartime system of purging undesirables, conduct trials of a few accused Loyalists, and require reparations from many Loyalists seeking reintegration.

Individual state laws were a hodgepodge of forms of punishments and limitations on former Loyalists after the war, and yet a careful examination makes it clear Americans settled on purges of a small minority and reparations from and incapacitations for many more. Further, over the first few years after the Revolution, all states increasingly relaxed both written laws and the application of those laws in favor of solutions compatible with the goals of transitional justice: to move society from purges and punishments to reincorporating Loyalists with full social and political belonging.

Wartime purges continued after the Revolution. Confiscation and treason acts passed during the war, listing specific Loyalists by name, were expanded after the war. South Carolina, for example, passed a confiscation act in 1782 with some three hundred names.[13] In almost all cases nationwide, the Loyalists who were targeted by these legislative purges were what Americans called "notorious," by which they meant Loyalists who had taken up arms against the United States or participated at a high level in wartime occupation administrations. Further, generally only those who had served as military officers, rather than enlisted men, were named in official legislative purge acts such as the confiscation acts. Massachusetts and South Carolina also crafted provisions for officially confiscating and selling estates left behind by Loyalists who, while not appearing on official legislative purge lists, had nonetheless left the state by the end of the war. In many cases these men had fought for the British and had been driven off by their Patriot neighbors through threats of extralegal justice.

Transitional justice in the postwar United States gradually moved from an emphasis on retribution, best epitomized by legislative policies pursuing property confiscation and expulsion, to a model of reintegration with significant incapacitations in order to both pacify angry people wanting retribution and to reassure more tolerant people that going forward reintegrated Loyalists could not pose either a military or political threat. These incapacitations were popular with the people, who saw them as a sensible method of containing possible threats and expected that former Loyalists should quietly accept such incapacitations of their full citizenship as a merciful and needed limitation that was part and parcel of a sane method of transitional justice. It was elite intellectuals who grudgingly acceded to the incapacitation model of transitional justice implemented by most American states only to try to move Americans to a model of full reintegration without limitation.

Retribution and incapacitations could go hand in hand in assuring Americans that justice was served to those who, as the instructions to the American negotiating team for the peace treaty explicitly said, "are considered here as the authors of the war." Robert R. Livingston continued in his charge to the treaty negotiating team that those who "have lost relations and friends . . . been robbed and plundered, or who have had their houses burned and their families ill treated by" the Loyalists would "in despite of all law or treaties, avenge themselves" if they had the power to do so and did not feel justice had been served.[14] Clear governmental retribution could head off more threatening postwar extralegal retribution. Samuel Adams, a leader of the opposition to Loyalist reintegration in Massachusetts, argued that the inevitable "Mutual Hatred and Revenge" between Patriots and Loyalists would mean endless conflict. He was representative of a common argument that the only real justice available was to continue the course of purging Loyalists and insisting on incapacitations.[15]

Postwar retribution could be, depending on one's vantage point, either capricious or the product of carefully thought-out, individualized, quasi-juridical evaluations. Loyalists often complained that retribution was levied without regard for the facts or justice, and some of their allies against confiscatory regimes agreed. In South Carolina antiretribution advocate Aedanus Burke characterized the place of retribution in a transitional justice scheme as necessary in very small doses but unpalatable in general. He argued that South Carolina's confiscation act functioned as an escape valve "to satisfy publick justice, and as you would throw a Tub to a whale to satisfy the vengeance of those who have suffered." Again and again Americans supported the necessity of visible retribution as a necessary part of healing after a brutal civil war and regime change. State-organized retribution was an important part of American's approach to transitional justice.[16]

Reparations are often popular in transitional justice schemes now as well as in the Revolutionary example. They serve the desire for justice as well as retribution. In the American Revolutionary example, reparations flowed to the state rather than to individuals. Nonetheless it is clear that property confiscation was in fact a system of reparations. The people as a whole collected the reparations through the mechanism of the state coffers. This becomes clearer when we consider the stated justifications and reasoning for both confiscation and for what they called amercement and we might term reparations through confiscatory extra taxes. In South Carolina the author of antiloyalist legislation Edward Rutledge advocated for amercement—a one-time tax penalty or reparation to the state of 12–25 percent of the total net worth of the family. Rutledge defended reparations since he did "not know one [Patriot] who would not be very glad to have lost no more than

25 per Cent^{m}" of his own net worth. American Patriots who had been plundered during the war, had their own property destroyed, or risked their life for the cause of the United States wanted to see Loyalists pay reparations. Some legislators justified reparations under a quarter of the estate as comparable to the cost of hiring a substitute soldier in one's own place (a legal practice during the war). In South Carolina one legislative committee defended maintaining the requirement for reparations even after the war ended by arguing that many Loyalists who were subject to reparations had unfairly profited from Patriots during the war. Or as they put it in the case of a Charleston blacksmith, we "think as he must have made large Profits by his Occupation during the British residence here, that he ought to pay Twelve per Cent."[17] A wide spectrum of American society approved of reparations and justified them again and again.

Patriot governments and leaders in all the states consistently hoped that reparations, through the mechanisms of confiscation and amercement, offered the government an easy source of "free" money. In Massachusetts, Joseph Palmer hoped that the sale of confiscated property "will Sink a very large part of the public debt." In South Carolina legislators used it as a slush fund for any pet project from mahogany chairs for the legislators to new schools and western land improvements. Individuals were not paid directly, but reparations could help them rebuild while lessening the overall tax burden. In Pennsylvania during the war, ordinary people petitioned to increase the tax burden on nonjurors and Loyalists, seeking to burden them with double taxes. Americans were certainly aware that the more the Loyalists contributed to the treasury in one way or another, the less everyone else would pay.[18]

This desire for easy money to lighten the load of driving the new nation forward may help explain why many Americans were increasingly receptive to allowing Loyalist refugees to return years after the war so long as they did not challenge the wartime and postwar confiscation of all their property. In Pennsylvania Loyalists who had been purged were later readmitted so long as they accepted the past confiscation of their property as a fait accompli and did not challenge that loss. In Massachusetts a British investigator from the Loyalist claims commission who was sent to comb through the confiscation records in that state concluded that the system had been "complicated and contradictory." In fact he eventually concluded that the Massachusetts legislators had deliberately tried to use complication and duplication in order to make confiscation secure. A complicated scheme made it much more difficult to use the court system effectively to unravel its legal intricacies and reclaim money. (Sally E. Hadden has shown in this volume that even if former Loyalists did not profit from these laws, entrepreneurial lawyers certainly did.) Of course by the time the investigator made this report in 1787, many Loyalists had found redress and reintegration in Massachusetts, and the remaining minority had already been recompensed at least in part by the British government. The British investigator was as interested in seeking evidence for the British government that they had been cheated out of money by the Americans as he was in establishing justice in the United States for those Loyalists.[19]

Individuals also sought reparations through personal plunder and graft. In Massachusetts the din of complaints over plunder grew so loud that the committees of safety were forced to "recommend" Congress consider the problem. One Massachusetts Patriot woman described the "pretty good picking" in the plunder of abandoned Loyalist property. Further Massachusetts allowed dishonest claims against confiscated estates while administering them for years, such that even wealthy estates ended up insolvent. Such widespread graft, affecting at least one-fifth of such estates, showed the way in which private plunder and public indifference guaranteed that Loyalists would render reparations to someone, even if it was through extralegal means.[20]

Incapacitations on political rights, either permanent or for a limited time, are common parts of transitional justice schemes. These incapacitations were an important part of the Revolutionary-era effort at transitional justice. The field of transitional justice generally studies transitions toward democratic regimes. Certainly the victorious American Patriots would have characterized their own regime change this way. Usually incapacitations are restrictions on political participation in the new democracy. They can assure that people who demonstrably do not share the values of the new democracy cannot subvert it from within the system. Such political incapacitations were central to persuading Americans to accept former Loyalists in their midst. As Robert Livingston had argued in opposing the forced return of Loyalist refugees, "should they be permitted to reside among us, they will neglect no means to injure and subvert our constitution and government and to sow divisions among us, in order to pave the way for the introduction of the old system. They will be dangerous partizans of the enemy." Members of the Pennsylvania legislature argued that it was "impolitic and dangerous" to offer full reintegration without significant political restrictions, even disabilities. They phrased it as disallowing "common participation in the government so soon after the war" and defended the idea of disenfranchisement as a crucial incapacitation protecting the country and enabling reconciliation as a later possibility.[21]

While some elite intellectuals later attacked these civic and political incapacitations as second-class citizenship unworthy of a democratic county, at the time they were a vital part of a just transition and necessary for Americans to buy into readmitting Loyalists. Loyalist disenfranchisement was popular in South Carolina—even among those otherwise supportive of efforts to reintegrate Loyalists. Aedanus Burke later turned against what he called second-class citizenship, but in 1782, early in the movement of transitional justice, he approved excluding what he called the "Tory dead weight" in state elections. He complimented Gov. John Rutledge's "good policy in excluding from voting all such persons as had not borne arms" for the Patriots. He fleshed out the argument of many thoughtful Americans in favor of at least a period of disenfranchisement for former Loyalists as a vital part of being willing to accept them. Burke reasoned it was "madness to allow men to influence our Elections who had borne arms against us without giving some Test of their attachmt. to us." His telling understanding of transitional justice underlined the necessity of a staged transition, beginning with quite stringent controls and incapacitations for former Loyalists and slowly bridging to full incorporation with the benefit of trust rebuilt over time, or what he termed evidence of "their attachment to us."[22]

Voting restrictions were common in almost every state after the Revolution. New York, Connecticut, Pennsylvania, North Carolina, South Carolina, and Georgia certainly stripped specific Loyalists from holding elective office or voting in elections. William Siebert calculated that as many as half the adult men in Pennsylvania may have been barred from voting by these antiloyalist voting restrictions, although this would be substantially higher than in other American states.[23] These states also forbade Loyalists from holding public elected office or even any public office that paid a public salary, so that they would not benefit from state service or hold any office of trust while the people at large did not trust them. In Pennsylvania exceptions were made to allow proscribed Loyalists to hold a handful of offices such as overseer of the poor and tax collector that were historically very unattractive and therefore difficult to fill. They were the kind of public positions taken out of duty, and therefore since they offered only disadvantage, Loyalists could still hold them. Pennsylvania may have also gone out of its way to make unwanted public offices open to non–oath takers because there were so many of them compared to other states.[24] (See Brett Palfreyman's essay in this volume for an explanation of why Pennsylvania's religious pacifist non–oath takers were so different from other Loyalists.)

South Carolina gradually relaxed voting restrictions on former Loyalists, and the last restrictions were swept away with the new state constitution of 1790. Other states also did away with voting restrictions around 1789–90 in the wake of the new US Constitution and new state constitutions in several states.[25] In effect Loyalists who sought to be reincorporated into the new republican United States faced restrictions on their ability to vote for just over a decade, which is a classic example of a time-limited incapacitation. These states then transitioned away from disenfranchisement and went forward allowing former Loyalists full rights in a participatory democracy. States did away with restrictions on office holding as well, ending all efforts at state-sanctioned degradation of former Loyalists. In South Carolina several districts that were majority Loyalist during the war sent former Loyalists to the state legislature as soon as the bans were lifted, and those former Loyalists were duly seated.[26]

Legislatures also experimented with other kinds of incapacitations, but only disenfranchisement was widespread. Several states forbade Loyalists from serving on juries. North Carolina forbade them from bringing civil suits. Pennsylvania forbade them from buying and selling real estate, although that was relaxed more quickly than other restrictions after the war. North Carolina at one time also forbade white Loyalists from carrying weapons—a restriction otherwise only levied on slaves. Pennsylvania even forbade Loyalists from teaching school for a while, in order to guarantee that children were not being inculcated in antidemocratic beliefs.[27] Such diversity of approaches to incapacitations speaks to the wide variety of aims they served—and perhaps as well to the creativity of the American mind.

State legislatures overall were actually careful to limit the kind of incapacitations they levied on former Loyalists, especially after the war. The limitations they did impose had clear support from the people not only as punishment but also as a vital control on maintaining the values of the new democratic nation. Americans never levied what might be termed incapacitations of the right to earn a living. Historians have long argued whether professionals such as doctors and lawyers were overrepresented among the Loyalists, and also whether they were more likely to be readmitted after the Revolution.[28] And we commonly imagine all artisans as members of the Sons of Liberty, when in fact plenty of Loyalists came from the ranks of the artisans. State legislatures could easily have restricted the ability of former Loyalists to ply their trade, and artisans and professionals would have been easy targets for such restrictions. Their Patriot competitors could certainly have found it in their self-interest to limit their competition. There were wartime examples in which the British, egged on by angry Loyalists, at least considered imposing such work restrictions on the Patriots. In South Carolina one widely reviled Loyalist earned the opprobrium of Patriots precisely because he tried to convince the British to make it impossible for Patriot artisans to ply their trade in occupied Charleston.[29] Yet Americans chose not to hurt former Loyalists badly by ending their ability to earn a living. Planters lost their land but got the chance to start over. Those who labored with their hands and minds could carry on their professions.

Transitional justice in the United States also relied on extralegal violence and public humiliation in order to create a feeling among the formerly victimized (the Patriots) that justice had been served. The desire for retribution also encouraged extralegal violence, including murders, looting, and those classics of the American Revolution—public humiliations such as tarring and feathering and public whippings. Public humiliation was an important part of the pre-Revolutionary organizing, and it continued as a tool in the hands of militias charged with suppressing dissent in the midst of civil war. After the war public humiliation became a potent (if rare) tool in the arsenal of transitional justice. Specifically in the American context it functioned as a way to target a few particular, publicly visible returning Loyalists who large swaths of the society deemed unacceptable or at least questionable and make their public humiliation (but not death) the focal point for the revenge instinct. One Massachusetts man who returned to his home state just after the peace treaty was made public found himself run back out of town "with a handspike under his crotch, and a halter around his neck." One local newspaper reprinted their legislature's 1778 act purging Loyalists from the state alongside a threat to string up returning Loyalists on a nearby gallows.[30]

Overall Americans moved from a wartime culture of retribution to a culture of reintegration that relied on assuring Americans that justice was served through incapacitations on former Loyalists and reparations. In many cases these restrictions were relaxed by 1784 (a mere three years after Yorktown), suggesting it had been more important to most former Patriots that Loyalists faced these restrictions than that they were always enforced.

WHEN TRANSITIONAL JUSTICE WORKS: AMERICAN RECONCILIATION

The overall goal of transitional justice is of course to move past the period of transition and to achieve a just situation, acceptable and inclusive for all. Americans worked in the postwar years to use the tools of transitional justice to move toward reconciliation between Patriots and Loyalists. Such a reconciliation would make their democratic government stronger and more long-lasting, which was an attractive goal. So they strove to achieve a workable reconciliation.

One thing that transitional justice studies make clear is that no solution needs to be perfect—it just needs to be workable. Americans ended up offering reintegration to a majority of Loyalists but not all. Purges were an important part of the eventual reconciliation. This was not merely because angry Patriots needed sacrificial lambs, as men such as Aedanus Burke had charged, but mainly because the Patriots, who considered themselves the victims of a war fueled by Loyalists (however unfair that may be), wished to separate a few Loyalists who had been very involved in British war efforts from the majority of them, who had been what Patriots often derisively called "trimmers." Using the analogy of a vessel trimming its sails to the prevailing wind, Patriots meant that these Loyalists were motivated to choose the winning side but lost their bet. American peace treaty negotiators had been in step with Patriot Americans when negotiator Benjamin Franklin characterized most Loyalists as men of no "Principle" who had chosen the strongest side to "secur[e] Safety with a Chance of Emolument & Plunder." Similarly John Jay characterized such men as the "less obnoxious" Loyalists.[31] In every state the logic of confiscation and expulsion was to winnow through Loyalists to find the majority who were acceptable to the body politic while expelling those few who were unacceptable. Other transitional justice schemes in the contemporary world often accept the purge of a small number of "undesirables" just as the American revolutionaries did. What is remarkable in the American context is not that a successful move to reconciliation required purging undesirables but that in the end so few were purged.

Expulsion through the confiscation and treason acts only purged a few hundred Loyalists per state. Pennsylvania, for example, issued eleven separate proclamations against Loyalists and disaffected persons between 1778 and 1781, and in those proclamations listed some 500 names—more than many other states.

Combing through all other accusations, only another 148 people were accused of treason outside of those proclamations, suggesting that no more than 650 people were singled out by legislative act. When we consider the role of the courts and the legislative acts targeting specific crimes generally undertaken by Loyalists against the war effort (counterfeiting, robbery, etc.), there were around 1,400 accusations, and a majority of those who went to trial were convicted—at least during the war. Yet most sentences were ended or reduced, so that the overall effect of the system mitigated against the worst outcomes. Anne Ousterhout consistently found that Pennsylvanians reduced sentences and mitigated the harshness of their laws and court decrees in order to offer Loyalists, even those who fought for the British, pardons and safe residence in the state. Even in Massachusetts, where Loyalists had been expelled early in the war, at least one third of Loyalists who had been publicly identified as such never left the state. In South Carolina approximately 300 Loyalists were expelled via specific legislative action. Others from all states had of course fled the United States based on divining that their own chances were not good, but they had never been formally expelled.[32]

Americans also imposed reparations schemes that sounded much harsher than they worked out to be in practice, as every state hesitated to sell confiscated properties and to collect smaller reparations payments. Disappointingly for some, the total dollar value of reparations never amounted to much. Massachusetts only confiscated about 15 percent of all Loyalist-owned real estate, and much of that was reduced by graft along the way. It never yielded the state treasury much.[33] Ousterhout calculated that in Pennsylvania only 0.1 percent of all land in the state was sold as confiscated property, taken from 0.05 percent of the people.[34] In South Carolina most properties were eventually returned.[35] Far more people were threatened with forced reparations than ever actually paid them. In fact no state seems to have made very much money off the sale of confiscated property, despite big dreams.

After the war even Loyalists who had been expelled formally, and many who had been expelled by the fear of extralegal violence but who had never been formally purged, sought to reconcile with their former friends and neighbors and then their states. Individual well-connected Loyalists could often find prominent people to write in support of their efforts to be taken off of retributive legislation, even if those supporters were commonly harsh toward Loyalists in general. Thomas Brattle of Massachusetts was able to get the written support of John Adams, for instance. Peter Van Schaack gained the support of treaty negotiator John Jay, who even greeted him when he disembarked ship in New York in 1785 as a returning Loyalist. Henry Laurens of South Carolina may have been adamantly opposed to any provision for Loyalists when he negotiated the peace treaty ending the war, but he supported his kin Elias Ball in his quest to return to the state and reclaim his confiscated property. Such support proved to be crucial for individual Loyalists who wished to return. The fact that multiple individuals, and not always well-connected ones, needed to support each individual Loyalist's drive to evade being permanently purged indicates that community support was vital to the transitional justice regime and to moving it toward reconciliation.[36]

Loyalists began the hard work of reconciling with their angry Patriot peers. In Massachusetts Thomas Aston Coffin and Ward Chipman were pleased when former friends, who were serving in such distinguished roles as the president of Yale and lieutenant governor of the state, greeted them in a "most polite, friendly manner." Yet they were easily dismayed when three other men avoided them and did not wish to speak to them. They did not have thin skins. Rather they understood the need for widespread support in their efforts to reestablish themselves on a safe and equal footing. Similarly in South Carolina former lieutenant governor Christopher Gadsden terrified two Loyalist brothers and former friends of his when he refused to shake their hands and muttered they should be "hang'd to be sure." It was not likely that he would actually have them executed, but they were terrified because they knew they needed broad support in their efforts to reintegrate.[37]

Pennsylvanians began to consider individual petitions for reintegration as early as 1782. By 1783 Pennsylvania was willing to countenance the return of many Loyalists so long as they did not have to restore their confiscated property. They were resistant to a mass amnesty, however, preferring to handle it case by case and often on a local level instead. Samuel Shoemaker had made his Loyalist inclinations known far and wide, and in consequence had to flee to New York for much of the war. Like many male Loyalists throughout America, he left his wife on the family property in order to maintain claim to it—despite the fact, as Kacy Tillman shows in this volume, that his wife was also clearly a Loyalist as well. His wife wrote her husband urging him to come home in late 1783. She reassured him it would be safe for him to return as the "general temper of the people" had so relaxed toward Loyalists that many could walk the streets "without meeting any incivility or insult." Yet despite these assurances, Shoemaker did not decide it was safe to return until 1786. Oddly when he arrived he declared himself a British subject still—in other words a resident alien in what had once been his own country. Yet he was tolerated and allowed to live in peace. In contrast when Salem, Massachusetts, merchants and artisans allowed exiled Loyalists to return, they demanded that they "are to get down on their knees . . . and ask pardon." In Virginia's coastal regions, even Loyalists formerly convicted of treason were readmitted through court appeals whose success depended on the submission of supporting petitions from Patriot neighbors.[38]

Why were Americans willing to reintegrate so many Loyalists, so long as they got the chance to choose whose reintegration they supported? One factor was the passage of time. As years passed they were more willing to open their arms to Loyalists, even those who they had initially been hostile toward. Laurens had counseled as early as December 1782 that "a decent Time for recovery and deliberation" would make it more likely that Americans would reconsider harsh decrees against

Loyalists. Timothy Pickering of Massachusetts believed that "time, which works wonders," would allow the anger to dissipate. Again and again Americans explained themselves using the analogy that their tempers were like objects cooling over time. Transitional justice scholars rarely take into account the value of the passage of time in allowing a fuller reintegration, despite the promise of studies in transition. The American Revolutionary method of transitional justice suggests that even a few years can allow a much fuller reintegration even while serving the pursuit of justice.[39]

As the years passed, more and more states relaxed their legal prohibitions on Loyalists. South Carolina ended most of their expulsions in 1784. By 1787 even Georgia was willing to readmit former Loyalists and allow "many of them to live among us at their ease." Yet "as to the restoration of confiscated estates, it is an operation that none of our politicians have as yet ventured to propose." In Massachusetts historian David E. Maas established a general pattern of increasing reintegration of Loyalists after the war and especially from 1784 on. The state legislature gradually revised confiscation laws and relaxed restrictions on those Loyalists who did return to the state. Massachusetts settled into reintegration with Loyalists who were deemed wartime moderates (did not fight in the war) but sometimes insisted their estates remain subject to confiscation—essentially return with the acceptance of heavy reparations. By 1785 advocates for reconciliation in the state legislature began to advocate for amnesty for former Loyalists. Various iterations of legislative amnesty over the next few years attempted to end confiscation and other incapacitations for Loyalists in the body politic.[40]

Despite the convergence of all the states in pursuing transitional justice, it was never a national policy. Even when Congress notified the states of the formal peace treaty, including the "recommendation" on Loyalist-confiscated property, it chose not to push the states on ending their own schemes of purges and lustration. It deliberately failed to provide any formal instructions on confiscation. Elite authors in every state came to argue against the forms transitional justice had taken, especially against reparations and incapacitations, and yet the national government, jealous of its powers in other contexts, never advocated or intervened in the state discussions moving toward reconciliation. Thomas Jefferson made this point to the British envoy George Hammond in his defense of America's adherence to the peace treaty. His May 29, 1792, letter has been regarded as a masterful diplomatic state paper—one of the finest ever produced.[41] Alexander Hamilton of New York attacked the people he termed proponents of "disqualification and expulsion" and "advocates for legislature discriminations." For Hamilton these laws made a mockery of the protections of citizenship all Americans should have, instead cheapening citizenship for all by creating a second-class citizenship from the beginning. Burke of South Carolina was outspoken in his condemnation of ongoing reparations payments in the guise of tax penalties. He felt that forcing residents to pay reparations would only "irritate one half of the people against the other, and disgrace both. It will also serve to keep alive the memory of the troubles of the present day, which should be buried in oblivion." While Burke did not support expulsion either, he did believe that reparations and incapacitations such as voting restrictions simply kept people from the healing necessary for reconciliation. Hamilton agreed, arguing it was actually the best way to ensure that "a large body of citizens in the state to continue enemies to the government." Hamilton and others also argued that the national honor demanded that the Loyalists be fully reintegrated (see Aaron N. Coleman's piece in this volume for more on this argument), but there is little evidence that it was what ultimately convinced Americans.[42] Instead the passage of time made them less angry, and as more Loyalists were readmitted, it became easier to trust them and therefore to imagine relaxing all prohibitions against them.

Conclusion

Nationally the United States belatedly called for a national policy of amnesty for Loyalists long after individual states had muddled through their own versions of transitional justice. Congress was finally moved to intervene due not to internal issues but to diplomatic concerns. The US Confederation Congress had trouble persuading the British to turn over western lands and western forts to the United States as well as securing continuing advantageous trade agreements. Given the need to continue tricky diplomatic negotiations with the British, the Americans were seeking advantages and found the appearance of refusing to honor the 1783 peace treaty's Loyalist provisions embarrassing in this new diplomatic push. The British also chose to make it an issue in the 1790s, because they saw it as a way to evade their own treaty obligations to turn over control of interior lands. States were urged to pass a law reiterating that states could not pass laws superseding the treaty—hoping that this window dressing would suffice to win new diplomatic spoils. States complied in passing this new law, largely because it was meaningless. The treaty had only "recommended" reintegration and economic restitution. Nothing legally compelled any state to return property or end incapacitations of any kind.

By the end of the 1780s, reconciliation had progressed far enough that states were even willing to contemplate general amnesty acts, even though the passage of the new US Constitution, with its explicit assurances of rights for all, should have made the question of incapacitations against Loyalists moot. For example the Pennsylvania legislature debated a general amnesty for all disaffected persons in 1792—some five years after the adoption of the Constitution theoretically struck down all civil incapacitations on former Loyalists.[43] Yet Americans were by and large reluctant to actually pass general amnesty acts, despite the fact that they had embraced the majority of Loyalists, been reluctant actually to collect most reparations, and gradually had relaxed all legal incapacitations against Loyalists. Transitional justice had done its work and brought back former Loyalists, paced their reintegration into American society, and allowed time to heal all wounds. In one short decade, Americans readmitted the majority of Loyalists and relaxed restrictions against them, even though neither the national government nor any external or international power made them do it. Transitional justice can work from within.

Plagiarism and the Nationalist Uses of Loyalist History

Alexander Hewatt and David Ramsay

In the preface to his history of South Carolina, published in 1809, the Revolutionary historian David Ramsay acknowledged his reliance on the Loyalist Alexander Hewatt's history when he declared that it "was read with much more advantage—on it greater reliance was placed—and of it more use has been made, than of all the histories which had preceded."[1] Yet Ramsay's acknowledgment failed to disclose that he had copied and paraphrased extensively from Hewatt without providing citations, committing what would be considered plagiarism by modern standards; nor did he give any indication that the historian he had plagiarized so heavily from was a Loyalist. But how could so staunch a supporter of the American Revolution and nationalist as Ramsay was plagiarize from someone he had himself described as a "a great tory," whose "strong national prejudices against the American character" made him "not a safe guide" on the Revolution?[2]

The same question could be asked of Ramsay's contemporaries, many of whom had likewise plagiarized from Hewatt or from other Loyalist historians. Adhering to an editorial conception of authorship in which the historian's role was to compile and synthesize the words and knowledge of his predecessors rather than to create a new and unique work of his own, early national historians copied freely from each other as well as from other sources such as the *Annual Register*.[3] What is striking, then, is not that these historians plagiarized but that they had no qualms about copying from their Loyalist opponents when their goal was to vindicate the Revolution and promote nationalism. Among the other historians who plagiarized from Hewatt were John Marshall, Hugh McCall, François Xavier Martin, and William Gilmore Simms, while Ramsay, Marshall, and George Bancroft all plagiarized from the Loyalist historian George Chalmers, suggesting that American nationalist historians and their Loyalist opponents had more in common than has been commonly assumed.[4] Therefore in his use of Hewatt, Ramsay was simply one of the most prominent and influential examples of a larger tendency that puts into question the image of the Loyalists as "losers," defeated by both the outcome of the Revolution itself and the battle for historical recognition afterward. Far from failing to propagate his own counternarrative of the Revolution, as Bernard Bailyn has argued was the case for the Loyalist historians, Hewatt was in some ways the victim of his own success, as Ramsay absorbed and coopted his attempt at such a counternarrative for nationalist ends.[5]

Hence rather than a sign of lax or uncritical scholarship, Ramsay's plagiarism of Hewatt was an interpretive choice that at once revealed his connection to Britain and enabled him to distance himself from it.[6] While scholars have widely noted America's persisting attachment to Britain in this period, they have varied over whether this attachment was a sign of postcolonial dependence and insecurity or of America's growing confidence in itself as a nation.[7] Both were the case in Ramsay's plagiarism of Hewatt, demonstrating how the same mechanisms that limited the development of American national consciousness could also contribute to it. Yet if in drawing from Hewatt, Ramsay revealed his attachment to his British roots, he was drawing on those roots at one remove, since as a Loyalist Hewatt himself occupied a liminal status as both British and not quite British.[8] Thus for Ramsay the process of becoming American was not just a matter of unbecoming British but also one of unbecoming Loyalist.[9] Paradoxically, however, Ramsay divested himself of his Loyalist proclivities not by repudiating them but by assimilating them into his nationalist perspective, as he sculpted the material provided by Hewatt into his exceptionalist vision of the United States.

But what did it mean for Ramsay to unbecome Loyalist when the Loyalists differed so much among themselves? Significantly he drew much more heavily from Hewatt than he did from the Loyalist historian Chalmers's scathingly critical portrayal of the colonies. What made Hewatt's work so appealing to Ramsay—and so malleable to his nationalist purposes—was Hewatt's ambivalence about the colonists' relationship to nature, Native Americans, and slavery. That ambivalence aligned his views more closely with Ramsay's and enabled Ramsay to convert his claims for the colonists' allegiance to Britain into a basis for the exceptionalist belief in American superiority and uniqueness simply by extending his assumptions and shifting their emphasis. Yet the very affinity between them was also what made Hewatt's Loyalist perspective so threatening to Ramsay. Precisely because Hewatt's concerns resonated so closely with his own uncertainties, he could not just ignore Hewatt altogether. For the same reason, however, neither could he openly acknowledge and confront Hewatt's dissenting point of view without putting into question the legitimacy of the Revolution. Ramsay's way out of this dilemma was to obscure and deny the validity—and indeed the existence—of Hewatt's opposition by absorbing it into his own analysis and using it to reaffirm his faith in the Revolution, thereby revealing the extent of and limits to the reintegration of the Loyalists into American national consciousness.[10] Thus where scholars of American nationalism have pointed to how the exclusion of others served as an instrument of inclusion among white men, Ramsay demonstrated how inclusion could serve to exclude as he incorporated Hewatt's analysis only to invalidate his perspective and legitimize the exclusion of Native Americans and slaves from the polity.[11]

I

Ramsay could rely so heavily on Hewatt partly because of the similarities in their social and historical vision. Like Hewatt he combined a desire to preserve social order with a dynamic vision of commercial progress and affirmed a belief in human agency while still holding onto a faith in the divine. But in his appropriations from Hewatt's discussion of natural history, Ramsay paradoxically converted these similarities into a basis for differentiating the United States from Britain, shaping what he took from Hewatt into his nationalist vision of America's capacity to prosper as an independent country without falling prey to the corruption or disorder that had destroyed other republics. Thus he turned Hewatt's ambivalence about the relationship between the human and the divine into a foundation for American exceptionalism simply through a shift of emphasis that gave primacy to human agency without repudiating a belief in providence altogether.

Neither Hewatt nor Ramsay came originally from the colony that was the subject of their histories. Hewatt migrated to South Carolina from Scotland in 1763 to serve as the minister of the First Presbyterian Church in Charleston, while Ramsay moved from Philadelphia to Charleston in 1774 after training as a doctor. Both men became part of Charleston's leading intellectual circles soon after their arrival there, alike becoming members of the Charleston Library Society, the town's intellectual center and a hub for its political elite, Hewatt in 1765 and Ramsay in 1776. But where Hewatt became a close associate of the colony's lieutenant governor William Bull and other prominent Loyalists, Ramsay became a leading figure in revolutionary circles, serving as a member of the South Carolina legislature and as a delegate to Congress during and after the Revolutionary War. Although he avoided expressing open opposition to the Revolution, Hewatt was exiled to Britain in 1777 because of his refusal to renounce royal authority and swear an oath of allegiance to Congress. After leaving for Britain, Hewatt completed his history of South Carolina and Georgia, publishing it in 1779. For his part Ramsay started his first historical work, his *History of the Revolution of South-Carolina*, while exiled to Saint Augustine during the British occupation of Charleston, publishing it in 1785, and followed with his history of the Revolution in 1789 and his history of South Carolina in 1809.[12]

Originally published in London, Hewatt's history did not appear in an American edition until 1836. Although it did not achieve the same regard as Ramsay's histories did, it was widely known to early national American historians, reflecting the continued dependence on imports of English books that characterized American culture after the Revolution.[13] Hence Hewatt's history was favorably mentioned by the *Monthly Anthology* in 1807 and served as a source for such historians as John Marshall, John Drayton, and Abiel Holmes, showing that its circulation extended beyond South Carolina.[14] Ramsay's letter to Jeremy Belknap referring to Hewatt's history shows that he had access to the work by 1794, though he did not specify how he had obtained it. If he did not purchase it for himself, he could have accessed it at the Charleston Library Society, which listed Hewatt's history among its holdings in its 1806 catalog.[15] Ramsay in turn further disseminated the influence of Hewatt's work through that of his own history of South Carolina. Although it did not achieve the same eminence as his best-known work, his history of the Revolution, going through a total of only two editions, it was an important source for other nineteenth-century historians of the state, including Robert Mills and William Gilmore Simms, who in turn plagiarized Hewatt either directly or indirectly through their use of Ramsay.[16]

While the language in his history of the American Revolution occasionally echoed Hewatt's, suggesting that he had come across Hewatt's history even before 1794, Ramsay did not make any direct reference to Hewatt in either this work or his history of the Revolution in South Carolina.[17] Ramsay's greater reliance on Hewatt for his history of South Carolina was partly a matter of chronological scope. Where both of his earlier histories focused on the Revolution, Ramsay's history of South Carolina encompassed the colony's entire history from its founding to 1808, coinciding more closely with the coverage of Hewatt's account, which extended from the beginnings of colonial settlement in South Carolina to the repeal of the Stamp Act. But Ramsay's turn to Hewatt's history was also a function of his changing social views and purposes. Adhering to the widely held view of history as "philosophy teaching by examples," in which the historian's purpose was to inculcate virtue and morality in his readers by providing them with examples to imitate or avoid, both men wrote in part to further their own political agenda.[18] Thus even their choice of what to include and emphasize in their histories reflected the political differences between them. Hewatt's decision to stop his account at the beginning of the Revolution, for example, revealed his inability to integrate it into his vision of a mutually beneficial relationship between Britain and its American colonies. Instead Hewatt made the royal takeover of South Carolina's government in 1719 the turning point of the colony's history, ending the first volume of his history with that event. By showing how the advent of royal government provided the colonists with both internal stability and protection against external threats, Hewatt underlined the colonists' dependence on Britain and portrayed the Revolution as a departure from colonial tradition.[19]

On his side, while the shift from the national orientation of his history of the American Revolution to the state focus of his 1809 work reflected his deepening sense of South Carolina identity, Ramsay saw no conflict between his national and state loyalties, pointing to how the traits that distinguished South Carolina actually made it the embodiment of the nation's republican ideals.[20] Hence unlike Hewatt, he ended the first volume of his history of South Carolina with the Revolution and made it the focal point of his work. Emphasizing its conservative character, he rooted it in earlier colonial developments and highlighted the continuities between them. Thus if Ramsay differed from Hewatt in viewing the Revolution as the culmination of, rather than a rupture with, colonial tradition, he shared Hewatt's concern with preserving social order. This concern became more acute as popular challenges to elite authority, along with escalating partisan and sectional divisions and what appeared to be a growing absorption in material gain, made Ramsay increasingly apprehensive by the 1780s and 1790s about the threat that Americans' love of freedom posed to social stability.[21] Such fears made Ramsay more receptive to Hewatt's message of social order by the time that he published his history of South Carolina. Where, then, in his history of the Revolution in South Carolina, he had unequivocally affirmed the right of the colonists to revolt against the proprietors in 1719 by appealing to the "law of nature," Ramsay adopted much of Hewatt's account of this event for his 1809 history to give his analysis a subtly more conservative cast than he had in his earlier work.[22] Consequently his history of South Carolina echoed Hewatt's in its somewhat apologetic defense of the revolt, which, he acknowledged, could not "be deemed conformable to the strict letter of the written law, yet necessity and self preservation justify their conduct."[23]

By dropping any reference to the law of nature in his history of South Carolina and justifying the revolution of 1719 solely on the basis of necessity, Ramsay qualified his earlier defense of such extralegal protests as an unconditional right derived from a higher law; only the particular circumstances of this dispute, he suggested, warranted the colonists' violation of the "strict letter" of the law. But even as his more qualified defense of the colonists' right to revolt and his use of Hewatt here reflected his transformation from a Revolutionary historian to a historian of the Revolution, as Peter Messer has termed it, Ramsay was no less ardent a defender of the Revolution of 1776 than he was when he published his first history.[24] Hence where Hewatt ended his account of the 1719 revolt with a list of the benefits the colonists derived from the royal takeover of the colony, Ramsay immediately followed this section with a discussion of the similarities between the two revolutions, which were so great that the revolutionaries themselves "must be struck with the resemblance of the measures adopted by their predecessors and themselves for accomplishing these great and similar events." Ramsay emphasized the orderly and peaceful character of both revolutions, describing how on both occasions, a "new government, without confusion or violence, virtually superseded the existing authority of the proprietary governor in one case and of the king's representative in the other." With this comparison he appropriated Hewatt's rendering of the 1719 revolt to show how the American Revolution was an extension of the revolution of 1719 rather than a repudiation of the regime it had established, as Hewatt believed.[25] Ramsay thereby endowed the Revolution of 1776 with the same conservative character that he had given the revolution of 1719 in adopting Hewatt's account of that event. By turning Hewatt's own words against him in this way, he provided the ultimate refutation of Loyalist arguments against independence. At the same time, his use of those words enabled him to express the qualms he shared with Hewatt about the social effects of the Revolution without fully owning that he was having qualms.

Yet it was not just Ramsay's growing conservatism that made him so receptive to Hewatt's work, for he also embraced Hewatt's dynamic vision of commercial progress. Subscribing to the four-stage theory of history associated with the Scottish conjectural historians, both men privileged commerce as the engine of and final stage of social progress and made its development a central theme in their accounts but turned this theme to opposing purposes.[26] Employing the language of commerce so integral to British identity in this period, Hewatt adhered to the view of Britain widely shared by metropolitan Britons and colonists alike as an empire distinguished by its reliance on trade and maritime power rather than military conquest.[27] Wishing to show the reciprocal relationship between Britain and its colonies in contributing to the prosperity of this empire, he opened his work by proclaiming his desire to demonstrate the "usefulness and importance" of the colonies to "a commercial nation."[28] Hewatt furthered this goal through the extensive discussions of South Carolina's economic development and resources that he wove into his political and military narrative, relying in particular on natural history. Interspersing detailed descriptions of the colony's climate, vegetation, geography, and natural resources throughout his narrative, he repeatedly pointed to how the colonists could contribute to their own and Britain's commercial prosperity by cultivating such resources, as he did in his lengthy discussion of how the colonists learned to cultivate indigo.[29] In this way he showed how the closeness to nature that distinguished the American colonists from the British could strengthen the basis for British distinctiveness and power and thereby serve as a basis for their own claims to British identity.[30]

Ramsay expanded on Hewatt's interest in South Carolina's social and economic development, allotting the first volume of his history to a chronological account of political and military developments and devoting his second volume to social and cultural life, divided into sections on such topics as the arts, medical history, fiscal history, and agricultural history.[31] Sharing Hewatt's concern with displaying South Carolina's natural resources and showing how humans could cultivate and use those resources for their own benefit, he privileged natural history to an even greater extent than Hewatt did, devoting one of the longest chapters of the second volume to the subject. Pointing, for example, to how the state's mountain streams could be used to power mills and "other labor-saving machinery," Ramsay, like Hewatt, used natural history to demonstrate South Carolina's capacity for commercial progress.[32] But where Hewatt pointed to South Carolina's abundance of natural resources to reveal how the colony could contribute to what he believed was the source of British greatness, Ramsay did so to show how South Carolina and by extension the United States could surpass Britain in its capacity for commercial development and prosperity.[33]

The greater attention that Ramsay gave to the cultivation of South Carolina's natural resources was in turn a function of a difference of emphasis in Ramsay's and Hewatt's understanding of the relationship between human agency and divine power. Hewatt revealed a certain ambivalence about human control over nature, as he alternated between depicting nature as a resource to be cultivated by humans and portraying it as a force beyond human control. Ramsay shared that ambivalence up to a point, borrowing directly from Hewatt as he veered between these two characterizations of nature. Yet he was ultimately less awed by the power of nature than was Hewatt and placed more emphasis than Hewatt did on human ability to harness that power because of his greater willingness to dissociate nature from the divine. His appropriation of Hewatt's description of South Carolina's thunderstorms revealed both his debt to Hewatt and the way that he was able to shift the emphasis of Hewatt's account to desacralize the power of nature through the subtle changes that he made to Hewatt's wording (see table 1).

TABLE 1:

HEWATT:	RAMSAY:
A thunder-storm here is a grand phenomenon, especially in the night; it is said to be the voice of the supreme Author of nature, whose command all the various elements obey, and it speaks his majesty and glory in the loudest and most exalted strain. The frequent balls of fire bursting from cloud to cloud; the forked flashes darting from the clouds to the earth, and from the earth to the clouds alternately, illuminating the whole surrounding atmosphere, and men, like so many worms, crawling in the dust in the midst of flaming fire, form a magnificent and striking scene. The continual muttering noise of thunder at a distance the dreadful explosion on the right hand, the repercussive roar on the left, while the solid foundations of the earth shake, and the goodly frame of nature seems ready to dissolve, to the eyes of an intelligent stranger must have appeared awful and great. The beasts of the field retire from the thicket, and shew evident	Though earthquakes in Carolina are harmless, thunder storms are not always so. When they take place, especially if in the night, their grandeur exceeds description. The frequent balls of fire bursting from cloud to cloud; the forked flashes darting between the clouds and the earth, and from the one to the other alternately, illuminate the whole surrounding atmosphere and form a magnificent and striking scene. The solemn sound of distant thunder, followed by the vast explosion on the one hand, and the repercussive roar on the other, appear tremendously awful. The beasts of the field start from the thicket and gaze at the surrounding prospect with evident symptoms of terror and astonishment, and the winged tribes seek the shelter of the groves.[B]

symptoms of silent awe and astonishment during the storm, and man's ultimate source of confidence is in the divine
protection.[A]

[A] Hewatt, *Historical Account*, 1: 82.

[B] Ramsay, *History of South Carolina*, 2: 305–306.

Viewing natural phenomena such as hurricanes and thunderstorms as mani-
festations of divine power, Hewatt's description of thunderstorms emphasized human helplessness in the face of the overwhelming grandeur of that power. Ramsay
directly copied Hewatt's phrasing when he spoke of how the "frequent balls of fire
bursting from cloud to cloud; the forked flashes darting between the clouds and
the earth, and from the one to the other alternately, . . . form a magnificent and
striking scene."[34] If in this description Ramsay shared Hewatt's admiration for the
grandeur of nature, he in the end made such grandeur seem less overwhelming
than it appeared in Hewatt's account, for he did not associate it with the divine in
the way that Hewatt did—hence he cut Hewatt's phrase that "men, like so many
worms, crawling in the dust in the midst of flaming fire" and omitted his references
to the "supreme Author of nature" and to "man's ultimate source of confidence is
in the divine protection."[35]

Yet here the difference between Hewatt and Ramsay was one of emphasis, not
an absolute one. Hewatt's use of the phrase "it is said" to refer to the belief that
thunderstorms represented the voice of the divine, which left ambiguous whether
this sentiment expressed his own view, would have made it easier for Ramsay to
dispense with providence altogether in this passage. Indeed Hewatt for the most
part emphasized the role of secular causes in his history, only occasionally referring to providential intervention or guidance. He thus provided Ramsay with a
vehicle for mediating the transition from a providential to a secular mode of explanation by bringing together these two causal frameworks and making Ramsay's
shift in favor of human agency seem less of a departure.[36] In turn Ramsay used his
affirmation of human agency to uphold the exceptionalist faith in America's ability to avoid the degeneration that had afflicted other republican societies. If people
had the ability to control and harness nature itself for their own purposes, he
suggested, then surely they could overcome and avert the natural cycles of decay
that had destroyed earlier republics. Ramsay believed that his work as a historian
could itself aid in this imperative by holding the revolutionaries up as exemplars
of republican virtue for present-day Americans to emulate, thereby enabling the
United States to ward off the corruption that classical republican thinkers considered so inimical to liberty.[37]

Yet Ramsay's sense of American exceptionalism at the same time prevented
him from relinquishing providence altogether as a force in history, for he attributed
to providential intervention the difference between the outcome of the American

Revolution and that of other revolutions. According to Ramsay South Carolina's ability to prevail against Britain during the Revolution and to "voluntarily impose on themselves the restraints of good government" afterward, in contrast to other countries that had undergone revolutions, could only be explained by appealing to "a superintending providence." Here, then, he appropriated Hewatt's providentialism not only to explain and sanction the Revolution but also to affirm his exceptionalist belief in the uniqueness of the Revolution and the nation it created. The duality in Hewatt on the relationship between providence and human agency thus allowed Ramsay to have it both ways—to proclaim his faith in human agency while at the same time maintaining a belief in the nation's divine mission.[38]

II

The plasticity of Hewatt's work likewise enabled Ramsay to mold it to his nationalist purposes as he grappled with his recognition of the casualties of this mission—the destruction and dispossession of Native Americans. While Ramsay was in the end more willing than Hewatt to accept this eventuality as the price of American expansion, his departure from Hewatt was rooted in Hewatt's own ambivalence on the subject. Hewatt thus provided him with a vehicle for mediating the exclusion of Native Americans from his vision of American destiny as he used his appropriations from Hewatt to at once express and resolve his uncertainties about the dispossession of Native Americans in favor of white American conquest.[39]

The ambivalence that both Hewatt and Ramsay expressed in their portrayals of Native Americans reflected the duality in Anglo-American perceptions of Native Americans more generally. As race became an increasingly accepted category of difference during the late eighteenth century, the deeply rooted view of Indians as brutal savages inherently inferior to Europeans gained added currency and legitimacy. At the same time, the idealization of the Indian as a noble savage who represented man in his natural state, uncorrupted by the materialism and vices of society, was also coming into vogue in this period.[40] Scottish stadial theory reinforced this duality in its assumption that all human societies progressed through the same series of stages—the hunter, the pastoral, the agricultural, and the commercial (in the most common variant of this scheme)—with each stage defined by its mode of subsistence and each one more civilized and advanced than the last.[41] Because they identified themselves with the more advanced stage of commercial development, Europeans could use stadial theory to justify the dispossession of Native Americans, who embodied for them the more primitive hunter stage, as necessary for the progress of humanity. Yet the idea that social progress was a function of different modes of subsistence also suggested—counter to the emerging belief in racial differences—that Indians were not inherently inferior to Europeans and that they could eventually attain the same level of civilization as Europeans.[42]

The duality in Hewatt's treatment of the subject revealed the double-edged implications of stadial theory for perceptions of Native Americans. Hence he followed stadial theory in identifying the Indians with a more primitive hunter stage of social development, but rather than justifying their dispossession on the basis that, as nomadic hunters, Native Americans did not possess any claims to private property, he argued that the European colonists had violated the Indians' prior claim to American lands.[43] His interpretation of stadial theory intersected with his providential perspective as he explained, "Their right was founded in nature and Providence: it was the free and liberal gift of heaven to them, which no foreigner could claim any pretension to invade."[44] Accordingly Hewatt made some effort to understand and convey the complexity of Native American culture, periodically offering quite detailed and lengthy descriptions of Indian customs. He reconciled his recognition of the Indians' right to their lands with his desire to uphold British imperial authority over the colonies through his faith in commerce, which he believed could at once civilize the Indians and enable them to coexist peacefully with the British in a mutually beneficial relationship. Thus he spoke approvingly of the hope that through "a fair and free trade" with the Indians, "their rude temper would in time be softened, their manners altered, and their wants increased," turning them into "good allies, both useful and beneficial to the trade of the nation."[45]

Yet the limits to Hewatt's sympathy for Native Americans were apparent in Ramsay's appropriation of his work. Ramsay had in his earlier works shared some of Hewatt's qualms about the injustice and brutality of the colonists' treatment of the Indians, even echoing Hewatt's logic and language in his history of the American Revolution when he, like Hewatt, affirmed the Indians' prior right to American lands: "The right of the Indian nations to the soil in their possession was founded in nature. It was the free and liberal gift of Heaven to them, and such as no foreigner could rightfully annul."[46] But Ramsay became more unwilling to acknowledge the injustice of the dispossession of the Indians from their land as the rapid westward expansion of the early nineteenth century made initial efforts by the US government to achieve "expansion with honor" through a policy of assimilation increasingly untenable and heightened the appeal of removal or extermination.[47] Ramsay made clear his increasingly unsympathetic view of the Indians in his history of South Carolina when he left out Hewatt's affirmation of the Indians' prior right to their land on the American continent, making a point of denying their rights to South Carolina territory, on the basis of their hunter state, in a footnote.[48]

Hence Ramsay departed from both Hewatt and his earlier work by putting more emphasis on Indian savagery in his history of South Carolina and his history of the United States. Yet this departure was rooted in the duality in Hewatt's own portrayal of Native Americans. For all his recognition of the provocations that incited Native American attacks on the colonists, Hewatt still displayed a fascination with the savagery and brutality of those attacks that provided Ramsay with a basis for his more unfavorable portrayal of Native Americans. Thus Hewatt repeatedly pointed to examples of Indian savagery, writing on these incidents with a vividness and detail that he rarely provided on other subjects, as he did in his description of how a group of Yamassee Indians during the Yamassee War "catched William Hooper, and killed him by degrees, by cutting off one joint of his body after another, until he expired. Another party surprised Henry Quinton, Thomas Simmons, and Thomas Parmenter, and, to gratify their revenge, tortured them to death. Dr. Rose afterwards fell also into their hands, whom they cut across his nose with their tomahawk." Ramsay copied almost word for word from this passage, employing Hewatt's graphic descriptions of Indian violence against the colonists to make his case for Indian savagery and inferiority. But where Hewatt used such descriptions to underline the colonists' need for British protection, Ramsay sought to justify white American conquest of Native American lands and soften the colonists' culpability in the destruction of the Indians.[49]

On the other side, while increasingly unsympathetic to the plight of the Indians, some of Ramsay's earlier qualms about the colonists' mistreatment of them persisted, and he appropriated directly from Hewatt for his acknowledgement of the colonists' responsibility for provoking Indian brutality and violence. His discussion of the colonists' war with the Cherokees in 1758–61 revealed how he used Hewatt to make this acknowledgement while at the same time subtly turning Hewatt's account to serve nationalist ends and affirm the belief in white American superiority that for him ultimately justified their conquest of the Indians. Thus even though much of his discussion of the Anglo-Cherokee War plagiarized directly from Hewatt, making only small changes in wording, those changes served to alienate the Indians more fully both from any claims to American or British identity and from any claims to a culture of their own (see table 2).

TABLE 2

HEWATT:	RAMSAY:
An unfortunate quarrel with the Virginians helped to forward their designs, by opening to them an easier access into the towns of the savages. In the different expeditions against Fort Duquesne, the Cherokees, agreeable to treaty, had sent considerable parties of warriors to the assistance of the British army. As the horses in those parts run wild in the woods, it was customary, both among Indians and white people on the frontiers, to lay hold on them and appropriate them to their own purposes. While the savages were returning home through the back parts of Virginia, many of them	An unfortunate quarrel with the virginians helped to forward their designs. In the successful expedition of 1758, against fort Duquesne, the cherokees had sent considerable parties of warriors to the assistance of the british army. While the savages were returning home from that expedition, through the back parts of Virginia, many of them having lost their horses took possession of such as came in their way. The virginians, instead of asserting their rights in a legal manner, resented the injury by force of arms and killed twelve or fourteen of these unsuspicious warriors. The cherokees, with

having lost their horses, laid hold of such as came in their way, never imagining that they belonged to any individual in the province. The Virginians however, instead of asserting their right in a legal way, resented the injury by force of arms, and killed twelve or fourteen of the unsuspicious warriors, and took several more prisoners. The Cherokees, with reason, were highly provoked at such ungrateful usage from allies, whose frontiers they had helped to change from a field of blood into peaceful habitations, and when they came home told what had happened to their nation. The flame soon spread through the upper towns, and those who had lost their friends and relations were implacable, and breathed nothing but fury and vengeance against such perfidious friends. In vain did the chieftains interpose their authority, nothing could restrain the furious spirits of the young men, who were determined to take satisfaction for the loss of their re-lations. . . . The scattered families on the frontiers of Carolina lay much exposed to scalping parties of these savages, who commonly make no distinction of age or sex, but pour their vengeance indiscrimi-nately on the innocent and guilty.[A]

reason, were highly provoked at such ungrateful usage; and when they came home, gave a highly colored account thereof to their nation. They became outrageous. Those who had lost friends and relations, resolved upon revenge. In vain did the chieftains interpose their authority. Nothing could restrain the ferocity of the young men. . . . Parties of young warriors took the field, and rush-ing down among the white inhabitants murdered and scalped all who came in their way.[B]

[A] Hewatt, *History Account*, 2:214–15.
[B] Ramsay, *Historical of South-Carolina*, 1:167–68.

In this passage Ramsay echoed Hewatt when he acknowledged that the exces-sive retaliation taken by the Virginia colonists against the Cherokees for stealing their horses and British treachery in imprisoning (and massacring) the chiefs who had come to negotiate for peace with them provoked the Cherokees into war. Even while recognizing that the colonists were partly to blame for instigating Cherokee anger and violence, Ramsay dropped phrases from Hewatt's narrative that ex-plained why the Cherokees were so incensed by the colonists' treatment of them. While, then, he used Hewatt's wording in pointing to the Cherokees' anger at their "ungrateful usage" by the colonists, he left out the next part of Hewatt's sentence, "from allies, whose frontiers they had helped to change from a field of blood into peaceful habitations."[50] By referring to the Cherokees' view of the colonists as allies and specifying what the Cherokees believed they had done for the colonists, Hewatt both made the Cherokees appear more rational in their sense of ill-usage than Ramsay did and highlighted their role in the development and prosperity of the colonies, thus making them in some sense part of the British Empire.[51] On his side Ramsay's addition of the phrase "highly colored" to describe the reaction of the Cherokees in the last part of this sentence, to read "and when they came home, gave a highly colored account thereof to their nation," followed by the addition of the sentence, "They became outrageous," made the Cherokees appear in his version more excessive and irrational than they did in Hewatt's account.[52] In this way, where Hewatt's account showed how the Cherokees acted according to the logic of their own culture and their relationship with the colonists, Ramsay's emphasis on their irrationality reinforced the view of them as savages governed by whatever impulses or emotions seized them rather than by an organized system of rules and principles.[53]

Likewise Ramsay both followed and departed from Hewatt in this explanation for the decline of the Indians. He shared some of Hewatt's qualms about that decline and his recognition of European culpability for this development when he, borrowing heavily from Hewatt's account, attributed their extinction to the "avarice and ambition of the professors of christianity," which have "debased the pristine habits and stern virtues of hardy, free, and independent savages," while the "vices of white people, falsely called christians," and the diseases brought on by these vices "have so nearly exterminated the native original owners of the soil, that many nations formerly populous are extinct."[54] But where Hewatt used his account of the decline of the Indians to underline the need for British protection and mediation, Ramsay drew the opposite conclusion from this development. Unlike Hewatt, who ended his analysis of Native American decline by pointing to the British government's "prudent plans" for "civilizing and managing those barbarous nations," which would both protect the colonists and prevent the further decline of the Indians, Ramsay made their extermination seem imminent and irreversible by emphasizing even more than Hewatt did how close to extinction they already were. He thus spoke of how the Cherokees were now "inconsiderable both in number and force" and the Catawbas were "fast sinking into insignificance."[55] In this way, directly contrary to Hewatt's purposes, he used his analysis of the decline of the Indians to show why Americans no longer needed the protection of the British and revealed that for all his recognition of European culpability in that decline, he was much more willing than Hewatt was to accept such destruction as the price of American independence and expansion.[56]

III

Ramsay found it more difficult to bend Hewatt's work to his purposes, however, when it came to the issue of slavery. While his own reluctance to criticize slavery prevented him from incorporating Hewatt's scathing condemnation of the institution into his account, neither could he completely disregard Hewatt's attack. Thus he reconciled slavery with American ideals and turned it into a basis for distinguishing himself from Hewatt and his British roots by reversing Hewatt's logic to emphasize the humanitarian benefits of slavery. Yet Ramsay's very departure from Hewatt revealed how important Hewatt was to crystallizing his views on slavery and American identity, as he at once defined his position in opposition to Hewatt and drew on him for the framework of that opposition.

Devoting much more attention to slavery than Ramsay did, Hewatt revealed both the extent and limits of his cosmopolitanism in his condemnation of the institution. Firmly convinced that Africans "have the same faculties with those of Europe," with minds "equally capable of cultivation, equally susceptible of the impressions of religion," he sharply condemned slavery as a violation of the natural rights of Africans and their claims to equality as human beings.[57] Writing at a time when antislavery sentiment had begun to develop in the Anglo-American world but had not yet crystallized into a widespread movement of activism against slavery, Hewatt revealed the roots of this sentiment in both commerce and religion—and its limits—in his attack on slavery. Partly a reaction to the rapid commercial expansion of this period, antislavery discourse served as a means of critiquing the excessive greed and materialism fostered by commercial society. Hewatt shared in this critique, arguing that to sanction such a cruel practice as slavery purely on the basis of its economic benefits was to give license to the unrestrained pursuit of greed and self-interest. Viewing the commercial motives and activities that drove slavery as a sign of moral corruption and degeneration, he summed up his view of slavery as an object lesson in the evils of avarice when he concluded, "in no instance can it be said to be a more plain and lamentable truth, that the love of money is the root of all evil, than when it urges men to trade in the bodies and souls of their fellow-creatures."[58]

Hewatt's argument that economic profit could never justify the enslavement of fellow human beings was predicated on a cosmopolitan perspective that recognized and privileged the shared humanity of African slaves over narrow considerations of national self-interest. He made that perspective explicit when he demanded, "Can the local circumstances of any province upon earth be pled in excuse for such a violent trade, and for such endless slavery in consequence of it?"[59] Founding the rights of Africans as human beings in divine origin, Hewatt made the religious basis for his cosmopolitan perspective clear when he condemned slavery as contrary to both "the grand rule of equity prescribed to Christians" and the will of providence, who had given to all human beings "an undoubted right to the means of self-preservation and happiness, and all the common rights and privileges of nature."[60] Accordingly he criticized the failure by Britain and its colonists to provide religious instruction to slaves as a violation of the cosmopolitan spirit of Christianity itself, which "breathes a spirit of benevolence, gentleness, and compassion for mankind in general, of what nation or complexion soever they be."[61]

Yet in urging the conversion rather than the emancipation of slaves as his solution to the evils of slavery, Hewatt backed away from and contradicted his condemnation of slavery as inherently wrongful and unjustifiable. For him the benefits of Christianity were so great that the oppression of slavery would be "much more tolerable and justifiable" if slaves were given instruction in Christian doctrines.[62] The limits to Hewatt's opposition to slavery (and the inconsistencies in his views on the issue) were even more apparent in his argument that the conversion of slaves would actually benefit their owners by making slave rebellion less likely and strengthen the institution through the softening influence of Christianity, which would make slaves "more faithful and diligent, and better reconciled to their servile condition." Thus the very force—his religious convictions—that enabled him to transcend national boundaries and recognize the shared humanity of African slaves and the British also limited the kind of action he was willing to advocate in support of that recognition.[63]

Hence even as he grounded his argument for the conversion of slaves in a cosmopolitan vision of Christianity, Hewatt at the same time expressed a chauvinistic belief in British superiority in his claims for its special responsibility as a Protestant nation to carry out this mission. Appealing to that sense of chauvinism, he criticized Britain's failure to promote the conversion of slaves as "a reproach to the subjects of Britain, who profess to be the freest and most civilized people upon earth."[64] Slaves, Hewatt believed, as "members of a great empire," deserved the benefits of Christianity in return for their contributions "to the improvement and opulence of the British dominions" and as part of the care and protection Britain was supposed to provide its subjects.[65]

Not only was Ramsay far less critical of slavery than Hewatt was; he in many ways seemed to be reacting directly against Hewatt in his treatment of the subject, taking Hewatt's cosmopolitan framework and using it to reconcile the institution with revolutionary ideals. Therefore, although he shared some of Hewatt's ambivalence about slavery, he departed much more sharply from Hewatt's treatment of the subject than he did in his discussion of nature and Native Americans. Ramsay's move away from a cautious recognition of the wrongfulness of slavery to an uneasy acceptance of the institution reflected the double-edged effects of the Revolution on slavery more generally. While the Revolution contributed to the erosion and questioning of slavery as a violation of its principles of equality and liberty in the northern states, it at the same time resulted in the hardening of slavery in other quarters, including Ramsay's state of South Carolina.[66] Hence Ramsay had during the 1770s and 1780s criticized slavery as a moral wrong and as a threat to republican ideals in his private correspondence. By the late 1780s, however, he had become increasingly unwilling to question slavery, as a result of both his own personal involvement in the institution through the slaves that his wife, Martha Laurens, had brought into their marriage and his belief that his reputation as an opponent of slavery had contributed to his defeat in his run for Congress in 1788. Consequently, he reversed his earlier position to conclude that slavery had become such a necessity that it would be fatal for South Carolina to do away with the institution, avoiding any mention of the subject even in his private letters after that point. Likewise he made little direct reference to slavery in his history of South Carolina, leaving slaves out altogether from his survey of South Carolina's population.[67]

This evasiveness at the same time betrayed Ramsay's lingering uneasiness about slavery, which is what made Hewatt's indictment of the institution so threatening to him. Sensitive to Hewatt's critique because of his own earlier qualms about slavery, Ramsay could not let it go undisputed. Yet those qualms also prevented him from directly challenging Hewatt with an overt defense of slavery. Instead he made his case against Hewatt largely by implication, omitting all of Hewatt's denunciations of slavery and making changes to his narrative that indirectly served to justify slavery, as in the case of their discussion of rice cultivation—a topic that received extensive treatment from both historians. But where Hewatt focused on the difficulty and labor involved in growing rice, Ramsay emphasized the power of technology to overcome those difficulties and the benefits of rice cultivation. Hewatt recognized the economic benefits of slavery for Britain and South Carolina when he pointed to how indispensable slave labor had been to the development of rice as one of the colony's staple crops. Not only did rice become "the chief support of the colony, and its great source of opulence," but as a source of provisions and labor, "it became also a source of naval strength to the nation, and of course more beneficial to it, than foreign mines of silver and gold." Rice was "so laborious" to grow that it could only have succeeded as a staple crop with the labor of African slaves, for "the utter inaptitude of Europeans" for such work would only have resulted in turning every rice plantation into "a burying ground to its European cultivators." Yet in Hewatt's view the necessity of slavery to the success of rice cultivation did not warrant their enslavement, for he demanded, "but, from such a consideration, what man will presume to vindicate the policy of keeping those rational creatures in perpetual exile and slavery."[68]

Whereas Hewatt pointed only to the economic benefits of rice cultivation for South Carolina and Britain, Ramsay made more far-reaching claims about its advantages. He began by echoing Hewatt's argument and language when he noted that rice, "besides furnishing provisions for man and beast, employs a number of hands in trade; and is therefore a source of naval strength. In every point of view it is of more value than mines of silver and gold."[69] But where Hewatt made this point only to set up his conclusion that the prosperity brought by rice cultivation had not been worth the cost in slave lives and suffering and that the colony could have prospered by relying on other crops, Ramsay suggested to the contrary that the benefits of rice cultivation for humanity were so great that they far outweighed such costs. By using rice as a stand-in for slavery, he could defend the institution without appearing to do so. Although he did not explicitly refer to Hewatt's critique of the use of slave labor in rice cultivation, his decision to omit these comments, while retaining Hewatt's opening statement about the economic benefits of rice, suggested that he was directly responding to that critique in his reversal of Hewatt's argument (see table 3).

Table 3

Hewatt:

From this small beginning did the staple commodity of Carolina take its rise, which soon became the chief support of the colony, and its great source of opulence. Besides provisions for man and beast, as rice employs a number of hands in trade, it became also a source of naval strength to the nation, and of course more beneficial to it, than foreign mines of silver and gold. . . .

So laborious is the task of raising, beating, and cleaning this article, that though it had been possible to obtain European servants in numbers sufficient for attacking the thick forest and clearing grounds for the purpose, thousands and ten thousands must have perished in the arduous attempt. The utter inaptitude of Europeans for the labour requisite in such a climate and soil, is obvious to every one possessed of the smallest degree of knowledge respecting the country; white servants would have exhausted their strength in clearing a spot of land for digging their own graves, and every rice plantation would have served no other purpose than a burying ground to its European cultivators. The low lands of Carolina, which are unquestionably the richest grounds in the country, must long have remained a wilderness, had not Africans, whose natural constitutions were suited to the clime and work, been employed in cultivating this useful article of food and commerce.

Ramsay:

From this small beginning the first staple commodity of Carolina took its rise. It soon after became the chief support of the colony. Rice, besides furnishing provisions for man and beast, employs a number of hands in trade; and is therefore a source of naval strength. In every point of view it is of more value than mines of silver and gold. Rice is said by Dr. Arbuthnot to support two thirds of the human race. No doubt can exist of its contributing extensively as nutriment to the great family of mankind.

Besides its consumption in Europe, Africa, and America, many millions of the inhabitants of Asia, live almost exclusively upon it. In plantations where it is cultivated, every domestic animal is usually fat and hearty. Among all the variety of grains none is more productive, nutritious, or wholesome than rice. In its simple state it is both a healthy and cheap food for the poor, and with proper preparation and additions it is one of the greatest delicacies at the tables of the rich; every particle of it is trebled in bulk and doubled in weight, and in its capacity for aliment, from the quantity of water it imbibes in boiling: for water is now known to be the principal ingredient in nutrition. He that eats rice at the same time receives mucilage and water, solid and fluid aliment of the most nourishing kind. Its emollient and glutinous qualities make it eminently

So much may be said for the necessity of employing Africans in the cultivation of rice; but great is the difference between employing negroes in clearing and improving those rich plains, and that miserable state of hardship and slavery to which they are there devoted, and which has been tolerated and established by the law of the land. If we view this race, first ranging over the hills of Africa, equally free and independent as other rude nations on earth, and from thence inveigled by fraud, or compelled by force, and then consigned over to a state of endless slavery, we must confess the change is great and deplorable, especially to an impartial and disinterested eye. Without them, it is acknowledged, slow must have been the progress of cultivation in Carolina; but, from such a consideration, what man will presume to vindicate the policy of keeping those rational creatures in perpetual exile and slavery. . . .

This navigation law, though it cramped the trade of the colonies, yet it has been attended with many beneficial consequences to Britain: and while she maintained the supreme power of legislation throughout the empire, and wisely regulated the trade and commerce of her foreign settlements, she might reap many and substantial advantages from them. . . . But should the planters in these colonies begin to think themselves entitled to the privileges of raising what productions they please, and of sending them to any market they judged most advantageous to themselves, they would then become colonies equally useful to all the world; and the mother country, who discovered, peopled and protected them, would share no more advantage

useful in bowel complaints, and as such it forms an important article in the stores of armies and other large bodies of men. . . . To those who from age or infirmity are deprived of their teeth, rice is a most convenient aliment, for it requires little or no mastication. When introduced into the stomach after being well boiled, it is more easily digested than almost any other solid food not thoroughly masticated. To that class of people whose deranged stomachs cannot digest bread, unless well raised and thoroughly baked, rice affords a safe and agreeable substitute, for it requires no fermentation, and when sufficiently boiled is as likely to agree with the stomach as crusts of bread or the best baked biscuits. To exhausted armies, starving navies, or even to the weary traveler, though far removed from the haunts of men, if fuel, water and an earthen or metallic pot can be procured, rice quickly affords a palatable and strengthening aliment. In voyages round the world, flour of every kind and every thing made from flour is apt to spoil, but rice sustains no injury from change of climate or the longest period of any voyage hitherto known. Such is the grain which was introduced into Carolina about 115 years ago, and has ever since been in high demand. . . .

After many attempts machines, worked by the tides, were contrived and erected by Mr. Lucas, which are equal to the beating out twenty barrels a day by the force of tide water with the help of a few hands. Before they were introduced, the labor of the negroes in doing the same business by hand was immense. It sometimes crippled the strength of the men, and often destroyed the fertility from them than rival states around her. On this principle Great Britain grounds her right to expect a market for her manufactures in the colonies she planted and nursed, and to regulate their produce and trade in such a channel as to render them only subservient to her own interest. Without this right they would not only be useless to her, but very prejudicial.[A]

of the women . . . All this mischief in a great measure has been done away for the last twenty years, in which period rice mills have become common in all parts of the state where rice is extensively cultivated.[B]

[A] Hewatt, *Historical Account*, 1:119–25.
[B] Ramsay, *History of South-Carolina*, 2:202–7.

Hence Ramsay departed from Hewatt by adding an extensive discussion of how the cultivation of rice was not just a matter of economic self-interest for South Carolina but a humanitarian endeavor, for rice "is said by Dr. Arbuthnot to support two thirds of the human race. No doubt can exist of its contributing extensively as nutriment to the great family of mankind." After pointing to how it was eaten all over the world, Ramsay followed with a lengthy disquisition on how there was no grain "more productive, nutritious, or wholesome than rice." In addition to "a healthy and cheap food for the poor," it was "eminently useful in bowel complaints," while it was easy to chew for "those who from age or infirmity" did not have teeth, to name just a few of its health benefits.[70] Like Hewatt, then, he did not consider it sufficient to justify slavery solely on economic grounds, for both shared a concern for humanity that transcended national boundaries. But unlike Hewatt, rather than concluding as a result that slavery was indefensible, he sought to justify slavery by showing how its products benefited humanity. In this way, whereas Hewatt condemned slavery as a violation of his humanitarian perspective, Ramsay paradoxically used that sense of cosmopolitan humanitarianism to sanction the exclusion of slaves from claims to humanity.

Hewatt's attack on slavery, coming as it did from a Loyalist, ironically facilitated this process of exclusion by enabling Ramsay to associate criticism of slavery with support for Britain and repudiate it as un-American.[71] Hewatt himself reinforced such an association, as he turned his humanitarian concern for the oppression of slaves into an instrument for asserting and legitimizing British imperial authority over the colonies in his argument for parliamentary intervention to promote the conversion of slaves. By his reasoning, since the British government was responsible for establishing slavery in the colonies in the first place, it was also responsible for doing what it could to alleviate its harmful effects by establishing institutions for the religious instruction of slaves.[72] Hewatt in turn extended the power that he claimed for Parliament to intervene on behalf of slaves into more far-reaching claims for parliamentary authority over other colonial matters, immediately following his condemnation of slavery with an affirmation of Britain's right to regulate colonial trade, on the basis that without such regulations the American colonies "would then become colonies equally useful to all the world."[73] The conjunction here of a humanitarian concern for slaves and the assertion of British imperial authority legitimized that authority as an extension of the cosmopolitan ideal of enlightened and civilized moderation that Britain sought to embody even as it revealed the limits to this ideal in denying the right of the colonies to become "equally useful to all the world."[74]

For Ramsay, rather than an argument against freedom from British trade regulations, the ability of South Carolina to be useful to all of the world if it were able to freely trade its rice demonstrated how independence would benefit not just the American colonies but humanity more generally. Thus he rebutted Hewatt by substituting his exposition on the humanitarian benefits of rice for Hewatt's defense of British trade regulations and his attack on slavery. When South Carolina could confer all the benefits that Ramsay listed through the export of its rice, he suggested, it was Hewatt—not the revolutionaries—who was being narrowly parochial in the qualms he expressed about the suffering of slaves who grew the crop and his defense of British trade restrictions. As Ramsay turned Hewatt's cosmopolitanism in on itself, the very strategy that Hewatt used to strengthen and legitimize British authority furthered the development of an American identity defined simultaneously by a larger concern for humanity and by the exclusion of slaves from that cosmopolitan vision. And by showing how slavery could actually help the nation fulfill its exceptionalist mission to advance the good of humanity, Ramsay simultaneously affirmed his own credentials as a loyal South Carolinian and his state's allegiance to American ideals when both were liable to question.[75]

Ramsay's plagiarism of Hewatt thus allowed him to have his cake and eat it too. Through his use of Hewatt, he at once affirmed the power of human agency to avert the cycles of decay that had destroyed other republics and maintained his belief in the nation's providential destiny, simultaneously expressed and assuaged his qualms about the Native American casualties of that destiny, and upheld slavery while proclaiming the nation's mission to benefit humanity. As he drew on Hewatt for the tenets of American exceptionalist ideology, he revealed how that ideology was as much the product of the nation's Loyalist—and British—origins as it was a repudiation of them.[76] Hewatt's condemnation of slavery, however, enabled Ramsay to establish a clearer sense of differentiation from those origins, as his differences with Hewatt on this issue allowed him to reconcile slavery with American ideals and turn it into a badge of national distinction. For Ramsay, then, the process of unbecoming Loyalist was partly a matter of becoming an apologist for slavery, as his treatment of the subject helped to crystallize and serve as a foundation for a unique American identity defined simultaneously by a cosmopolitan humanitarianism and racial exclusion.[77]

Postwar Loyalist Hopes

To Be "Parts and Not Dependencies of the Empire"

The experience of revolution shaped the white Loyalist response to British North America during the 1780s and early 1790s. Exiled from their homes, the Loyalists hoped for security and stability in place of disorder and violence. In September 1778, as Loyalist Eliza Byles adjusted to her new home in Halifax, Nova Scotia, she recorded despondency but also possibility:

> I am a young Exile from my native Shore;
> Start at the Flash of Arms and dread the Roar;
> my Softer Soul, not form'd for Scenes like these;
> Flies to the Arms of Innocence and Peace.[1]

Like Eliza Byles, many Loyalists contrasted the "arms and roar" of the American states with the potential for stability and peace in the north. But the threat of an expanding and republican United States was as apparent as the marginal position of colonies in British North America. The Loyalists returned to the question that had remained unresolved during the Revolution: what was required to maintain a long-lasting union between the colonies and the empire? They looked back at the late rebellion and identified the problems that had led to the secession of the "old thirteen." They hoped to stabilize their new world in three ways: through increasing the population of the British provinces, making the provinces economically integral to the empire, and, finally, establishing a political structure that could compete successfully with US republicanism.

Understanding the Revolution

The 1783 Treaty of Paris produced a permanent cleavage on the North American continent. It cut off the older portion of the British colonial empire and, at the same time, preserved the northern half, consisting of the provinces of Quebec and Nova Scotia. To secure their hold over the North Atlantic and deter US expansionism, the British government encouraged the settlement of up to ten thousand

Loyalists (including three thousand Aboriginals) to Quebec and thirty-five thousand Loyalists (including five thousand black people) to Nova Scotia.[2] These loyal subjects would populate the British provinces and ensure British dominion.[3]

The Loyalist migration to Nova Scotia represented part of a long and evolving relationship between peopling the region and securing the interests of the British state.[4] Two decades earlier, during the Seven Years' War, the British had expelled the Acadians because their multiple and mixed loyalties represented a threat. In their place the British had encouraged more than seven thousand New Englanders to settle in the Maritimes. The New Englanders met the empire's need for trustworthy subjects during an earlier postwar consolidation. By 1766 these New Englanders represented the largest majority in peninsular Nova Scotia.[5]

As the New Englanders had taken over the lands of the exiled Acadians, the overwhelming presence of white Loyalists in the Maritimes, along with their political capital, undermined the claims of the Aboriginals.[6] Until 1782 the Aboriginals had retained some negotiating power in relation to the empire. The migration of the New England planters did not compare with the weight of the Loyalist settlement, which doubled the population of Nova Scotia. The massive presence of the king's friends ended two hundred years of imperial-Aboriginal treaties and undermined Aboriginal economies. Nova Scotia moved from a pattern of imperial-native relations to one resembling a settlement colony.[7]

The Loyalist influx between 1775 and 1784 significantly strengthened the British position in the Maritimes. In 1755 the total population of Nova Scotia and Cape Breton was 25,000. By 1767, with the Acadian expulsion and in spite of planter migration, the population was only 11,800. The arrival of the Loyalist refugees raised the population: by 1791 the peninsula had 55,500 people (along with 1,500 more in Cape Breton), and by 1811, 70,000. To some extent emigration continued to check the growth in the Maritimes: white Loyalist refugees returned to the States and more than 1,000 black refugees left for Freetown, Sierra Leone, in 1792.[8]

The Loyalist immigration elevated the importance of the Maritimes. Transformed from marginal to strategic importance, the Canadian colonies represented an ideal point of a new trade triangle, West Indies to British North America to Britain. These colonies were not only closest to England but located strategically near the sugar colonies. Timber, provisions, and fish from the Maritimes offered Britain a chance to lower its reliance on supplies from the thirteen seceded colonies. Populated by a large number of English-speaking inhabitants who swore allegiance to the empire, the Maritimes could act as a buffer to US growth and, indeed, show the Americans that their experiment in republicanism was inferior to unification with the British imperial state.[9] In July 1783, Loyalist officer Brook Watson celebrated the settlement of the Maritimes by "good people of property." Thirty years earlier Watson had helped in expelling the Acadians from Nova Scotia. He believed that those with the "most settled love to the Constitution of England will form a barrier against those of opposite principle and become the envy of all their neighbors."[10]

As exiles in London, the Loyalists assessed the causes and consequences of the Revolution. Many who continued to imagine a new life within a revised and flourishing empire were Loyalist moderates. They had survived the war better than those who had become hardliners. For example Gov. William Franklin of New Jersey could not mask his bitterness toward the revolutionary leaders or Britain and remained outside the inner circles of London and of British North America.[11] Franklin's experience of imprisonment and his transformation into a hardline Loyalist in war-torn New York City did not resemble the experience of more moderate Loyalists, especially those who had made themselves indispensable to the British establishment or who had escaped to England at the first violence.

New York attorney William Smith Jr. was the most articulate of the mid-Atlantic Loyalist moderates during and after the rebellion. Trusted by the British government during the Revolution, Smith was appointed chief justice of New York. He left for England in 1783 with the British commander in chief, Sir Guy Carleton, who in 1786 acquired the title Baron Dorchester and a new position as governor in chief of Quebec, New Brunswick, and Nova Scotia.[12]

In 1785, as Smith awaited his appointment as chief justice of Quebec under Carleton, he jotted down his reflections on the causes and success of the American Revolution. Smith criticized the loose structure of imperial governance in the colonies and the weak powers of colonial executives. He regretted that the empire had not asserted more control over colonial governance prior to the revolutionary troubles. He disregarded those who believed that the war was caused by the "Stamp Act, Duty Acts or Tea Acts." Instead he argued that the "matches to the train [were] laid long before." The infant colonies had matured in growth, opulence, education, and spirit, and the older system of government had long been inadequate for them. To counteract the slide toward possible anarchy, the British government long ago should have strengthened the power of the governors, upper houses, and courts. These institutions would have checked immediately the reach of those who promoted the idea of liberty outside of the British Empire.

Other Loyalists also blamed British imperial governance as creating conditions for rebellion. A Loyalist essay, published anonymously between 1785 and 1790 and titled "Brief Observations on the Expediency of Granting a Charter to the Inhabitants of Nova Scotia," drew attention to the same causes. The essayist encouraged closer metropolitan control, smaller assemblies, and a restriction on town meetings. In Nova Scotia the councillors and the chief justices should be appointed by His Majesty. Indeed the "neglect of this measure in the original formation" led to "great evils." The assemblies should have been smaller, as the larger numbers— comprising "fool and knaves" —assumed a "false importance" that rendered them "vain and refractory." Town meetings in the thirteen colonies had clearly exceeded their power. Henceforth a statute or charter should make null and void all the votes and business of such meetings.[13]

Although Smith lamented the long-term misrule of American colonies, he was most bitter about the British handling of the revolutionary situation after 1775. He regretted Parliament's rigidity and its unwillingness to cede local control to appointed executives in times of emergency. In particular he expressed dismay at Britain's handling of the peace overtures in the spring of 1778. Short of independence, the Carlisle Peace Commission had granted the colonies all the concessions they had demanded before the Declaration of Independence. But Smith complained about the lack of authority vested in the Carlisle Commission. Even by that late date, Parliament had not authorized the commission to make final and abiding decisions about a "generous and lasting reunion" based on their firsthand knowledge of the colonial context. The powers of these commissioners, he lamented, were not "decisive and irreversible" because Parliament controlled the final authority "to confirm or reject" their conclusions. If the 1778 concessions could have been circulated as law and not as mere proposals, he insisted, the "party of independence would have been broken and ruined."[14] Here Smith blamed Britain for not offering the Loyalists a timely and substantive alternative to republicanism.

Most assuredly Britain's loss of the thirteen colonies lay with the measures adopted by the government—long-term and short-term—and not with the actions of the king's friends in the colonies. Smith was most enraged about Britain's negligence of the king's friends during the Revolution. He emphasized that Loyalist support was powerful during the years of war. He observed that the revolt had never been the wish of the "Continent." Indeed he lamented that Britain, by ignoring the strength of support for the unity of empire, did not "avail herself of the aid of the Friends." By failing to set up a civil government in cities such as New York, and refusing to organize and arm the Loyalists, the empire had left the king's most devoted friends to the "mercy of their enemies."

From his criticisms of the government during the Revolution, Smith offered recommendations for strengthening British North America. The government should encourage and reward the allegiance of its most loyal subjects lest these people become "impatient and disappointed" and become the "exasperated foes" of Britain."[15] These local executives could assist in maintaining peace and securing allegiance. Smith wanted the agents of the government in British North America to be committed to a "discreet vigilance on the spot." As long as it was consistent with the weal of the whole empire, the agent should "be adequate to everything he may see expedient to grant."[16] It was the "inattention" to this local aspect of executive power, Smith argued, that brought on the late rebellion. All the common threads of language, religion, and interest were inadequate if an executive was not placed to "quicken" these bonds into activity. With the right "head," the British government could, under one banner, have collected not only the Loyalists but "all the overflowings of Great Britain and the dispersions of Europe."[17]

Smith's view that Loyalists should lead the development of British North America was echoed by others. In "Brief Observations," the anonymous essayist also promoted the settlement of Loyalists, "principled men, with their families and property" who would accelerate the growth of an "eligible asylum." The "*true* Loyalists" would function as "the pole star" for the expansion of the new colony. The British would reap great benefits "by fixing them in as free and advantageous a situation as the nature of the government can admit."[18]

The ideal of establishing a separate and distinct Loyalist haven ruled by men of proven loyalty and superior intelligence was not a postwar development. In 1780 an establishment in the northern portion of what is now Maine had been proposed for "meritorious and distressed" Loyalists who could not return to their former homes. New Ireland, as the colony would be called, would also promote the settlement of Loyalist regiments who could enlist as the need arose. Most of all, New Ireland would become self-sustaining and relieve the British government from the continual expense of supporting the Loyalists and their families.[19]

Surprisingly the Loyalist understanding of the rebellion—as caused by ambitious schemers who manipulated a large populace—led them to imagine common Americans as adding to British strength. The Loyalists did not perceive ordinary people as having fixed republican principles that inevitably threatened constitutional government. Disappointed at the republican experiment, many would happily exchange the chaos of their world to live under British protection. According to Smith, the principles, habits, friendships, connections, and the "temper raised by their afflictions" meant that Americans were the most "eligible to become citizens" of the Canadian provinces. The anonymous author of "Brief Observations" also emphasized that instability, the "internal boils" and "natural evils," would encourage many Americans to migrate to the British colonies. Many were more than ready to abandon their "once darling wish of independency." They would not sacrifice their lives a second time for imaginary blessings. They would not be "impudent nor dangerous" subjects.[20]

This anonymous essayist invited nonloyalist Americans from the seceded colonies to British North America. The "paternal goodness" of Britain would encourage the zeal and ambition of true subjects and "operate most forcibly on the revolted Americans by proving . . . what they might have enjoyed on a reunion with their careful and gracious Sovereign, and fellow-subjects."[21] To encourage large-scale American migration to Nova Scotia, the British must immediately offer "unsolicited" a legal guarantee to reassure the Americans that they would "enjoy all the rights and privileges of real British subjects." Procrastination could have "fatal consequences." The large migration would help to establish Nova Scotia to its "proper height of strength and influence." The success of the Maritimes depended not only on political stability but on a substantially larger population.[22]

Writing years before the ratification of the Constitution stabilized the relations between the thirteen states and their new federal government, Smith imagined a reconnection between the seceded colonies and the British Empire. From his first-hand experience in New York, he knew that that government of the United States was shaky. If Britain set up a proper system of constitutional government as an example to the southern nation, it would invite those unhappy with the American system to consider reuniting with the empire. Among the unhappy Smith called out the quiet Loyalists of New York and Pennsylvania, the debtors to British subjects, the provinces that opposed the creation of a centralized establishment, the merchants suffering without credit, the soldiers denied adequate compensation for their services, and the landlords who "condemn the equality, hate the insolence, and dread the rapacity of the poor."[23] He mocked as "fallacious" those who painted the new country as the "hope and refuge of Humanity" and emphasized that America "seems to be in the wildest confusion."[24] The outbreak of Shays' Rebellion in Massachusetts confirmed Loyalists' pessimism about the future of the United States. In October 1786 Anglican reverend Mather Byles, formerly of New England, observed cynically that the "public disturbances are no more than it was natural to expect."[25] Like Smith, Byles predicted turmoil and lawlessness for the new nation.

Smith's concern with populating British North America echoed in other Loyalist proposals. Dr. Silvester Gardiner, the seventy-eight-year old New England Loyalist, stressed the relationship between population and dominion. On the eve of the Revolution, Gardiner was a wealthy man with many houses in Kennebec, Maine, and close political ties to Boston's elites. During the pre-Revolutionary crisis, he had faced being tarred and feathered and possible banishment. He sought safety in Boston in 1776. Unwilling to go too far from home, he went to Halifax and then British-governed New York City the following year. For two years he tried to set up a small business selling drugs and his own silver and to make some income collecting outstanding debts. By 1778, when his Massachusetts property was confiscated, he abandoned hope of returning to New England and left for England. When the war ended, Gardiner was settled in Poole, England, because he had become interested in trade with Newfoundland that was controlled by the merchants there.[26]

Gardiner promoted Newfoundland as not only a commercial but also a settlement colony. He underlined the strategic importance of naval power and, hence, the reliance on skilled seamen, nurtured in Newfoundland's fisheries, who could man England's mercantile, marine, and fishing fleets.[27] Gardiner criticized the disadvantages of Britain's existing policy because it encouraged these seamen, at the end of their service, to migrate to the "ambitious rival nation" to the South. He had been eyewitness to at least five hundred who had left Newfoundland and come to Boston.[28] The emigration of these fishermen removed their naval talents from the British, and the loss of their numbers weakened the British colony.

A permanent population, Gardiner insisted, was the source not only of great riches but provided for the "strength and security" of every country. These laborers, "poor miserable wretches," could contribute to the creation of a "flourishing colony," and if provided with property and civil government, they would create manufactures, build whaling ships, and "retire to little cottages with their wives and children and enjoy every domestic felicity in common with their fellow inhabitants."[29] Content and secure in Newfoundland, they would be less likely to migrate to the United States and add to the talents and strength of the rival nation. In the long term, the colonization of Newfoundland was essential to protecting the British Empire in the North Atlantic.

Since John Cabot's first voyages to Newfoundland in 1497 and 1498, the English had maintained a continuing interest in the region. Treating Newfoundland as an extension of Europe and not as a settlement colony, West Country merchants had long sent seasonal labors to work in its fisheries.[30] The merchants opposed long-term settlement of the island and treated it primarily as maritime fishery. In a region where economic activity outpaced demographic or political development, the West Country merchants prevailed.[31] The regulation of the economy and the limited settlement permitted in Newfoundland was legislated by the Parliament and not by a colonial assembly. Understanding that supremacy at sea required trained seamen to man fleets in times of war, the British government's interests aligned with those of the merchants.

Yet despite strict regulations, the requirement for compulsory return to England of Newfoundland fishermen was constantly broken. By 1783 Newfoundland had twelve thousand residents. Third-generation families lived in the island, and some independently carried on trade with Southern Europe.[32] But the imperial government refused to recognize the transformation of the island. In 1784 the only concession was the arrival of James O'Donnell as the first Roman Catholic priest on the island.[33] Despite the large number of long-term residents, the lack of clear title to land made inhabitants resistant to improving their conditions or establishing lasting institutions. In 1783 there were no roads, public schools, hospitals, postal service, or newspapers. In the 1783 Treaty of Paris, Britain showed its lack of interest for the Newfoundland colonists by permitting New England to continue its participation in the Newfoundland fisheries and France to maintain fishing rights on the northern shore.[34]

Gardiner's thoughts about the benefits of colonization came at a time when the British Empire was weighing the economic significance of American independence: Was the expense of colonization necessary for the commercial expansion of the empire? Was mercantilism more profitable than free trade?[35] With the loss of the thirteen colonies, Britain had lost a valuable domain. As much as a third of its merchant marine as well as its control over raw materials such as timber and naval stores was gone forever. Most important, the British sugar islands, heavily dependent on lumber, dairy, and meat from the former colonies, needed a new supplier.

Planning Ahead

During the Revolutionary years, the Loyalists had not disregarded the colonies' economic role when they proposed plans for imperial union. In 1780 Pennsylvania assemblyman Joseph Galloway, a longtime protégé of Benjamin Franklin, began his discourse on the subject of reunion with two questions: "What is the best system of policy by which America, in future, be governed by the British state, to the longest period of time? And, secondly, what advantages of commerce the colonists ought to injoy as members of that State?"[36] Without doubt Galloway gave the political question more weight.[37] The economic question would acquire a new prominence for the exiled Loyalists in British North America.

The British government had to decide the terms for a new relationship with the seceded colonies. Already in the peace negotiations of 1782, Lord Shelburne had expressed interest in moving Britain toward a commercial partnership with the new nation. He felt "deep concern" in the "separation of countries, united by blood, by principles, habits and every tie." To "avoid all future risk of enmity," he supported a "foundation . . . better adapted to the present temper and interests in both countries."[38] Shelburne wanted to restore the economic privileges the thirteen colonies had formerly enjoyed as part of the empire.[39] In place of settlement colonies, the United States would become a trading ally. Continued US consumption of British goods would ensure a market for rapidly expanding British manufactures, and US shipments to the Caribbean would mean an uninterrupted supply of sugar.

After Shelburne was forced out of office in February 1783, the new minister, William Pitt the Younger, also introduced a bill "for the provisional establishment and regulation of trade and intercourse between the subjects of Great Britain and those of the United States of America." This would have permitted American ships to export and import goods to the West Indies and Great Britain on the footing established prior to the Revolution.[40]

Some British politicians objected to the lenient commercial policy advocated by Shelburne and Pitt. In 1783 Lord Sheffield, another member of the British Parliament, believed that maintaining a self-sufficient empire required mercantilism. The Navigation Act, "the guardian of prosperity of Britain," if abandoned would reduce the "Naval Power of Britain." Only the West India planters would "derive any benefit, however partial and transient, from their open intercourse directly with the American States, and indirectly with the rest of the world."[41] To maintain naval supremacy and employ six hundred thousand seamen, British ships must be the mechanism for moving goods from British ports. Those in the West Indies had to learn to manage their plantations with more economy and efficiency for the long-term benefit of the nation.[42]

The Loyalist George Chalmers, an Edinburgh-trained lawyer, shared Sheffield's views. Chalmers had fled Maryland in 1775, when the outbreak of revolutionary hostilities made it impossible for prominent Loyalists to remain in the northern colonies. Chalmers was bitter about his losses and his treatment during the Revolution. Like Gardiner he resented a policy that would permit the United States to prosper commercially. Chalmers wished explicitly to exclude American goods by legislation rather than to trust British success to open competition. Along with

Loyalist officer Brook Watson, William Smith Jr., and the anonymous Loyalist essayist, Chalmers wanted the North American colonies with their Loyalist settlers to rise to prominence.[43] With the help of Loyalists and Loyalist exports from British North America, the truncated British Empire would be as self-sufficient as it was in 1775.

Chalmers laid the blame for the rebellion first with Britain and then with New England. He observed that the threat of revolution had brewed since the founding of the colonies. The "original defects" of the colonial constitutions did not sufficiently control the colonies.[44] In addition the economic independence of the thirteen colonies had long posed a threat to Britain. "From the date of their successive settlements," he raged, "they have generally framed their commercial regulations rather as the opponents than the subjects of a trading empire."[45] Chalmers lamented the division of interests between the colonies and Britain by the early eighteenth century. During the War of Jenkins' Ear (King George's War), New Englanders had demanded cash for military services, as mercenaries, instead of acting as "subjects of a great empire." They had profited from "illicit and undutiful" traffic with the enemy while their fellow subjects in Britain had carried the burden of the war.[46] In fact the "New-English" had aimed at independence from the earliest period. While England was engaged in a civil war, they "extended their plantations, and established their independence. . . . [They] derided the authority of their native land and neglected the jurisprudence of their fathers."[47] These New Englanders "disseminated their peculiar principles among the colonies of the south either by their communication or their example."[48]

Like other Loyalists, Chalmers regarded the growth of the US population as an ominous sign. The "successive augmentation of their populousness" was encouraged by the "importation of the African Negro, the German refugee, the Irish emigrant, the English convict, and the Scotch adventurer."[49] The weakness of the imperial political hold combined with the large population had led "by a natural progress" toward "revolt and civil war."[50]

Like Smith, Chalmers accused the British of negligence. He believed that the British government could have taken measures to check the "encroaching spirit" of the thirteen colonies.[51] Most recently, the British Parliament had not given "permanent energy" to the 1754 Albany Plan of Union. When the colonial delegates had asked the government to "compel" a plan because the colonies would disagree among themselves on quotas and measures, Britain "cautiously avoided all political regulation as either dangerous or unnecessary."[52]

Inspired by the necessity of common defense against the French and Indians, the Albany Plan proposed a union of contiguous colonies in a local confederation. Emanating from the directives of the Lords of Trade, the Albany conference led colonists such as Benjamin Franklin to suggest the creation of an in-between authority that would mediate between the Crown and the colonies for the purpose of protecting the colonists against the Aboriginals and the British against the French. In this proposal, a Crown-appointed president general and a grand council of delegates elected by the colonial assemblies would bridge between the realities of the colony and the interests of the Crown. Far from the harbinger of an American national identity, the proponents of the Albany Plan envisioned a future in which Britain would establish a coordinated system of imperial governance in North America. Smith's father, the elder William Smith, had participated in the Albany conference.

In the spring of 1783, Chalmers published his *Observations on the Commerce of the American States with Europe and the West Indies.* He challenged any policy that strengthened those who had given up their birthright in violent rebellion. Under no circumstances must Americans "act as rivals in the commerce of the West Indies," a trade that the British nation "is still bound to defend."[53] The king had already declared the United States as a free, independent, and sovereign nation. Hence "it did not require a great lawyer to tell that the soil of such a nation was alien; that the ships of such a nation were alien; and that the navigators of such ships were, ex prima facie, aliens."[54] Britain must cease imagining itself as related to the colonies. The father who ceased to be a father by the death of his son was different than the father who cast off his son.[55] In the strongest tone, Chalmers insisted that the seceded colonies "had no claim to anything beyond independence."[56]

Chalmers's hope for the Loyalists and the Maritimes clashed with the interests of the Caribbean planters. The loss of the thirteen colonies had alarmed the merchants, who worried about supplying lumber and food to the planters and slaves in the sugar islands. They hoped to continue with what they considered the cheapest option: providing American supplies in American ships to the Caribbean. In response Chalmers insisted that the islands could thrive without dependence on the United States. In the short term, the West Indies could receive salt meats from Ireland, fish from Newfoundland, horses from England, and poultry from Bermuda.[57] Within three years Nova Scotia and Canada would be able to furnish the supplies required by the Caribbean planters.[58] Based on his long experience in the colonies, Chalmers reassured the government that United States would not retaliate by prohibiting all trade with Britain because the Americans were addicted to British manufactures and West Indian rum.[59]

Voices such as Chalmers's had some influence on British policy. Between 1782 and 1784, Shelburne's and Pitt's vision of economic liberalization was partially rejected. To maintain an exclusive imperial trade in the West Indies, British North America would play a more central role. In July 1783 American shipping was excluded from the West Indies trade, and staples such as meat, dairy, and fish were not allowed to be carried to the islands, even in British ships.[60] But an important statute specified that the United States could supply these items if they were in short supply in the North American colonies. Moreover, in an effort to gain a monopoly on the carrying trade, the British specified that the Americans could export and import enumerated items as long as they did so in British ships: they could export naval stores, lumber, flour, and grain to the sugar colonies and import rum, sugar, molasses, and coffee. These orders were passed continuously until 1788, when they became embodied in an act of Parliament.[61]

The Loyalist vision of the Maritimes as a colonial granary, a large reserve of timber, and a potential market for British manufactures and West India rum did not materialize. In 1783 Gov. John Parr of Nova Scotia had found it necessary to import timber, provisions, and livestock from the United States to meet the needs of Loyalists.[62] In 1789 exports to the West Indies declined further.[63] It was clear that the Maritimes did not have the resources, especially interior transportation, to compete with the more mature economy of the United States. Nova Scotia, in terms of the recentness of its settlement, the newness of its political structures, its lack of urban networks, and the thin reach of its institutional establishments, resembled the backcountry South more than the well-connected regions from which so many settlers had migrated.[64] The New England Loyalist Mather Byles commented on the "hissing wilderness": there was not a single quadruped that howled, but there was an abundance of rattlesnakes.[65]

Arriving from urban towns, many of the new immigrants to the Maritimes were inexperienced farmers. Some looked down on agricultural labor. Local consumption left little for export in the first years after the war.[66] Fishing remained more profitable than cultivating crops, and the high cost of growing grain could not compete with the lower cost and higher profits of cattle raising. In addition the Nova Scotians found it easy to import provisions from the coastal towns in United States, where the flour was superior and also cheaper because of the United States' reliance on slave labor.[67]

The British partnership with the United States—politically unnatural but economically indispensable—left the Loyalists in British North America economically unprotected.[68] The theory of a self-sustained empire remained, but the practical needs of supplying the West Indies were paramount. Because the health of fifty thousand whites and five hundred thousand blacks depended on the reliable supply of food, cattle, and lumber, and because British mercantile interests lobbied for the protection of the sugar islands, the British compromised the Maritimes. Caught between the long-term interests of the British North America and the short-term needs of the West Indies, they chose to protect their immediate sugar interests. The West Indian trade led to years of extraordinary prosperity for the United States and of lost potential for the Maritimes.[69]

The 1807 US embargo changed the commercial possibilities for British North America. Without the benefit of the United States as supplier to the West Indies, the British opened free trade ports, and Nova Scotia became the entrepôt for North Atlantic trade. For the first time, British North American ports handled more shipping than the ports of the United States.[70] Historian Gerald Graham argues that the continuation of the embargo would have created a long-term basis for systematized West Indies trade.[71] But the embargo was repealed in March 1, 1809. And again the Maritimes struggled to align their interests with those of the empire.

Imagining Intercolonial Union

Although the Albany Plan did not receive intercolonial or imperial support, the idea of a union under the Crown became a source of inspiration for moderates during the pre-Revolutionary crisis twenty years later. These Americans were concerned about the brittle and uncompromising tone that had crept into the imperial debate. They continued to believe that an American supergovernment could act as an ideal intermediary between the colonies and London and provide a constitutional solution to imperial conflicts. In February 1774 Joseph Galloway expressed his anxiety about the future of the colonies if cast without the unifying influence of the empire. Galloway worried that the various colonies acted as independent communities that shared nothing in common. They had "different forms of government, productions of soil, and views of commerce; different religions, tempers, and private interests." Their only hope of mutual harmony and stability lay within the empire.[72]

In a letter written to Galloway, Gov. William Franklin also proposed a written constitution to define more clearly the colonies' relationship to Parliament: "I wish most sincerely with you that a Constitution was formed and settled for America, that we might know what we are and what we have, what our Rights and what our Duties are, in the Judgment of this country as well as our own. Till such a Constitution is settled, different sentiments will ever occasion Misunderstanding."[73] Galloway called for a Crown-appointed president-general to serve as the chief executive for the colonies. This president-general would govern with a grand council chosen by the colonial assemblies for a period of three years. The grand council would exercise "all the legislative rights, powers and authorities necessary for regulating and administering all the general police & affairs of the colonies." Together the president-general and grand council would constitute "an inferior branch of the British legislature." To mediate potentially conflicting interests among the colonies, the president-general could veto any acts passed by the grand council. Galloway's proposal gave the colonies veto power over imperial taxes but preserved the ultimate sovereignty of the Crown and Parliament. To deny the supreme authority of Parliament over the colonies, he believed, would be a "manifest contradiction while we confess that we are subjects of the British Government."[74]

Despite his respect for the sovereignty of Parliament, Galloway recognized its limits in times of war. The government's panoramic observations about the American colonies did not offset the disadvantages of distance and imperfect local knowledge. In the last passage of his plan, he recognized the urgent problem of distance between the colonies and Britain and went so far as to dismiss the need for parliamentary approval in times of crisis: "That in Time of War all Bills for granting Aids to the Crown prepared by the Grand Council and approved by the president General shall be valid and passed into a Law *without* the Assent of the British Parliament."[75] In 1779 Galloway tempered the radicalism of his earlier proposal by suggesting that Parliament issue a temporary act that granted the king's local representative permission to pass laws in times of war.[76]

In 1780 he continued to believe that proper measures could bridge the distance between the two sides and lead to successful reunion. He insisted that distance did not mean that the components of the "beautiful if not the most powerful system in the world" should be severed.[77] Instead he insisted that the greater distance necessitated a more perfect union. If governed with "uniformity and vigor," the state's authority would reach "all parts of society, without regard to their locality in the empire." Galloway likened the empire's authority to the "powers of the human will," which could keep many extremities in order.[78] In 1779 he had noted the "peace and Harmony and perfect submission" that resulted from the union between England and Scotland.[79] Again in 1780 he cited that union as the "magical charm" that suddenly transformed discontent and rebellion into peace and order.[80]

The political explanation for British failure offered by exiled Loyalists did not differ radically from Galloway's observations during the war. Despite the problem of distance and local decision-making, the exiles saw nothing inevitable about American victory. They believed that British policies, short-term and long-term, had enabled the conditions for the unnatural break with the empire, and if proper political measures were not taken in the future, Britain would again face the risk of disloyalty and another colonial revolt.

Jonathan Sewell, former attorney general of Massachusetts, diagnosed the causes of the Revolution from London. Sewell's experience in Patriot Boston—in contrast to Smith's wartime experience in Loyalist New York City—may have shaped his more bitter recollections of the war. Significantly he did not consider the possibility of adding numbers to British North America by winning the Americans. His essay expressed a mixture of emotions—clarity about the conditions that had led to successful rebellion, anger at the government's disregard for Loyalists, and, finally, faith that Loyalists could set an example for a revised political structure in British North America.[81]

Sewell blasted Britain's handling of Boston during the pre-Revolutionary years. He had escaped harassment from Patriotic mobs in Boston by fleeing to London in the summer of 1775. Sewell was among another eight thousand Loyalists who sought refuge in England during the war.[82] In a 1776 letter to fellow Loyalist Edward Winslow, Sewell expressed his rage at the American revolutionaries and his desire for the government to take retributive action: "I wish the vengeance of Great Britain may speedily overtake their base deluders." He never wished to see Massachusetts again "till I return at the millennium."[83]

In 1785 Sewell observed that "nothing" contributed more to the rebellion than the distance of the country from Great Britain. He noted that the replies from Britain had taken so long that small issues had turned into "real evils." Indeed "local circumstances shifted so suddenly and violently between the giving information and receiving instructions how to act" that the government was powerless to avoid acting on "erroneous principles." When an immediate remedy was necessary to stop disorders, it could not be constitutionally procured in sufficient time. The "lapse," he thought, gave "full scope for such disorders to increase and rage so universally" as to "render the intended remedy ineffective." To guard against this in the future, Sewell proposed the appointment of a lord-lieutenant or governor general who would have authority, in any emergency, to make final decisions.[84]

Sewell ended his essay on a note of optimism. He proposed "His Majesty's colonies on the Continent of America." As Benjamin Franklin had offered suggestions for a unification of the colonies in 1754 in his "Short Hints towards a Scheme for Uniting the Northern Colonies," Sewell offered "some general hints on the subject."[85] Like Franklin in 1754, William Smith Jr. in 1767, and Galloway in 1774, Sewell proposed the appointment of a Crown-appointed executive and a legislative council with the power to tax. The Albany Plan had proposed "one general government" for North America; Sewell proposed one general act like the Magna Carta for all the British colonies.[86] For him the threat of separatism was strong and real, and the possibility of union, though difficult, was essential. The creation of a new American republic made union of the northern colonies necessary.

But Sewell's expectation of a united British North America was not shared by the British government. In 1784 Col. Robert Morse of the Royal Engineers expressed the minority opinion when he wrote: "In the course of this Report, my mind has been strongly impressed with the idea of uniting these Provinces with Canada, to the advantage of both countries, and that by establishing the same laws, inducing a constant intercourse and mutual interest, a great country may yet be raised up in North America."[87] The tendency of the British government was toward particularism rather than amalgamation of the Northern colonies. In 1784 New Brunswick and Cape Breton were separated from Nova Scotia, and each was given its own government. In 1791 Upper Canada as an English-speaking province was set apart from Lower Canada, which remained French.

Instead of supporting intercolonial union, the British government gave impetus to the Church of England as a means of fostering loyalty. Membership in the church would promote loyalty to Britain. Civil disobedience, the government believed, had resulted from the absence of correct religious principles. Without Episcopal supervision, the church could not combat revolutionary propaganda. In 1787 the Reverend Charles Inglis, former rector of Trinity Church in New York, was appointed bishop of Nova Scotia. Significantly he had jurisdiction not only over Nova Scotia but also Canada, Newfoundland, and New Brunswick.

In 1789 Bishop Inglis promoted the idea of an Anglican seminary for American refugees. He linked Anglican theology with British constitutionalism. Nova Scotia was an "asylum of Loyalists who wish to have their children educated in constitutional principles."[88] If proper encouragement was not given to Anglican establishments, the next generation would not be indoctrinated in constitutional principles. They would go to churches run by Methodists, who "get drunk and blaspheme like atheists."[89] The church would assure "diffuse salutary effects" so that "pure religion, virtue, order and loyalty may prevail."[90] Like Inglis, the author of "Brief Observations" also underscored the importance of Anglicanism as a means of establishing political allegiance. An Anglican Church would increase the loyalty of the subjects, although no compulsory methods should be adopted. Religion, the essayist wrote, was "politically essential in every system of government." Those whose tenets point them to republicanism had a great influence over youth and should be prevented from being heads of colleges and seminaries of learning.[91]

William Smith did not share Inglis's view on the importance of Anglicanism. More than twenty years earlier, Inglis and Smith had clashed over the question of an American bishopric. Ten years before that, Smith had promoted a secular state university (King's College) for New York. In British North America, he appealed to his patron, Lord Dorchester, to establish schools where no theology was taught, while Inglis appealed to the church hierarchy in England to promote an Anglican educational establishment. Instead of religion serving as a binding glue, Smith anticipated that British "liberal government . . . without any contracted preference or religious discriminations" would help to assimilate the French in Quebec and create to a bicultural region protected by English law.[92]

It took the next generation of American Loyalists to elaborate on Jonathan Sewell's idea that governments could maintain their essential autonomy and at the same time retain membership in the empire. In 1824 Sewell's son, the younger Jonathan Sewell, along with John Beverly Robinson, son of Virginia Loyalist Christopher Robinson, emphasized that the empire faced no threat from the union of the British North American provinces. They tried to convince the British government that the union would lead neither to separation nor revolt.

In 1785 Loyalists such as the older Sewell had supported union because they had hoped to transform the British provinces from their marginal position as scattered settlements to an indispensable part of the empire. They had promoted optimistically the provinces' potential. The empire had everything to gain from a united British North America. Almost forty years later, the Loyalist ideal had not come to pass. Ironically they now stressed the economic disappointment of the provinces to promote colonial union. Sewell and Robinson assured the British government that the united colonies would not abandon imperial connections because they could not survive commercially outside them. Nor did they have the means to protect themselves against a rival nation such as the United States. The British American colonies, they emphasized, had "no rational hope of preserving their independence by their own strength."[93] The empire had nothing to fear from a united British America.

Somewhat sharply the Loyalists reminded the government that there was no connection between intercolonial union and rebellion. The late American revolt had not arisen because of the consolidation of the colonies. The colonies had separate governments at the time of the revolt, and in fact the "violence of particular states would have been moderated by the more steady counsels of the whole united."[94] They advocated union because the combined strength would make them feel more as "parts rather than dependencies of Britain."[95]

CONCLUSION

During the Revolution Loyalist spokesmen hoped a single coalition would speak on behalf of Loyalist interests. Writing in December 1779, Maryland Loyalist Anthony Stewart wrote the importance of establishing a board that would collect and disseminate information favorable to the Loyalist cause. Stewart explained that "refugees from the several revolted colonies should chuse Representation to sit in a general committee to watch over their mutual interests . . . to convey a true state of the present situation of America and the practicability of conquering this country by pursuing proper measures."[96] But no united Loyalist voice emerged during the Revolution.

After the Revolution the exiled Loyalists did not organize under a single official or administrative structure. Yet there emerged a growing convergence about their vision for British North America. Although not in direct or intimate contact with one another, the exiled Loyalists diagnosed the problems of the Revolution similarly, revised older solutions, and, most of all, imagined a world where they would one day outpace the United States economically and demographically. They hoped the British government would stabilize their political world, promote their economic advancement, and protect them against rival nations. They anticipated that their progress would advance Britain's interests in the North Atlantic. Unlike the British the Loyalists did not look upon intercolonial union as a dangerous tendency. Intimately aware of the US presence to the south, they saw union as protection against US expansionism.

During the 1760s and 1770s, the British government moved toward more centralized political control over its North American colonies. The violent reaction to this control had led to the secession of thirteen colonies. Devoted to the ideal of colonial prosperity and imperial union, the Loyalists were exiled from their homes. In the Maritimes they were caught in yet another British transformation. During the 1780s and 1790s, the empire began to move away from mercantilism and toward free trade. The security given to the commercial expansion of the thirteen colonies in the seventeenth century was denied to the Loyalists in British North America. Thus the Americans who had compelled the Loyalists into exile benefitted most from Britain's new policies. With cheaper goods, a more mature economy, and millions of consumers, the United States was a better trading partner to Britain than the economically limited provinces.

Warren R. Hofstra

Afterword

Robert McCluer Calhoon—The Politics
of Moderation and a Passion for Teaching

That Robert McCluer Calhoon's students and fellow scholars have organized a festschrift for him is hardly surprising. The testimonial essays in this volume speak eloquently to the profound influence that Calhoon has had on these authors as they developed their ideas and careers. It is my hunch, however, that at work behind this festschrift is the greater inspiration of a master at conveying history's deeper meaning to others because his own scholarship has arisen from a deep well of personal experience that he learned to craft as history in the course of a long and distinguished career. Bob Calhoon has certainly influenced me in this way, and I am honored to write this afterword.

Like so many others, I became acquainted with Bob first through his work and reputation in the field of Revolutionary War history. Our friendship as colleagues grew at various history conferences, seminars, and other meetings. Much of Bob's early work focused on the British Loyalists during the American Revolution. By the 1980s, however, his interests began to shift to the region of the eighteenth-century backcountry. Most of the events where we encountered one another concerned this frontier region and the rising field of scholarship on it. We obviously shared this interest. Only gradually, however, did I begin to grasp the scope and depth of his fascination for the backcountry. For Bob it was a source of political moderation in an American political history otherwise dominated by accounts of party politics and policies. Moderates did not fit in—nor did Robert McClure Calhoon. His work on them is sui generis.

It was for this reason that I turned to him for collaboration in a project of mine about the eighteenth-century migration of people from the north of Ireland to the British New World colonies—literally from Ulster to America, as indicated in the title of the resulting collection of essays.[1] These people came to call themselves the Scotch-Irish, although the term is laden with political freight in the culture wars of our own day. Many writers attribute the contemporary lifeways of southern, rural, and working-class people to an essentialist Scotch-Irish culture that purportedly persisted from the eighteenth century to today as defined by country music, gun rights, social violence, evangelicalism, and deeply conservative politics.[2] The heartland of this culture resides in the Appalachian highlands of West Virginia, western Virginia, North and South Carolina, and Georgia in addition to eastern Kentucky and Tennessee.

This is the region that scholars of early America have been calling the backcountry and to which Bob Calhoon turned in midcareer. His theme of political moderation made much greater sense out of it and the experience of backcountry Scotch-Irish than did the essentialist arguments of the apologists for southern conservatism. Although large numbers of the Scotch-Irish migrated and settled there between the late 1720s and the end of the eighteenth century, the defining cultural characteristic of the backcountry was diversity, not homogeneity. The continued presence of Native Americans had profoundly influenced the settlement history of the region and helped define its role in the evolving imperial politics of British colonialism and early American nationalism. But constituting a truly polyglot culture there were large numbers of Europeans, including the Scotch-Irish but also English, Anglo-American, and German migrants intermixed with smaller numbers of Dutch, Scandinavian, French, and other European settlers along with a relatively small number of African American slaves they acquired or brought with them. Pluralism and change, not static essentialism, shaped the cultural trajectory of the backcountry and Appalachia from the eighteenth century to the present. Although many residents today align with conservative causes, Democrats and Republicans, liberals and conservatives, evangelicals and humanists have mutually created a dynamic and evolving political culture there.

It was this diversity and dynamism that attracted Calhoon's attention. The counterpart of diversity is accommodation. To live together, culturally diverse people must by necessity learn to compromise. And the story that Calhoon found in the backcountry entailed people with different languages, values, politics, and cultures. They shared, however, a common economy—the means of living off the land—that to make work required constant trade, negotiation, and mediation. Their religions and denominations differed, but they shared a common commitment to reconciling differences lawfully and peacefully. Here was a formula for moderation. For Calhoon moderation is not simply a political posture or tendency to occupy the middle of the political road. Moderates are not those who avoid political extremes, steer clear of strong political philosophies, and shun conflict. To be a moderate is itself not moderate, but it is to moderate. Political moderates, according to Calhoon, are people "who intentionally undertake civic action, at significant risk or cost, to mediate conflicts, conciliate antagonisms, or find middle ground."[3]

Although not a political party, moderation is a distinct political philosophy. Moderates are not uncertain, indecisive people with their mugs on one side of the fence and their wumps on the other. "The substantial core of political moderation expressed itself as a political philosophy at the core of civil society," writes

Calhoon.[4] Moderates tend the fences in a political world in which fences do make for better neighbors. Thus moderation is a "synonym for political reasonableness."[5] Moderates are negotiators, conciliators, mediators, arbitrators, and go-betweens. They are not appeasers; they compromise but are not easily compromised or bought off. As pragmatists they stand for what works and can be achieved. One North Carolina moderate, whom Calhoon studied, counseled Hampden-Sydney students in 1866 that "only what is rational and attainable should be the object of our desires."[6] By not taking sides, moderates can attain the greatest good for the greatest numbers, promote the public welfare, and secure the commonweal.

Diversity, as the defining feature of the eighteenth-century backcountry, transformed the region into "an incubator of moderate politics," according to Calhoon.[7] His argument in his most important work on the subject, *Political Moderation in America's First Two Centuries,* and reiterated in his afterword for *Ulster to America,* holds that ethnic, religious, and cultural diversity throughout the broad region of the southern uplands owing to its settlement by Scotch-Irish and many other ethnic and national groups created an environment where political success required political participation by people with widely varying identities and political leadership could be founded only on the common ground of their religion and their economic interdependence. "The backcountry was moderate because it was conflicted," argues Calhoon, "conflicted because it was demographically dynamic, and demographically dynamic because ethnic identities in the backcountry were grounded in religion."[8] He is wholly unique in seeing this connection between moderation and the backcountry. During the past quarter century, the backcountry has provided the subject for a great deal of scholarship, but only Calhoon has been able so effectively to draw this scholarship out of the eighteenth century and render moderation meaningful in the twentieth and twenty-first centuries as a profoundly relevant political philosophy. No wonder his students are so receptive and responsive.

Where, we might ask, did he get his ideas? What experiences brought them to mind? If, for Bob Calhoon, scholarship is lived experience, then where has life led him in their development? How did they inspire the passion of his writing and teaching? Some anecdotes are in order. Bob grew up in Pittsburgh, the northern hub of the southern backcountry. According to historian David Cannadine, "Western Pennsylvania [in the eighteenth and early nineteenth centuries] was very much a cultural extension of Protestant Ulster, and that was in turn an extension of Presbyterian Scotland."[9] As one local story had it, in answering John Knox's request for Scotland, God threw in Ulster and Pittsburgh for good measure. The irony—the joke—lies in the reputation Pittsburgh earned by the end of the nineteenth century as "Hell with the lid off." It was an inferno of industrial development—steel, railroads, oil, aluminum, Carborundum. It sucked in immigrant workers from all over the world. By the twentieth century, it was one of the most diverse cities in the United States. It may have taken the soft corruption and ward heeling of machine politics to keep it running in the industrial era, but it was the conflict between capital and labor, not quarrels within or among immigrant groups, that shaped its history during the period of Calhoon's upbringing. The working people of Pittsburgh learned to live together under great tension and stress.

Bob's next stop on the way to academia lay at the College of Wooster, in Wooster, Ohio. Named for Gen. David Wooster, of Revolutionary War fame, the city and its eponymous college may have nurtured Calhoon's interest in the American Revolution. But perhaps more influential was the open-to-everyone atmosphere promoted at the institution. Diversity was its keystone. It prides itself for granting its first PhD degree to a woman, Annie B. Irish, in 1882 and opening its doors to African Americans shortly thereafter. The Revolution carried Calhoon into graduate school at Case Western Reserve University, where he achieved distinction as the first student to earn a PhD under eminent colonialist and Revolutionary War scholar Jack P. Greene. According to Bob, "the coming of the Revolution was the 'hot' topic in the 1960s and that meant research trips to Boston, New York, Philadelphia, and Charleston."[10]

At this point Calhoon's career took a series of what might best be called providential turns. In 1964, with doctorate in hand, he received two job offers. One from DePaul University in Chicago provided a tenure track in his field of early American and Revolutionary War history. The other from the University of North Carolina at Greensboro (UNCG) was a one-year instructorship teaching European and American surveys. Like Paul on the road to Damascus, Bob Calhoon embraced the unexpected. "For reasons I could not articulate clearly at the moment, I declined the DePaul offer," he later reflected. "Although I never regretted my choice, I sometimes wondered why I made it."[11] If he had decided otherwise, this festschrift would, no doubt, never have come into existence, and his scholarship would probably have taken quite different directions. Greensboro was critical to what came next.

For exceptional and perhaps equally providential reasons, Richard Nelson Current had been drawn to UNCG to head the history department in 1955. That was the year in which Current, already a full professor at the University of Illinois, had won the Bancroft Prize for his work on Abraham Lincoln, *The Man Nobody Knows.* As Calhoon reflected, Current chose Greensboro as his next stop on a career leading eventually to the University of Wisconsin because he thought it "would be a really nice place to live and he would have more time for research."[12] Bob was deep in his extended work on Loyalism and the Revolutionary War, and Current occasionally chided him for ignoring local sources from the Greensboro "backcountry." Then one day in 1974 Current showed Calhoon his copy of *The Life and Character of the Rev. David Caldwell,* by Eli Washington Caruthers, and commented that "there's stuff on the Tories" in Caldwell's "politically sophisticated" sermons. It was one of those brief moments of realization that shaped an entire career. "How, I wondered in 1974," Bob later reflected, "did those sermons get written and preached in the wilds of the Carolina frontier, of all places. . . . Answering that question occupied much of my subsequent career."[13] The line from Current to Caldwell to Calhoon led from the eighteenth-century backcountry directly to the subject of political moderation. Making the connection, however, took quite some time.

Then "in 1995," writes Calhoon, "I experienced an epiphany."[14] The oracle of the moment was William Edward Moran, chancellor of UNCG from 1979 to 1994. Bob had just given a talk on James Sharbrough Ferguson, Moran's predecessor as UNCG chancellor from 1964 to 1979. He had compared Ferguson to David Caldwell, "who played a similar role in the late eighteenth century at Chapel Hill" to the role that history forced upon Ferguson during the civil rights era of the 1960s and 1970s. "I thought [that] was a neat comparison," commented Bob. After the talk Moran came up to Calhoon and observed that "something else tied these two men together—Ferguson and this earlier figure—that you didn't tell us about." And epiphany: "Suddenly it hit me," Calhoon recalled, "and something that I said to him, well, they were both 'historic moderates'. . . . I thought that's exactly what Ferguson was. Not a moderate, but a historic moderate. That is, someone who understood this long history."[15] Ferguson's responses to the challenges the civil rights movement presented to UNCG during his chancellorship, in other words, did not arise in a vacuum but as an expression of that long line of history linking the backcountry world of ethnic and racial diversity in which the town of Greensboro was founded to the conundrums its university confronted in meeting the test of civil rights and social justice in the perplexing diversity persisting there two centuries later.

Calhoon expected a follow-up query from Moran on the meaning or definition of historic moderation. And Bob had planned to say, "Well, that's a long story." But no rejoinder followed—Moran "just smiled and [said] he liked that answer a lot." The next morning Bob's waking thought was "long story, that'd be a book."[16] And *Political Moderation in America's First Two Centuries* was conceived. In drafting this book during the following decade, Bob was living out in many complex and subtle ways his own experiences at UNCG and the personal implications of his scholarship. What had crystallized in his mind was a unique sense of moderation's presence and power in his own life as well as in American history. Studying with Bob and writing a dissertation during this period must have been an exhilarating and deeply fulfilling experience.

When Bob and James Sharbrough Ferguson arrived in Greensboro in the mid-1960s, UNCG was undergoing a deep transition of its own that was provoked and compounded by the turmoil of the times. This situation, too, had a long history. Charles Duncan McIver, a crusader for women's education, had founded the institution in 1881 as the State Normal and Industrial School. Changes in its name to the North Carolina College for Women in 1919 and thirteen years later to the Woman's College of the University of North Carolina speak of its dedication to the education of women as teachers and as citizens. By the post–World War II era, it had become the largest all-woman's college in the United States. But changes came quickly in the 1960s. A year before Calhoon and Ferguson arrived, it assumed its current identity as the University of North Carolina at Greensboro and began admitting men. Few came at first. Clarence Shipton, a former coach, became the first dean of men. And with only a single male student admitted that first year, Shipton became the subject of some mirth as the "Dean of Man." But diversity among the student body was increasing. During Bob's first semester, there were eight men and thirty-five hundred women. The first African Americans had been admitted in 1956. For UNCG coping with this measure of diversity was a new and challenging experience.

One of Bob's first lessons in moderation at a diversifying institution came within the history department. Richard Bardolph served as chair, and according to Bob he ran the "department the way I think departments were run in the Midwest in the 1940s—with a strong hand, with giving faculty a lot of autonomy . . . but to leave administrative matters entirely in the hands of the strong, assertive, active department head." Moreover the "idea of having department meetings with votes or with any policy set by the faculty was just totally foreign to Dick's way of thinking." But to the younger faculty, "it seemed only sensible that things should be done in a democratic, open, cooperative way."[17] One of the first issues this faculty faced was the "growing hostility in the university to the history department's apparent privileged position" as one of its largest departments. Sociology, for instance, had as few as three faculty members. "Dick tried to warn us that this [challenge] was coming—that we needed to prepare as a department." He cautioned moderation. "Soften up a little bit," he counseled, "and give ground." Compromise would be in the "interest of maintaining the larger institutional strength of the department."[18]

The emerging university soon faced more confounding issues that far exceeded the significance of intramural struggles over departmental allocations. In 1968 the cafeteria workers went on strike. At this still predominantly white institution, all these workers were either older African Americans from the community or younger students at the nearby North Carolina Agricultural and Technical University, a historically black college famous for the Greensboro lunch counter sit-ins in 1960.

This strike was the first in a series of three racially and politically charged incidents James Ferguson had to address and resolve. Faced with the initial strike, he created a Racial Policies Committee to seek a negotiated solution. And he appointed Bob as one of the three faculty representatives to this committee. The respect that Ferguson had for Calhoon was mutual. "What a wonderful thing for students to be able to hear someone talking in this slow, casual, Southern, dignified way about things of great power and intensity, and somehow, you know, conveying the vitality of history without raising your voice or getting away from this typical Mississippi cadence," Bob observed about Ferguson.[19] For a boy from Pittsburgh and a scholar of revolutions, listening to Ferguson must have been a remarkably calming and clarifying experience. Ferguson was "an old line Mississippi liberal." His father had been a Methodist minister who worked for racial reconciliation in his preaching and throughout his career. And the son had taught in Mississippi for fourteen years before "he was sort of chased out of Mississippi by white citizen's councils because he stood up to them."[20]

The "dignity and modesty [that] were the hallmarks of [Ferguson's] personality" clearly impressed the young faculty member. The threat of violence at UNCG was real and present. Any disturbance "could have led to police coming on [the campus] in riot gear and making arrests," observed Calhoon. Yet Ferguson "was able to find creative ways to prevent that from happening."[21] He mediated; he arbitrated; he conciliated. He took an uncompromising and aggressive stand against violence at the same time he brokered reforms and protected civil rights. "In all three instances, Ferguson appointed a committee of people widely respected on campus—got their advice and acted in a way which kept peace on campus when things were very tense. And he was really a superb crisis manager in racial confrontation." Calhoon, of course, served on these committees. He observed how Ferguson "learned in each one" of the confrontations. In "each one he would see things that he had learned in the earlier ones."He put these lessons to use. All the while "he was trying to work behind the scenes to keep this body of student activists from precipitating violence."[22]

What Bob realized in 1995 in the aftermath of his talk on Ferguson and Moran's question was that in resolving racial crises at UNCG, Ferguson was drawing on a long history of political moderation traceable among the Scotch-Irish and others who had settled the southern backcountry. The ways they found to get along and prosper collectively could be identified in the sophisticated sermons of David Caldwell. These ways took root and resurfaced consistently throughout the backcountry region even in the strife-torn labor disputes of industrial Pittsburgh. Bob's epiphany embraced his experiences there, but UNCG in the 1960s and 1970s became his own backcountry. It was diverse in ways that even his upbringing and education could not comprehend at first. It was riven by conflicts that must have appeared baffling and confusing. But out of this turmoil and upheaval a powerful leader—a voice for reason and moderation—emerged. Ferguson didn't call for tear gas and fire hoses. But on the other hand, he didn't quail before the threat of broken glass and bloodied heads. He was a moderate, a pragmatist, and a conciliator. And he stood in a long line of political moderation born in the diversity of the American backcountry and constituting a posture much older than any American political party. Ferguson indeed stood for what Bob had been living through and at the same time working on as a historian. This conjunction of self and subject, experience and the critical thinking of learning from it, made Robert Calhoon into the powerful teacher that is so evident in the work of the students represented in the essays of this volume.

Notes

ABBREVIATIONS

AO	Audit Office Papers, TNA
DLAR	David Library of the American Revolution
HSP	Historical Society of Pennsylvania
NARA	National Archives and Records Administration
NCA	State Archives of North Carolina
NHPL	Petitions to the Legislature, New Hampshire State Archives
NHPSP	*New Hampshire Provincial and State Papers,* Nathaniel Bouton et al., eds. (Concord, NH, 1874–96)
NSA	Nova Scotia Archives
NYHS	New-York Historical Society
NYPL	New York Public Library
PRO	The Public Record Office, TNA
PYM	Philadelphia Yearly Meeting (Arch Street) Meeting for Sufferings, Minutes 1775–1785, Haverford Special Collections, Pennsylvania
SRNC	*The State Records of North Carolina,* vols. 11–25, ed. Walter Clark (Raleigh: P. M. Hale et al., 1886–1907)
T	*Treasury Papers,* TNA
TJP	*Thomas Jefferson Papers*
TNA	The National Archives of UK
WMQ	*William and Mary Quarterly*

INTRODUCTION

1. Ruma Chopra, "Enduring Patterns of Loyalist Study: Definitions and Contours," *History Compass* 11, no. 11 (2013): 983.

2. John Adams to James Lloyd, January 28, 1815, *Founders Online,* National Archives, last modified July 12, 2016, http://founders.archives.gov/documents/Adams/99-02-02-6401 [accessed July 24, 2016]; Henry Laurens to Edward Bridgen, Nantes, August 10, 1782, in *The Papers of Henry Laurens,* 16 vols., ed. Philip M. Hamer, George C. Rogers, and David R. Chesnutt (Columbia: Published for the South Carolina Historical Society by the University of South Carolina Press, 1968–2003), 15: 554–55.

3. Robert M. Calhoon, *The Loyalists in Revolutionary America, 1760–1781* (New York: Harcourt Brace Jovanovich, 1973), ix; Paul H. Smith, "The American Loyalists: Notes on Their Organization and Numerical Strength," *WMQ* 3rd. ser., 25, no. 2 (1968): 267–70.

4. Maya Jasanoff, *Liberty's Exiles: American Loyalists in the Revolutionary World* (New York: Knopf, 2011), 351–358; Philip Ranlet, "How Many American Loyalists Left the United States?" *Historian* 76, no. 2 (2014), 291–306.

5. Patrick Spero and Michael Zuckerman, eds., *The American Revolution Reborn* (Philadelphia: University of Pennsylvania Press, 2016), 5–6; David Armitage, *Civil Wars: A History in Ideas* (New York: Knopf, 2017), 121–158.

6. Jim Piecuch, *Three Peoples One King: Loyalists, Indians, and Slaves in the Revolutionary South, 1775–1782* (Columbia: University of South Carolina Press, 2008).

7. Ruma Chopra, *Choosing Sides: Loyalists in Revolutionary America* (Lanham, MD: Rowman & Littlefield, 2013), 37, 49; Harvey Amani Whitefield, *North to Bondage: Loyalist Slavery in the Maritimes* (Vancouver: University of British Columbia Press, 2016); Cassandra Pybus, *Epic Journeys of Freedom: Runaway Slaves of the American Revolution and Their Global Quest for Liberty* (Boston: Beacon, 2006).

8. Robert M. Calhoon, "The Reintegration of the Loyalists and the Disaffected," in *The American Revolution: Its Character and Limits,* ed. Jack P. Greene (New York: New York University Press, 1987), 51–74; David E. Maas, *The Return of the Massachusetts Loyalists* (New York: Garland, 1989); David E. Maas, "The Massachusetts Loyalists and the Problem of Amnesty, 1775–1790," in *Loyalists and Community in North America,* ed. Robert M. Calhoon, Timothy M. Barnes, and George A. Rawlyck (Westport, CT: Greenwood, 1994), 65–75.

9. Michael A. McDonnell and David Waldstreicher. "Revolution in the *Quarterly*? A Historiographical Analysis." *WMQ* 3d ser., 74, no. 4 (October 2017): 661.

10. Calhoon, *Loyalists in Revolutionary America,* ix.

11. Robert M. Calhoon, *Political Moderation in America's First Two Centuries* (Cambridge: Cambridge University Press, 2009).

"The Success of Either Lies in the Womb of Time"

1. John Randolph to Thomas Jefferson, September 1775, *The Papers of Thomas Jefferson* (hereafter TJP), 42 vols., ed. Julian P. Boyd (Princeton: Princeton University Press, 1950), 1:244.

2. Thomas Jefferson to John Randolph, August 25, 1775, TJP 1:241.

3. John Randolph, *Considerations on the Present State of Virginia* (Williamsburg, 1774).

4. Samuel Crisp, *Virginia: A tragedy, as it is acted at the Theatre-Royal in Drury-Lane, by His Majesty's servants* (London: Printed for J. and R. Tonson and S. Draper, 1754) Act I, Scene II, 50. This play intentionally illustrates, in grand metaphor, the idea of Virginia as a place in the mid-eighteenth-century British mind.

5. "Sacred knot" was a common 18th-century British reference to loyalty. Ibid and Anon., "Loyalty to our King," (London, 1745), preface.

6. Samuel Crisp, *Virginia: A tragedy.*

7. Edmund Randolph, "History of Virginia," *Journal of American History* 57, no. 3 (1970): 176.

8. Andrew Jackson O'Shaughnessy, *An Empire Divided: The American Revolution and the British Caribbean* (Philadelphia: University of Pennsylvania Press, 2000). O'Shaughnessy describes a strikingly similar set of characteristics and political perceptions among British West Indians, who were able to keep the island provinces in the empire, and metropolitan Virginians, who could not.

9. Michael McKeon, *The Secret History of Domesticity: Public, Private, and the Division of Knowledge* (Baltimore: Johns Hopkins University Press, 2005), 74–80.

10. Thomas Jefferson, Declaration of Independence (1776), https://www.loc.gov/exhibits/jefferson/jeffdec.html, accessed February 23, 2018; Robert Munford, *The Patriots*, in *A Collection of Plays and Poems, by the Late Col. Robert Munford, of Mecklenburg County, in the State of Virginia* (Petersburg, VA: William Prentis, 1798).

11. Letter from Francis Atterbury to Sir Jonathan Trelawny, June 13, 1702, in *The Epistolary Correspondence, Visitation Charges, Speeches, and Miscellanies of the Right Reverend Francis Atterbury* (London, 1784), 69; Paul Langford, *A Polite and Commercial People: England, 1727–1783* (New York: Oxford University Press, 1992), esp. chap. 3; David S. Shields, *Civil Tongues and Polite Letters in British America* (Chapel Hill: University of North Carolina Press, 1997), xviii; J. G. A. Pocock, "Virtues, Rights, and Manners," in *Virtue, Commerce, and History: Essays on Political Thought and History, Chiefly in the Eighteenth Century* (Cambridge: Cambridge University Press, 1985), 49–50. Shields's analysis of discursive practices in the context of gentility unfortunately overlooks the salient characteristics of Augustan political praxis and its focus on moderation.

12. Robert M. Calhoon, *Political Moderation in America's First Two Centuries* (Cambridge: Cambridge University Press, 2009), 24–81; Erin Skye Mackie, ed., *The Commerce of Everyday Life: Selections from "The Tatler" and "The Spectator"* (London: Bedford/St. Martin's, 1998); Julian Hoppit, *A Land of Liberty? England 1689–1727* (Oxford: Oxford University Press, 2002), 430–34; Paul Langford, "The Uses of Eighteenth-Century Politeness," *Transactions of the Royal Historical Society*, 6th ser. 12 (2002): 311–31; J. G. A. Pocock, "The Varieties of Whiggism from Exclusion to Reform: A History of Ideology and Discourse," in *Virtue, Commerce, and History: Essays on Political Thought and History, Chiefly in the Eighteenth Century* (Cambridge: Cambridge University Press, 1985), 215–51; Lawrence E. Klein, "Joseph Addison's Whiggism," in *"Cultures of Whiggism": New Essays on English Literature and Culture in the Long Eighteenth Century*, ed. David Wormersley (Newark: University of Delaware Press, 2005), 108–26; Tone Sundt Urstad, *Sir Robert Walpole's Poets: The Use of Literature as Pro-Government Propaganda, 1721–1742* (Newark: University of Delaware Press, 1999), esp. 110–15.

13. Pocock, "Virtues, Rights, and Manners."

14. See O'Shaughnessy, *Empire Divided.*

15. Joanne B. Freeman, *Affairs of Honor: National Politics in the New Republic* (New Haven: Yale University Press, 2001), 8.

16. Alison Gilbert Olson, *Making the Empire Work: London and American Interest Groups, 1790–1890* (Cambridge, MA: Harvard University Press, 1992).

17. J. G. A. Pocock, "Hume and the American Revolution: The Dying Thoughts of a North Briton," in *Virtue, Commerce, and History: Essays on Political Thought and History, Chiefly in the Eighteenth Century* (Cambridge: Cambridge University Press, 1985), 125–41; William L. Hedges, "Telling Off the King: Jefferson's Summary View as American Fantasy," *Early American Literature* 22, no. 2 (1987): 166–74.

18. James Conniff, "Hume on Political Parties: The Case for Hume as a Whig," *Eighteenth-Century Studies* 12, no. 2 (1978–79): 150–73.

19. Ibid.; Pocock, "Varieties of Whiggism from Exclusion to Reform," 215–310; Langford, "Old Whigs, Old Tories, and the American Revolution," *Journal of Imperial and Commonwealth History* 8 no. 2 (1980): 106–30; Reed Browning, *Political and Constitutional Ideas of the Court Whigs* (Baton Rouge: Louisiana State University Press, 1982), 176–80, 201–2; Peter N. Miller, *Defining the Common Good: Empire, Religion, and Philosophy in Eighteenth-Century Britain* (New York: Cambridge University Press, 1994), 73–92.

20. Conniff, "Hume on Political Parties"; H. T. Dickinson, *Liberty and Property: Political Ideology in Eighteenth-Century Britain* (London: Methuen, 1977), 127–33; Pocock, "Hume and the American Revolution."

21. David Hume, "Whether the British Government Inclines More to Absolute Monarchy, or to a Republic," in *Essays Moral, Political, Literary*, ed. Eugene F. Miller (Indianapolis: Liberty Fund, 1987), 47–50.

22. Emory G. Evans, *A "Topping People": The Rise and Decline of Virginia's Old Political Elite, 1680–1790* (Charlottesville: University of Virginia Press, 2009), 87–89; Edmund S. Morgan, *American Slavery, American Freedom: The Ordeal of Colonial Virginia* (New York: Norton, 1995), 366–67.

23. "The Speech of Sir John Randolph, Upon His Being Elected Speaker of the House of Burgesses," Printed by William Parks (Williamsburg, Va., 1734). https://www.loc.gov/item/rbpe.17800010e/.

24. *Journals of the House of Burgesses of Virginia, 1727–1740* (Richmond: Library of Virginia, 1915), 175–76.

25. Ibid.

26. Warren M. Billings, John E. Selby, and Thad W. Tate, *Colonial Virginia: A History* (New York: KTO, 1985), 301–9.

27. *An Appeal to the Public in Relation to the Tobacco * * * [Bill]: And a Revival of the Old Project, to establish a General Excise* (London, 1751), 55, 58.

28. *An Essay on Political Lying, &c.* (London, 1757), 4.

29. Horace Walpole to Lady Ossory, January 6, 1772, manuscript in unpublished correspondence of Walpole, Lewis Walpole Library, Yale University.

30. William Beverley to Lord Fairfax, August 9, 1742, *WMQ* 3, no. 4 (1895): 230–31. Beverley might well have been posturing with Fairfax for favor in distinguishing himself from his metropolitan competitors in the colony. He went on in the letter to observe that "as yr Ldp's friends are now in play, I hope you will have Justice done you without delay, & yt you will obtain all ye Lands according to ye most extensive bounds of your Grant" and then proceeded to ask obliquely Fairfax's assistance in obtaining the newly vacant office of secretary of the colony.

31. Ibid.

32. Peyton Randolph to John Custis IV, [February] 1742. Original at NYHS, copy at Virginia Historical Society.

33. David John Mays, *Edmund Pendleton, 1721–1803: A Biography*, vol. 1 (Richmond: Library of Virginia, 1752), appendix 2, 358–69. An incident that opponents to Robinson made a great deal of political hay out of, the affair deserves another look, if for no other reason than the sheer vastness of the community of people who benefitted from Robinson's largesse with public funds, and the economic circumstances that might have justified it as a "Reason of State," defined by Nathan Bailey as, "in political affairs, a rule or maxim, whether it be good or evil, which may be of service to the state; properly, something that is expedient for the interest of the government; but contrary to moral honesty and justice." *Dictionarium Britannicum*, 2d ed. (London, 1736).

34. J.G.A. Pocock, *Three British Revolutions: 1641, 1688, 1776* (Princeton, NJ: Princeton University Press, 2014).

35. David Shields has persuasively described the "disingenuous identification of reason with one's political affections" that began to pervade transatlantic communications as a

reaction "against the tendency for politeness to calcify into 'correctness.'" This essay differs from Shields's work in two key areas but otherwise embraces and builds on his explanation of sociability and sentiment. First Shields explicitly denies the Habermasian claim that an "age of sense" and reason existed, arguing instead that politicocultural discourse was determined by sentimentality and "communities of conscience" from the late seventeenth century through the eighteenth century. While I agree that sentimental politics were always present in the British Atlantic in the period, I believe that reason, sense, and moderation were the defining characteristics of British political culture until the 1760s. Second, his analysis focuses on Charleston, Boston, and Philadelphia because "conversation and literary communication" of the sort he describes coalesced around institutions, such as coffeehouses, clubs, and salons, "wherever urbanization occurred." Urbanization, of course, was conspicuously absent in the Chesapeake in the eighteenth century. Shields, *Civil Tongues and Polite Letters in British America*, xv–xvi, xvii.

36. Shields, *Civil Tongues and Polite Letters in British America*, xv–xvi, xvii.

37. Billings, Selby, and Tate, *Colonial Virginia*, 301.

38. Shields, *Civil Tongues and Polite Letters in British America*, xv–xvi, xvii.

39. See, for example, William Makepeace Thackeray, *The Virginians, a Tale of the Last Century* (London: Bradbury & Evans, 1857).

40. Langford, "Old Whigs, Old Tories, and the American Revolution," 106–30; Julie Flavell, "American Patriots in London and the Quest for Talks, 1774–5," *Journal of Imperial and Commonwealth History* 20 (1992): 335–69.

41. *Virginia Gazette* (Parks), June 1, 1775.

42. Randolph, "History of Virginia," 219.

43. Whitney A. Martinko, "Progress and Preservation: Representing History in Boston's Landscape of Urban Reform, 1820–1860," *New England Quarterly* 82, no. 2 (2009), 304–334.

44. See Calhoon, *Tory Insurgents: The Loyalist Perception and Other Essays* (Columbia: University of South Carolina Press, 1989). This criticism remains true for the historiography of colonial Virginia. Even the best works have not been immune. E.g., John E. Selby, *The Revolution in Virginia: 1775–1783* (Charlottesville: University of Virginia Press, 1988), xi.

45. William A. Benton, *Whig Loyalism: An Aspect of Political Ideology in the American Revolutionary Era* (Madison, NJ: Fairleigh Dickinson University Press, 1966).

46. Samuel Johnson, *A Dictionary of the English Language* (London, 1755).

47. Horace Walpole, *Book of Miscellany* [1786?], 57, mss, Lewis Walpole Library, Yale University.

48. Adam Smith, *The Wealth of Nations* (New York: Bantam Books, 2003), 1027–28. For Jefferson's political thought and imperial vision, see Peter S. Onuf, *Jefferson's Empire: The Language of American Nationhood* (Charlottesville: University of Virginia Press, 2000).

49. Randolph, *Considerations*, 15.

50. Dumas Malone, *Jefferson the Virginian* (Charlottesville: University of Virginia Press, 1948), 128–53.

51. Ibid., 3.

52. Marie G. Kimball, *Jefferson, the Road to Glory: 1743–1776* (United States: Coward-McCann, 1943), 12–13.

53. John Thornton, "A New Map of Virginia, Maryland, Pensilvania, New Jersey, Part of New York, and Carolina," ca. 1723–28 (originally published ca. 1701), in *Degrees of Latitude:*

Mapping Colonial America, ed. Margaret Beck Pritchard and Henry G. Taliaferro (Williamsburg, VA: Abrams, 2002), 102–5.

54. "Council of Trade and Plantations to the King, 8 September 1721," *Calendar of State Papers: Colonial North America and the West Indies, 1574–1739* 32 (2000): 408–49.

55. Ibid.

56. Kimball, *Jefferson, the Road to Glory,* 16.

57. "Randolph, William," *Dictionary of American Biography,* vol. 8, ed. Dumas Malone (1963), 371–72; Margaret D. Sankey, "Randolph, William (1650–1711)," *Oxford Dictionary of National Biography* (2004). Among William Randolph's sons were Isham and John. John had two sons, John and Peyton, the first of which is part of the subject of this essay. The younger John, therefore, was the first cousin of Jefferson's mother.

58. Parish register St. Paul Shadwell, XO 24/128.

59. It is presumed that Jane accompanied the family at this time, though there is no evidence that she did not join them later. Gerald S. Cowden, "The Randolphs of Turkey Island: A Prosopography of the First Three Generations, 1650–1806" (PhD diss., College of William and Mary, 1977), 36. Unless she was left with her mother's relatives in London—which is possible—then she was probably in Virginia by October 1725, when her younger sister, Mary, was born in Williamsburg (Jefferson Bible, Small Special Collections Library, University of Virginia).

60. Malone, *Jefferson the Virginian,* 17.

61. *Goochland County Deed Book,* May 18, 1736. It appears that this exchange was merely a temporary one to ensure the legal delivery of the property from Randolph to Jefferson. A more proper deed was later recorded that makes it clear that Jefferson paid Randolph fifty pounds for the tract.

62. Malone, *Jefferson the Virginian,* 17.

63. Millicent Rose, *The East End of London* (London: Cresset, 1951), 67; Ben Weinreb and Christopher Hibbert, eds., *The London Encyclopedia* (New York: St. Martin's, 1983), 780. See contra Susan Kern, "The Material World of the Jeffersons at Shadwell," *WMQ,* 3rd ser., 62, no. 2 (2005): 2–5.

64. James Horn, "The British Diaspora: Emigration from Britain, 1680–1815," in *The Oxford History of the British Empire,* vol. 2, *The Eighteenth Century,* ed. P. J. Marshall (Oxford: Oxford University Press, 1998), 31. See also Alison Games, "Migration," in *The British Atlantic World, 1500–1800,* eds. David Armitage and Michael J. Braddick (London: Palgrave Macmillan, 2002), 38–39.

65. Billings, Selby, and Tate, *Colonial Virginia,* 201; Breen, "An Empire of Goods: The Anglicization of Colonial America, 1690–1776," *Journal of British Studies* 25, No. 4 (1986), 467–499.

66. Jacob M. Price, "The Rise of Glasgow in the Chesapeake Tobacco Trade, 1707–1775," *WMQ* 11, no. 2 (1954): 179–80.

67. Jack P. Greene, *Pursuits of Happiness: The Social Development of Early Modern British Colonies and the Formation of American Culture* (Chapel Hill: University of North Carolina Press, 1988), 179, table 8.1.

68. Qtd. in Maldwyn A. Jones, "The Scotch-Irish in British America," in *Strangers within the Realm: Cultural Margins of the First British Empire,* ed. Bernard Bailyn and Philip D. Morgan (Chapel Hill: University of North Carolina Press, 1991), 284.

69. Edmund S. Morgan, *American Slavery, American Freedom: The Ordeal of Colonial Virginia* (New York: Norton, 1995), 341–42.

70. Anthony S. Parent, *Foul Means: The Formation of a Slave Society in Virginia, 1660–1740* (Chapel Hill: University of North Carolina Press, 2003), 181; Morgan, *American Slavery,* 344; Games, "Migration," 41; Greene, *Pursuits of Happiness,* 179; Jack P. Greene, "Empire and Identity from the Glorious Revolution to the American Revolution," in *The Oxford History of the British Empire,* vol. 2, *The Eighteenth Century,* ed. P. J. Marshall (Oxford: Oxford University Press, 1998), 225; Onuf, *Jefferson's Empire,* 14–15.

71. Philip D. Morgan and Michael L. Nicholls, "Slaves in Piedmont Virginia, 1720–1790," *WMQ,* 3d ser., 46, no. 2 (1989): 211–51; Ian K. Steele, *The English Atlantic, 1675-1740: An Exploration f Communication and Community* (New York: Oxford University Press, 1986), 252 .

72. Joshua Fry and Peter Jefferson, "A Map of the Inhabited Part of Virginia Containing the whole Province of Maryland with part of [Pennsylvania], New Jersey and North Carolina," London, 1751, Special Collections, University of Virginia. The likelihood is that neither Fry nor Jefferson ever saw the cartouche, as it was engraved in London.

73. Emily J. Salmon and Edward D. C. Campbell, *The Hornbook of Virginia History: A Ready-Reference Guide to the Old Dominion's People, Places, and Past* (Richmond: Library of Virginia, 1994), 159–71.

74. Actually the source of the cartouche is difficult to determine. The map was engraved and published for the Board of Trade in Charing Cross, London, in 1751 by Thomas Jeffreys. Whether the cartouche is a product of Virginia or a London addition is unknown, as is the artist.

75. James A. Bear and Lucia C. Stanton, eds., *Jefferson's Memorandum Books: Accounts, with Legal Records and Miscellany, 1767–1826,* vol. 2 (Princeton: Princeton University Press, 1997), 7n22, 84n42; Kimball, *Jefferson, the Road to Glory,* 24.

76. John Gibson, *The History of Glasgow, from the Earliest Accounts to the Present Time* (Glasgow: Chaplin & Duncan, 1777), 212; Price, "Rise of Glasgow in the Chesapeake Tobacco Trade," 183–84.

77. Roger Atkinson to [Lionel] Lyde, July 5, 1769, Atkinson Papers, Small Special Collections Library, University of Virginia.

78. Douglas preached first at Dover Church in Goochland on September 15, 1750. *WMQ* 15, no. 4 (1907), 24; Malone, *Jefferson the Virginian,* 39–40.

79. Malone, *Jefferson the Virginian,* 31.

80. Thomas Jefferson, *Autobiography of Thomas Jefferson, 1743–1790: Together with a Summary of the Chief Events in Jefferson's Life,* ed. Paul Leicester Ford (New York: Dover, 2005), 5–7.

81. Malone, *Jefferson the Virginian,* 51–52; William and Mary Bursar Boarding Accounts, 1760–1762, John D. Rockefeller Library, Colonial Williamsburg Foundation.

82. Jefferson, *Autobiography,* 5–7.

83. Benjamin Rush, *The Autobiography of Benjamin Rush,* ed. George W. Corner (Philadelphia: American Philosophical Society, 1948), 151. For a contemporary critical view of Wythe, see "Satirical letter from Tim Pastime to William Hunter, editor of the Virginia Gazette" (1761), 1990.4, Special Collections Manuscript, Colonial Williamsburg Foundation. See also William E. Hemphill's often overlooked but quite informative and perceptive

work "George Wythe the Colonial Briton: A Biographical Study of the Pre-Revolutionary Era in Virginia" (PhD diss., University of Virginia, 1937).

84. Joan Lane, "Small, William (1734–1775)," in *Oxford Dictionary of National Biography,* vol. 50, ed. H. C. G. Matthews and Brian Harrison (Oxford: Oxford University Press, 2004); Kimball, *Jefferson, the Road to Glory,* 46–48.

85. Thomas Jefferson to John Page, February 20, 1770, *TJP.* There is considerable question over the extent of the conflagration at Shadwell. Though Jefferson reported to Page that he was "burned out of a home" and to other correspondents that he had lost everything, his memorandum books show that a number of his possessions survived the fire, and more tellingly, there is no evidence that his mother and the rest of the family did not continue to live there. See Memorandum Book, 22, 158–59n43. There is also no mention in his or his mother's surviving financial records of any expense laid out to reconstruct a house. In fact, on March 1, 1770, less than two weeks after the fire, Jefferson notes work to be done on Monticello (then referred to as Hermitage), but nothing about Shadwell (Malone, *Jefferson the Virginian,* 30). The only information is a much later note by Jefferson's daughter, Martha, that her parents could not spend their wedding night at Shadwell because the house that Thomas had "fitted up" for his mother was too small to accommodate the newlyweds, his mother, and his remaining brother and sisters. The archaeological record has also proven less than helpful, revealing evidence that a fire had indeed occurred at one time but nothing more specific than that. Fiske Kimball, "The Search for Jefferson's Birthplace," *Virginia Magazine of History and Biography* 51, no. 4 (1943), 381–406. Indeed the inventory of the house at Shadwell that followed the death of Jefferson's mother in 1776 shows a number of pieces of furniture that can be found on Peter Jefferson's inventory of 1757, strongly suggesting that the fire might not have been too extensive. Albemarle County Will Book, Albemarle County Court House, Charlottesville, VA.

86. *TJP,* 1:42.

87. *TJP,* 1:63. Jefferson refers here to the southern pavilion at Monticello.

88. Cowden, "Randolphs of Turkey Island," 229, 233, 471, 580; R. A. Austen-Leigh, ed., *Eton College Lists 1678–1790* (Eton: Spottiswoode, 1907); R. A. Austen-Leigh, ed., *The Eton College Register 1753–1790* (Eton: Spottiswoode, Ballantyne, 1921). Beverley Randolph died at Eton and was buried at the chapel there in 1762.

89. Austen-Leigh, *Eton Register,* 490; Cowden, "Randolphs of Turkey Island," 218; Matthew Henry Peacock, *History of the Free Grammar School of Queen Elizabeth at Wakefield* (Wakefield: Milne, 1892), 213; *The Bland Papers: Being a Selection from the Manuscripts of Col. Theodorick Bland* (Petersburg, Va., 1840–1843); John Venn, E. S. Roberts, and Edward John Gross, *Biographical History of Gonville and Caius College, 1349–1897,* 4 vols. (Cambridge: Cambridge University Press, 1897–1901), previous citation; J. A. Lemay, ed., *Robert Bolling Woos Anne Miller: Love and Courtship in Colonial Virginia* (Charlottesville: University Press of Virginia, 1990), 17; Alumni Oxoniensis: The Members is the University of Oxford, 1715–1886 (Univ. of Oxford, 1888); H. A. C. Sturgess, ed., *Register of Admissions to the Honourable Society of the Middle Temple* (London: Butterworth, 1949); R. A. Roberts, ed., *A Calendar of the Inner Temple Records* (London: Sotheran, 1933).

90. Rush, *Autobiography,* 152.

91. Thomas Jefferson to John Page, July 15, 1763, *TJP,* 1:9–11. "Belinda" was a sobriquet used by Jefferson in his correspondence to refer to Burwell, whom he intended to marry. In fact Jefferson went so far as to ask her guardian, William Nelson, for permission, but

he was told that such permission would depend entirely on Burwell's wishes, which she was not inclined to grant. Jefferson to Page, January 1764, *TJP*.

92. Malone, *Jefferson the Virginian*, 83–84.

93. James Ogilvie to Jefferson, February 20, 1771, *TJP*, 1:38–39.

94. Jefferson to Thomas Adams, *TJP*, 1:48–49.

95. Jacob M. Price, "Who Cared about the Colonies? The Impact of the Thirteen Colonies on British Society and Politics, circa 1714–1775," in *Strangers within the Realm: Cultural Margins of the First British Empire*, ed. Bernard Bailyn and Philip D. Morgan (Chapel Hill: University of North Carolina Press, 1991), 436. See also Michael Kammen, *Empire and Interest: The American Colonies and the Politics of Mercantilism* (Philadelphia: Lippincott, 1970), 124, 130; Michael Kammen, "British and Imperial Interests in the Age of the American Revolution," in *Anglo-American Political Relations, 1675–1775*, ed. Richard Maxwell Brown and Alison Gilbert Olson (New Brunswick, NJ: Rutgers University Press, 1970), 151; Jack M. Sosin, *Agents and Merchants: British Colonial Policy and the Origins of the American Revolution, 1763–1775* (Lincoln: University of Nebraska Press, 1965), xv. For the full scope of North American ties to metropolitan opposition groups in the 1760s and 1770s and the problematic political position in which those placed North American interests, see Pauline Maier, *From Resistance to Revolution: Colonial Radicals and the Development of American Opposition to Britain, 1765–1776* (New York: Norton, 1991), esp. 163, 168–69.

96. William Palfrey to John Hancock, February 15, 1771, Palfrey Papers, mss 1704.4(32/2), Houghton Library, Harvard University.

97. Ralph Wormeley Jr. to Landon Carter, October 7, 1772, Landon Carter Papers, Small Special Collections Library, University of Virginia.

98. Randolph, *Considerations on the Present State of Virginia*, 23.

99. Jack P. Greene, ed., *The Diary of Colonel Landon Carter of Sabine Hall, 1752–1778*, 2 vols. (Charlottesville: University Press of Virginia, 1965), 2:1029; "Voluntarious" letter, June 1, 1775, *Virginia Gazette* (Parks).

100. Randolph, *Considerations on the Present State of Virginia*, 44.

101. Robert Beverley to William Fitzhugh, July 20, 1775, in Robert Calhoon, "A Sorrowful Spectator of These Tumultuous Times: Robert Beverley Describes the Coming of the Revolution," *Virginia Magazine of History and Biography* 73 (1965): 41–55.

102. See also, more generally, Sarah Knott, *Sensibility and the American Revolution* (Chapel Hill: University of North Carolina Press, 2009).

103. Munford.

104. Gwenda Morgan, "Randolph, Sir John (1693–1737)," *DNB*.

105. John J. Reardon, *Peyton Randolph, 1721–1775: One Who Presided* (Durham, NC: Carolina Academic, 1982), 1–10; "Randolph, John," *Dictionary of American Biography*, 362.

106. *Newcastle Courant*, October 19, 1745; November 2, 1745, quoted in Kathleen Wilson, *The Sense of the People: Culture and Imperialism in England, 1715–1785* (New York: Cambridge, 1995).173.

107. Horace Walpole to Horace Mann, April 25, 1746 (os),Wilmarth S. Lewis, ed., *Horace Walpole's Correspondence* (New Haven: Yale University Press, 1967), 19:249.

108. *Daily Advertiser*, April 26, 1746, qtd. in *Horace Walpole's Correspondence*, 19:249n22.

109. Randolph, *Considerations on the Present State of Virginia*, 3.

110. It has been argued that "few people identified themselves as Loyalists in Revolutionary Virginia," a conclusion that is inconsistent in the face of more recently available

evidence. See Michael A. McDonnell, *The Politics of War: Race, Class, and Conflict in Revolutionary Virginia* (Chapel Hill: University of North Carolina Press, 2007), 4n4.

111.   Randolph, *Considerations on the Present State of Virginia.*

112.   Jefferson to John Randolph, August 1775, *TJP,* 1:241.

113.   Peter Wilson Coldham, *American Loyalist Claims* (Arlington: National Genealogical Society, 1980); Lorenzo Sabine, *The American Loyalists: Biographical Sketches of Adherents to the British Crown in the War of the Revolution* (Boston: Little & Brown, 1847).

114.   Simon Schama, *Rough Crossings: Britain, the Slaves and the American Revolution* (New York: HarperCollins, 2006), 17.

115.   Coldham, *American Loyalist Claims,* 158.

116.   Wormeley Family Papers, Special Collections, University of Virginia.

117.   Emory G. Evans, "Byrd, William," *Dictionary of Virginia Biography,* vol. 2 (2001): 470–72.

118.   Lord George Germain to Sir Edward Walpole, August 17, 1778, Mss2 G3173 a1, Virginia Historical Society.

119.   Mary Beth Norton, "John Randolph's 'Plan of Accommodations,'" *WMQ,* 3rd ser., 28, no. 1 (1971): 109.

120.   Ibid., 110–11.

121.   Leonard L. Mackall, ed., "A Letter from the Virginia Loyalist John Randolph to Thomas Jefferson Written in London in 1779," *American Antiquarian Society Proceedings* 30 (1920): 30.

122.   *TJP,* 1:66–67.

123.   Sandor Salgo, *Thomas Jefferson: Musician and Violinist* (Chapel Hill: University of North Carolina Press, 2002).

Reexamining Loyalist Identity during the American Revolution

1.   Research for this essay was made possible through fellowships and grants from the University of Stirling, the William L. Clements Library at the University of Michigan, the John D. Rockefeller Jr. Library at Colonial Williamsburg, the British Library, the Houghton Library at Harvard University, the David Library of the American Revolution, the New York State Archives, the New York State Library, the Huntington Library, the United Empire Loyalists' Association, the New-York Historical Society, and Eugene Lang School of Liberal Arts at The New School. I would also like to thank Heather Lonks Minty, Michael D. Hattem, Matthew Dziennik, Colin Nicolson, Emma Macleod, and my colleagues at the Adams Papers at the Massachusetts Historical Society for their valuable assistance.

2.   Robert M. Calhoon, review of *The King's Friends: The Composition and Motives of the American Loyalist Claimants* by Wallace Brown. *Virginia Magazine of History and Biography* 74, no. 2 (1966): 220; emphasis in original. Wallace Brown, *The King's Friends: The Composition and Motives of the American Loyalist Claimants* (Providence: Brown University Press, 1965).

3.   Brown noted in 1970 that "some of a renaissance in Loyalist studies is now taking place and all indicates the movement will grow"; Brown, "The View at Two Hundred Years: The Loyalists of the American Revolution," *American Antiquarian Society Proceedings* 80, pt. 1 (1970): 47. Brown highlighted the publication of William H. Nelson's *The American Tory* (Oxford: Clarendon Press, 1962) and *Peter Oliver's Origins and Progress of*

the American Rebellion: A Tory View, ed. Douglass Adair and John A. Schultz (Stanford: Stanford University Press, 1961), as the starting points of the renaissance.

4. Henry J. Young, review of *The King's Friends: The Composition and Motives of the American Loyalist Claimants* by Wallace Brown, *WMQ,* 3rd. ser., 23, no. 3 (1966): 503–5; Gordon S. Wood, review of *The King's Friends: The Composition and Motives of the American Loyalist Claimants* by Wallace Brown, *Journal of Southern History* 32, no. 2 (1966): 242–43. See also Eugene R. Fingerhut, "Uses and Abuses of the American Loyalists' Claims: A Critique of Quantitative Analyses," *WMQ* 25, no. 2 (1968): 245–58.

5. Brown, *King's Friends,* conclusion; Maya Jasanoff, *Liberty's Exiles: American Loyalists in the Revolutionary World* (New York: Knopf, 2011), 386n65, 8; Aaron N. Coleman, "Loyalists in War, Americans in Peace: The Reintegration of the Loyalists, 1775–1800" (PhD diss., University of Kentucky, 2008), 4; Aaron Sullivan, "In But Not of the Revolution: Loyalty, Liberty, and the British Occupation of Philadelphia," (PhD diss., Temple University, 2014), 6.

6. Quoted in John Shy, *A People Numerous and Armed: Reflections on the Military Struggle for American Independence* (Ann Arbor: University of Michigan Press, 1990), 208–9.

7. Charles Inglis to Myles Cooper, July 24, 1775, Fettercairn Papers, box 75, folder 3, National Library of Scotland; Mercy Otis Warren, *History of the Rise, Progress, and Termination of the American Revolution,* 3 vols. (New York: AMS, 1970), 3:259; George Otto Trevelyan, *The American Revolution,* 3 vols. (New York: Longmans, Green, 1922–26), 1:377.

8. Robert M. Calhoon, *The Loyalists in Revolutionary America, 1760–1781* (New York: Harcourt Brace Jovanovich, 1973), "Epilogue: A Special Kind of Civil War," 500–506.

9. Loyalists were identified from *New-York Gazette: and the Weekly Mercury,* April 17, 1775, January 1, 1776; November 11, 1776; December 2, 9, 1776; "Declarations of Dependence," Y1776, NYHS; CO 5/1108, ff. 71–101, TNA; CO 5/ 1109, ff. 1–49, TNA; vol. 274, Henry Clinton Papers, 1736–1850, William L. Clements Library, University of Michigan. Also of use were Esther Clark Wright, *The Loyalists of New Brunswick,* rev. ed. (Windsor: Lancelot, 1955), 253–345; Henry J. Young Collection, William L. Clements Library, University of Michigan. It should be noted that Loyalists often signed multiple declarations or took the oath of allegiance on more than one occasion.

10. For further discussion of this and for a broad-based evaluation of the sources used in this analysis, see Christopher F. Minty, "Mobilization and Voluntarism: The Political Origins of Loyalism in New York" (PhD diss., University of Stirling, 2014), chaps. 1–2.

11. Given that the British occupied Staten Island, it is probable that the inhabitants of Richmond County were either tendered the oath of allegiance or that they furnished declarations upon or during the British occupation. However, despite a thorough examination of newspapers in conjunction with private correspondence and the papers of prominent British generals, which is how all the other documents were located, no such documents relating to Richmond County have been located.

12. Identifying race is an issue that plagues eighteenth-century African American history because it is seldom possible to identify people of color unless they were referred to as such. Compounding this situation, if racial characteristics were discussed, it often occurred in either a negative or sensational context—slave runaways or acts of violence, for instance—or when discussing African Americans as an economic commodity. But this is not to suggest that it was not possible for African Americans to sign lists or that Loyalism

in the colonies or New York was not racially diverse. On the contrary there is an impressive and growing body of scholarship on African American Loyalists. The absence of significant numbers of identifiable African Americans from Loyalist declarations offers an intriguing insight into not just how wartime forces shaped Loyalism but also how British officials interpreted race in a province where they were attempting to restore authority and stability. See Shane White, *Somewhat More Independent: The End of Slavery in New York City, 1770–1810* (Athens: University of Georgia Press, 1991), 64–65, 153. For works on African American Loyalists, see, for instance, Michael E. Groth, "Black Loyalists and African American Allegiance in the Mid-Hudson Valley," in *The Other Loyalists: Ordinary People, Royalism, and the Revolution in the Middle Colonies, 1763–1787*, ed. Joseph S. Tiedemann, Eugene R. Fingerhut, and Robert W. Venables (Albany: State University of New York Press, 2009), 81–104; Simon Schama, *Rough Crossings: Britain, the Slaves, and the American Revolution* (London: BBC, 2005); Jim Piecuch, *Three Peoples, One King: Loyalists, Indians, and Slaves in the Revolutionary South, 1775–1782* (Columbia: University of South Carolina Press, 2008); Douglas R. Egerton, *Death or Liberty: African Americans and Revolutionary America* (New York: Oxford University Press, 2009); Gary B. Nash, "The African Americans' Revolution," in *Oxford Handbook of the American Revolution*, ed. Edward G. Gray and Jane Kamensky (New York: Oxford University Press, 2013), 254–64.

13. See Claim of William Brown, AO 12/24, ff. 176–81, TNA.

14. Markham Scrapbook Collection, vol. 2, MC1868, microfilm no. F10048, Provincial Archives of New Brunswick, Fredericton, NB.

15. For Heron and his associates, see Minty, "Mobilization and Voluntarism."

16. See *New-York Gazette: and the Weekly Mercury*, June 26, 1775; July 1, 1776; November 3, 1777; August 17, 1778.

17. In Norfolk, for instance, merchants made up a significant portion of the city's loyal population. Of 361 identified Loyalists, 178, or 49 percent, left the colony, and 63 percent of them were merchants. In Massachusetts, of the 308 Loyalists named in the Banishment Act of 1778 whose occupations could be identified (233), nearly one-fifth were merchants (45). See Robert East, *Business Enterprise in the American Revolutionary Era* (New York: Columbia University Press, 1938), 218–20; Adele Hast, *Loyalism in Revolutionary Virginia: The Norfolk Area and the Eastern Shore* (Ann Arbor: UMI Research Press, 1982), 177, 175; Colin Nicolson, "Governor Francis Bernard, the Massachusetts Friends of Government, and the Advent of the Revolution," *Proceedings of the Massachusetts Historical Society* 103 (1991): 34; James H. Stark, *The Loyalists of Massachusetts and the Other Side of the American Revolution* (Salem, MA: Salem Press, 1910), 137–40.

18. See Robert V. Wells, *The Population of the British Colonies before 1776: A Survey of Census Data* (Princeton: Princeton University Press, 1975).

19. See C. James Taylor, "John Watts and Revolutionary New York" (PhD diss., University of Tennessee, 1981). For Bancker, Nicoll, and Rhinelander, see Bancker's Account and Survey Books, 1760–1815, NYHS; Charles Nicoll, Account Books, 1753–1801, NYHS; Rhinelander Family Papers, 1771–1848, NYHS.

20. See Minty, "Mobilization and Voluntarism," chap. 2. See also John J. McCusker, *Money and Exchange in Europe and America, 1600–1775: A Handbook* (Chapel Hill: University of North Carolina Press, 1978).

21. Gary B. Nash, "Urban Wealth and Poverty in Pre-Revolutionary America," *Journal of Interdisciplinary History* 6, no. 4 (1976): 545–84; Raymond A. Mohl, "Poverty in Early

America, a Reappraisal: The Case of Eighteenth-Century New York City," *New York History* 50, no. 1 (1969): 5–27.

22. Brown, *King's Friends,* 308. Probate of Abraham Furman, March 22, 1779, Probated Wills, vol. 32, 295, New York State Archives; Probate of Walter Franklin, August 22, 1780, Probated Wills, vol. 32, 308–14, New York State Archives.

23. Identifying children as Loyalists is problematic: see Philip Ranlet, "How Many American Loyalists Left the United States?" *Historian* 76, no. 2 (2014): 295–96.

24. On the father-son experience in the American Revolution, see, for instance, Robert M. Weir, "Rebelliousness: Personality Development and the American Revolution in the Southern Colonies," in *The Southern Experience in the American Revolution,* ed. Jeffrey R. Crow and Larry E. Tise (Chapel Hill: University of North Carolina Press, 1978), 25–54.

25. Colin Nicolson, "The Friends of Government: Loyalism, Ideology and Politics in Revolutionary Massachusetts" (PhD diss., University of Edinburgh, 1988), 368–69.

26. Joseph Kett argues that young men were not perceived as fully independent adults until they were self-employed, married, and had established their own (stable) household. Men could remain semidependent until their mid to late twenties, if not later. See Joseph F. Kett, *Rites of Passage: Adolescence in America, 1790 to the Present* (New York: Basic Books, 1977), 29–31, 93–102.

27. See Jasanoff, *Liberty's Exiles,* and Ranlet, "How Many American Loyalists Left the United States?"

28. Brown, *King's Friends,* 9–10, 98–101; Philip Ranlet, *The New York Loyalists* (Knoxville: University of Tennessee Press, 1986), 173; Virginia D. Harrington, *The New York Merchant on the Eve of the Revolution* (New York: Columbia University Press, 1935), 349–51. For other historians who have made the correlation between Loyalism and Anglicanism, see, for instance, Alexander C. Flick, *Loyalism in New York during the American Revolution* (New York: Columbia University Press, 1901), esp. 9–10; Nelson, *American Tory,* 3; Leopold S. Launitz-Schürer, *Loyal Whigs and Revolutionaries: The Making of the Revolution in New York, 1765–1776* (New York: New York University Press, 1980), 178–79; Janice Potter, *The Liberty We Seek: Loyalist Ideology in Colonial New York and Massachusetts* (Cambridge, MA: Harvard University Press, 1983); Joseph S. Tiedemann, *Reluctant Revolutionaries: New York City and the Road to Independence, 1763–1776* (Ithaca: Cornell University Press, 1997), 208; Ruma Chopra, *Unnatural Rebellion: Loyalists in New York City during the Revolution* (Charlottesville: University of Virginia Press, 2011), 47–48.

29. For a detailed breakdown of all sources consulted here, see Minty, "Mobilization and Voluntarism," chap. 2. Marriage and baptismal records were consulted at http://registers .trinitywallstreet.org/files/history/registers/registry.php (accessed November 2, 2016).

30. Anglicans made up around 10 percent of the province's population. In 1750, 20 out of 164 of New York's congregations were Anglican, and on the eve of the Revolution, 26 out of 239 were. Though the Church of England was not numerically hegemonic, its political and economic power was buoyed by constant support from the province's governor and the Society for the Propagation of the Gospel. See Chopra, *Unnatural Rebellion,* 13; James B. Bell, *The Imperial Origins of the King's Church in Early America, 1607–1783* (Basingstoke: Palgrave Macmillan, 2004), 214–15; James B. Bell, *Empire, Religion and Revolution in Early Virginia, 1607–1786* (Basingstoke: Palgrave Macmillan, 2013), 165–66.

31. Holly Brewer, "Subjects by Allegiance to the King? Debating Status and Power for Subjects—and Slaves—through the Religious Debates of the Early British Atlantic," in

State and Citizen: British America and the Early United States, ed. Peter S. Onuf and Peter Thompson (Charlottesville: University of Virginia Press, 2013), 29–35.

32. For more, see Minty, "Mobilization and Voluntarism," appendix.

33. Tiedemann, *Reluctant Revolutionaries,* 24–25; Joyce D. Goodfriend, "The Social Dimensions of Congregational Life in Colonial New York City," *WMQ* 46, no. 2 (1989): 273.

34. Sydney V. James, *A People among Peoples: Quaker Benevolence in Eighteenth-Century America* (Cambridge, MA: Harvard University Press, 1963), 142, 145.

35. Quotes taken from Arthur J. Mekeel, "New York Quakers in the American Revolution," *Bulletin of Friends' Historical Association* 29, no. 1 (1940): 50, 51n5.

36. Thomas Jones, *History of New York during the Revolutionary War: And of the Leading Events in the Other Colonies at That Period,* 2 vols., ed. Edward Floyd DeLancey (New York: Printed for the NYHS, 1879), 1:2; Tiedemann, *Reluctant Revolutionaries,* 23–24; Joyce D. Goodfriend, "Archibald Laidlie and the Transformation of the Dutch Reformed Church in Eighteenth-Century New York City," *Journal of Presbyterian History* 81, no. 3 (2003): 149–62; Goodfriend, "Social Dimensions of Congregational Life in Colonial New York City," 268–69; Randall Herbert Balmer, *A Perfect Babel of Confusion: Dutch Religion and English Culture in the Middle Colonies* (New York: Oxford University Press, 2002), esp. vii–ix, 38–39, 106–8, 141–56.

37. Michael Kammen, *Colonial New York: A History* (New York: Scribner, 1975), 238; Tiedemann, *Reluctant Revolutionaries,* 22–23. For Livingston, McDougall, and Scott during the imperial crisis, see Dorothy R. Dillon, *The New York Triumvirate: A Study of the Legal and Political Careers of William Livingston, John Morin Scott, William Smith, Jr.* (New York: Columbia University Press, 1949); Roger J. Champagne, *Alexander McDougall and the American Revolution in New York* (Schenectady: New York State American Revolution Bicentennial Commission with Union College Press, 1975); Milton M. Klein, *The American Whig: William Livingston of New York,* rev. ed. (New York: Garland, 1993), 429–542.

38. J. C. D. Clark, *The Language of Liberty 1630–1832: Political discourse and social dynamics in the Anglo-American world* (New York: Cambridge University Press, 1994), esp. chap. 4.

39. On Lutherans and New York City's other religions, see Arnold J. H. Van Laer, *The Lutheran Church in New York, 1649–1772: Records in the Lutheran Church Archives at Amsterdam, Holland* (New York: New York Public Library, 1946); Goodfriend, "Social Dimensions of Congregational Life in Colonial New York City"; Joyce D. Goodfriend, *Before the Melting Pot: Society and Culture in Colonial New York City, 1664–1730* (Princeton: Princeton University Press, 1992).

40. Nancy L. Rhoden, *Revolutionary Anglicanism: The Colonial Church of England Clergy during the American Revolution* (Basingstoke: Palgrave Macmillan, 1999), 88–89, 149, 180n4; Bell, *War of Religion,* 222–40 (for New York, 226–27). Moore, Bloomer, and Cutting were identified as signatories to a declaration from Queens County (*New York Gazette: and the Weekly Mercury,* December 2, 1776) and Moore was also administered the oath of allegiance in New York City in March 1777 (see William Tryon to Lord George Germain, March 28, 1777, CO 5/1108, ff. 71–101, TNA). Loyalist Anglican ministers included Samuel Auchmuty, Luke Babcock, Joshua Bloomer, John Bowden, Myles Cooper, Leonard Cutting, John Doty, Charles Inglis, James Lyon, John Milner, Benjamin Moore, John Ogilvie, Samuel Seabury, John Vardill, and Isaac Wilkins.

41. The extent of Anglican ministers' Loyalism in New York was matched or surpassed in Connecticut, Delaware, Georgia, Maryland, Massachusetts, New Hampshire, New Jersey, and Rhode Island. In Virginia and South Carolina, proportionally more Anglican ministers became Patriots.

42. Hast, *Loyalism in Revolutionary Virginia,* 175; Bell, *War of Religion,* 205–6; Nicolson, "Friends of Government," 370–71.

43. Isaac Wilkins to Myles Cooper, October 2, 1778, Fettercairn Papers, box 75, folder 3, National Library of Scotland.

44. "A. W. Farmer" [i.e., Samuel Seabury], *A View of the Controversy between Great-Britain and Her Colonies in a Letter to the Author of a Full Vindication of the Measures of the Congress* (New York: Rivington, 1774), 10–11; "An American" [i.e., Charles Inglis], *The True Interest of America Impartially Stated, in Certain Strictures on a Pamphlet Intitled Common Sense,* 2nd ed. (Philadelphia: Humphreys, 1776), 10, 18. The last quote ("endearing connection") is taken from a testament from Isaac Wilkins as he departed New York in May 1775: see *The Price of Loyalty: Tory Writings from the Revolutionary Era,* ed. Catherine S. Crary (New York: McGraw-Hill, 1973), 35.

45. Charles Inglis to Myles Cooper, July 24, 1777, Fettercairn Papers, box 75, folder 3, National Library of Scotland; Charles Inglis to Robert Lowth, June 11, 1781, Robert Lowth Letters, Charles Inglis Letters, MS Am (3), Houghton Library, Harvard University; [John Wetherhead] to Myles Cooper, February 7, 1778, Fettercairn papers, box 75, folder 4, National Library of Scotland.

46. Edward Larkin, "What Is a Loyalist?," *Common-Place* 8, no. 1 (2007), http://www.common-place-archives.org/vol-08/no-01/larkin/; Ranlet, "How Many American Loyalists Left the United States?"; Jasanoff, *Liberty's Exiles.* See also Philip Ranlet and Maya Jasanoff, "Communications," *WMQ* 66, no. 1 (2009): 229–31.

47. Christopher F. Minty, "The Future of Loyalist Studies," *Borealia: A Group Blog on Early Canadian History,* November 23, 2015, http://earlycanadianhistory.ca/2015/11/23/the-future-of-Loyalist-studies/.

48. Calhoon, *Loyalists in Revolutionary America,* 503, 506.

Constructing Female Loyalism(s) in the Delaware Valley

1. This research was made possible thanks to a research fellowship with the Library Company/Historical Society of Philadelphia and a Delo grant from the University of Tampa. Many thanks to the librarians at the Library Company of Philadelphia/HSP and the Haverford Special Collections who helped with this project. Thanks also to my writing group members—Caroline Wigginton, Abram Van Engen, Michele Navakas, Angie Calcaterra, Greta LaFleur, Travis Foster, and Wendy Roberts—and the editors of this collection for their invaluable feedback concerning my revisions.

2. "Fighting Quakers" proved the exception to the majority of friends who disapproved of the Revolution because of their belief in pacifism. A total of 1,276 members were disowned from the Society of Friends for getting involved in the war in one way or another: "758 for military deviations, 239 for paying taxes and fines, 125 for subscribing loyalty tests, 69 for assisting the war effort, 32 for accepting public office and 42 for miscellaneous deviations including watching military drills and celebrating independence." William C. Kashatus III, *Conflict of Conviction: A Reappraisal of Quaker Involvement in the American Revolution* (New York: University Press of America, 1990), 38, 101–2, 108–9.

3. The following texts provide a solid foundation for understanding Quaker pacifism during the American Revolution: Adair P. Archer, "The Quaker's Attitude toward the Revolution," *WMQ* 1, no. 3 (1921): 167–82; Harry E. Seyler, "Pennsylvania's First Loyalty Oath," *History of Education Journal* 3, no. 4 (1952): 114–26; Richard Wilson Renner, "Conscientious Objection and the Federal Government, 1787–1792," *Military Affairs* 38, no. 4 (1974): 142–45; Arthur J. Mekeel, *The Quakers and the American Revolution* (York: Sessions Book Trust, 1996); and, most recently, Sarah Crabtree, *Holy Nation: The Transatlantic Quaker Ministry in an Age of Revolution* (Chicago: University of Chicago Press, 2015).

4. John Sullivan, *Letters and Papers of Major General John Sullivan* (Concord: New Hampshire Historical Society, 1930), 433–34.

5. On May 15, 1776, Congress passed a resolution requiring special committees to draft and administer the test oaths. County committees chose representatives for this purpose, and all representatives met in Philadelphia on June 18, 1776, to comply with this request. The convention delegates at this event drafted the test oaths discussed here. Seyler, "Pennsylvania's First Loyalty Oath," 116–17.

6. Mekeel, *Quakers and the American Revolution*, 2–3.

7. Ethyn Williams Kirby, "The Quakers' Efforts to Secure Civil and Religious Liberty, 1660–96," *Journal of Modern History* 7, no. 4 (1935): 412. Quakers did, however, have the option to affirm instead of swearing, but for a number of reasons such an alternative was still unappealing.

8. Richard Bauman, *Let Your Words Be Few: Symbolism of Speaking and Silence among Seventeenth-Century Quakers* (Cambridge: Cambridge University Press, 1983), 97. For more on the history of Quakers and oath taking, see chapter 7 of Bauman's book.

9. For more on what constituted "Loyalism," see Robert M. Calhoon, *The Loyalists in Revolutionary America* (New York: Harcourt Brace Jovanovich, 1965); Wallace Brown, *The King's Friends: The Composition and Motives of the American Loyalist Claimants* (Providence: Brown University Press, 1965); W. S. MacNutt, "The Loyalists: A Sympathetic View," *Acadiensis* 6, no. 1 (1976): 3–20; Janice Potter, "The Lost Alternative," *Humanities Association Review* 27, no. 2 (1976): 89–193; Esmond Wright, *Red, White and True Blue: The Loyalists in the Revolution* (New York: AMS, 1976); Elisa Tamarkin, *Anglophilia: Deference, Devotion, and Antebellum America* (Chicago: Chicago University Press, 2008); Maya Jasanoff, *Liberty's Exiles: American Loyalists in the Revolutionary World* (New York: Knopf, 2011); and Ruma Chopra, *Unnatural Rebellion: Loyalists in New York City during the American Revolution* (Charlottesville: University of Virginia Press, 2011).

10. Sullivan, *Letters and Papers*, 433–34.

11. Robert F. Oaks, "Philadelphians in Exile: The Problem of Loyalty during the American Revolution," *Historical Society of Pennsylvania* 96, no. 3 (1972): 303.

12. Crabtree, *Holy Nation*, 46. See also Mekeel, *Quakers and the American Revolution*, 4–5, 198–99; and Thomas Gilpin, *Exiles in Virginia: With Observations on the Conduct of the Society of Friends during the Revolutionary War, Comprising the Official Papers of the Government Relating to That Period 1777–1778* (Bowie, MD: Heritage Books, 2003), 38, 42.

13. Owen S. Ireland, *Religion, Ethnicity, and Politics: Ratifying the Constitution in Pennsylvania* (University Park: Pennsylvania State University Press, 1995), 221.

14. Other women in the Delaware Valley and the surrounding area held similar viewpoints concerning (and used similar strategies to resist) being forced to choose one side or another during the war. Letter writers and journalists who engaged in similar

rhetorical performances include Elizabeth Graeme Fergusson, Elizabeth Drinker, Elizabeth Murray, Grace Growden Galloway, Hannah Griffitts, Rebecca Shoemaker, Deborah Norris (Logan), and Sally Wister. The exiles' experiences—most notably those of Margaret Mascarene Hutchinson, Margaret Holyoke Mascarene, Sarah Winslow Deming, Sarah Frost, Elizabeth Lichtenstein Johnston, and Martha I'ans Walker, to name a few—differ somewhat, though they still vacillate along the political spectrum. Crabtree, *Holy Nation*, 19.

15. Margaret Morris, *Private Journal Kept during a Portion of the Revolutionary War for the Amusement of a Sister* (Philadelphia: Privately printed, 1836), 11.

16. Cynthia Dubin Edelberg, *Jonathan Odell: Loyalist Poet of the American Revolution* (Durham, NC: Duke University Press, 1987), 57.

17. Morris, *Private Journal*, 11.

18. Society of Friends, 9 mo. 27, 1776; 9th Month to the 4th of the Tenth Month, 1777; 16th 9 month 1778, "To the Meeting for Sufferings," PYM (Arch Street) Meeting for Sufferings, Minutes 1775–1785, Haverford Special Collections, Pennsylvania. I have preserved the Quakers' unique dating system.

19. PYM, 9 mo. 27, 1776; PYM, 9th Month to the 4th of the Tenth Month, 1777.

20. Margaret Morris, *Journal of Margaret Hill Morris* in *Letters of Doctor Richard Hill and His Children; or, The History of a Family, as Told by Themselves*, ed. John Jay Smith (Philadelphia: Privately printed, 1854), 67.

21. "Count de Nope" refers to Count Carl von Donop, a Hessian colonel who commanded garrisons in Burlington at the time that Morris kept her journal.

22. Morris, *Journal of Margaret Hill Morris*, 222.

23. Ibid., 220.

24. She called them "gondola men" because they sailed in gundalow boats. For more on the gundalow boats, see Nancy Coffey Heffeman and Ann Page Stecker, *New Hampshire: Crosscurrents in its Development* (Lebanon, NH: University Press of New England, 2004), 71; and Alan Axelrod, *The Real History of the American Revolution: A New Look at the Past* (New York: Sterling, 2009), 121.

25. The PYM confirm that Quakers decided to banish from the Society anyone who participated in the war for either side. Participation for the Quakers included requisitions, quartering, correspondence, military action, political office, or participating in crowd action, celebrations, or protests (PYM, 29th day of the 9th Month to the 4th of the Tenth Month 1777).

26. Morris, *Private Journal*, 28.

27. Ibid.

28. For Quaker debates about what constituted gray-area engagement, see PYM, "To the Meeting for Sufferings 16th 9 mo 1778," 174–83, which discusses requisitions; PYM, "At the Monthly Meeting for Sufferings 16th of the 9th mo. 1779," 216–17, which discusses test oaths and paying fines for refusing oath taking; and PYM, "To the Comittee [*sic*] appointed by the yearly meeting," 16, which talks about the ethics of caring for sick and injured Bostonians during the war. About the Meeting for Sufferings, see Crabtree, *Holy Nation*, 15.

29. Morris, *Private Journal*, 36.

30. By "generic," I mean "genre." The letter-journal is a letter, a diary, and a political proclamation, a familiar, intimate writing form as well as a publicly circulated document.

31. Samuel Shoemaker was Anna Rawle's stepfather. An excellent resource for the Rawle/Shoemaker biography is Rebecca Warner Rawle Shoemaker, Anna Rawle, and Margaret Rawle, *Letters and Diaries of a Loyalist Family of Philadelphia*, 1780–86, Pemberton Papers, TS, HSP, 1284–1300.

32. Shoemaker, *Letters and Diaries*, HSP, 1291.

33. William Brooke Rawle, "Laurel Hill and Some Colonial Dames Who Once Lived There," *Pennsylvania Magazine of History and Biography* 35, no. 4 (1911): 395; Judith Van Buskirk, "They Didn't Join the Band: Disaffected Women in Revolutionary Philadelphia," *Pennsylvania History* 62, no. 3 (1995): 320.

34. Whether or not Rawle and the Shoemakers were targeted because they were subversives, Loyalists, or Quakers is a really interesting line of inquiry; the answer is probably yes to all three. And while I am not particularly interested in answering that question here, given that I am most concerned with how Rawle identified herself, I do think this slippage between political identities—and the ways in which the rebels navigated that slippage—is worthy of another study.

35. Rawle, "Laurel Hill and Some Colonial Dames Who Once Lived There," 397.

36. Anna Rawle to Mrs. [Rebecca] Shoemaker, [October 1781], Pemberton Papers, *Letters and Diaries of a Loyalist Family of Philadelphia*, 70.63, HSP, 120–21. Subsequent references to this collection will be cited as author to recipient, date, HSP, and page number when available.

37. Rawle to Shoemaker, June 7, 1780, HSP.

38. Rawle to Shoemaker, October 27 [1781], HSP.

39. For more on the loaded etymology of the word "mob," see Dirk Hoerder, *Crowd Action in Revolutionary Massachusetts 1765–1780* (New York: Academic Press, 1977), 6–9.

40. Rawle may have framed the crowd action as random and chaotic (which was typical of the way a Loyalist would view the rebels), but rebels rarely smashed and burned houses spontaneously or at will. Rather they carefully selected their targets so they might serve as symbols, usually identifying people who supported, implemented, or enforced what they saw to be unfair policies created by the Crown. The candles in the window, which would protect a house from being looted, were an important symbol as well. Crowds used large fires, such as bonfires, to signal the start of a march or riot and small flames, such as candles, to mark houses because flames of all sizes had providential significance. For more on fire and crowd action during the American Revolution, see Robert Blair St. George, *Conversing by Signs: Poetics of Implication in Colonial New England Culture* (Chapel Hill: University of North Carolina Press, 1998), 243.

41. Anna Rawle to Rebecca Shoemaker, October 27 [1781], HSP. Robert Shewell lived in a house on Second Street, near Anna Clifford's grandmother's estate, the Edward Warner house on Front Street, which is where this incident took place.

42. In a letter to the Pennsylvania Executive Council, the Society of Friends explained its stance on war-related celebrations: "As they could not join with others in shedding the blood of their fellow-men, . . . neither could they unite in rejoicing for the advantages gained by such blood-shed . . . ; therefore they were not . . . to make a shew of conformity in such rejoicings by placing lights in any part of the fronts of their houses, or other compliances of the like nature and tendency; well knowing . . . such things to be inconsistent with religious gravity and sobriety." John Drinker, 12th Month 6th, 1781, "To the President and Executive Council, the General Assembly of Pennsylvania, and others whom it may

concern," Epistles Issued and Received 1668–1821, folder 1774–1797, Haverford Special Collections, Haverford College, Haverford, Pennsylvania.

43. Rawle to Shoemaker, October 27 [1781], HSP.

44. Susan Klepp, "Rough Music on Independence Day, Philadelphia, 1778," in *Riot and Revelry in Early America,* ed. William Pencak, Matthew Dennis, and Simon P. Newman (University Park: Pennsylvania State University Press, 2002), 161.

45. Ibid., 161, 165.

46. Gilpin, *Exiles in Virginia,* 38. Anyone interested in the Virginia Exile Crisis should also read Elizabeth Sandwith Drinker, *The Diary of Elizabeth Drinker,* ed. Elaine Foreman Crane (Boston: Northeastern University Press, 1991).

47. Sarah Logan Fisher, April 5, 1778, Belfield Family Papers, Sarah Logan Fisher Diaries 1776–1795, vol. 5, HSP. Henry Drinker, who was imprisoned with Tommy Fisher, confirmed that the prisoners were receiving letters from Robert Pleasants, John Parrish, John James, and other Friends in a letter to Mahlon Jenney, 12 mo. 22 1777, Letters of American Friends: George Dillwyn and Henry Drinker, Haverford Special Collections, Haverford College, Haverford, Pennsylvania.

48. Fisher, 22nd Day of the 12th Month, vol. 1, HSP.

49. Fisher, the 4th day [1777]), vol. 2, HSP.

50. Fisher, 1777, vol. 5, HSP.

51. Fisher, May 12–September 24 1777, vol. 3, HSP.

52. Fisher, n.d., vol. 2, HSP, 43.

53. Fisher, Oct 9 [1777], vol. 4, HSP.

54. Fisher, [Sept 1777], vol. 4, 2, HSP.

Loyalist Refugee Camp

1. Guy Carleton, First Baron Dorchester: The National Archives of the UK (TNA), PRO: 30/55/17/1946.

2. TNA: PRO 30/55/19/2358.

3. TNA: PRO 30/55/20/2472.

4. Oscar Theodore Barck Jr., *New York City during the War for Independence, with Special Reference to the Period of British Occupation* (Port Washington, NY: Friedman, 1966), 74.

5. Marion Balderston and David Syrett, eds., *The Lost War: Letters from British Offices during the American Revolution* (New York: Horizon, 1975), 103.

6. Barck, *New York City during the War for Independence,* 76; Philip Ranlet, *The New York Loyalists* (Lanham, MD: University Press of America, 2002), 72.

7. For the latest interpretation of the garrison model, see Ranlet, *New York Loyalists.*

8. The Loyalist citadel thesis appears in the biographical work of prominent individuals. A good general example is William Smith in *Historical Memoirs of William Smith,* ed. William H. W. Sabine (New York: New York Times, 1958).

9. The opportunist model appears in the most recent work on Revolutionary New York City. For the best of this work, see Judith L. Van Buskirk, *Generous Enemies: Patriots and Loyalists in Revolutionary New York* (Philadelphia: University of Pennsylvania Press, 2002); and Ruma Chopra, *Unnatural Rebellion: Loyalists in New York City during the Revolution* (Charlottesville: University of Virginia Press, 2011).

10. Robert M. Calhoon, *The Loyalists in Revolutionary America, 1760–1781* (New York: Harcourt, Brace, Jovanovich, 1973), 370–87.

11. For an introduction to forced migration, see works by the Refugee Studies Centre at Oxford University: Noahiko Omata, "Home-Making during Protracted Exile: Diverse Responses of Refugee Families in the Face of Remigration," *Transnational Social Review* 15 (2016): 26–40; Diana Ihring, *Human Mobility as a Resource in Conflict: The Case of Syria*, RSC Working Paper Series, no. 115 (2016), www.rsc.ox.ac.uk/publications/human-mobility-as-a-resource-in-conflict-the-case-of-syria; and Evan Easton-Calabria, "'Refugees Asked to Fish for Themselves': The Role of Livelihoods Trainings for Kampala's Urban Refugees," New Issues in Refugee Research, no. 277 (2016), www.unhcr.org/en-us/research/working/56bd9ed89/refugees-asked-fish-themselves-role-livelihoods-trainings-kampalas-urban.html.

12. Simon Turner, *Politics of Innocence: Hutu Identity, Conflict and Camp Life* (New York: Berghahn Books, 2010).

13. "Benetton Group—Corporate Website," http://www.benettongroup.com/archive/press-release/colors-41-lukole-camp (accessed May 09, 2016). For information about the closure of the camp, see "UNHCR Prepares Transition Ahead While Camps Are Closing," *UNHCR News*, June 17, 2008, http://www.unhcr.org/4857de172.html.

14. Turner, *Politics of Innocence*, 1–21.

15. Van Buskirk, *Generous Enemies*, 2.

16. Ibid., 2–3.

17. The 1771 census estimated that 21,863 civilians lived in New York City. The population just before and after the war was closer to 25,000. See Barck, *New York City during the War for Independence*, 75.

18. American Loyalist Claims, AO 13, series 2, 1780–1785, reel 5, vol. 45, Claim of William Waddell, NYPL.

19. Benjamin L. Carp, "The Night the Yankees Burned Broadway: The New York City Fire of 1776," *Early American Studies* 4, no. 2 (2006): 475, 477.

20. Cynthia Dubin Edelberg, "Jonathan Odell and Philip Freneau: Poetry and Politics in the Garrison Town of New York City," in *Loyalists and Community in North America*, ed. Robert M. Calhoon, Timothy M. Barnes, and George A. Rawlyk (Westport, CT: Greenwood, 1994), 106.

21. John Smyth, Accounts, 1778–83, NYHS.

22. Sir Guy Carleton Papers, 1767–1867, box 1, item 384, dated January 21, 1777, NYPL.

23. Van Buskirk, *Generous Enemies*, 25.

24. Barck, *New York City during the War for Independence*, 77.

25. Abraham Tomlinson and Henry B. Dawson, *New York City during the American Revolution: Being a Collection of Original Papers (now First Published) from the Manuscripts in the Possession of the Mercantile Library Association, of New York City* (New York: Privately printed for the Association, 1861), 154.

26. Ibid.

27. Nicholas Cresswell, *The Journal of Nicholas Cresswell, 1774–1777* (New York: Dial, 1924), 244–45.

28. Sir Guy Carleton Papers, box 1, item 507, NYPL.

29. Sabine, *The American Loyalists*, 1: 464.

30. Philip Papas, *That Ever Loyal Island: Staten Island and the American Revolution* (New York: New York University Press), 87–88.

31. Sabine, *Biographical Sketches*, 211.

32. Qtd. in Papas, *That Ever Loyal Island,* 214.

33. Cresswell, *Journal of Nicholas Cresswell,* 244–45.

34. Barck, *New York City during the American Revolution,* 94–95.

35. James Rivington's *New York Gazetteer,* September 17, 1783.

36. American Loyalist Claims, AO 13, series 2, 1780–1785, reel 5, nol. 17, Claim of Thomas Bosworth, NYPL.

37. Sir Guy Carleton Papers, box 1, item 444, NYPL.

38. Qtd. in Chopra, *Unnatural Rebellion,* 73.

39. For example see TNA: PRO 20/55/41/4663/1–16, titled "Returns for the District of New York Commencing the 1 July, 1781."

40. John Smyth, Accounts, 1778–83, NYHS.

41. Billy G. Smith, *Down and out in Early America* (University Park: Pennsylvania State University Press, 2004).

42. Linda S. Stuhler, "A Brief History of Government Charity in New York (1603–1900)," —Social Welfare History Project, Virginia Commonwealth University (2013), http://www.socialwelfarehistory.com/eras/brief-history-state-charity-new-york-1603-1900.

43. American Loyalist Claims, AO 13, series 2, reel 5, vol. 45, Claim of William Waddell, NYPL.

44. Balderston and Syrett, *Lost War,* 131.

45. Qtd. in Chopra, *Unnatural Rebellion,* 70–71.

46. Balderston and Syrett, *Lost War,* 108.

47. Qtd. in Chopra, *Unnatural Rebellion,* 140.

48. The primary Loyalist regiment raised in New York was the King's Royal Regiment from June 1776. For further information, see "Loyalist Regiments," On-Line Institute for Advanced Loyalist Studies (2001), http://www.royalprovincial.com/military/rlist/rlist.htm (accessed May 9, 2016).

49. TNA: PRO 30/55/18/2207.

50. TNA: PRO 30/55/21/2576.

51. TNA: PRO 30/55/19/2358.

52. TNA: PRO 30/55/88/9854.

53. TNA: PRO 30/55/21/2527.

54. TNA: PRO 30/55/33/3822.

55. TNA: PRO 30/55/24/2823.

56. TNA: PRO 30/55/15/1833.

57. TNA: PRO 30/55/17/2012.

58. TNA: PRO 30/55/17/1903.

59. TNA: PRO 30/55/18/2237.

60. TNA: PRO 30/55/18/2253.

61TNA: PRO 30/55/65/7271

62. TNA: PRO 30/55/15/1735.

63. TNA: PRO 30/55/13/1558.

64. See, for example, TNA: PRO30/55/35/4010–4011; TNA: PRO 30/55/41/4702; TNA: PRO30/55/ 43/4491–4942.

65. Jabez Fitch, *The New-York Diary of Lieutenant Jabez Fitch,* ed. W. H. W. Sabine (New York: New York Times & Arno, 1971), 148.

Before and After Ramsour's Mill

1. Quoted in Piers Mackesy, *The War for America 1775–1783* (Cambridge, MA: Harvard University Press, 1965), 518. Jim Piecuch's conclusion, following his careful focus on British interactions with potential allies, details "negative myths about the Loyalists." Piecuch, *Three Peoples One King: Loyalists, Indians, and Slaves in the Revolutionary South, 1775–1782* (Columbia: University of South Carolina Press, 2008), 328–31. See also R. Kent Newmyer, "Charles Stedman's History of the American War," *American Historical Review* 63 (1958): 106–8.

2. Charles, Earl Cornwallis to Francis, Lord Rawdon, June 29, 1780, in *Correspondence of Charles, First Marquis Cornwallis,* 3 vols., ed. Charles Ross (London: Murray, 1859), 1:49.

3. The "British" force included about 120 provincials recruited in northern colonies. About one-half of the revolutionaries had come from west of the Appalachians. Following well-publicized hangings, more than 100 prisoners slipped away while moving through heavy woods, and others were exchanged. At least 200 Loyalist veterans of Kings Mountain were still active in South Carolina Loyalist militia units in 1782. Their pay lists name an additional 400 men who had served with Ferguson and had died at Kings Mountain or later. Treasury Papers (T) 50/1–2, TNA, microfilm in North Carolina Collection, Wilson Library, University of North Carolina, Chapel Hill; Carole Hammett, "Kings Mountain Prisoners of War," Combs &c. Research Group, http://www.tngenweb.org/revwar/kingsmountain/prisoners.html (accessed October 16, 2014); Piecuch, *Three Peoples One King,* 198–202; Bobby Gilmer Moss, *Roster of the Loyalists in the Battle of Kings Mountain* (Blacksburg, SC: Scotia-Hibernia, 1998); John Buchanan, *The Road to Guilford Courthouse: The American Revolution in the Carolinas* (New York: Wiley, 1997), 230–41.

4. Robert Wilson Gibbes, comp., *Documentary History of the American Revolution* (New York: Arno, 1971), 247; Hugh Franklin Rankin, *The North Carolina Continentals* (Chapel Hill: University of North Carolina Press, 1971), 28–31; Paul Hubert Smith, *Loyalists and Redcoats: A Study in British Revolutionary Policy* (Chapel Hill: University of North Carolina Press, 1964), 23, 26–28; William Meek claim, Audit Office Papers, TNA (AO) 12/49/257, AO 12/68/55; William Ritenhouse claim, AO 12/49/110, AO 12/68/20; Eli Branson claim, AO 12/34/386, AO 13:117.

5. Carole Watterson Troxler, "Allegiance without Community: East Florida as the Symbol of a Loyalist Contract in the South," in *Loyalists and Community in North America,* ed. Robert M. Calhoon, Timothy M. Barnes, and George A. Rawlyk, Contributions in American History, no. 158 (Westport, CT: Greenwood, 1994), 121–26.

6. *SRNC,* 14:866.

7. Adelaid L. Fries, ed., *Records of the Moravians in North Carolina,* 6 vols. (Raleigh: North Carolina Historical Commission, 1922), 5:1590.

8. Andrew Hamm claim, AO 12/35/155, AO 65/23, AO 13/138; Carole Watterson Troxler, *Farming Dissenters: The Regulator Movement in Piedmont North Carolina* (Raleigh: Department of Cultural Resources, 2011), 47–48; Fries, *Records of the Moravians,* 1:457.

9. Fries, *Records of the Moravians,* 5:1590 (quotation). Jeffrey J. Crow explored the role of the Revolutionary militia as an enforcer of order for the backcountry Whig elite and showed that disarming the uncooperative was a widespread practice; Crow, "Liberty Men and Loyalists: Disorder and Disaffection in the North Carolina Backcountry," in *An Uncivil*

War: The Southern Backcountry during the American Revolution, ed. Ronald Hoffman, Thad W. Tate, and Peter J. Albert (Charlottesville: University Press of Virginia, 1985), 137–47.

10. Emphasis added. Patrick Tonyn to Lord George Germain, December 9, 1780, Colonial Office Papers, TNA (CO) 5/560: 52.

11. "Case of the Loyalists in North Carolina," *Political Magazine and Parliamentary, Naval, Military, and Literary Journal* 4 (1783): 266; Carole Watterson Troxler, "Refuge, Resistance, and Reward: The Southern Loyalists' Claim on East Florida," *Journal of Southern History* 55 (1989): 563–95.

12. Lincoln County Minute Docket, Court of Pleas and Quarter Sessions, 1780–1781, CR.060.301.1, NCA; Tryon County Minute Docket, Court of Pleas and Quarter Sessions, 1769–1779, CR.094.301.1- CR.094.301.2, NCA; Gertrude MacKinney, ed., *Pennsylvania Archives, Eighth Series, Volume IV, House of Representatives Proceedings, October 14, 1741–September 11, 1753* (Harrisburg, 1931), 3325–26, www.portal.state.pa.us, (accessed March 10, 2015); Bobby Gilmer Moss, *Journal of Capt. Alexander Chesney, Adjutant to Major Patrick Ferguson* (Blacksburg, SC: Scotia-Hibernia, 2002), 138.

13. William Alexander Graham, *General Joseph Graham and His Papers on North Carolina Revolutionary History* (Raleigh: Edwards & Broughton, 1904), 214.

14. Ibid., 215–16.

15. David Scheck, writing in the 1880s, took a generous view of the Ramsour's Mill Loyalists, regarding them as naive fellow Germans who wanted only to do their duty. *North Carolina, 1780–'81: Being a History of the Invasion of the Carolinas by the British Army under Lord Cornwallis in 1780–'81* (Raleigh: Edwards & Broughton, 1889), 63. Pay abstract of Lt. Col. John Moore's Regiment, North Carolina Militia, Treasury Papers, 50/1, TNA.

16. Emphasis added. *SRNC*, 14: 866.

17. John Hamilton designated a bull pen as "a place Built by the Rebells for the reception of Torries." Neil Colbreath claim, AO 13/118; Archibald McDougald claim, AO 12/102/124,223, AO 13/25; Daniel McNeill claim, AO 13/138; Neil McArthur claim, AO 13/121; Neil McArthur receipt, March 1782, British Headquarters Papers 4211, William L. Clements Library, Ann Arbor, Michigan.

18. Samuel Bryan recruited it: the North Carolina Volunteers. James Hamilton claim, AO 12/71/66, AO 13/79/119/120 pp. 315–316; Samuel Bryan claim, AO 12/99/314, AO 13/117.

19. Charles Stedman, *The History of the Origin, Progress, and Termination of the American War*, 2 vols. (London: Printed for the author, 1794), 2:385.

20. Cornwallis to Clinton, 30 June 1780, Cornwallis Papers, TNA 30/11/72, 18 (first and third quotations); Cornwallis to Rawdon, June 29, 1780, Cornwallis Papers, TNA 30/11/77/20 (second quotation).

21. He spelled his name *Welsch* and used German script. Brent Holcomb, *Deed Abstracts of Tryon, Lincoln, and Rutherford Counties, North Carolina 1769–1786* (Greenville, SC: Southern Historical Press, 1977), 48.

22. Eli Branson claim.

23. After militia recruits reached him, Cornwallis did not have enough muskets or rifles for them. Before he took command, a powder magazine in Charleston had exploded, destroying between two and three thousand muskets and an unknown number of rifles, said to have been "intended to arm the back-country people." Johann Hinrichs, "Diary of Captain Hinrichs," in *The Siege of Charleston*, trans. Bernhard A. Uhlendorf (Ann Arbor: University of Michigan Press, 1938), 297–99.

24. Crow, "Liberty Men and Loyalists," 138–42.

25. *SRNC*, 14:867 (first quotation); *SRNC*, 15:265 (second quotation); Bryan's recruits told Francis, Lord Rawdon "that they had been drafted to serve in the Militia, and, refusing to march, had no alternative but joining us or going to prison." Qtd. in Smith, *Loyalists and Redcoats*, 144. [Banastre Tarleton], *Campaigns of 1780 and 1781 in the Southern Provinces* (Dublin: Coles et al., 1787), 88.

26. Emphasis added. *SRNC*, 14: 868.

27. Cornwallis Papers, TNA 30/11/2/44–45; Piecuch, *Three Peoples One King*, 189.

28. Cornwallis to Clinton, April 10, 1781, in Charles, Marquis Cornwallis, *An Answer to That Part of the Narrative of Lieutenant-General Sir Henry Clinton, K.B., Which Relates to the Conduct of Lieutenant-General Earl Cornwallis, during the Campaign in North-America, in the Year 1781* (London: Printed for J. Debrett, 1783), 10 (first quotation); *Gentleman's Magazine* 53, no. 155 (second quotation).

29. Earlier Cornwallis had observed South Carolina militiamen switching to new provincial units. Piecuch, *Three Peoples One King*, 194–95. James Monroe, *Edinburgh Magazine and Literary Miscellany* 44 (1782): 294–98; John Hamilton claim, AO 12/36/242, AO 12/73, 277, AO 12/76, 95, 96, 101, AO 13/84/85, 95,120.

30. Stedman, *History of the Origin*, 2:197.

31. Bryan Sr.'s "mansion house" headquarters was near the Shallow Ford on the Yadkin River. Grants, Anson County, Morgan Bryan, 1752, Granville Proprietary Land Office, Secretary of State, NCA; Land Entries, Warrants, and Plats of Survey, Anson County, Morgan Bryan Sr., 1752–53, Granville Proprietary Land Office, Secretary of State, NCA. For Bryan's other settlements, see posting by J. Michael Frost, "Frost, Gilchrist and Related Families," www.frostandgilchrist.com (accessed October 2015).

32. I treated the Orange County dynamic of this question in *Farming Dissenters*, 133–48, and further in "Land Tenure as Regulator Grievance and Revolutionary Tool," in *New Voyages to Carolina: Toward a Reinterpretation of North Carolina History*, ed. Larry E. Tise and Jeffrey J. Crow (Chapel Hill: University of North Carolina Press, 2017).

33. Leslie Hall, *Land and Allegiance in Revolutionary Georgia* (Athens: University of Georgia Press, 2001), 109–36; Harvey H. Jackson, "The Rise of the Western Members: Revolutionary Politics and the Georgia Backcountry," in Hoffman, Tate, and Albert, *Uncivil War*, 276–320; Thomas Cooper and David J. McCord, eds., *The Statutes at Large of South Carolina*, 10 vols. (Columbia: Johnston, 1836–41), 4:568–70; May–June 1783 Militia Reports, South Carolina Historical Commission, Charleston, in "Reports on Loyalist Exiles from South Carolina, 1783," ed. Robert W. Barnwell Jr., *Proceedings of the South Carolina Historical Association* (1937): 43–46; Carole Watterson Troxler, *The Loyalist Experience in North Carolina* (Raleigh: North Carolina Department of Cultural Resources, 1976), 29–35; Surry County, North Carolina, Minutes of Court of Pleas and Quarter Sessions, August 15, 1782, NCA.

34. January–February 1779, Joint Papers, Correspondence, Remonstrances, and Resignations Sent to the Assembly, General Assembly Session Records, box 1, NCA.

35. *SRNC*, 14:261 mistranscribes "Enoree" as "Enroll."

36. Nicholas Welsh [*sic*] to Treasury, March 20, 1786, Treasury Papers, TNA, 1:629 (quotation); Nicholas Welch claim, AO 12/34/ 374, AO 12/109/ 306–307, AO 13/124; General Assembly Session Records, NCA, January–February 1779, box 1.

37. Robert Scott Davis Jr., "The Loyalist Trials at Ninety Six in 1779," *South Carolina Historical Magazine* 80 (1979): 175–80.

38. "Case of the Loyalists in North Carolina," 266.

39. John Richard Alden, *The South in the Revolution 1763–1789* (Baton Rouge: Louisiana State University Press, 1957), 235.

40. Contemporaries referred to the Loyalist leader at Kettle Creek as "Boyd," and near-contemporary sources use both James and John for the same person. James and John Boyd may have been related, as both names occur in land records in North Carolina's Orange County in the 1750s and 1760s and on tributaries of the Saluda River in South Carolina in 1772. Davis, "Loyalist Trials," 172 (quotation); Ruth Herndon Shields, *Orange County, N.C. Abstracts of the Minutes of the Court of Pleas and Quarter Sessions of Sept. 1752–Aug. 1766* (Greenville, SC: Southern Historical Press, 1965); Plats 12.12.56.20, 12.12.56.22, 12.12.56.24, 12.12.56.25, 12.13.84.3, 12.13.84.4, Granville Proprietary Land Office, Secretary of State, NCA; *Orange County Records,* 13 vols., ed. William D. Bennett and Ruby Grant Bennett (Raleigh and Rocky Mount, 1987–93), vols. 1–4; Robert S. Davis, "Loyalism and Patriotism at Askance: Community, Conspiracy, and Conflict on the Southern Frontier," in *Tory Insurgents: The Loyalist Perception and Other Essays,* ed. Robert M. Calhoon, Timothy M. Barnes, and Robert S. Davis (Columbia: University of South Carolina Press, 2010), 229–83; Survey Plats 13:305, 3, and 13:306, 1–2, South Carolina Department of Archives and History.

41. Land records for 1772–73 at Raeburn Creek show Lindley's land adjacent to James and John Boyd's holdings. Memorial Books 12: 36, 12:64, South Carolina Department of Archives and History; Survey Plats 13:293, 460, South Carolina Department of Archives and History; Record Books of Cane Creek Monthly Meeting, Friends Historical Society Library, Guilford College, Greensboro, North Carolina; Deposition of William Millen, January 28, 1779, Miscellaneous Papers, 1776–1789, War of Revolution, Military Collection, NCA, cited in Davis, "Loyalism and Patriotism"; *DNCB* s.v. "James Lindley"; Troxler, *Farming Dissenters,* 151.

42. Davis and I have shared references and assessments during four decades, and some of our publications have leapfrogged. Most pertinent for the Raeburn Creek–Wrightsborough culture is his "Loyalism and Patriotism at Askance," 249–52 (quotation 259). Memorial of James Harvey, January 2, 1780, Sir Henry Clinton Papers, 83:4, William L. Clements Library, Ann Arbor, Michigan; Christopher Coleman Jr. et al., certificate for half-pay for James Harvey, Chancery 106, vol. 89, pt. 1, copy courtesy of Todd Braisted.

43. Griffith John McRee, *Life and Correspondence of James Iredell, One of the Associate Justices of the Supreme Court of the United States,* 2 vols. (New York: Appleton, 1857), 2:408 (quotation); Lincoln County Deed Book 17:334, 379, NCA; Lincoln County Deed Book 18:142, NCA; Rowan County Will Book D:121–123, NCA; Granville Proprietary Land Office, Secretary of State, NCA, Grant Book 6:106, Grant Book 51:66; Revolutionary War Army Accounts, A:54, 185, B:224, Military Papers, State Comptroller, State Treasurer's Record Group, NCA; Petition of Andrew Hamm, 1798, New Brunswick Land Grants and Petitions, Library and Archives Canada; Revolutionary War pension statements S30966, W3976, S8803, Library of Congress, transcribed by Will Graves, www.southerncampaign.org/pen (accessed September 2015); Robert Scott Davis, "The Incident at Cherokee Ford and the Battle of Vann's Creek. February 1779," http://www.kettlecreekbattlefield.org/sitebuilder-content/sitebuilderfiles/cherokeefordandvanncreekbattle.pdf (accessed October 16, 2015); 1783 Spanish census, East Florida Papers, Library of Congress; *SRNC* 17:261; James E. Wooley and Vivian Wooley, *Rutherford County, North Carolina, Wills and Miscellaneous*

Records, 1783–1868 (Easley, SC: Southern Historical Press, 1984), 4–5; Walter Lowrie, *Early Settlers of Mississippi as Taken from Land Claims in the Mississippi Territory* (1834; rpt. Easley, SC: Southern Historical Press, 1986), 628–29; J. H. Roberts, November 22, 1880, Lyman Copeland Draper, Kings Mountain Papers, Series DD, 4DD 70, Draper Manuscript Collection, State Historical Society of Wisconsin, Madison, microfilm in Davis Library, University of North Carolina, Chapel Hill; *City Gazette,* July 10, 1816 (Saint John, New Brunswick); "Case of the Loyalists in North Carolina," 266; author's correspondence with Miss Sylvia Hamm, Sussex Corner, New Brunswick, 1995; Nicholas Welch claim; Andrew Hamm claim; John Hamilton claim.

44. Initial probing of hazards in North Carolina appears in Crow, "Liberty Men and Loyalists"; Troxler, *Loyalist Experience,* 18–20; and Troxler, "Land Tenure as Regulator Grievance and Revolutionary Tool." In the South Carolina upcountry, large districts continued as administrative units until 1786, when the organization of new counties helped maintain the 1783–85 reconciliation explored by Rebecca Brannon in *From Revolution to Reunion: The Reintegration of the South Carolina Loyalists* (Columbia: University of South Carolina Press, 2016), 111–39.

45. Minutes of the Tryon County Committee of Safety, Secretary of State, NCA; Mecklenburg County Court Minutes, April 1778, NCA; Jonas Bedford claim, AO 13/108; Jacob, Peter, and John Blewer claims, AO 13/35. The pattern is documented further in my "A Loyalist Life: John Bond of South Carolina and Nova Scotia," *Acadiensis* 19 (1990): 72–91, and "Origins of the Rawdon Loyalist Settlement," *Nova Scotia Historical Review* 8 (1988): 62–76.

46. Matthew H. Spring, *With Zeal and with Bayonets Only: The British Army on Campaign in North America, 1775–1783* (Norman: University of Oklahoma Press, 2008), 22.

47. [John Cruden] to [Moses Kirkland], 18 September 1780, Winslow Family Papers, II: 11 ff., University of New Brunswick Archives, Fredericton, New Brunswick; Cruden to Cornwallis, September 29, 1780, Cornwallis Papers, TNA 30/11/64/126.

PRAGMATISM AND PRINCIPLE

1. Alexander Chesney's second and third sons were Francis Rawdon Chesney (1789–1872) and Charles Cornwallis Chesney (1791–1830).

2. Charles Cornwallis Chesney, *Essays in Military Biography* (New York: Holt, 1874), 323; Alexander Chesney, "Journal of Captain Alexander Chesney," Diaries and Journals, Public Record Office, Northern Ireland, Treasury Papers, TNA 1095/3/1; CMSIED 8909192, transcript: http://www.dippam.ac.uk/ied/records/41002 (accessed May 2, 2015); Alexander Chesney, *The Journal of Alexander Chesney, a South Carolina Loyalist in the Revolution and After,* ed. E. Alfred Jones, *Ohio State University Bulletin* 26, no. 4 (1921) (hereafter *Chesney Journal*). In 1874 Chesney's son Charles Cornwallis Chesney published a portion of his father's memoir.

3. *Chesney Journal,* 41, 126–27, 129–44; A. Chesney, "Journal of Captain Alexander Chesney."

4. Robert M. Calhoon, Timothy M. Barnes, and Robert Scott Davis, eds., *Tory Insurgents: The Loyalist Perception and Other Essays* (Columbia: University of South Carolina Press, 2010), 370–71.

5. *Chesney Journal,* 1–5, 1n1, 4n20, 60–63, 127–28; Mark James Gomsak, "Alexander Chesney: Loyalism and Leadership in the Carolina Backcountry" (MA thesis, University of South Carolina, 2002), 4, 6–7, 7n6; Jean Stephenson, *Scotch-Irish Migration to South*

Carolina, 1772: Rev. William Martin and His Five Shiploads of Settlers (Baltimore, MD: Clearfield, 1999), 27–31; *South Carolina Gazette* (Charleston), October 22, 1772; Alexander Chesney, plat for 100 acres in Colleton County, June 20, 1773, and Robert Chesney, plat for 350 acres in Ninety Six District, May 26, 1773, South Carolina Surveyor General's Office, Colonial Plat Books (Copy Series), 1731–75, series 213184, vol. 14, p. 71, microfilm, South Carolina Department of Archives and History. The Chesney farm was located near the juncture of today's Union, Spartanburg, and Cherokee Counties.

6. Jerome A. Greene, *Historic Resource Study and Historic Structure Report, Ninety Six: A Historical Narrative* (Denver: US Dept. of the Interior, 1978), 57; Rebecca Nathan Brannon, "Reconciling the Revolution: Resolving Conflict and Rebuilding Community in the Wake of Civil War in South Carolina, 1775–1860" (PhD thesis, University of Michigan, Ann Arbor, 2007), 16; Wallace Brown, *The King's Friends: The Composition and Motives of the American Loyalist Claimants* (Providence, RI: Brown University Press, 1965), 219–21, 337–40; Gomsak, "Alexander Chesney," 56–61.

7. *Chesney Journal*, 1n2, 43n299; Jac Weller, "The Irregular War in the South," *Military Affairs* 24, no. 3 (1960): 131 (first quote); Gomsak, "Alexander Chesney," 10, 15, 16 (second quote).

8. *Chesney Journal*, iii, 5–6, 5n25, 100–101, 135–37; Statement of Obedience to the King from the Loyalists on the Pacolet River (in the claim of Alexander Chesney), PRO: American Loyalist Claims, series 2, reel 134, AO 13/126, p. 325.

9. *Chesney Journal*, 6–7, 130–31; "Chesney, Alexander," Compiled Service Records of Soldiers Who Served in the American Army during the Revolutionary War, 1775–83, NARA Microfilm M881, roll 886. In September 1776 Chesney became a private in the Continental Army when South Carolina's provincial regiments were absorbed into the Continental establishment.

10. *Chesney Journal*, 7 (quoted), 131.

11. Ibid., 7, 7n46, 131.

12 Ibid., 7.

13 Ibid., 7 (quoted); Andrew Williamson to William Henry Drayton, August 22, 1776, in *Documentary History of the American Revolution: Consisting of Letters and Papers Relating to the Contest for Liberty, Chiefly in South Carolina, from Originals in the Possession of the Editor, and Other Sources, 1776–1782*, ed. Robert W. Gibbes (New York: Appleton, 1857), 32.

14. *Chesney Journal*, 7–8; Gomsak, "Alexander Chesney," 20.

15. *Chesney Journal*, 8 (quoted), 9, 9n63, 127–29, 134; Alexander Chesney, account audited (file no. 1224), September 6, 1779, Accounts Audited of Claims Growing out of the Revolution in South Carolina, 1775–1856 (Microcopy No. 8), series 108092, reel 22, microfilm, South Carolina Department of Archives and History.

16. Thomas Cooper, *The Statutes at Large of South Carolina*, vol. 1 (Columbia, SC: Johnston, 1836), 147–51 (quoted); *Chesney Journal*, 131.

17. *Chesney Journal*, 8–9, 8n57, 131; Gomsak, "Alexander Chesney," 20.

18. *Chesney Journal*, 8–9, 131.

19. Ibid., 9, 9n62.

20. Ibid., 8, 9–10, 9n64, 10n65, 128, 134; Alexander Chesney, *Journal of Capt. Alexander Chesney: Adjutant to Major Patrick Ferguson*, ed. Bobby Gilmer Moss and E. Alfred Jones (Blacksburg, SC: Scotia-Hibernia, 2002), 17, 17n108, 147. William Hodge and his son William served at various times in the South Carolina Patriot militia.

21. *Chesney Journal*, 10.

22. Ibid., 10 (quoted), 67–68, 70, 72, 113, 131; Chesney *Journal of Capt. Alexander Chesney*, 117–18, 113; Murtie June Clark, *Loyalists in the Southern Campaigns of the Revolutionary War*, vol. 1, *Official Rolls of Loyalists Recruited from North and South Carolina, Georgia, Florida, Mississippi, and Louisiana* (Baltimore: Genealogical Publishing, 1981), 324, 326.

23. *Chesney Journal*, 11–12, 82–83, 126, 131–32; Wade S. Kolb and Robert M. Weir, eds., *Captured at Kings Mountain: The Journal of Uzal Johnson, a Loyalist Surgeon* (Columbia: University of South Carolina Press, 2011), 90.

24. *Chesney Journal*, 12–14, 13n96.

25. Ibid., 14 (quoted); Pension file for William Hodge, W. 4233, Revolutionary War Pension and Bounty-Land Warrant Application Files, RG 15, Microfilm series M804, roll 1295, NARA.

26. Chesney Journal, 14–15 (quoted); Banastre Tarleton, *A History of the Campaigns of 1780 and 1781, in the Southern Provinces of North America* (Dublin, Ireland: Colles, Exshaw, White, H. Whitestone, Burton, Byrne, Moore, Jones, and Dornin, 1787), 70–72.

27. *Chesney Journal*, 14–15.

28. Ibid., 17–18 (quoted); Chesney, *Journal of Capt. Alexander Chesney*, 35.

29. *Chesney Journal*, 18.

30. Ibid., 17–18 (quoted), 17–18nn121–22.

31. Ibid., 18; Lyman Copeland Draper, *King's Mountain and Its Heroes: History of the Battle of King's Mountain, October 7th, 1780, and the Events Which Led to It* (Cincinnati: P. G. Thomson, 1881), 318–19, 326.

32. *Chesney Journal*, 18–19; Anthony Allaire, *Diary of Lieut. Anthony Allaire* (New York: Arno, 1968), 31–32. Chesney claimed twenty-four were sentenced to death and that ten were hanged; Allaire gives the numbers of nine and three, respectively.

33. *Chesney Journal*, 12, 19–20 (quoted); Chesney, *Journal of Capt. Alexander Chesney*, 35, 35n208; Allaire, *Diary*, 32; Draper, *King's Mountain and Its Heroes*, 270.

34. *Chesney Journal*, 20 (quoted), 20n124, 142, 143.

35. Ibid., 20–21.

36. Ibid., 21, 138–39; Chesney, *Journal of Capt. Alexander Chesney*, 39.

37. *Chesney Journal*, 21, 141–42; Louisa Chesney and Jane Chesney O'Donnell, *The Life of the Late General F. R. Chesney*, ed. Stanley Lane-Poole (London: Allen, 1885), 12–13 (quoted).

38. *Chesney Journal*, 21–22.

39. Ibid., 22 (quoted); pension file for William Hodge, W. 4233, RG 15, Microfilm series M804, roll 1295, NARA.

40. *Chesney Journal*, 9n62, 22.

41. Ibid., 23.

42. Ibid., 23 (quoted), 23n162, 139.

43. Ibid., 23–24 (quoted), 108, 139.

44. Ibid., 24–26.

45. Ibid., 26. Chesney estimated the distance of his ride to be eighty miles.

46. Ibid.

47. Ibid., 27 (quoted), 139–40.

48. Ibid., 138 (first quote), 129, 27 (second quote).

49. Ibid., 27; Chesney, *Journal of Capt. Alexander Chesney*, 17n108; Chesney and O'Donnell, *Life of the Late General F. R. Chesney*, 12–13, 16.

50. *Chesney Journal,* 28, 129; Chesney and O'Donnell, *Life of the Late General F. R. Chesney,* 16–17.

51. *Chesney Journal,* ix, 43 (first quote), 54, 56; Chesney and O'Donnell, *Life of the Late General F. R. Chesney,* 16n (second quote).

52. *Chesney Journal,* v–xi, 1, 28–56, 43n299; 125–44; Chesney and O'Donnell, *Life of the Late General F. R. Chesney,* 32–33, 376; Chesney, *Journal of Capt. Alexander Chesney,* 172. Chesney's wife and daughter give the year of his death as 1843.

53. Sworn testimony of John Phillips [n.d.] and Zacharias Gibbs [n.d.], *Chesney Journal,* 135–37.

54. John Cruden testimonial, February 8, 1782; Nisbet Balfour testimonial, April 1, 1782; Francis Rawdon testimonial, August 18, 1782; and Charles Cornwallis testimonial, November 20, 1783, *Chesney Journal,* 139–40.

55. *Chesney Journal,* 143.

"New Hope" in Shelburne

1. Eleanor Robertson Smith, ed., *Remarks and Rough Memorandums: Captain William Booth, Corps of Royal Engineers, Shelburne, Nova Scotia, 1787, 1789* (Shelburne: Shelburne County Archives and Genealogical Society, 2008), 36–37, 50. The original William Booth diaries (1787 and 1789) are located in the Moore Collection in the Esther Clark Wright Archives at Acadia University, Wolfville, Nova Scotia.

2. Edward Gray, "Liberty's Losers," *WMQ,* 3rd ser., 70 (2013): 188.

3. Robert M. Calhoon, "The Loyalist Perception," in *Tory Insurgents: The Loyalist Perception and Other Essays,* eds. Robert M. Calhoon, Timothy M. Barnes, and Robert S. Davis (Columbia: University of South Carolina Press, 2010), 3, 10.

4. Barry Cahill, preface to Smith, *Remarks and Rough Memorandums,* v. Also see Bonnie Huskins, "'Remarks and Rough Memorandums': Social Sets, Sociability, and Community in the Journal of William Booth, Shelburne, 1787 and 1789," *Journal of the Royal Nova Scotia Historical Society* 13 (2010): 103–32; Bonnie Huskins, "'Shelburnian Manners': Gentility and the Loyalists of Shelburne Nova Scotia," *Early American Studies* 31, no.1 (2015): 151–88.

5. The phrase 'Loyalist dream' was used by Ann Gorman Condon in her book *The Envy of the American States: The Loyalist Dream for New Brunswick* (Fredericton: New Ireland Press, 1984). The phrase 'new hopes' is a modification of the name of the vessel owned by the Holderness family as discussed in the introduction of this essay.

6. Edward Winslow to Ward Chipman, July 7, 1783, Edward Winslow Papers, MG H2, vol. 2, pt. 2, 104, Harriet Irving Library, University of New Brunswick.

7. Murray Barkley, "The Loyalist Tradition in New Brunswick," *Acadiensis* 4, no. 2 (1975): 3–45; Norman Knowles, *Inventing the Loyalists: The Ontario Loyalist Tradition and the Creation of a Usable Past* (Toronto: University of Toronto Press, 1997); Cecilia Morgan, *Creating Colonial Pasts: History, Memory, and Commemoration in Southern Ontario, 1860–1980* (Toronto: University of Toronto Press, 2015). Also see my blog: "Let's Work Together: A Loyalist Historian from Canada Responds to American Scholars," March 7, 2016, https:// earlycanadianhistory.ca/2016/03/07/overlooked-Loyalists/.

8. Barry Cahill, preface to Smith, *Remarks and Rough Memorandums,* v–vii.

9. Huskins, "'Remarks and Rough Memorandums.'"

10. Benjamin Marston qtd. in Maya Jasanoff, *Liberty's Exiles: American Loyalists in the*

Revolutionary World (New York: Knopf, 2011), 169; Ruma Chopra, *Unnatural Rebellion: Loyalists in New York City during the Revolution* (Charlottesville: University of Virginia Press, 2011), 15.

11. Smith, *Remarks and Rough Memorandums,* 37, 52.

12. "Middling gentility" is used by Huskins in "Shelburnian Manners," 151, 158.

13. The phrase "revolution in manners" is taken from C. Dallett Hemphill, ''Manners and Class in the Revolutionary Era: A Transatlantic Comparison,'' *WMQ.* 3rd ser. 63, no. 2 (2006): 365.

14. Neil Mackinnon, "A Caustic Look at Shelburne Society in 1787," *Acadiensis* 17, no. 2 (1988): 139; Hemphill, "Manners and Class in the Revolutionary Era," 365; Peter Borsay, *The English Urban Renaissance: Culture and Society in the Provincial Town, 1660–1770* (Oxford: Oxford University Press, 1989), 224–27.

15. Maya Jasanoff, *Liberty's Exiles: American Loyalists in the Revolutionary World* (New York: Alfred A. Knopf, 2011), 152.

16. Neil MacKinnon, *This Unfriendly Soil: The Loyalist Experience in Nova Scotia, 1783–1791* (Montreal: McGill-Queen's University Press, 1986), 31–32, 35–36, 38–39, 172–73; Huskins, "'Remarks and Rough Memorandums,'" 104.

17. This is similar to the cost of building the Holdernesses' home: eleven hundred pounds. Smith, *Remarks and Rough Memorandums,* 60.

18. Ibid., 138

19. Calhoon, "Loyalist Perception," 10.

20. MacKinnon, *This Unfriendly Soil,* 17–20, 74; Marion Robertson, *King's Bounty: A History of Early Shelburne* (Halifax: Nova Scotia Museum, 1983), 64–66.

21. Smith, *Remarks and Rough Memorandums,* 18

22 Ibid., 61.

23. Calhoon, "Loyalist Perception," 10.

24. Smith, *Remarks and Rough Memorandums,* 21–22.

25. See ibid, 23n33 and 41.

26. Ibid., 86.

27. This phrase is found in Jasanoff, *Liberty's Exiles,* 172.

28. Laird Niven, *Was This the Home of Stephen Blucke? The Excavation of AkDi-23, Birchtown, Shelburne County,* Curatorial Report no. 93 (Halifax: Nova Scotia Museum and Nova Scotia Department of Tourism and Culture, 2000), 14.

29. Robertson, *King's Bounty,* 88.

30. Barry Cahill, "The Black Loyalist Myth in Atlantic Canada," *Acadiensis* 29, no. 1 (1999): 76–87; James W. St. G. Walker, "Myth, History and Revisionism: The Black Loyalists Revisited," *Acadiensis* 29, no. 1 (1999): 89.

31. Smith, *Remarks and Rough Memorandums,* 145–46.

32. Entries for Stephen Blucke and Margaret Blucke, *Book of Negroes,* Guy Carleton, First Baron Dorchester Papers, TNA: PRO 30/55/100, 10427, https://novascotia.ca/archives/Africanns/BNpages.asp?ID=46 (accessed October 19, 2016).

33 Barry Cahill, "Stephen Blucke: The Perils of Being a 'White Negro' in Loyalist Nova Scotia," *Nova Scotia Historical Review* 11 (1991): 129–34.

34. Niven, *Was This the Home of Stephen Blucke?,* 15; James W. St. G. Walker, *The Black Loyalists: The Search for a Promised Land in Nova Scotia and Sierra Leone, 1783–1870* (Toronto: University of Toronto Press, 1992), 22.

35. Walker, *Black Loyalists,* 22–23; John Parr to Robert Morris and others, warrant to survey, 28 April 1786, Nova Scotia Land Papers, https://novascotia.ca/archives/landpapers/archives.asp?ID=870&Doc=warrant&Page=201107118 (accessed October 14, 2016).

36. Cahill, "Stephen Blucke," 131; Smith, *Remarks and Rough Memorandums,* 45; "Stephen Blucke," *Black Loyalists: Our History, Our People,* http://blackloyalist.com/cdc/people/secular/blucke.htm (accessed November 11, 2016); Walker, *Black Loyalists,* 69–70.

37. The phrase "white negro" is found in the title of Barry Cahill's article: "Stephen Blucke: The Perils of Being a 'White Negro'," 129.

38. Smith, *Remarks and Rough Memorandums,* 45.

39. Niven, *Was This the Home of Stephen Blucke?,* 14, 24, 27, 29, 32, 33, 36. Also see "Objects, 1775–1800," *Remembering Black Loyalists, Black Communities in Nova Scotia,* http://novascotia.ca/museum/blackloyalists/17751800/Objects1775/cufflink.htm (accessed November 11, 2016).

40. Walker, *Black Loyalists,* 19.

41. Robertson, *King's Bounty,* 97–98; Walker, *Black Loyalists,* 20.

42. Nathan O. Hatch, "The Second Great Awakening and the Transformation of American Christianity (1989)," *Thinking Through the Past: A Critical Approach to U.S, History Volume I: To 1877,* 5th ed. , ed. John Hollitz (Stamford: Cengage Learning, 2015), 155.

43. Boston King, "Memoirs of the Life of Boston King," *Methodist Magazine, for April, 1798,* http://antislavery.eserver.org/narratives/boston_king (accessed November 11, 2016).

44. Walker, *Black Loyalists,* 79.

45. Ibid., 83.

46. Ibid., 83.

47. Ibid.

48. Cahill, "Stephen Blucke," 133; Robertson, *King's Bounty,* 97–98.

49. Jasanoff, *Liberty's Exiles,* xii–xiii, xv.

50. Ibid., 172.

51. Cahill, "Black Loyalist Myth in Atlantic Canada," 77.

52. Jasanoff, *Liberty's Exiles,* 291–92.

53. "Free Settlement on the Coast of Africa," *Black Loyalists: Our History, Our People,* http://blackloyalist.com/cdc/documents/official/free_settlement_coast_of_africa.htm (accessed November 11, 2016).

54. Walker, *Black Loyalists,* 19.

55. Qtd. in A. F. Walls, "The Nova Scotian Settlers and Their Religion," *Sierra Leone Bulletin of Religion* 1 (1959): 19–31.

56. Jasanoff, *Liberty's Exiles,* 284.

57. Robertson, *King's Bounty,* 104.

58. Ira Berlin qtd. in Randy J. Sparks, prologue to *The Two Princes of Calabar: An Eighteenth-Century Odyssey* (Cambridge, MA: Harvard University Press, 2008), 3–4.

59. Casandra Pybus, *Epic Journeys of Freedom: Runaway Slaves of the American Revolution and Their Global Quest for Liberty* (Boston: Beacon, 2006); Simon Schama, *Rough Crossings: Britain, the Slaves and the American Revolution* (Toronto: Penguin Canada, 2008).

60. Lawrence Hill, *The Book of Negroes* (Toronto: Harper Collins, 2007). This novel was published under the title *Someone Knows My Name* in the United States, Australia, and

New Zealand. It was adapted as an eleven-part miniseries by the Canadian Broadcasting Corporation in 2015.

61. "Clarkson's Mission to America, 1791–1792," *Black Loyalists: Our History, Our People:* see pp. 67–68 (http://blackloyalist.com/cdc/documents/diaries/mission/63-72.htm; accessed September 20, 2016) and 73–82 (http://blackloyalist.com/cdc/documents/diaries/mission/73-82.htm; accessed September 20, 2016); Walker, *Black Loyalists,* 117.

62. [Walker, *Black Loyalists,* 128.]; Eleanor Robertson Smith and Kim Robertson Walker, *Founders of Shelburne Who Came, 1783–1793, and Stayed* (Shelburne: Shelburne County Archives & Genealogical Society, 2008), 11; Robertson, *King's Bounty,* 105, Cahill, "Stephen Blucke," 131–32.

63. For more on Sierra Leone, see Walker, *Black Loyalists,* 145–380.

64. Margaret Blucke to Rev. Mr. Marrant, New York, 12 October 1789, *Black Loyalists: Our History, Our People,* http://blackloyalist.com/cdc/documents/letters/mrs_blucke_to_marrant.htm (accessed November 11, 2016); Niven, *Was This the Home of Stephen Blucke?,* 16.

65. Carole Watterson Troxler, "Re-enslavement of Black Loyalists: Mary Postell in South Carolina, East Florida, and Nova Scotia," *Acadiensis* 37 (2008): 70–85.

66. "The Narrative of Hannah Ingraham," *Loyalist Women in New Brunswick,* http://preserve.lib.unb.ca/wayback/20141205153708/http://atlanticportal.hil.unb.ca/acva/loyalistwomen/en/context/biographies/ingraham.html (accessed November 11, 2016).

67. Smith and Walker, *Founders of Shelburne,* 11; Cahill, "Stephen Blucke," 132.

68. Smith, *Remarks and Rough Memorandums,* 45–46.

69. Harvey Amani Whitfield, *North to Bondage: Loyalist Slavery in the Maritimes* (Vancouver: University of British Columbia Press, 2016), 58; Walker, *Black Loyalists,* 19.

70. Smith, *Remarks and Rough Memorandums,* 45.

71. Huskins, "Shelburnian Manners," 177.

72. Jasanoff, *Liberty's Exiles,* 91.

73. Ibid., 175.

74. Ibid.

75. Robertson, *King's Bounty,* 91; Walker, *Black Loyalists,* 47; Niven, *Was This the Home of Stephen Blucke?,* 31.

76. Smith, *Remarks and Rough Memorandums,* 45.

77. Ibid., 70.

78. Ibid., 144.

79. Whitfield, *North to Bondage,* 109.

80. Ibid., 58.

81. Robertson, *King's Bounty,* 103.

82. Whitfield, *North to Bondage,* 100–101; Troxler, "Re-enslavement of Black Loyalists," 70–85.

83. Cahill, preface to Smith, *Remarks and Rough Memorandums,* vi.

84. Catherine M.A. Cottreau-Robins, "Exploring the Landscape of Slavery in Loyalist Era Nova Scotia," in this volume.

85. Whitfield, *North to Bondage,* 4, 16, 20, 42, 49, 53, 112, 116; Catherine M. A. Cottreau-Robins, "Searching for the Enslaved in Nova Scotia's Loyalist Landscape," *Acadiensis* 43, no. 1 (2014): 125–36.

86. Whitfield, *North to Bondage,* 8, 10, 43, 65–67.

87. Whitfield, *North to Bondage,* 27, 107; to Robertson, *King's Bounty,* 96.

88. Smith, *Remarks and Rough Memorandums,* 32.

89. Ibid., 52; Cahill, preface to Smith, *Remarks and Rough Memorandums,* vi–vii.

90. Smith, *Remarks and Rough Memorandums,* 110–11.

91. Ibid., 44.

92. Ibid., *Memo,* 52.

93. Ibid.; copy of letter from Booth to Samuel Proudfoot, Shelburne, August 31, 1789, in ibid., 31–32. Thanks to Barry Gaspar from Duke University for decoding the term *Teefee.* The Creole term is a reduced form of the French term *petite fille: petite* becomes *tee* or *ti,* and *fille* becomes *fee* or *fi.* Email correspondence, September 7, 2012.

94. Cahill, preface to Smith, *Remarks and Rough Memorandums,* 60, 91.

95. Whitfield, *North to Bondage,* 114.

96. Cottreau-Robins, "Searching for the Enslaved," 133

Exploring the Landscape of Slavery in Loyalist Era Nova Scotia

1. Many individuals and institutions supported the research noted above. Regarding this essay, I thank the volume editors, Rebecca Brannon and Joseph Moore, as well as Jerry Bannister of the History Department, Dalhousie University, for their review and guidance. I also recognize the contributions of the Nova Scotia Museum, the United Empire Loyalist Association of Canada, the Black Loyalist Heritage Center, Young Canada Works Program, and the generous communities of Hardwick, Massachusetts, and Wilmot and Summerville, Nova Scotia.

2. For the range of scholarship, see James W. St. G. Walker, *The Black Loyalists: The Search for the Promised Land in Nova Scotia and Sierra Leone, 1783–1870* (Toronto: Longman, 1976); Ellen Gibson Wilson, *The Loyal Blacks* (New York: Capricorn Books, 1976); David G. Bell, *Early Loyalist Saint John: The Origin of New Brunswick Politics, 1783–1786* (Fredericton: New Ireland, 1983); Ann Gorman Condon, *The Envy of the American States: The Loyalist Dream for New Brunswick* (Fredericton: New Ireland, 1984); J. M. Bumsted, *Understanding the Loyalists* (Sackville: Mount Allison University Press, 1986); Neil MacKinnon, *This Unfriendly Soil: The Loyalist Experience in Nova Scotia 1783–1791* (Montreal: McGill-Queen's University Press, 1988); Simon Schama, *Rough Crossings: Britain, the Slaves and the American Revolution* (Toronto: Viking Canada, 2005); Jerry Bannister and Liam Riorden, eds., *The Loyal Atlantic: Remaking the British Atlantic in the Revolutionary Era* (Toronto: University of Toronto Press, 2012); Ruth Holmes Whitehead, *The Black Loyalists: Southern Settlers of Nova Scotia's First Free Black Communities* (Halifax: Nimbus, 2013); Ken Donovan, "Slavery and Freedom in Atlantic Canada's African Diaspora: Introduction," *Acadiensis* 43, no. 1 (2014): 109–15; and Harvey Amani Whitfield, *North to Bondage: Loyalist Slavery in the Maritimes* (Vancouver: University of British Columbia Press, 2016).

3. *Black Loyalist* is a term that has been debated intensely. See Barry Cahill, "The Black Loyalist Myth in Atlantic Canada," *Acadiensis* 29, no. 1 (1999): 76–87; and James W. St. G. Walker, "Myth, History and Revisionism: The Black Loyalists Revisited," *Acadiensis* 29, no. 1 (1999): 88–105. Similar to Walker, I draw from the larger definition of *Loyalist* in the *Canadian Encyclopedia.* Specifically "Loyalists are among the American colonists of varied ethnic backgrounds who supported the British cause during the American Revolution . . . for highly diverse reasons." The black Loyalists were among this widely defined group

and consisted of enslaved, indentured, and free individuals. I also use the term *black Loyalist* to appreciate the significant and diverse cultural experience of the group during and following the Revolutionary period.

4. Nova Scotia was much larger geographically during the American Revolution period. New Brunswick and Upper Canada were created after the conflict (1784 and 1791, respectively), to accommodate the influx of Loyalists. See R. Cole Harris, ed., *Historical Atlas of Canada,* vol. 1 (Toronto: University of Toronto Press, 1987), plate 32. Approximately thirty-two thousand Loyalist refugees immigrated to Nova Scotia following the American Revolution. The Loyalist migration represented an unprecedented arrival of enslaved persons to the province and with that the unprecedented arrival of a political and ideological framework that carried within it perceptions of race and seeds of discrimination that took root. Estimated numbers vary in the documentary record. Generally by 1784 more than three thousand free black Loyalists had arrived in Nova Scotia, New Brunswick, and Prince Edward Island. For a basic summary of the arrival and settlement of the black Loyalists, see "African Nova Scotians," NSA, https://novascotia.ca/archives/virtual/?Search=THans&List=all (accessed May 2012).

5. The full study of the Loyalists, from which this paper is drawn, is available through Dalhousie University. See Catherine M. A. Cottreau-Robins, "A Loyalist Plantation in Nova Scotia, 1784–1800" (PhD diss., Dalhousie University, 2012).

6. Historian Robins Winks was one of the first academics to raise the issue of slavery in Canada in his volume *The Blacks in Canada: A History* (New Haven: Yale University Press, 1971). Another early article is T. Watson Smith, "The Slave in Canada," *Collections of the Nova Scotia Historical Society* 10 (1899): 1–161.

7. Two copies of *The Book of Negroes* were developed in 1783. The British copy is on file with the Sir Guy Carleton Papers at the National Archives in Kew, Great Britain, and the American copy is on file at the National Archives in Washington, DC. A copy of the original British version is at the Nova Scotia Archives (NSA) and was used for my dissertation. See *Book of Negroes,* Bound Manuscript, RG1, vol. 423, NSA. For a searchable index, see *Book of Negroes,* NSA, https://novascotia.ca/archives/Africanns/archives.asp?ID=26 (accessed August 2012). It is important to note that not all enslaved African Americans landing in Maritime Canada were recorded in *The Book of Negroes.* Those so recorded arrived mainly from the Lowland South, Chesapeake, and New England regions.

8. See Cottreau-Robins, "Loyalist Plantation in Nova Scotia," for complete historical and archival sources linked to Timothy Ruggles. Given his activity on many fronts, the record is rich. Only brief portions are noted here. Also Catherine M. A. Cottreau-Robins, "Searching for the Enslaved in Nova Scotia's Loyalist Landscape," *Acadiensis* 43, no. 1 (2014): 125–36; and Catherine M. A. Cottreau-Robins, "The Loyalist Plantation: An Interdisciplinary Approach to Informing Early African Nova Scotian Settlement," *Journal of the Royal Nova Scotian Historical Society* 17 (2014): 32–56.

9. For further portrayal of a Massachusetts gentleman of the era, see Alexandra A. Chan, *Slavery in the Age of Reason: Archaeology at a New England Farm* (Knoxville: University of Tennessee Press, 2007), 96–102.

10. Often noted as "servants" in the archival record particular to Ruggles.

11. Deborah Navas, *Murdered by His Wife* (Amherst: University of Massachusetts Press, 1999); Ivan Sandrof, "Forgotten Giant of the Revolution: The Story of Brigadier General Timothy Ruggles of Hardwick," *Worcester Historical Society,* n.s., 3, no. 6 (1952),16–28.

References can be found in the diary of Dr. Elihu Ashley of Deerfield, Massachusetts, who describes stopping at Brigadier General Ruggles's Hardwick home. See Amelia F. Miller and A. R. Riggs, eds., *Romance, Remedies, and Revolution: The Journal of Dr. Elihu Ashley of Deerfield, Massachusetts, 1773–1775* (Amherst: University of Massachusetts Press, 2007), 86–87.

12. The ultimate success of British forces in the Seven Years' War cemented for Ruggles his "uniform attachment" to Great Britain and influenced his vigorous declaration from Boston in April 1775 "to contribute everything in my power to convince these rebellious wretches of their folly and wickedness in despising the best Government both in Theory and administration that ever yet bles'd the earth we inhabit and if it causes me as many wearisome days and sleepless nights, as five campaigns did in the last War, I pray God my constitution may endure it; and my Country will be happy if success extends his Majesty's arms; if not many of us will lose our lives and be put out of our present miserable situation." See CO 5/154, TNA.

13. Ruggles was chosen as a delegate from Massachusetts, and when the general Stamp Act Congress (also known as the First Colonial Congress) met in New York in October 1765, he was elected president. Edmund S. Morgan and Helen M. Morgan, *The Stamp Act Crisis: Prologue to Revolution* (Chapel Hill: University of North Carolina Press, 1953), 105; Ruma Chopra, *Unnatural Rebellion: Loyalists in New York City during the Revolution* (Charlottesville: University of Virginia Press, 2011), 19–28.

14. "Brigadier Ruggles' Reasons for His Dissent from the Resolutions of the Congress at New York, as Given into the House, February 19, 1766," in *History of Hardwick, Massachusetts*, ed. Lucius R. Paige (Boston: Houghton, Mifflin, 1883), 62–64. This is one of several occasions Ruggles published his views or explained his actions in the Boston papers. For example in the *Boston News-letter and New-England Chronicle*, he listed the reasons he voted nay when the Sons of Liberty resolved and the House of Representatives adopted measures to prevent the consumption of foreign goods and to encourage the manufactures of the province. *Boston News-letter and New-England Chronicle*, no. 3363, March 17, 1768, American Antiquarian Society, Historic Newspaper Collections, Worcester, Massachusetts.

15. Ibid. In the later period, also see Ruggles's call to "The Association" published in the *Boston News-letter*, no. 3718, December 29, 1774, 2. The announcement for a Loyalist Association reinforces Ruggles's commitment to the Loyalist cause and the unwavering value he placed on parliamentary rule and the authority of the king. This public call spoke directly to his Loyalist ideology. It was a statement of rules and actions to perform "our indispensable duty" and uphold "the good and wholesome Laws of Government." The Loyalist subscribers "associate and mutually covenant, and engage to . . . stand by and assist in the defense of Life, Liberty and Property, whenever the same shall be attacked . . . not acknowledge, or submit to the pretended authority, of any Congress, Committees of Correspondence or other unconstitutional Assemblies of Men . . . we will . . . enforce obedience to the rightful Authority of our most Gracious King George, the third, and of his laws."

16. Condon, *Envy of the American States*, 4–6.

17. In 1774 the governor, recognizing Ruggles's support, appointed him mandamus councillor, which he accepted with hesitation given that the position was associated with unequivocal supporters of the Crown in a volatile climate of anti-British sentiment. The position gave Ruggles authority as a member of the King's Council. See "List of the

Gentlemen Appointed by His Majesty, Counsellor of This Province," *Essex Journal*, August 10, 1774, 3.

18. See *Massachusetts Spy, or, American Oracle of Liberty*, no. 391, October 29, 1778, 1, Historic Newspaper Collections of the American Antiquarian Society, Worcester, Massachusetts.

19. Annapolis Royal and Granville are not far from Wilmot Township, which is also in Annapolis County, where Ruggles got his principal land grant.

20. Ruggles's thoughts can be best imagined, while waiting in Annapolis for word of his grant, through a letter he sent to his friend Edward Winslow Sr. in New York dated July 17, 1783. He described in detail the agricultural possibilities. See W. O. Raymond, *Winslow Papers, 1776–1826* (Saint John: Sun, 1901), 106–9. The "Plan of Wilmot Township" shows the thousand-acre grant only, whereas Crown Land Index Sheets nos. 35 and 28 indicate Ruggles's having two parcels, a thousand-acre piece and a nine-thousand-acre piece. His sons Richard and John had lots directly north and adjacent to their father. See Old Book 14, p. 19, reel 13041 for the original land grant dated April 24, 1784. "Being Lotts number 45 & 46 . . . containing together 1000 acres . . . being all wilderness lands." "Plan of Wilmot Township," MG1 vol. 1299, no. 19, NSA. The Crown Land Index Sheets provided by the Department of Lands and Forest for Nova Scotia provide the original grant book numbers and page references. Ruggles's memorial documents are highly detailed and accompanied by letters of support and testimony.

21. See the monument near the town center in Hardwick recognizing Ruggles as a pioneer in scientific agriculture and his efforts to establish the Hardwick Fair in 1762, "the oldest in the US."

22. Cousins, "Brigadier General Timothy Dwight Ruggles," 3.

23. *Royal Gazette and Nova Scotia Advertiser*, August 11, 1795, MFM 8167, NSA. Reverend Wiswall also noted in his personal journal at Wilmot, October 12, 1795, "There is now no gentleman of property left in Wilmot." See "Journal of Reverend John Wiswall, 1771–1812," call no. 1900.008, manuscript on file, Acadia University Archives, Wolfville.

24. The Ruggles Road is the main thoroughfare through the Wilmot/North Mountain land grant.

25. See Leland Ferguson's discussion of colonoware ceramics in *Uncommon Ground: Archaeology and Early African America, 1650–1800* (Washington, DC: Smithsonian Institution Press, 1992). See also Mark P. Leone's discussion of spiritual caches at the Charles Carroll House in Annapolis, Maryland, in *The Archaeology of Liberty in an American Capital: Excavations in Annapolis* (Los Angeles: University of California Press, 2005), 192–244, and see the work of several contributors in *"I Too Am America": Archaeological Studies of African-American Life*, ed. Theresa A. Singleton (Charlottesville: University Press of Virginia, 1999). Of particular note is part 1 of the latter volume, titled "African-American Identity and Material Culture."

26. It is important to recognize that the slaveholder would have had considerable control over not only daily life and work but also the shaping of the living quarters, the use of the space, and the material culture within. All would reflect the British colonial influence of the day as well as elements of the British North American plantation complex. Trevor Bernard, *Planters, Merchants, and Slaves: Plantation Societies in British America, 1650–1820* (Chicago: University of Chicago Press, 2015); Justin Roberts, *Slavery and the Enlightenment in the British Atlantic, 1750–1807* (Cambridge: Cambridge University Press, 2013).

For a thorough description and analysis of the artifacts collected, see Cottreau-Robins, "Loyalist Landscape in Nova Scotia," 153–225.

27. It is notable that the interdisciplinary dissertation work (Ruggles) was the first and remains the only comprehensive study of slavery, slaveholding, and slavery landscape that includes the excavation of a slave dwelling in Nova Scotia. The recent Grant landscape fieldwork is the first step to testing the model and the Ruggles findings. As more fieldwork is completed and the archaeological record develops, there will be opportunities to explore new questions and paradigms specifically linked to the enslaved such as the archaeology of agency and resistance and the archaeology of race. Charles E. Orser Jr., *The Archaeology of Race and Racialization in Historic America* (Gainesville: University Press of Florida, 2007); Marcia-Anne Dobres and John E. Robb, eds., *Agency in Archaeology* (New York: Routledge, 2000).

28. Iain Robertson and Penny Richards, eds., *Studying Cultural Landscapes* (London: Oxford University Press, 2003), 3. Robertson and Richards agree this is possible in the study of landscape and discuss several examples in England.

29. Ibid., 1–3. The complexity of studying landscapes is emphasized in archaeology by Christopher C. Fennell; see Fennell, "Carved, Inscribed and Resurgent: Cultural and Natural Terrains as Analytical Challenges," in *Perspectives from Historical Archaeology: Revealing Landscapes,* ed. Christopher C. Fennell (N.p.: Society for Historical Archaeology, 2011), 1–11.

30. Bishop Charles Inglis Papers, September 16, 1791, book 5 for 1791, p. 17, MG1, vol. 480, NSA.

31. The similarities are numerous and cover key elements regarding the configuration and use of space, the position of buildings, agricultural pursuits, community statement, and composition of the labor force. See Cottreau-Robins, "Loyalist Plantation in Nova Scotia," for specific details.

32. Janice Potter, *The Liberty We Seek: Loyalist Ideology in Colonial New York and Massachusetts* (Cambridge, MA: Harvard University Press, 1983), 12–14. Ideology, as described by Potter, is an argument on behalf of a cause, which is coherent, cohesive, and comprehensive. A key element of Loyalist ideology was the vision of an Anglo-American empire: Britain and America. Loyalists believed the two were united by history, trade, and a shared attachment to the empire and the British government. A continued link would also bring unity and prosperity. This was not a sudden ideology for Ruggles that came along as war tensions increased. He was a long-standing Anglo-American. He wrote, published, and coordinated military engagements not only to cultivate action and provide explanation or clarification, but also, as Potter states, to affect choice.

33. Interplay of the evidence and an examination of similarities and differences is key to the interdisciplinary process. See Allen F. Repko, *Interdisciplinary Research: Process and Theory* (Los Angeles: Sage, 2008).

34. Memorial of Brigadier General Timothy Ruggles, October 16, 1783, AO 13/75, 403–8, TNA.

35. In the specific time frame noted here, the 1760s, approximately two hundred enslaved individuals arrived in Nova Scotia with New England planters who migrated to the province to resettle lands emptied following the expulsion of the Acadians in 1755. Also, in the mid-eighteenth century, slavery was part of daily life at the French fortress Louisbourg in Cape Breton, Nova Scotia, until its final fall in 1758. See "Slavery and Freedom, 1749–1782," NSA, https://novascotia.ca/archives/africanns/results.asp

?Search=&SearchList1=1&Language=English (accessed January 2016); and Ken Donovan, "Slaves in Ile Royale, 1713–1758," *French Colonial History* 5 (2004): 25–42.

36. Comparable, for example, in social position, land ownership, military and political connections, and associations with doctors, clergy, the financially advantaged, and those linked to industry. Several archival documents provided clues, such as muster roles, township records, church records, tax records, census records, *The Book of Negroes,* and journals. This is a preliminary analysis given that the scope reaches well beyond Ruggles's North Mountain plantation.

37. The scholarship regarding slavery in Maritime Canada is actively building, and there have been publications and public exhibitions that have expanded discussion and recognition. For examples see Whitfield, *North to Bondage;* Whitehead, *Black Loyalists;* and Carole Watterson Troxler, "Re-enslavement of Black Loyalists: Mary Postell in South Carolina, East Florida, and Nova Scotia," *Acadiensis* 37, no. 2 (2008): 70–85. See also the Black Loyalist Heritage Center in Birchtown, Nova Scotia, and the Africville Museum in Halifax, Nova Scotia. Still for the most part and especially outside Maritime Canada, the story of Canada's slave past, particularly among the general population, remains largely unknown.

38. See George Stoddard Ruggles, *General Timothy Ruggles 1711–1795* (Wakefield, MA: Privately printed, 1897) and Franklin L. Bailey, *The Genealogy of Thomas Ruggles of Roxbury, Massachusetts,* (1896).

39. For a comprehensive family history, see Edith Mosher and Nellie Fox, *Land of a Loyalist* (Hantsport, Nova Scotia: Lancelot, 1988), and T. Watson Smith, "Loyalist History—John Grant," *Acadiensis* 1 (1901): 7–18.

40. Smith, "Loyalist History," 7–18; Mosher and Fox, *Land of a Loyalist,* 17.

41. Mosher and Fox, *Land of a Loyalist,* 18.

42. Ruggles's lengthy memorial estimated sixteen thousand pounds and detailed everything from his sugar tongs to the leashes for his hounds.

43. Mosher and Fox, *Land of a Loyalist,* 20. Sarah, in an effort to gain compensation for their losses, described the original farmhouse as 150 acres lying in the town of Brookland, Long Island, on which stood a valuable mansion house measuring 48 by 36 feet, with a kitchen adjoining as well as barns and outbuildings in good repair. Hay, grain, cattle, and horses were also seized or driven away.

44. See Crown Land Index Sheet no. 53 and Old Book 12, p. 229, Hants County Registry of Deeds, Nova Scotia.

45. Old Book 12, p. 229; Mosher and Fox, *Land of a Loyalist,* 22.

46. Mosher and Fox, *Land of a Loyalist,* 31. The *Halifax Journal* printed a brief notice stating that on Sunday, November 2, 1817, Mr. Grant of Newport accidentally shot himself with his own pistol.

47. Field survey is also planned for the forested area that surrounds the family cemetery. An old cart road nearby leads to the gypsum quarry initially developed by Michael Grant at turn of the nineteenth century and an associated wharf on the riverbank near the beach to the southwest. The importance of the Avon River that abuts the western edge of the land grant cannot be minimized. This was the principal highway for transportation, communication, and commerce in the evolving countryside.

48. Mosher and Fox, *Land of a Loyalist,* 22. Mosher and Fox note a slave for each family member.

Lawyering for Loyalists in the Post–Revolutionary War Period

1. My thanks to the staff at Harvard Business School, who offered superb assistance in locating the materials used in this study, particularly Christopher Gore's postwar account book, Mss 83 1785–1810 G666 (microfilm reel group 85–3960, reel 7). I would also like to thank the organizers of the 2014 annual meeting of the Omohundro Institute for Early American History and Culture, which convened in Halifax, Nova Scotia, where an earlier version of this paper was delivered. That presentation was partially funded by the Burnham-Macmillan Endowment of Western Michigan University History Department.

2. Harrison Gray Otis to Robert Hallowell, January 2, 1789, Harrison Gray Otis Letterbook 1788–1807 (reel 11), Harrison Gray Otis Papers, Massachusetts Historical Society.

3. Thomas Hutchinson to "Dear Sir," January 8, 1770, vol. 27, 92–93, Massachusetts Archive Collection, Massachusetts State Archive.

4. Clifford Shipton, *Sibley's Harvard Graduates: Biographical Sketches of Those Who Attended Harvard College, 1756–1760, with Bibliographical and Other Notes*, vol. 14, 1756–60 (Boston: Massachusetts Historical Society, 1968), 650–61.

5. Samuel Eliot Morison, *The Life and Letters of Harrison Gray Otis, Federalist 1765–1848*, vol. 1 (Boston: Houghton, Mifflin, 1913), 28.

6. Ibid., 1: 29.

7. James H. Stark, *The Loyalists of Massachusetts and the Other Side of the American Revolution* (Boston: Stark, 1910), 337.

8. Harrison Gray to Harrison Gray Otis, February 12, 1821, Harrison Gray Otis Papers, Massachusetts Historical Society.

9. Samuel Eliot Morison, "The Property of Harrison Gray, Loyalist," *Publications of the Colonial Society of Massachusetts* 14 (1911/1913): 331.

10. Samuel Eliot Morison, *Life and Letters of Harrison Gray Otis*, 1:1–14, 39.

11. Ibid.

12. Morison, "Property of Harrison Gray, Loyalist," 328.

13. Ibid., 328–29.

14. Qtd. in ibid., 331.

15. Ibid., 341–42.

16. Ibid., 343.

17. Qtd. in ibid., 345.

18. Morison, *Life and Letters of Harrison Gray Otis*, 1: 39–40.

19. Morison, "Property of Harrison Gray, Loyalist," 349.

20. Ibid., 329.

21. Ibid., 330.

22. Qtd. in ibid., 350.

23. Ibid., 335.

24. Ibid., 336–37.

25. Helen R. Pinkney, *Christopher Gore: Federalist of Massachusetts, 1758–1827* (Waltham, MA: Gore Place Society, 1969), 3.

26. Ibid., 10.

27 Ibid.

28. E. Alfred Jones, *The Loyalists of Massachusetts: Their Memorials, Petitions and Claims* (Baltimore: Genealogical Publishing, 1969), 150.

29. Under the October 1, 1778, act of the Massachusetts General Court. Pinkney, *Christopher Gore*, 12–13.

30. Confiscated estates reproduced with locations and names of purchasers in *Proceedings of Massachusetts Historical Society*, 2nd ser., 10:162–85. David E. Maas, ed., *Divided Hearts, Massachusetts Loyalists, 1765–1790: A Biographical Directory* (Boston: Society of Colonial Wars in the Commonwealth of Massachusetts/New England Historic Genealogical Society, 1980), 67; Pinkney, *Christopher Gore*, 13.

31. Gore's individual memorial at AO 13/73, TNA, cited in Jones, *Loyalists of Massachusetts*, 150. Gore signed a collective memorial with twenty-eight other Loyalist refugees. AO 13/46, reprinted in ibid., 309.

32. Pinkney, *Christopher Gore*, 11.

33. Ibid., 14–15. The commander of his regiment was also his brother-in-law, Thomas Craft.

34. "Memoir of Christopher Gore," *Collections of the Massachusetts Historical Society*, 3rd ser., 3 (1833): 206.

35. Pinkney, *Christopher Gore*, 13.

36. Ibid.

37. Jones, *Loyalists of Massachusetts*, 150; Pinkney, *Christopher Gore*, 13.

38. Harrison Gray Otis to Harrison Gray, June 2, 1789, Harrison Gray Otis Letterbook 1788–1807, reel 11, Massachusetts Historical Society.

39. Robert Troup to Christopher Gore, October 21, 1795, John Lowell Papers, bMS AM 1582, Houghton Library, Harvard University.

40. Maas, *Divided Hearts*, xxiii–xxiv.

41. Pinkney, *Christopher Gore*, 16.

42. Ibid., 17.

43. Christopher Gore to Daniel Newcomb, July 16, 1780, Mellen Chamberlain Collection, Boston Public Library, cited in Pinkney, *Christopher Gore*, 16.

44. Christopher Gore to Rufus King, August 22, 1789, Rufus King papers, NYHS, cited in Pinkney, *Christopher Gore*, 17.

45. Debits for November 23, 1785; January 29, 1786; and May 18, 1786, Christopher Gore, Christopher Gore Account Book, Mss 83 1785–1810 G666, microfilm Reel Group 85–3960, reel 7, n.d., Harvard Business School Historical Collections, Boston.

46. Woody Holton, "Abigail Adams, Bond Speculator," *WMQ* 64, no. 4 (2007): 821–38.

47. Pinkney, *Christopher Gore*, 19.

48. Anthony J. Connors, "Andrew Craigie," *Harvard Magazine*, December 2011, http://harvardmagazine.com/2011/11/andrew-craigie (accessed November 5, 2016).

49. Pinkney, *Christopher Gore*, 34–37. Pinkney estimated, from incomplete records, that Gore held $135,000 in securities, for which he paid less than half that to acquire them originally. Ibid., 38.

50. John Adams to John Quincy Adams, September 13, 1790, in *Adams Family Correspondence*, vol. 9, ed. Margaret A. Hogan et al. (Cambridge MA: Harvard University Press, 2009), 112, http://www.masshist.org/publications/apde/portia.php?id=ADMS-04-09-02-0059 (accessed November 5, 2016).

51. John Quincy Adams to John Adams, September 21, 1790, in Hogan et al., *Adams Family Correspondence*, 9: 117–18.

52. "Memoir of Christopher Gore," 194.

53. Pinkney, *Christopher Gore*, 48.

54. "Memoir of Christopher Gore," 201.

55. Annie Thwing, "Inhabitants and Estates of the Town of Boston, 1630–1822," Thwing Collection (Boston, n.d.), NEHGS online archival collections, www.americanancestors .org (accessed November 5, 2016).

56. Gore's amassed wealth enabled him to live on a mediocre government salary in London and Paris for the better part of eight years. He was present while Jay's Treaty was negotiated. In 1804 he returned to Boston, where he continued to work in private practice until his election as governor in 1809. Thereafter he did not practice law again as a full-time advocate. "Memoir of Christopher Gore," 195–96.

57. Ibid., 200.

58. Morison, *Life and Letters of Harrison Gray Otis.*

"That Abundant Infamous Roach"

1. *American Loyalist Claims Commission Papers, 1780–1835,* Great Britain, AO, vol. 90, 78–80, microfilm edition, 1973, housed at DLAR, Washington Crossing, Pennsylvania (originals are in the National Archives, London); hereafter AO 13, followed by volume and pages: AO 13/90/78–80. On the imagery of patriotic attachment to the king in particular and also British government in Loyalist claims, see Keith Mason, "The American Loyalist Problem of Identity in the Revolutionary Atlantic World," in *The Loyal Atlantic: Remaking the British Atlantic in the Revolutionary Era,* ed. Jerry Bannister and Liam Riordan (Toronto: University of Toronto Press, 2012), 39–74.

2. See Maya Jasanoff, *Liberty's Exiles: American Loyalists in the Revolutionary World* (New York: Knopf, 2011), 9–12.

3. *The Case of Thomas Packer Batcheller, Eldest Son of Major Breed Batcheller, late of New Hampshire in New England,* pamphlet (London: Meyers, 1798), 12; held at NYHS.

4. Robert Calhoon, "The Loyalist Perception," in *Tory Insurgents: The Loyalist Perception and Other Essays,* ed. Robert M. Calhoon, Timothy M. Barnes, and Robert S. Davis (Columbia: University of South Carolina Press, 2010), 3–14.

5. On the rapid Revolutionary acquisition of power in New Hampshire, see Jere R. Daniell, *Experiment in Republicanism: New Hampshire Politics and the American Revolution, 1741–1794* (Cambridge, MA: Harvard University Press, 1970), 74–112; and Paul W. Wilderson, *Governor John Wentworth and the American Revolution: The English Connection* (Lebanon, NH: University Press of New England, 1994), 221–65.

6. Perhaps because of the absence of civil war in New Hampshire, there are few relatively recent monograph studies of New Hampshire Loyalists. Robert Munro Brown, "Revolutionary New Hampshire and the Loyalist Experience: 'Surely We Have Deserved a Better Fate'" (PhD diss., University of New Hampshire, 1983), argues that Loyalism in New Hampshire was weak and devoid of leadership after Governor Wentworth left. James Leslie Walsh, "Friend of Government or Damned Tory: The Creation of Loyalist Identity in Revolutionary New Hampshire, 1774–1784" (PhD diss., University of New Hampshire, 1996), offers an analysis largely based on Loyalist claims of a unified identity as suffering victims and patriotic supporters of the Crown.

7. On New England's emphasis on monitoring and controlling the threat of "Tory language," see Robert M. Calhoon, *The Loyalists in America, 1760–1781* (New York: Harcourt Brace Jovanovich, 1973), 320–25.

8. On the centrality of household and contractual marriage metaphors in Revolutionary politics, see Jay Fliegelman, *Prodigals and Pilgrims: The American Revolution against Patriarchal Authority, 1750–1800* (New York: Cambridge University Press, 1985); and Jan Lewis, "The Republican Wife: Virtue and Seduction in the Early Republic," *WMQ*, 3rd ser., 44 (1987): 689–721. On myriad meanings of seduction in literature in this period and its relation to familial and political identities, see Elizabeth Barnes, *States of Sympathy: Seduction and Democracy in the American Novel* (New York: Columbia University Press, 1997), 18–39. On the fusion of familial and governmental authority, see Kathleen Wilson, "Rethinking the Colonial State: Family, Gender, and Governmentality in Eighteenth-Century British Frontiers," *American Historical Review* 116, no. 5 (2011): 1294–322, and Carole Shammas, *A History of Household Government in America* (Charlottesville: University of Virginia Press, 2002), 52–82.

9. J. H. Temple, *A History of North Brookfield, Massachusetts* (North Brookfield, MA, 1887), 452; Jonas Reed, *A History of Rutland, Worcester County, Massachusetts* (Worcester, MA: Mirick & Bartlett, 1836), 114–15.

10. Otis Grant Hammond, *Tories of New Hampshire in the War of the Revolution* (Concord: New Hampshire Historical Society, 1917), 43; Memorial of Breed Batcheller to Sir Guy Carleton, July 5, 1778, Sir Frederick Haldimand Papers, microfilm, DLAR (originals are in the British Library, London), reel 109: Memorials from the Provincial and Loyalist Corps, 1777–1785, vol. 1, p. 19.

11. S. G. Griffin's 1870 and 1871 histories of Nelson (Packersfield) originally published in the *Nelson Clarion*, reprinted in *Celebration by the Town of Nelson, New Hampshire of the One Hundred and Fiftieth Anniversary of Its First Settlement, 1767–1917* (Nelson, NH, 1917), 6–12, https://archive.org/stream/celebrationbytowoonels (accessed May 14, 2015). Batcheller's survey in *NHPSP*, ed. Nathaniel Bouton et al. (Concord, NH, 1874–96), 28:8–9.

12. See the series of petitions in *NHPSP*, 28:31–48.

13. *Batcheller vs. Wright*, December 7 and December 25, 1773, Manuscript, Cheshire County Inferior Court Records, no. 5 Manuscripts researched while housed at Cheshire County Courthouse, Keene, NH, and are now housed at the New Hampshire State Archives, Concord.

14. *New Hampshire Gazette*, March 16, 1766.

15. *New Hampshire Gazette*, February 13, 1767.

16. Daniell, *Experiment in Republicanism*, 3–33, 74–112; Wilderson, *Governor John Wentworth*, 13–22, 221–65.

17. "Evidence against Breed Batcheller Taken at a Special Session at Keene, June 10, 1777," NHPL, folder "Petitions: Tory: Packersfield: Breed Batchelor."

18. Ibid.

19. Griffin, *Celebration by the Town of Nelson*, 18.

20. Ibid., 19.

21. Packersfield Committee of Inspection to General Assembly, March 19, 1776: Report on Dec. 13, 1775 attempt to question Batcheller, folder "Petitions: Tory: Packersfield: Breed Batchelor," NHPL.

22. Meshech Weare to the Continental Congress, July 8, 1775, *NHPSP*, vol. 7, 561.

23. Petition of William Start to New Hampshire Committee of Safety, December 5, 1775, NHPL.

24. AO 13/52/268–269.

25. Proclamation of General Thomas Gage, June 12, 1775, Library of Congress, http:// memory.loc.gov/cgi-bin/query/r?ammem/rbpe:@field(DOCID+@lit(rbpe03801700)) (accessed May 24, 2015).

26. Packersfield Committee of Inspection to General Assembly, March 19, 1776.

27. Fitzwilliam Committee of Inspection to General Assembly, March 6, 1776, folder "Petitions: Tory: Packersfield: Breed Batchelor," NHPL.

28. Packersfield Committee of Inspection to General Assembly, March 19, 1776.

29. New Hampshire Constitution, January 5, 1776, *NHPSP,* vol. 8, 2–4.

30. Thomas Paine, "Reflections on Unhappy Marriages," in *Common Sense and Related Writing,* ed. Thomas P. Slaughter (Boston: Bedford/St. Martin's, 2001), 71–72.

31. Clare A. Lyons, *Sex among the Rabble: An Intimate History of Gender and Power in the Age of Revolution, Philadelphia, 1730–1830* (Chapel Hill: University of North Carolina Press, 2006), 14–26. Also see Mary Beth Sievens, *Stray Wives: Marital Conflict in Early National New England* (New York: New York University Press, 2005), 86–101.

32. Thomas Paine, "Common Sense," in *Common Sense and Related Writing,* 91.

33. Ibid., 109.

34. Ibid., 90.

35. Public broadside, March 19, 1776, reprinted in Daniell, *Experiment in Republicanism,* 113.

36. Association Test, *NHPSP,* vol. 8, 204–5.

37. Returns of the Association Test, *NHPSP,* vol. 8, 263, 244.

38. *Freeman's Journal,* June 29, 1776.

39. *New Hampshire Gazette,* August 5, 1780; August 12, 1780.

40. Treason Act passed by General Assembly, April 6, 1781, *New Hampshire Gazette,* May 21, 1781.

41. Quotes from "An Act for Taking Up, Imprisoning or Otherwise Restraining Persons Dangerous to This State," in *NHPSP,* vol. 8, 592–93. On the power of committees of safety, see Daniell, *Experiment in Republicanism,* 99–128.

42. Jeremiah Clough to his father, September 6, 1777, box 2, folder "Aug. 1777," New Hampshire Records and Archives (NH State Archives), Early Documents, General Court Records, Committee of Safety (RG 111) General Court, boxes 1 and 2.

43. Lois K. Stabler, ed., *Very Poor and of Lo Make: The Journal of Abner Sanger* (Portsmouth, NH: Randall, 1986), 129.

44. *NHPSP,* vol. 8, 515.

45. On Weare's moderation and that of the New Hampshire legislature committee as a whole in dealing with Loyalists, see Calhoon, *Loyalists in Revolutionary America,* 290–94. On the overall development of pragmatic political moderation among both Loyalists and Revolutionaries over the course of the war, see Timothy Barnes and Robert Calhoon, "Loyalist Discourse and Moderation of the American Revolution" in *Tory Insurgents,* 160–203.

46. John Langdon to Josiah Bartlett, June 24, 1776, in *Josiah Bartlett Papers, 1743–1795,* microfilm (Concord: New Hampshire Historical Society, 1976), ed. Frank C. Mevers, microfilm item D831, F882. Originals housed in various repositories.

47. "Surrey" Committee to Meshech Weare, March 10, 1777, Meshech Weare Papers, 1776–1785, 1 reel, microfilm, Massachusetts Historical Society, Boston.

48. Josiah Bartlett to William Whipple, April 21, 1777, in *Josiah Bartlett Papers*, item D3251, F1156–57. Also see Elizabeth Fenn, *Pox Americana: The Great Small Pox Epidemic of 1775–82* (New York: Hill & Wang, 2001), 91–92.

49. Memorial of Packersfield to Committee of Safety, May 8, 1777, New Hampshire State Archives, Concord, folder "May 1777."

50. On the pervasiveness of counterfeiting among Loyalists in New Hampshire (in which there is no evidence that Batcheller was involved), see Munro, "Revolutionary New Hampshire and Loyalist Experience," 172–78.

51. For example witnesses testified that Elijah King, Samuel Smith, and Abner Sanger had said that if forced, they would fight for the British; see "Dispositions and Orders of Justices in the County of Cheshire Relative to Tories," June 3, 1777, *NHPSP*, vol. 8, 593–96.

52. Evidence against Breed Batcheller, NHPL.

53. Ibid.

54. "Depositions and Order of Justices in the County of Cheshire Relative to Tories," June 3, 1777, *NHPSP*, vol. 8, 594.

55. Resolution of the House, June 12, 1777, *NHPSP*, vol. 8, 582–83.

56. Breed Batcheller and Robert Gilmore to Colonel Wyman, July 14, 1777, NHPL, folder "Petitions: Tory: Packersfield: Breed Batchelor." The letter is in Batcheller's handwriting and has all the initial first-person references crossed out and replaced with second person to include Gilmore. The particulars of the letter are Batcheller's; I retain the original first person here to indicate his voice.

57. Griffin, *Celebration by the Town of Nelson*, 23–24.

58. Memorial of Breed Batcheller to Sir Guy Carleton, July 5, 1778, in Sir Frederick Haldimand Papers (microfilm, DLAR, originals are in the British Library, London), reel 109: Memorials from the Provincial and Loyalist Corps, 1777–1785, vol. 1, p. 19.

59. "Case of Thomas Packer Batcheller," 12.

60. Memorial of Breed Batcheller, September 24, 1783, British Headquarters (Sir Guy Carleton) Papers, 1747–1783 (PRO 30/55) (originals in the Public Records Office, London), microfilm, DLAR, Document 9193, pp. 1–2; and "Pay Bill of the Extra Guides of the Army and for Sundry Other Persons for Services Done by Order of the Commander in Chief, under the Direction of Colonel Beverly Robinson Commanding at Different Periods and Ending the 24th June 1782," ibid., Document 5074, p 1.

61. The New Hampshire Proscription and Confiscation Acts of 1778 are reprinted in Henry Harrison Metcalf, *Laws of New Hampshire*, vol. 4, *Revolutionary Period* (Bristol, NH: Musgrove, 1916), 177–80, 191–93.

62. Janice Potter-MacKinnon, *While the Women Only Wept: Loyalist Refugee Women in Eastern Ontario* (Montreal: McGill-Queen's University Press, 2003), 69–77.

63. Assessment and Confiscation of Breed Batcheller's Land in Hollis, May 15, 1778; Inventory of Confiscated Estate of Breed Batcheller at Packersfield, May 18, 1778; and Inventory of Breed Batcheller's Marlborough Lands, October 15, 1778, NHPL, folder "Petitions: Tory: Packersfield: Breed Batchelor."

64. Sanger, *Very Poor and of Lo Make*, 194.

65. Petition of Mary Ann Bourn, October 23, 1778, NHPL, folder "October 21–31, 1778."

66. Petition of Ruth Batcheller, October 26, 1778, NHPL, folder "October 21–31, 1778."

67. Journal of the House, *NHPSP*, vol. 8, 796–814.

68. Petition of Ruth Batcheller, June 2, 1789, *NHPSP*, vol. 12, 640.

69. Linda K. Kerber, *Women of the Republic: Intellect and Ideology in Revolutionary America* (Chapel Hill: University of North Carolina Press, 1980), 136.

70. Petition of Prudence Baxter, May 13, 1778, NHPL, folder "May 1–15, 1778."

71. Baxter recounted his detention for treason in Boston in "Records of the American Loyalist Claims Commission, 1776–1831," Great Britain, AO, vol. 12, p. 44, microfilm edition, 1972, housed at DLAR (originals are in NAUK) and Petition of Prudence Baxter, December 14, 1778, NHPL, folder "Dec. 1778."

72. Petition of Simon Baxter, December 25, 1781, NHPL, folder "Dec. 1781."

73. Petition of Jane Holland, August 13, 1778, NHPL, folder "August 1778."

74. Petition of the Selectmen of Londonderry, May 19, 1778, NHPL, folder "May 16–30, 1778."

75. AO13/53/102.

76. Sanger, *Very Poor and of Lo Make,* 460.

77. Ibid., vii–xxiv.

78. Memorial of Breed Batcheller, September 24, 1783, British Headquarters (Sir Guy Carleton) Papers, 1747–1783 (PRO 30/55), document 9193, pp. 1–2.

79. Muster Roll of Disbanded Officers Discharged and Disbanded Soldiers and Loyalists Mustered at Digby the 29th May 1784, vol. 24, p. 6, MG 23 D1, ser. 1, item 112, Ward Chipman Papers: Muster Master General's Papers, 1776–1785, Library and Archives of Canada, Ottawa, http://www.bac-lac.gc.ca/eng/discover/military-heritage/loyalists/loyalists-ward-chipman/pages/item.aspx?IdNumber=112& (accessed May 15, 2015).

80. AO 13/90/78.

81. An Inventory of the Estate of the Late Captain Breed Bachelor, Deceased Taken August the 10th, 1786, microfilm 19005, Annapolis County Probate, File B-5, NSA and Management.

82. Philip Gould, *Writing the Rebellion: Loyalist and the Literature of Politics in British America* (New York: Oxford University Press, 2013), 10.

83. Petition of Ruth Batcheller, June 2, 1789, *NHPSP*, vol. 12, 640–41.

84. Journal of the Senate, 1789, *NHPSP*, vol. 21, 562.

85. Petition of Ruth Batcheller, June 2, 1789, *NHPSP*, vol. 12, 640.

86. *Heads of Families at the First Census of the United States Taken in 1790, New Hampshire* (Washington, DC: Government Printing Office, 1907), 21, https://www.census.gov/prod/www/decennial.html (accessed May 28, 2015).

87. See Potter-MacKinnon, *While the Women Only Wept,* 140–60, and Nancy Christie, "'He Is the Master of His House': Families and Political Authority in Counterrevolutionary Montreal," *WMQ* 3, no. 2 (2013): 341–70.

88. "Case of Thomas Packer Batcheller," 3–16.

89. Ibid., 5.

90. Ibid., 13.

91. Ibid., 16.

92. Ibid., 3.

93. Frank H. Whitcomb, *Vital Statistics of the City of Keene* (Keene, NH: Sentinel, 1905), 103.

94. Josiah Lafayette Seward, *A History of Sullivan, New Hampshire, 1777–1917,* 2 vols. (Keene, NH: Sentinel, 1921), 2:843, and Whitcomb, *Vital Statistics of the City of Keene,* 149.

95. Samuel Wadsworth, "Breed Batcheller," unpublished manuscript, n.d., Historical Society of Cheshire County, New Hampshire, Keene, NH.

96. *New Hampshire Sentinel,* July 1, 1840.

97. T.H. Breen, *American Insurgents, American Patriots: The Revolution of the People* (New York: Hill and Wang, 2010), 185–240, quote on 186. Breen's work draws heavily on New Hampshire sources in making its arguments regarding the power of local committees.

98. Judith L. Van Buskirk, *Generous Enemies: Patriots and Loyalists in Revolutionary New York* (Philadelphia: University of Philadelphia Press, 2002), focuses on families with divided loyalties in and around occupied New York, and Jasanoff, *Liberty's Exiles,* casts light on the experiences of families during the Loyalist diaspora.

99. Lewis, "Republican Wife," 720.

The Nonjuror Problem in Pennsylvania

1. Shortly after the war, most commentators suggested that as many as half of the otherwise eligible voters in Pennsylvania were disenfranchised by the Test Laws; see, for example, *(Philadelphia) Freeman's Journal,* October 6, 1784. Later in the 1780s, the majority of estimates settled closer to two-fifths; see *Independent Gazetteer* (Philadelphia), January 1, 1785, and *Carlisle Gazette,* October 3, 1785. These estimates were almost definitely influenced by political preferences. Supporters of the nonjurors had an incentive to claim that a substantial proportion of the population was disenfranchised, thus amplifying the apparent magnitude of the injustice. Likewise opponents had equally strong incentives to minimize the extent of the problem. Historian Robert Brunhouse seemingly accepts the highest of contemporary estimates, writing that the "test law excluded nearly one-half of the inhabitants of the State from citizenship"; Brunhouse, *The Counter-Revolution in Pennsylvania, 1776–1790* (Harrisburg: Pennsylvania Historical Commission, 1942), 155. Owen Ireland speculates more cautiously, saying only that the nonjurors represented a "sizable portion of the population of the state"; *Religion, Ethnicity, and Politics: Ratifying the Constitution in Pennsylvania* (University Park: Pennsylvania State University Press, 1995), 54–55.

2. "An Act for Securing to This Commonwealth the Fidelity and Allegiance of the Inhabitants Thereof, and for Admitting Certain Persons to the Rights of Citizenship," March 4, 1786, found in *Laws Enacted in the Second Sitting of the Tenth General Assembly of the Commonwealth of Pennsylvania* (Philadelphia, 1786), 35–37; "An Act to Alter the Test of Allegiance to This Commonwealth . . . ," March 29, 1787, found in *Laws Enacted in the Second Sitting of the Eleventh General Assembly of the Commonwealth of Pennsylvania* (Philadelphia, 1787), 304–6; "An Act to Repeal All of the Laws of the Commonwealth Requiring Any Oath of Affirmation of Allegiance from the Inhabitants Thereof," March 13, 1789, found in *Laws of the Thirteenth General Assembly of the Commonwealth of Pennsylvania, Enacted in the Second Sitting* (Philadelphia, 1789), 43–45.

3. Though Brunhouse admits that early "parties" in Pennsylvania were "loose, nebulous affairs," he argues that during the course of the war and especially into the 1780s, "there was a greater tendency to consider these party organizations as permanent structures"; *Counter-Revolution in Pennsylvania,* 9–10. Owen Ireland agrees that these factions could be considered "relatively modern political parties" in terms of overall stability and continuity; *Religion, Ethnicity, and Politics,* xvi.

4. For a brief summary of party politics in Pennsylvania during the war years and into the 1780s, see Owen Ireland, "The Crux of Politics: Religion and Party in Pennsylvania, 1778–1789," *WMQ* 42, no. 4 (1985): 454–56.

5. Pauline Maier, *Ratification: The People Debate the Constitution, 1787–1788* (New York: Simon & Schuster, 2010), 99; Owen Ireland, "Crux of Politics," 459. Ireland repeats this demographic and electoral argument in *Religion, Ethnicity, and Politics,* xix, and "The People's Triumph: The Federalist Majority in Pennsylvania, 1787–1788," *Pennsylvania History* 56 (1989): 93–113.

6. Brunhouse, *Counter-Revolution in Pennsylvania,* 191–228; Jackson Turner Main, *Political Parties before the Constitution* (Chapel Hill: University of North Carolina Press, 1973), 174–211; and Terry Bouton, *Taming Democracy: "The People," the Founders, and the Troubled Ending of the American Revolution* (New York: Oxford University Press, 2007).

7. Ireland, *Religion, Ethnicity, and Politics,* xvii; Ireland, "Crux of Politics," 454, 471.

8. Maya Jasanoff has compiled by far the most exhaustive estimate of the total Loyalist migration. Loyalist refugees carried with them an additional fifteen thousand slaves; Jasanoff, *Liberty's Exiles: American Loyalists in the Revolutionary World* (New York: Vintage, 2011), 351–58. For more on the fortunes of the Loyalist diaspora, see Mary Beth Norton, *The British-Americans: The Loyalists Exiles in England, 1774–1789* (New York: Little, Brown, 1974); James W. St. G. Walker, *The Black Loyalists: The Search For a Promised Land in Nova Scotia and Sierra Leone, 1783–1870* (Toronto: University of Toronto Press, 1992); Maya Jasanoff, "The Other Side of the American Revolution: Loyalists in the British Empire," *WMQ* 65, no. 2 (2008): 205–32; and Simon Schama, *Rough Crossings: Britain, the Slaves and the American Revolution* (New York: Harper Perennial, 2009).

9. *Minutes of the First Session of the Ninth General Assembly of the Commonwealth of Pennsylvania, 1784* (Philadelphia, 1784), April 8, 1784, 303.

10. Though the experience of Loyalists who remained in the states after the American Revolution remains seriously understudied, all the primary accounts agree that most lingering Loyalists successfully reintegrated back into American society. See esp. David E. Maas, "The Return of the Massachusetts Loyalists" (PhD diss., University of Wisconsin, 1972), 467–505; Robert M. Calhoon, "The Reintegration of the Loyalists and the Disaffected," in *The American Revolution: Its Character and Limits,* ed. Jack P. Greene (New York: New York University Press, 1987), 51–74; Aaron N. Coleman, "Loyalists in War, Americans in Peace: The Reintegration of the Loyalists, 1775–1800" (PhD diss., University of Kentucky, 2008); Brett Palfreyman, "Peace Process: The Reintegration of the Loyalists in Post-Revolutionary America" (PhD diss., Binghamton University, 2014); and Rebecca Brannon, *From Revolution to Reunion: The Reintegration of the South Carolina Loyalists* (Columbia: University of South Carolina Press, 2016).

11. According to statistics compiled by Anne Ousterhout, a total of 491 Pennsylvanians were "proclaimed"—that is, identified by name by the legislature or executive council, charged with treason, and subjected to attainder should they fail to appear to answer the charges before a certain date. See Ousterhout, "Controlling the Opposition in Pennsylvania during the American Revolution," *Pennsylvania Magazine of History and Biography* 105 (1981): 3–34. Pennsylvania's bill of attainder was "An Act for the Attainder of Divers Traitors, if They Render Not Themselves by a Certain Day . . . ," March 6, 1778, in *The Statutes at Large of Pennsylvania from 1682 to 1801,* 18 vols., ed. James T. Mitchell and Henry Flanders (Harrisburg: Clarence M. Busch, State Printer of Pennsylvania,

1896–1915), 9:201–15. All ten proclamations issued by the executive council can be found in *The Pennsylvania Archives*, 3rd ser., 10:519–44.

12. "An Act, Obliging the Male White Inhabitants of This State to Give Assurances of Allegiance to the Same . . . ," Jun. 13, 1777, found in *Laws Enacted in a General Assembly of the Representatives of the Freemen of the Commonwealth of Pennsylvania* (Philadelphia, 1777), 37–39.

13. Ibid., 37.

14. According to Owen Ireland, the three central issues that "defined partisan politics" in postwar Pennsylvania were the fate of the Test Laws, the conversion of the Anglican-dominated College of Philadelphia to the Presbyterian-dominated University of Pennsylvania, and the future of the Revolutionary State Constitution of 1776. See *Religion, Ethnicity, and Politics,* xvi.

15. *Freeman's Journal,* September 29, 1784. A group of nonjurors in Philadelphia referred to their status as "vassalage" in a petition submitted to the General Assembly and read aloud on the floor, November 3, 1785; *Minutes of the First Session of the Tenth General Assembly of the Commonwealth of Pennsylvania, 1785* (Philadelphia, 1785), 15.

16. *Pennsylvania Evening Herald,* December 21, 1785.

17. Benjamin Rush, *Considerations upon the Present Test-Law of Pennsylvania: Addressed to the Legislature and Freemen of the State* (Philadelphia, 1784), 21.

18. A Ploughman," *Carlisle Gazette,* March 29, 1786; John Smilie, *Pennsylvania Evening Herald,* December 21, 1785.

19. *Minutes of the First Session of the Ninth General Assembly . . . , 1784,* April 8, 1784, 303; *Pennsylvania Evening Herald,* December 21, 1785.

20. *Minutes of the First Session of the Ninth General Assembly . . . , 1784,* April 8, 1784, 303; *Freeman's Journal,* September 9, 1784; "To Representatives of Bucks County," *Pennsylvania Packet* (Philadelphia), August 17, 1783; "Lucullus to the Western People, No. 1," *Pennsylvania Packet* (Philadelphia), July 21, 1784. On continuing violence along the frontier, see Peter Silver, *Our Savage Neighbors: How Indian War Transformed Early America* (New York: Norton, 2008), 261–92.

21. "J.B.," *Carlisle Gazette,* February 21, 1786; *Pennsylvania Evening Herald,* March 11, 1786.

22. *Pennsylvania Evening Herald,* December 21, 1875; "Mentor," *Pennsylvania Mercury* (Philadelphia), February 4, 1785; *Pennsylvania Evening Herald,* December 21, 1875.

23. "J.B."; "To the Honorable the Representatives of the Freemen of the Commonwealth of Pennsylvania, in General Assembly met," *Independent Gazetteer* (Philadelphia), May 7, 1785.

24. *Pennsylvania Evening Herald,* December 21, 1785; "J.B."

25. "A Pennsylvanian," *Pennsylvania Evening Packet* (Philadelphia), December 28, 1785.

26. *Pennsylvania Evening Herald,* December 21, 1785.

27. According to historian Edward Countryman, victorious Patriots in nearby New York also linked the punishment of suspected enemies of the Revolution with the rights of conquest. "Independence, republicanism, and the confiscation of the great Tory estates would be permanent," Countryman wrote, "not because there had been no opposition, but because opposition had been crushed"; Countryman, *A People in Revolution: The American Revolution and Political Society in New York, 1760–1790* (Baltimore: Johns Hopkins University Press, 1981), 175.

28. *Pennsylvania Evening Post,* June 17, 1783.

29. *Pennsylvania Evening Herald,* December 21, 1785; "To Thomas Long, Joseph Savitz, James Wilkinson, James Tate, and Joseph Thomas, Esquires, the Representatives in the General Assembly of This Commonwealth for the County of Bucks," *Pennsylvania Packet* (Philadelphia), August 17, 1783; *Freeman's Journal,* September 29, 1784.

30. "To Representatives of Bucks County," *Pennsylvania Packet* (Philadelphia), August 17, 1783; "A Ploughman."

31. "J.B."; "Mentor." Note that Republicans' understanding of "the liberty of the whole" reflected an eighteenth-century notion of inclusiveness and did not extend to women, African Americans (free or slave), or Native Americans.

32. A number of Constitutionalists charged that Republicans' efforts to repeal or revise the Test Laws were part of a larger "design to reconcile the minds of the people to the restoration of [Loyalist] property," if not a plan to "place the government again in their hands." Worse yet, Constitutionalists intimated that Republicans in the assembly had received an "insidious petition from the late proprietaries"—a request from members of the Penn family for restoration of certain confiscated lands in western Pennsylvania. See *Freeman's Journal,* September 29, 1784. Given the long history of conflict between Pennsylvania's colonial assemblies and the propriety governors, most contemporary Pennsylvanians would recognize the mere suggestion of preferential treatment for the Penns as an extremely serious accusation. According to Robert Brunhouse, these political attacks proved effective, contributing to Republicans' initial failure to revise the Test Laws in 1784; *Counter-Revolution in Pennsylvania,* 140–41, 154–55. Republicans, for their part, claimed that these charges were distorted; they had no intention of pardoning attainted Loyalists or restoring property, particularly to the Penns. For more on pre-Revolutionary political disputes in Pennsylvania, see Richard R. Beeman, *The Varieties of Political Experience in Eighteenth-Century America* (Philadelphia: University of Pennsylvania Press, 2004), 204–42.

33. Rush, *Considerations upon the Present Test-Law,* 18.

34. "J.B."; *Pennsylvania Evening Herald,* December 21, 1785.

35. Brunhouse, *Counter-Revolution in Pennsylvania,* 154–55. For Constitutionalists' overwhelmingly negative response to petitions from nonjurors, see esp. *Minutes of the First Session of the Ninth General Assembly of the Commonwealth of Pennsylvania,* April 8, 1785.

36. "An Act for Securing to This Commonwealth the Fidelity and Allegiance of the Inhabitants Thereof, and for Admitting Certain Persons to the Rights of Citizenship," March 4, 1786, found in *Laws Enacted in the Second Sitting of the Tenth General Assembly of the Commonwealth of Pennsylvania* (Philadelphia, 1786), 35–37. See note 3 above for a complete summary of legislation related to the dismantling of the oath system.

Justice and Moderation?

1. Until recently scholars have neglected the topic of Loyalist reintegration. Early attempts at the subject include Oscar Zeichner, "The Rehabilitation of Loyalists in Connecticut," *New England Quarterly* 11 (1938): 308–30; Merrill Jensen, *The New Nation: A History of the United States during the Confederation, 1781–1789* (New York: Vintage, 1950). The topic remained dormant until the 1970s: Mary Beth Norton, *The British-Americans: The Loyalists Exiles in England: 1774–1789* (Boston: Little, Brown, 1972); David E. Maas, "The Return of the Massachusetts Loyalists" (PhD diss., University of Wisconsin, 1972); Rick Ashton, "The

Loyalist Experience: New York, 1763–1789" (PhD diss., Northwestern University, 1973); Roberta Tansman Jacobs, "The Treaty and the Tories: The Ideological Reaction to the Return of the Tories, 1783–1787" (PhD diss., Cornell University, 1973). Contributions in the 1980s include Phillip Ranlet, *The New York Loyalists* (Knoxville: University of Tennessee Press, 1986), and Robert S. Lambert, *South Carolina Loyalists in the American Revolution* (Columbia: University of South Carolina Press, 1987). Starting with Judith Van Buskirk, *Generous Enemies: Patriots and Loyalists in New York* (Philadelphia: Pennsylvania University Press, 2002), 155–96, the topic has started to attract more attention of historians. See Aaron N. Coleman, "Loyalists in War, Americans in Peace: The Reintegration of the Loyalists, 1775–1800" (PhD diss., University of Kentucky, 2008); Ruma Chopra, *Unnatural Rebellion: Loyalists in New York City during the Revolution* (Charlottesville: University of Virginia Press, 2011); Maya Jasanoff, *Liberty's Exiles: American Loyalists in the Revolutionary War* (New York: Knopf, 2011); and Rebecca Brannon, *From Revolution to Reunion: The Reintegration of South Carolina Loyalists* (Columbia: University of South Carolina Press, 2016). Of particular importance to this essay is Robert M. Calhoon, "The Reintegration of the Loyalists and Disaffected" in *The American Revolution: Its Character and Limits,* ed. Jack P. Greene (New York: New York University Press, 1987), 51–74.

2. The literature on transitional justice is extensive. An excellent primer on the field's origins and developments is Ruti G. Teitel, "Transitional Justice Genealogy," *Harvard Human Rights Journal* 16 (2003): 69–94.

3. Ronen Steinberg, "Transitional Justice in the Age of the French Revolution," *International Journal of Justice* 7 (2013): 267–85. I thank Rebecca Brannon for pointing me to this source.

4. John Elster, *Closing the Books: Transitional Justice in Historical Perspective* (Cambridge: Cambridge University Press, 2004), 1–2.

5. Roman David, *Lustration and Transitional Justice: Personnel Systems in the Czech Republic, Hungary, and Poland* (Philadelphia: University of Pennsylvania Press, 2011); Luc Huyse, "Justice after Transition: On the Choices Successor Elites Make in Dealing with the Past," *Law and Social Inquiry* 20 (1995): 51–78.

6. Robert M. Calhoon, *The Loyalists in Revolutionary America, 1760–1781* (New York: Harcourt Brace, 1973); Bernard Bailyn, *The Ordeal of Thomas Hutchinson* (Cambridge, MA: Harvard University Press, 1976); Norton, *British-Americans;* and Jasanoff, *Liberty's Exiles.*

7. "The Association," October 20, 1774, in *Sources and Documents Illustrating the American Revolution and the Formation of the Federal Constitution, 1764–1788,* 2nd ed., ed. Samuel Eliot Morison (New York: Oxford University Press, 1972), 124.

8. Claude H. Van Tyne, *The Loyalists in the American Revolution* (New York: Smith, 1953), 190–212; James Westfall Thompson, "Anti-Loyalist Legislation during the American Revolution," *Illinois Law Review* 3 (1908–9): 81–90, 147–171; Coleman, "Loyalists in War, Americans in Peace," 191–209; and Brett Palfreyman, "The Loyalists and the Federal Constitution: The Origins of the Bill of Attainder Clause," *Journal of the Early Republic* 35 (2015): 451–73.

9. *New York Gazette and Weekly Mercury,* February 27, 1775.

10. An Inhabitant," May 19, 1775, in *American Archives,* 4th ser., vol. 2, ed. Peter Force, 644.

11. Nathaniel Whittaker, *Discourses against Toryism* (Massachusetts: John Mycall, 1777), 14, 19.

12. Thomas Paine, *The American Crisis, Number 1*, December 19, 1776, in *Common Sense and Related Writings*, ed. Thomas P. Slaughter (Boston: Bedford, 2001), 129.

13. William Whipple to John Langdon, February 1, 1779, in *Letters of Delegates to Congress, 1774–1789*, 25 vols., ed. Paul L. Smith (Washington, DC: Government Printing Office, 1976–90), 12:43.

14. "An Act Obliging the Male White Inhabitants of This State to Give Assurances of Allegiance to the Same, and for Other Purposes Therein Mentioned," June 13, 1777, in *Statutes at Large of Pennsylvania from 1682 to 1801*, 18 vols., ed. James T. Mitchell and Henry Flanders (Harrisburg: Clarence M. Busch, State Printer of Pennsylvania, 1896–1915), 8:18–19; "Act to Punish Certain Crimes and Misdemeanors, and to Prevent the Growth of Toryism," in *Laws of Maryland, February 5, 1777–April 20, 1777* (Annapolis, 1777), chap. 20; "An Act of Free Pardon," June 26, 1778, in *Delaware, Laws, Statues, etc. 1778* (Wilmington, 1778), 1–8. Also see New Hampshire's "Oath of Allegiance" broadside issued in 1776.

15. "The Tory Act," January 2, 1776, in *Journals of Continental Congress, 1774–1789*, 34 vols., ed. Worthington C. Ford (Washington, DC: Government Printing Office, 1906), 4:23.

16. "Instructions to the Honourable Representatives in Assembly, for the City and County of New York, from the Mechanics Body, the Grocers, Retailers, and Innkeepers, Electors within Said City," January 9, 1784, *Independent Gazette or the New York Journal Revived*, January 29, 1784; "At a Meeting of the Inhabitants of the District of Saratoga, in the County of Albany Held on Tuesday the 6 Day of May, 1783," *New York Gazetteer or Northern Intelligencer*, May 26, 1783; "At a Meeting of the Good People of Rombout's Precinct," May 27, 1783, in *South Carolina Gazette and General Advertiser*, July 22, 1783; "A Meeting of the Freeholders and Other Inhabitants of This Town," April 24, 1783, *Boston Gazette*, May 5, 1783; "The Observer," *Massachusetts Centinel*, February 9, 1785.

17. Nathaniel Whittaker, *The Reward of Toryism* (Newburyport: John Mycall, 1783), 8–9; emphasis in the original.

18. Richard Oswald to Thomas Townshed, November 6–7, 1782, in *John Jay: The Winning of the Peace: Unpublished Papers, 1780–1784*, 2 vols., ed. Richard B. Morris (New York: Harper & Row, 1980), 2:406–7.

19. Benjamin Franklin and John Adams to Robert Livingston, December 4, 1782, in *The Revolutionary Diplomatic Correspondence of the United States*, 6 vols., ed. Francis Wharton (Washington DC: Government Printing Office, 1889), 6:106–7.

20. E. Alfred Jones, ed., *The Loyalists of Massachusetts: Their Memorials, Petitions, and Claims* (Baltimore: Genealogical Publishing, 1969), 35; Boston Town Meeting, April 7, 1783, in Record Commission, *A Report of the Record Commissioners of the City of Boston Containing the Boston Town Records, 1778–1783* (Boston: Rockwell & Churchill, 1895), report 80, 306–7; Thomas Jones, *History of New York during the Revolution, and of the Leading Events in Other Colonies during That Period*, ed. Edward de Lancey, 2 vols. (New York: New-York Historical Society, 1879), 2:244, 505; Alexander Flick, *Loyalism in New York during the Revolution* (New York: Columbia University Press, 1901), 163; Ashton, "Loyalist Experience," 174; and *Charleston Gazette*, July 8, 15, 22, 30, 1783; *Gazette of the State of South Carolina*, July 23, 1783. For a take on the events in Charleston that sees these actions as muted and limited, see Brannon, *From Revolution to Reunion*.

21. Joseph Jones to James Madison, June 8, 1783, in *Letters of Joseph Jones of Virginia 1777–1787*, ed. Worthington C. Ford (Washington, DC: Department of State, 1889), 116; May 24, 1783, May 26, 1783, December 2, 1783, *Journal of the House of Delegates of Virginia*

(Richmond, 1783): May Session, 31, 34, and October session, 76; and Proclamation of December 19, 1782, in *Calendar of Virginia State Papers,* 11 vols., ed. William P. Palmer (Richmond: Goode, 1881), 3:400.

22. Walter Clark, ed., *The State Records of North Carolina,* 26 vols. (Raleigh: Hale, 1886–1907), 24:488–90; 19:343; Archibald Maclaine to George Hooper, April 29, 1783, May 29, 1783, in Clark, *State Records of North Carolina,* 25:957–59, 963; New Jersey, *Journal of the Proceedings of the Legislative Council of the State of New Jersey,* October session (Trenton: Collins, 1784), 24; Maryland, *House of Delegates,* May 27, 1783 (Annapolis: Green, 1783), 42. New York actually passed two bills for the sales of confiscated property: "An Act for the Immediate Sale of Certain Forfeited Estates," April 6, 1784, and "An Act for the Speedy Sale of the Confiscated and Forfeited Estates within This State and for Other Purposes Therein Mentioned," May 12, 1784, both in *Laws of the Legislature of State of New York in Force against Loyalists* (London: Reynell, 1786), 122, 41–85; Maas, "Return of the Massachusetts Loyalists"; and Thomas Cooper, ed., *Statutes at Large of South Carolina,* 10 vols. (Columbia: Johnston, 1836–41), 4:553–54, 568–70. For a breakdown of the various measures the States adopted against Loyalists during 1783, see Jacobs, "Treaty and the Tories," 90–115; Allan Nevins, *The American States during and after the Revolution, 1775–1789* (New York: Macmillan, 1927), 644–56; and, Coleman, "Loyalists in War, Americans in Peace," 97–109.

23. "Proceedings of the Freeholders and Inhabitants of Amenia Precinct, in Dutchess County," *Pennsylvania Packet,* July 19, 1783.

24. "A Meeting of the Freeholders and other Inhabitants of the Town of Worchester (Massachusetts), May 22, 1783," *Pennsylvania Packet,* June 19, 1783. Also see the "Petition of Inhabitants and Freeholders of Amherst County, Virginia" and "Petition of the Inhabitants of Essex County, Virginia," June 6, 1783, in Virginia Legislative Assembly, Petitions, 1782–1789.

25. James Iredell to Hannah Iredell, May 21, 1783, in *The Life and Correspondence of James Iredell,* 2 vols., ed. Griffith McGree (New York: Appleton, 1858), 2:51–52; Thomas Jefferson to Phillip Turpin, July 29, 1783, in *The Papers of Thomas Jefferson,* 41 vols., ed. Julian P. Boyd et al. (Princeton: University of Princeton Press, 1951), 6:330; John Jay to Egbert Benson, September 12, 1783, in Morris, *John Jay,* 586–87. Other examples include George Mason to Patrick Henry, May 6, 1783, in *The Papers of George Mason,* 3 vols., ed. Robert A. Rutland (Chapel Hill: University of North Carolina Press, 1970), 2:770; John Dickinson, "Message to the General Assembly," November 10, 1783, in *Minutes of the First Session of the Eighth General Assembly of the Commonwealth of Pennsylvania* (Philadelphia: Halls & Sellers, 1783), 22; "A Patriot," July 15, 1783, and "A Planter," August 9, 1783, both in *South Carolina Gazette and General Advertiser;* and Arthur Lee to James Monroe, August 23, 1783, in Smith, *Letters of Delegates,* 20:581–82.

26. Alexander Hamilton, "A Letter from Phocion to the Considerate Citizens of New York," January 1–27, 1784, and "Second Letter from Phocion," April 1784, in *The Papers of Alexander Hamilton,* 27 vols., ed. Harold Coffin Syrett and Jacob Ernest Cooke (New York: Columbia University Press, 1961–87), 3:483–97, 530–58.

27. "Phocion," in Plutarch, *Lives of the Noble Grecians and Romans,* ed. Arthur Hugh Clough (New York: Benediction Classics, 2015), 530–543.

28. Hamilton, "Letter from Phocion," 3:485, 491.

29. Ibid., 3:484.

30. Ibid., 3:485, 487, 494.

31. Ibid., 3:495.

32. Ibid., 3:494.

33. Hamilton, "Second Letter from Phocion," 3:556–57.

34. Aedanus Burke to the Governor of South Carolina, *American Museum* 1 (1787): 121–23.

35. Aedanus Burke, *An Address to the Freemen of South-Carolina* (Charleston: Bell, 1783), 3–4.

36. Ibid., 17, 9, 1.

37. Ibid., 16.

38. Ibid., 25.

39. Ibid., 7, 10, 16.

40. Ibid., 28–29.

41. Ibid., 28.

AMERICA'S REVOLUTIONARY EXPERIENCE WITH TRANSITIONAL JUSTICE

1. Jon Elster, *Closing the Books: Transitional Justice in Historical Perspective* (Cambridge: Cambridge University Press, 2004), 1.

2. Ruti G. Teitel, *Transitional Justice* (Oxford: Oxford University Press, 2000). Also see her more recent essays on the importance of globalization in moving transitional justice forward: Teitel, *Globalizing Transitional Justice: Contemporary Essays* (Oxford: Oxford University Press, 2014).

3. Ronen Steinberg, "Transitional Justice in the Age of the French Revolution," *International Journal of Transitional Justice* 7 (2013): 267–85.

4. David E. Maas, *The Return of the Massachusetts Loyalists* (New York: Garland, 1989), 185; Anne M. Ousterhout, *A State Divided: Opposition in Pennsylvania to the American Revolution* (New York: Praeger, 1987), 161.

5. Roberta Tansman Jacobs, "The Treaty and the Tories: The Ideological Reaction to the Return of the Loyalists, 1783–1787" (PhD diss., Cornell University, 1974), 5–20.

6. Rebecca Brannon, *From Revolution to Reunion: The Reintegration of the South Carolina Loyalists* (Columbia: University of South Carolina Press, 2016), 55–56.

7. O. T. Murphy, "The Comte de Vergennes, the Newfoundland Fisheries, and the Peace Negotiation of 1783: A Reconsideration," *Canadian Historical Review* 46, no. 1 (1965): 32–46.

8. Treaty of Paris (1783), International Treaties and Related Records, 1778–1974, General Records of the United States Government, Record Group 11, NARA.

9. Maas, *Return of the Massachusetts Loyalists*, 432; Jacobs, "Treaty and the Tories," esp. chap. 3; John Adams to Henry Laurens, Paris, March 12, 1783, in *The Papers of Henry Laurens*, 16 vols., ed. Philip M. Hamer, George C. Rogers, and David R. Chesnutt (Columbia: Published for the South Carolina Historical Society by the University of South Carolina Press, 1968–), 16:161.

10. Maas, *Return of the Massachusetts Loyalists*, 435.

11. Henry Laurens to James Laurens, Paris, December 17, 1782, in Hamer, Rogers, and Chesnutt, *Papers of Henry Laurens*, 16:84. "The American Peace Commissioners to Robert R. Livingston, 18 July 1783," Founders Online, NARA, last updated March 28, 2016, http://founders.archives.gov/documents/Franklin/01-40-02-0197 (accessed January 1, 2017). Original source: Ellen R. Cohn, ed., *The Papers of Benjamin Franklin*, vol. 40, May 16 through

September 15, 1783 (New Haven: Yale University Press, 2011), 325–30; "From George Washington to Guy Carleton, 22 June 1782," *Founders Online*, NARA, last modified June 29, 2016, http://founders.archives.gov/documents/Washington/99-01-02-08751 (accessed January 1, 2017).

12. Elster, *Closing the Books*, 14, 39.

13. Act. no. 1153, "An Act for Disposing of Certain Estates, and Banishing Certain Persons, Therein Mentioned," in *Statutes at Large of South Carolina*, 10 vols., ed. Thomas Cooper and David J. McCord (Columbia: Johnston, 1836–41), 4:516–23.

14. Robert R. Livingston to Benjamin Franklin, January 7, 1782, in *The Revolutionary Diplomatic Correspondence of the United States*, 6 vols., ed. Francis Wharton et al. (Washington, DC: Government Printing Office, 1889), 5:92–94.

15. Samuel Adams to John Adams, qtd. in Maas, *Return of the Massachusetts Loyalists*, 448.

16. Aedanus Burke to Arthur Middleton, May 14, 1782 in Joseph Barnwell, ed., "Correspondence of Hon. Arthur Middleton, Signer of the Declaration of Independence," *South Carolina Historical and Genealogical Magazine* 26, no. 4 (1925): 200.

17. Edward Rutledge to Arthur Middleton, Jacksonborough, February 26, 1782, in Barnwell, "Correspondence of Hon. Arthur Middleton," 7; Theodora J. Thompson and Rosa S. Lumpkin, eds., *Journals of the House of Representatives, 1783–1784* (Columbia: Published for the South Carolina Dept. of Archives and History by the University of South Carolina Press, 1977), 221.

18. Maas, *Return of the Massachusetts Loyalists*, 307; Brannon, *From Revolution to Reunion*, 49; Ousterhout, *State Divided*, 204–5.

19. John Anstey to the Commissioners on American Loyalists, November 4, 1787, qtd. in Maas, *Return of the Massachusetts Loyalists*, 270–71.

20. Maas, *Return of the Massachusetts Loyalists*, 275–77, 293–94.

21. Jon Elster, *Retribution and Reparation in the Transition to Democracy* (Cambridge: Cambridge University Press, 2006), 52–53. Robert R. Livingston to Benjamin Franklin, January 7, 1782, in Wharton et al., *Revolutionary Diplomatic Correspondence of the United States*, 5:92–94. Brett Palfreyman, "The Nonjuror Problem in Pennsylvania," this volume.

22. Aedanus Burke to Arthur Middleton, Jacksonborough, January 25, 1782, in Barnwell, "Correspondence of Hon. Arthur Middleton," 193.

23. Wilbur H. Siebert, *The Loyalists of Pennsylvania* (Columbus: Ohio State University, 1920), 72, 88–90; Oscar Zeichner, "The Rehabilitation of Loyalists in Connecticut," *New England Quarterly* 11, no. 2 (1938): 308–30; Oscar Zeichner, "The Loyalist Problem in New York after the Revolution," *New York History* 21, no. 3 (1940): 284–302; Ousterhout, *State Divided*, 161–62; Robert O. DeMond, *The Loyalists in North Carolina during the Revolution* (Durham, NC: Duke University Press, 1940), 156.

24. Ousterhout, *State Divided*, 205.

25. Brannon, *From Revolution to Reunion*, 60–61, 139; Siebert, *Loyalists of Pennsylvania*, 88–90.

26. Robert Stansbury Lambert, *South Carolina Loyalists in the American Revolution* (Columbia: University of South Carolina Press, 1987), 302.

27. DeMond, *Loyalists in North Carolina during the Revolution*, 156; Ousterhout, *State Divided*, 161–62; Siebert, *Loyalists of Pennsylvania*, 88–90.

28. David E. Maas argues that professionals were much more likely to return to the United States and be reintegrated. In his study of Massachusetts, he suggests that men

who possessed rare skills were usually welcomed back with few restrictions because their skills were so valuable. Yet Kathy Roe Coker found no professional or economic differences between those who stayed and those who left in her study of South Carolina. Maas, *Return of the Massachusetts Loyalists*, 134–48; Kathy Roe Coker, "The Punishment of Revolutionary War Loyalists in South Carolina" (PhD diss., University of South Carolina, 1987).

29. Adele Stanton Edwards, ed., *Journals of the Privy Council, 1783–1789* (Columbia: Published for the South Carolina Dept. of Archives and History by the University of South Carolina Press, 1971), 117. For further discussion of the case of James Cook, see Brannon, *From Revolution to Reunion*, 123–24.

30. Maas, *Return of the Massachusetts Loyalists*, 446–47.

31. Benjamin Franklin to Henry Laurens, Passy, March 20, 1783, in Hamer, Rogers, and Chesnutt, *Papers of Henry Laurens*, 16:167; Richard Oswald to Thomas Townshend, November 6–7, 1782, in *John Jay: The Winning of the Peace: Unpublished Papers, 1780–1784*, 2 vols., ed. Richard B. Morris (New York: Harper and Row, 1980), 2:406–7. Thanks to Aaron N. Coleman's essay in this volume for pointing me to this Jay correspondence.

32. Ousterhout, *State Divided*, 287–92; Maas, *Return of the Massachusetts Loyalists*, 210.

33. Maas, *Return of the Massachusetts Loyalists*, 318.

34. This figure does consciously exclude all the property held by and confiscated from William Penn's heirs, who were not Loyalists but British nonresident landowners and therefore in a very different legal and moral position. Even if those properties are included, state authorities only sold 0.6 percent of all lands in the state as confiscated. Ousterhout, *State Divided*, 295–96.

35. Brannon, *From Revolution to Reunion*, 118–25.

36. Maas, *Return of the Massachusetts Loyalists*, 412; Aaron N. Coleman, "Loyalists in War, Americans in Peace: The Reintegration of the Loyalists, 1775–1800" (PhD diss., University of Kentucky, 2008), 47–49. Henry Laurens to John Owen, London, August 9, 1783, and Henry Laurens to Elias Ball, London, September 11, 1783, in Hamer, Rogers, and Chesnutt, *Papers of Henry Laurens*, 16:260, 336. For a longer discussion of the importance of community support for the reintegration of the Loyalists, see my state-level study: Brannon, *From Revolution to Reunion*, esp. chap. 3.

37. Maas, *Return of the Massachusetts Loyalists*, 455. Edward Rutledge to Arthur Middleton, December 12, 1781, in Barnwell, "Correspondence of Hon. Arthur Middleton," 187–93.

38. Maas, *Return of the Massachusetts Loyalists*, 489; Ousterhout, *State Divided*, 217–19; Adele Hast, *Loyalism in Revolutionary Virginia: The Norfolk Area and the Eastern Shore* (Ann Arbor: UMI Research, 1982), 159–60.

39. Henry Laurens to William Manning, Parish, December 4, 1782, in Hamer, Rogers, and Chesnutt, *Papers of Henry Laurens*, 16:67–68; Timothy Pickering qtd. in Maas, *Return of the Massachusetts Loyalists*, 453.

40. Maas, *Return of the Massachusetts Loyalists*, 467–73, 80–82.

41. "From Thomas Jefferson to George Hammond, 29 May 1792," *Founders Online*, NARA, last modified October 5, 2016, http://founders.archives.gov/documents/Jefferson/01-23-02-0506. (accessed January 1, 2017). Original source, *The Papers of Thomas Jefferson*, vol. 23, *1 January–31 May 1792*, ed. Charles T. Cullen (Princeton: Princeton University Press, 1990), 551–613.

42. Maas, *Return of the Massachusetts Loyalists*, 440–41. Alexander Hamilton, "A Letter from Phocion to the Considerate Citizens of New York," January 1–27, 1784, in *The Papers*

of Alexander Hamilton, 27 vols., ed. Harold Coffin Syrett and Jacob Ernest Cooke (New York: Columbia University Press, 1961–87), 3:493–95; Alexander Hamilton, "A Second Letter from Phocion," April 1784, in Syrett and Cooke, *Papers of Alexander Hamilton,* 3:549; Aedanus Burke, Charge to the Grand Jury of Ninety Six District, November 26, 1783, as reprinted in the *South Carolina Gazette and General Advertiser,* December 18, 1783; Aedanus Burke, *An Address to the Freemen of the State of South-Carolina* (Philadelphia: Bell, 1783), 25.

43. Ousterhout, *State Divided,* 220–21.

Plagiarism and the Nationalist Uses of Loyalist History

1. David Ramsay, *The History of South-Carolina: From Its First Settlement in 1670, to the Year 1808* (Charleston: Longworth, 1809), 1: x.

2. David Ramsay to Jeremy Belknap, March 13, 1794, in Robert Brunhouse, ed., "David Ramsay, 1749–1815: Selections from His Writings," *Transactions of the American Philosophical Society,* n.s., no. 55, part 4 (Philadelphia: American Philosophical Society, 1965), 137.

3. See Jay Fliegelman, *Declaring Independence: Jefferson, Natural Language, and the Culture of Performance* (Stanford: Stanford University Press, 1993), 164–81, on the relationship between plagiarism and this editorial conception of authorship. On its implications for ideas about the historian's role in early national historiography, see Eileen Ka-May Cheng, *The Plain and Noble Garb of Truth: Nationalism and Impartiality in American Historical Writing, 1784–1860* (Athens: University of Georgia Press, 2008), 106–20. On the prevalence of plagiarism among the Revolutionary historians, see George Callcott, *History in the United States, 1800–1860: Its Practice and Purpose* (Baltimore: Johns Hopkins University Press, 1970), 134–38; Orin G. Libby, "Some Pseudo-Historians of the American Revolution," *Transactions of the Wisconsin Academy of Sciences, Arts, and Letters* 13 (1900): 419–25; R. Kent Newmyer, "Charles Stedman's History of the American War," *American Historical Review* 63 (1958): 924–34.

4. On Ramsay's plagiarism, see Elmer Johnson, "David Ramsay: Historian or Plagiarist?" *South Carolina Historical Magazine* 57 (1956): 189–98; and Orin Libby, "Ramsay as a Plagiarist," *American Historical Review* 7 (1902): 697–703. On the plagiarism of Hewatt by Ramsay and his successors, see Elmer Johnson, "Alexander Hewat: South Carolina's First Historian," *Journal of Southern History* 20 (1954): 57–59. On Marshall's plagiarism, see William A. Foran, "John Marshall as a Historian," *American Historical Review* 43, no. 1 (1937): 51–64. On how Bancroft and his early national predecessors plagiarized from Chalmers, see Richard Vitzthum, *The American Compromise: Theme and Method in the Histories of Bancroft, Parkman, and Adams* (Norman: University of Oklahoma Press, 1974), 51–53, 62–65; and Eileen Ka-May Cheng, "Plagiarism in Pursuit of Truth: George Chalmers and the Patriotic Legacy of Loyalist History," in *Remembering the Revolution: Memory, History, and Nation Making from Independence to the Civil War,* ed. Michael A. McDonnell et al. (Amherst: University of Massachusetts Press, 2013), 144–61.

5. On Ramsay's influence see Arthur Shaffer, *To Be an American: David Ramsay and the Making of the American Consciousness* (Columbia: University of South Carolina Press, 1991), 88–189; and Peter C. Messer, "From a Revolutionary History to a History of Revolution: David Ramsay and the American Revolution," *Journal of the Early Republic* 22 (2002): 205–33. On the marginalization of the Loyalists from American historical consciousness, see Wallace Brown, "The View at Two Hundred Years: The Loyalists of the

American Revolution," *American Antiquarian Society Proceedings* 80 (1970): 25–47; George A. Billias, "The First Un-Americans: The Loyalists in American Historiography," in *Perspectives on Early American History: Essays in Honor of Richard B. Morris,* ed. George A. Billias and Alden T. Vaughan (New York: Harper & Row, 1973), 282–324; and Bernard Bailyn, "The Losers: Notes on the Historiography of Loyalism," in *The Ordeal of Thomas Hutchinson* (Cambridge. MA: Harvard University Press, 1974), 383–408. For recent challenges to this marginalization, see Edward Larkin, "What Is a Loyalist? The American Revolution as Civil War," *Common-Place* 8, no. 1 (2007), http://www.common-place-archives .org/vol-08/no-01/larkin/ (accessed November 12, 2016); Maya Jasanoff, *Liberty's Exiles: American Loyalists in the Revolutionary World* (New York: Knopf, 2011); and Philip Gould, *Writing the Rebellion: Loyalists and the Literature of Politics in British America* (New York: Oxford University Press, 2013).

6. For critical perspectives on Ramsay's plagiarism, see Johnson, "David Ramsay"; Libby, "Ramsay as a Plagiarist."

7. For the former view, see Sam W. Haynes, *Unfinished Revolution: The Early American Republic in a British World* (Charlottesville: University of Virginia Press, 2010); and Kariann Yokota, *Unbecoming British: How Revolutionary America Became a Postcolonial Nation* (New York: Oxford University Press, 2011). For the latter view, see Elisa Tamarkin, *Anglophilia: Deference, Devotion, and Antebellum America* (Chicago: University of Chicago Press, 2008).

8. On this attachment and on how the colonists occupied this liminal status, see Leonard Tennenhouse, *The Importance of Feeling English: American Literature and the British Diaspora, 1750–1850* (Princeton: Princeton University Press, 2007), 1–18. On the importance of copying to American nationhood, see William Huntting Howell, *Against Self-Reliance: The Arts of Dependence in the Early United States* (Philadelphia: University of Pennsylvania Press, 2015).

9. On the importance of "unbecoming British" to the development of American identity, see Yokota, *Unbecoming British.*

10. On the reintegration of the Loyalists, see Robert M. Calhoon, "The Reintegration of the Loyalists and the Disaffected," in *The Loyalist Perception and Other Essays,* ed. Robert Calhoon (Columbia: University of South Carolina Press, 1989), 195–215.

11. On the importance of exclusion to American nationalism, see Sacvan Bercovitch, *The Rites of Assent: Transformations in the Symbolic Construction of America* (New York: Routledge, 1993), 14–28, 50–51; Rogers Smith, *Civic Ideals: Conflicting Visions of Citizenship in U.S. History* (New Haven: Yale University Press, 1997); and Carroll Smith-Rosenberg, *This Violent Empire: The Birth of an American National Identity* (Chapel Hill: University of North Carolina Press, 2010).

12. For background on these historians, see Geraldine M. Meroney, "Alexander Hewat's *Historical Account,*" in *The Colonial Legacy: Loyalist Historians,* ed. Lawrence Leder (New York: Harper Torchbooks, 1971), 135–63; George D. Terry, "Alexander Hewat," in *Dictionary of Literary Biography 30: American Historians, 1607–1865* (Detroit: Gale Research, 1984), 111–15; and Shaffer, *To Be an American.*

13. On this dependence see Hugh Amory and David D. Hall, *A History of the Book in America,* vol. 1, *The Colonial Book in the Atlantic World* (Chapel Hill: University of North Carolina Press, 2009), 183–97, 296–98, 420, 477–78, 482.

14. "Misnomers," *Monthly Anthology* 4, no. 8 (1807): 429.

15. Charleston Library Society, *A Catalogue of Books Belonging to the Charleston Library Society: May, 1806* (Charleston: Young, 1806), 17.

16. Johnson, "Alexander Hewat," 58–62.

17. See below, this essay, for an example.

18. On the Revolutionary historians' belief in the moral function of history, see Lester Cohen, *The Revolutionary Histories: Contemporary Narratives of the American Revolution* (Ithaca: Cornell University Press, 1980), 161–211; and Arthur Shaffer, *The Politics of History: Writing the History of the American Revolution, 1783–1815* (Chicago: Precedent, 1975), 31–48, 96–102. On Ramsay's social purposes, see Shaffer, *To Be an American*, 105–27, 147–53, 188–206, 231–47; and Lester Cohen, foreword to David Ramsay, *The History of the American Revolution*, ed. Lester Cohen (1789; Indianapolis: Liberty Fund, 1990), xiii–xxv. On Hewatt's didactic understanding of history, see Meroney, "Alexander Hewat's *Historical Account*," 135–39.

19. For Hewatt's emphasis on the benefits of royal protection, see Meroney, "Alexander Hewat's *Historical Account*," 144–50.

20. On the relationship between these loyalties, see Messer, *Stories of Independence*, 122–23, 174–75; Eve Kornfeld, "From Republicanism to Liberalism: The Intellectual Journey of David Ramsay," *Journal of the Early Republic* 9 (1989): 306–12; Shaffer, *To Be an American*, 172–76, 231–47.

21. For Ramsay's emphasis on the orderly and traditional character of the Revolution and his growing fears of social disorder, see Shaffer, *To Be an American*, 120–23, 191–96.

22. David Ramsay, *The History of the Revolution of South-Carolina from a British Province to an Independent State*, 2 vols. (Trenton, NJ: Collins, 1785), 1:5. On Ramsay's growing conservatism, see Messer, "From a Revolutionary History," 205–33.

23. Ramsay, *History of South-Carolina*, 1:86; Alexander Hewatt, *An Historical Account of the Rise and Progress of the Colonies of South Carolina and Georgia*, 2 vols. (London: Donaldson, 1779), 1:291.

24. Messer, "From a Revolutionary History," 205–33.

25. Ramsay, *History of South-Carolina*, 1:90–91. On how Ramsay interpreted the revolt of 1719 as a precursor to the American Revolution, see Shaffer, *To Be an American*, 239–40.

26. On the role of commerce in Scottish conjectural history, see J. G. A. Pocock, "Cambridge Paradigms and Scotch Philosophers: A Study of the Relations between the Civic Humanist and the Civil Jurisprudential Interpretation of Eighteenth-Century Social Thought," in *Wealth and Virtue: The Shaping of Political Economy in the Scottish Enlightenment*, ed. Istvan Hont and Michael Ignatieff (New York: Cambridge University Press, 1983), 240–45. On Ramsay's commitment to commerce, see Shaffer, *To Be an American*, 243–45.

27. Jack P. Greene, *Evaluating Empire and Confronting Colonialism in Eighteenth-Century Britain* (New York: Cambridge University Press, 2013), 20–49.

28. Hewatt, *Historical Account*, 1:iii. For the Loyalists' belief in the importance of commerce to this mutually beneficial relationship, see Janice Potter, *The Liberty We Seek: Loyalist Ideology in Colonial New York and Massachusetts* (Cambridge, MA: Harvard University Press, 1983), 121–31. On Hewatt's belief in the importance of imperial government to the colonies' commercial growth, see Messer, *Stories of Independence*, 56.

29. Hewatt, *Historical Account*, 2:138–145. On Hewatt's interest in these topics, see Meroney, "Alexander Hewat's *Historical Account*," 136.

30. On how the American colonists used natural history to claim a place for themselves within the British Empire, see Joyce Chaplin, "Nature and Nation: Natural History in Context," in *Stuffing Birds, Pressing Plants, Shaping Knowledge: Natural History in North America 1730–1860*, ed. Sue Ann Prince (Philadelphia: American Philosophical Society, 2003), 75–79; and Susan Parrish, *American Curiosity: Cultures of Natural History in the Colonial British Atlantic World* (Chapel Hill: University of North Carolina Press, 2006), 27–33.

31 On the structure and content of Ramsay's history of South Carolina, see Shaffer, *To Be an American*, 231–47.

32. Ramsay, *History of South-Carolina*, 2:295–96. On Ramsay's interest in natural history and the environment, see Shaffer, *To Be an American*, 235–40.

33. On Ramsay's portrayal of South Carolina as a model of the nation's economic development, see Shaffer, *To Be an American*, 243–45.

34. Ramsay, *History of South-Carolina*, 2:306; Hewatt, *Historical Account*, 1:82. On the identification of electricity with divine power, see James Delbourgo, *A Most Amazing Scene of Wonders: Electricity and Enlightenment in Early America* (Cambridge, MA: Harvard University Press, 2006), 102–9.

35. Hewatt, *Historical Account*, 1:82.

36. On the Revolutionary historians' shift to a secular mode of explanation and their faith in human agency, see Cohen, *Revolutionary Histories*, 57–127, 205–11.

37. On classical republican fears of corruption, see Bernard Bailyn, *The Ideological Origins of the American Revolution* (Cambridge, MA: Harvard University Press, 1967); J. G. A. Pocock, *The Machiavellian Moment: Florentine Political Thought and the Atlantic Republican Tradition* (Princeton: Princeton University Press, 1975), 462–552; Gordon Wood, *The Creation of the American Republic, 1776–1787* (New York: Norton, 1969), 3–124. On the Revolutionary historians' hopes that their work would enable Americans to escape these cycles of decay, see Cohen, *Revolutionary Histories*, 185–211. On how Ramsay sought to achieve this goal, see Cohen, foreword to Ramsay, *History of the American Revolution*, xiii–xxv.

38. Ramsay, *History of South-Carolina*, 2:450. See Shaffer, *To Be an American*, 110–12, 152–53, on Ramsay's commitment to exceptionalist assumptions and the way that he brought together a naturalistic interpretation of history with occasional references to providence. In contrast see O'Brien, "David Ramsay," 1–15, on Ramsay's departure from exceptionalist assumptions and their providential basis. See Messer, *Stories of Independence*, 110, 114–17, on how the Revolutionary historians combined a faith in providential design with their belief in human agency. On how the Revolutionary historians reconciled these beliefs and the nationalist function of their faith in providential destiny, see Shaffer, *Politics of History*, 49–50, 59–66. On Ramsay's use of providential language and its British roots, see Nicholas Guyatt, *Providence and the Invention of the United States, 1607–1876* (New York: Cambridge University Press, 2007), 95–114, but my analysis departs from Guyatt's emphasis on the failure of the Loyalists to articulate a viable alternative to Revolutionary providentialism.

39. On the exclusion of Native Americans from definitions of America, see Jack P. Greene, *The Intellectual Construction of America* (Chapel Hill: University of North Carolina Press, 1993), 92–94, 124, 186–93.

40. On this duality see Robert Berkhofer, *The White Man's Indian: Images of the American Indian from Columbus to the Present* (New York: Vintage Books, 1978), 1–28, 72–80,

86–96; Roy Harvey Pearce, *Savagism and Civilization: A Study of the Indian and the American Mind* (Berkeley: University of California Press, 1988), 76, 135–50. On the myth of the noble savage in the Jeffersonian era, see Bernard W. Sheehan, *Seeds of Extinction: Jeffersonian Philanthropy and the American Indian* (Chapel Hill: University of North Carolina Press 1973), 89–116, 207–10. On the growing importance of race as a category of difference in this period, see Roxann Wheeler, *The Complexion of Race: Categories of Difference in Eighteenth-Century British Culture* (Philadelphia: University of Pennsylvania Press, 2000).

41. On this four-stage theory, see Ronald Meek, *Social Science and the Ignoble Savage* (Cambridge: Cambridge University Press, 1976); Karen O'Brien, *Narratives of Enlightenment: Cosmopolitan History from Voltaire to Gibbon* (Cambridge: Cambridge University Press, 1997), 132–36; J. G. A. Pocock, *Barbarism and Religion: Narratives of Civil Government* (Cambridge: Cambridge University Press, 1999), 2:309–29.

42. On the mixed implications of stadial theory for Native Americans, see the differing views of George Dekker, *The American Historical Romance* (Cambridge: Cambridge University Press, 1987), 73–98; Pearce, *Savagism and Civilization*, 82–100; Wheeler, *Complexion of Race*, 35–36, 181–90; Berkhofer, *White Man's Indian*, 38–49; and Sheehan, *Seeds of Extinction*, 15–44.

43. See Pearce, *Savagism and Civilization*, 66–73; Greene, *Intellectual Construction*, 92–93; and Berkhofer, *White Man's Indian*, 120–21, 138, on the denial of Indian rights to their land based on their status as hunters.

44. Hewatt, *Historical Account*, 1:14.

45. Ibid., 2:277. On Hewatt's desire for trade with the Indians, see Meroney, "Alexander Hewat's *Historical Account*," 149. On how Hewatt and other Loyalist historians viewed Native Americans as potential members of the British Empire, see Messer, *Stories of Independence*, 61–69.

46. Ramsay, *History of the American Revolution*, 1:4. On Ramsay's earlier sympathy for Native Americans, see Greene, *Intellectual Construction*, 189–91; and Messer, "From a Revolutionary History," 211, 226.

47. Berkhofer, *White Man's Indian*, 134–66; and Sheehan, *Seeds of Extinction*, 3–12, 185–279.

48. Ramsay, *History of South-Carolina*, 1:150–51n. On Ramsay's changing view of Native Americans, see Messer, "From a Revolutionary History," 226–29.

49. Hewatt, *Historical Account*, 1:223; Ramsay, *History of South-Carolina*, 1:164. For Hewatt's portrayal of the Indians as a threat to the colony's stability, see Meroney, "Alexander Hewat's *Historical Account*," 141–42. More generally on the fascination with Indian violence and savagery, see Sheehan, *Seeds of Extinction*, 185–201.

50. Ramsay, *History of South-Carolina*, 1:167; Hewatt, *Historical Account*, 2:214.

51. See Messer, *Stories of Independence*, 63–64, on how Hewatt and other Loyalist historians recognized the rationality of Native Americans and their rights as members of the empire.

52. Ramsay, *History of South-Carolina*, 1:167; Hewatt, *Historical Account*, 2:214.

53. On how Ramsay increasingly attributed conflicts between whites and Indians to the "savagery" of the Indians in his history of the United States, see Messer, "From a Revolutionary History," 227–28.

54. Ramsay, *History of South-Carolina*, 1:197; Hewatt, *Historical Account*, 2:279. See Messer, *Stories of Independence*, 65–66, 124–25, on how Hewatt and Ramsay attributed this

development to white American corruption. On white perceptions of the decline of the Indians, see Sheehan, *Seeds of Extinction*, 213–42.

55. Hewatt, *Historical Account*, 2:280; Ramsay, *History of South-Carolina*, 1:197–98.

56. On Ramsay's earlier recognition of European culpability for the decline of the Indians and its limits, see Greene, *Intellectual Construction*, 189–93.

57. Hewatt, *Historical Account*, 2:101. See Terry, "Alexander Hewat," 113, and Meroney, "Alexander Hewat's *Historical Account*," 145–46, on Hewatt's critique of slavery.

58. Hewatt, *Historical Account*, 1:123. On how antislavery sentiment served to express anxieties about commerce, see Philip Gould, *Barbaric Traffic: Commerce and Antislavery in the Eighteenth-Century Atlantic World* (Cambridge, MA: Harvard University Press, 2003).

59. Hewatt, *Historical Account*, 1:121.

60. Ibid., 1:122, 2:95. On how religion intersected with natural rights arguments in Hewatt's challenge to slavery, see Winthrop D. Jordan, *White over Black: American Attitudes toward the Negro, 1550–1812* (New York: Norton, 1977), 293–94. On the religious basis for this sense of humanitarianism, see Christopher Brown, *Moral Capital: Foundations of British Abolitionism* (Chapel Hill: University of North Carolina Press, 2006), 56–57.

61. Hewatt, *Historical Account*, 2:98.

62. Ibid. On Hewatt's concern with the religious conversion of slaves, see Meroney, "Alexander Hewat's *Historical Account*," 146.

63. Hewatt, *Historical Account*, 2:102–3. On the importance of religious conversion as a solution for the evils of slavery among early British critics of slavery, see Brown, *Moral Capital*, 55–75. For the growing recognition in Britain of the inhumanity of its colonial slave system and its limits, see Greene, *Evaluating Empire*, 156–71.

64. Hewatt, *Historical Account*, 2:99. On the mixture of chauvinism and cosmopolitanism that characterized the British conservative response to the American Revolution, see Eliga H. Gould, "American Independence and Britain's Counter-Revolution," *Past and Present* no. 154 (1997): 110–11. On the importance of religion to British identity and on how the idea of Britain's civilizing mission served to justify colonial conquest, see Jack P. Greene, "Empire and Identity from the Glorious Revolution to the American Revolution," in *The Oxford History of the British Empire*, vol. 2, *The Eighteenth Century*, ed. P. J. Marshall (Oxford: Oxford University Press, 1998), 213–15, 218–20; Linda Colley, *Britons: Forging the Nation, 1707–1837* (New Haven: Yale University Press, 1992), 5, 11–54, 367–68.

65. Hewatt, *Historical Account*, 2:98. On the precedents for Hewatt's recognition of slaves as subjects, see Brown, *Moral Capital*, 212–28.

66. Ira Berlin, *Many Thousands Gone: The First Two Centuries of Slavery in North America* (Cambridge, MA: Harvard University Press, 1998), 219–324; Douglas Egerton, *Death or Liberty: African Americans and Revolutionary America* (New York: Oxford University Press, 2009), 148–68.

67. On the change in Ramsay's views on slavery, see Messer, "From a Revolutionary History," 213–15, 219–20, 228–29; Messer, *Stories of Independence*, 119–20, 130–31, 174–75; Shaffer, *To Be an American*, 165–87; Arthur H. Shaffer, "Between Two Worlds: David Ramsay and the Politics of Slavery," *Journal of Southern History* 50 (1984): 175–96; Kornfeld, "From Republicanism to Liberalism," 298–311. On Ramsay's omission of slaves from his survey of South Carolina's population, see Jordan, *White over Black*, 340.

68. Hewatt, *Historical Account*, 1:119–121. See Terry, "Alexander Hewat," 113, on Hewatt's discussion of the importance of slaves to rice cultivation.

69. Ramsay, *History of South-Carolina*, 2:202; Hewatt, *Historical Account*, 1:119.

70. Ramsay, *History of South-Carolina*, 2:202–4.

71. On the nationalist reaction against British attacks on American slavery, see Matthew Mason, *Slavery and Politics in the Early American Republic* (Chapel Hill: University of North Carolina Press, 2009), 87–105, 219–23; and Haynes, *Unfinished Revolution*, 41–42, 183–203.

72. Hewatt, *Historical Account*, 2:98–99. On how Hewatt's critique of slavery stemmed from and buttressed his support for British imperial authority, see Messer, *Stories of Independence*, 67–68.

73. Hewatt, *Historical Account*, 1:125. On how British antislavery proposals in this period functioned as a means of asserting imperial authority over the colonies, see Brown, *Moral Capital*, 240–58.

74. On how British claims to represent a cosmopolitan humanitarianism served to justify imperial authority, see Gould, "American Independence," 110–21, 134–41.

75. For a different view that points to the problems slavery created for exceptionalist assumptions, see Greene, *Intellectual Construction*, 154–56, 186–89. On how Ramsay reconciled slavery with American ideals, see also Messer, *Stories of Independence*, 123, 130–31, 174–75.

76. On the European origins of American exceptionalist ideology, see Greene, *Intellectual Construction*. On the British roots of the belief in America's providential destiny, see Guyatt, *Providence and the Invention of the United States*, 1–94.

77. On the importance of race to the process of unbecoming British, see Yokota, *Unbecoming British*, 213–25, 238–39.

Postwar Loyalist Hopes

1. Eliza Byles, September 29, 1778, in MG 1, vol. 163, #4, in NSA.

2. Of the legitimately American, 40 percent came from New York, 15 percent from the Middle Colonies, 20 percent from New England, and the remaining 25 percent (black and white) from the southern colonies. About 20 percent were disbanded British regulars and their dependents. See William G. Godfrey, "Loyalist Studies in the Maritimes: Past and Future Directions," *London Journal of Canadian Studies* 9 (1993): 5. Slightly more than half the Loyalists settled in what became Canada. See Stephen Conway, "Britain and Revolutionary Crisis, 1763–1791," in *The Oxford History of the British Empire*, vol. 2, *The Eighteenth Century*, ed. P. J. Marshall (New York: Oxford University Press, 1998), 344; J. M. Bumsted, "The Consolidation of British North America, 1783–1860," in *Canada and the British Empire*, ed. Philip Buckner (Oxford: Oxford University Press, 2008), 44.

3. Thousands of Loyalists also settled in Caribbean Islands.

4. At this time Nova Scotia meant New Brunswick, the islands of the Prince Edward Island province, and Cape Breton, together with the province of Nova Scotia.

5. The census showed 6,913 Americans, mostly New Englanders, living in Nova Scotia, the majority of 13,374 people listed. See Elizabeth Mancke, "Another British America: A Canadian Model for the Early Modern British Empire," *Journal of Imperial and Commonwealth History* 25, no. 1 (1997): 19.

6. Fifteen years after the establishment of New Brunswick, Thomas Carleton, on October 3, 1798, wrote from Fredericton: "I cannot pretend to judge but if any proper arrangement for affording some occasional relief to the Indians in this province could be made, it

would relieve me at the same time from a very considerable embarrassment." See Thomas Carleton to General Prescott, October 3, 1798, in MG 23 D3 (now R6173-0-9-E), Public Archives of Canada, Ottawa.

7. John G. Reid, "Pax Britannica or Pax Indegena? Planter Nova Scotia (1760–1782) and Competing Strategies of Pacification," *Canadian Historical Review* 85, no. 4 (2004): 688–90.

8. In 1755 Nova Scotia and Cape Breton had twenty-five thousand inhabitants: of these fourteen thousand were Acadians, fewer than thirty-eight hundred were English (including soldiers), sixteen hundred were Germans, and two thousand were Micmacs. See Julian Gwyn, "Economic Fluctuations in Nova Scotia," in *Making Adjustments: Change and Continuity in Planter Nova Scotia, 1759–1800*, ed. Margaret Conrad (Fredericton: Acadiensis, 1991),, 69, 71.

9. Ann Gorman Condon, "1783–1800: Loyalist Arrival, Acadian Return, and Imperial Reform," in *The Atlantic Region to Confederation: A History*, ed. Phillip A. Buckner and John G. Reid (Toronto: University of Toronto Press), 187–88.

10. Brooke Watson to Joshua Mauger, between January and July 1783, Gilder Lehrman Society Papers, NYHS.

11. Brig. Henry E. Fox to Edward Winslow, April 14, 1784, in *Winslow Papers A.D. 1776–1826*, ed. William O. Raymond (Boston: Gregg, 1972), 177. As Fox wrote, "Governor Franklin might be appointed governor; but it met with so little encouragement from them that he dropped it on the second day having got only three or four names to it."

12. Carleton was recommended for his military and political experience but also for "the more ready determination of Subjects upon which instant decision might be requisite." See Lord Sydney to Lieutenant Governor Hope, April 6, 1786, in *Documents Relating to the Constitutional History of Canada, 1759–1791*, ed. Adam Shortt and Arthur G. Doughty (Ottawa: De L. Tache, 1918), 810.

13. Stephen Conway, "Britain and Revolutionary Crisis, 1763–1791," in *Oxford History of the British Empire, Volume II: Eighteenth Century*.

14. Oscar Zeichner, "Documents: William Smith's Observations on America," *New York History* 23 (1942): 337.

15. Ibid., 339.

16. Ibid., 340.

17. Ibid.

18. Stephen Conway, "Britain and Revolutionary Crisis, 1763–1791," in *Oxford History of the British Empire, Volume II: Eighteenth Century*.

19. George Germaine to Sir Henry Clinton, September 2, 1778, in *Documents of the American Revolution*, ed. K. G. Davies (Dublin: Irish University Press, 1976), 193.

20. Conway, "Britain and Revolutionary Crisis," 345; Oscar Zeichner, "Documents: William Smith's "Observations on America"," *New York History* XXIII (1942), 339.

21. Nova Scotia Charter, 1785, MG 23 C 20, in Nova Scotia Archives.

22. "Brief Observations," NSA, 6. In the younger Sewell's proposal of 1810, he also imagined that "descendants of Englishmen" who "profess the same religion, and speak the same language" would be "more easily assimilated" than other groups such as the Catholic French.

23. Zeichner, "William Smith's Observations on America," 331–40.

24. Ibid., 315.

25. Mather Byles to his sisters, October 7, 1786, in Byles Family Papers, DLAR.

26. Olivia E. Coolidge, *Colonial Entrepreneur: Dr. Silvester Gardiner and the Settlement of Maine's Kennebec Valley* (Gardner, ME: Tilbury House, 1999), 197, 201–2, 207, 243–44.

27. Patrick K. O'Brien, "Inseparable Connections: Trade, Economy, Fiscal State, and the Expansion of Empire, 1688–1815," in *The Oxford History of the British Empire*, vol. 2, *The Eighteenth Century*, ed. P. J. Marshall (New York: Oxford University Press, 1998), 74.

28. Dr. Silvester Gardiner, "Some Facts Collected and Observations Made on the Fisheries, and Government of Newfoundland, Showing the Many Advantages, Which Will Arise to This Kingdom on Colonizing That Island, to Which Is Added a Plan for a Speedy Settling of It," in MG 21 Add. Mss, vol. 10, PAC, Ottawa.

29. Ibid.

30. Elizabeth Mancke and John G. Reid, "Elites, States, and the Imperial Conquest of Acadia," in *The Conquest of Acadia, 1710: Imperial Colonial and Aboriginal Constructions*, ed. John G. Reid, Maurice Basque, Elizabeth Mancke, Barry Moody, Geoffrey Plank, and William Wicken (Toronto: University of Toronto Press, 2004), 32.

31. Elizabeth Mancke, "Negotiating an Empire: Britain and Its Overseas Peripheries, 1550–1780," in *Negotiated Empires: Centers and Peripheries in the Americas, 1500–1820*, ed. Christine Daniels and Michael V. Kennedy (New York: Routledge, 2002), 240; Mancke, "Another British America," 4.

32. Gerald S. Graham, "Fisheries and Sea Power," in *Historical Essays on the Atlantic Provinces*, ed. G. A. Rawlyk (Toronto: McClelland & Stewart, 1967), 11; Mancke, "Another British America," 27; Condon, "1783–1800," 188.

33. Bumsted, "Consolidation of British North America," 44.

34. Condon, "1783–1800," 188–89.

35. P. J. Marshall, "Britain without America—A Second Empire," in *The Oxford History of the British Empire*, vol. 2, *The Eighteenth Century*, ed. P. J. Marshall (New York: Oxford University Press, 1998), 577.

36. Joseph Galloway, 1780 Plan, in *Anglo-American Union: Joseph Galloway's Plan to Preserve the British Empire, 1774–1788*, ed. Julian Boyd (Philadelphia: University of Pennsylvania Press, 1941), 127.

37. Ibid., 128.

38. Lord Shelburne to Richard Oswald, July 27, 1782, in *British Colonial Developments, 1774–1834: Select Documents*, ed. Vincent Harlow and Frederick Madden (Oxford: Clarendon, 1953), 246.

39. Helen Taft Manning, *British Colonial Government after the American Revolution, 1782–1820* (New Haven: Yale University Press, 1933), 47.

40. Grace Amelia Cockroft, *The Public Life of George Chalmers* (New York: Columbia University Press, 1939), 67; Chalmers was appointed as chief clerk to the Board of Trade in 1786.

41. Manning, *British Colonial Government*, 42.

42. Cockroft, *Public Life of George Chalmers*, 73, 75.

43. Manning, *British Colonial Government*, 44.

44. George Chalmers, *An Introduction to the History of the Revolt of the American Colonies*, 2 vols. (Boston: Munroe, 1845), 2:119.

45. Ibid., 2:120.

46. Ibid., 2:253–54, 257.

47. Ibid., 1:221.

48. Ibid., 2:113.

49. Ibid., 2:116.

50. Ibid., 2:119.

51. Ibid., 2:261.

52. Ibid., 2:253–54, 273.

53. Cited in Cockroft, *Public Life of George Chalmers,* 72; Gerald S. Graham, *Sea Power and the British North America, 1783–1820* (Cambridge, MA: Harvard University Press, 1941), 27, 25.

54. George Chalmers, *Opinions of Eminent Lawyers on Various Points of Jurisprudence Chiefly Concerning the Colonies* (Burlington, VT: Goodrich), 652.

55. Ibid.

56. Ibid., 697.

57. Grace Amelia Cockroft, *The Public Life of George Chalmers* (New York: Columbia University Press, 1939), 72; George Chalmers, "Opinions of Eminent Lawyers on Various Points of Jurisprudence Chiefly Concerning the Colonies," NSA, 697.

58. Ibid., 73.

59. Ibid., 70.

60. Graham, *Sea Power and the British North America,* 20.

61. Ibid., 27. In the absence of a unified federal government or constitution in the United States, these experimental and ad hoc British policies met with no joint or unified protest from the United States.

62. Ibid., 33.

63. Ibid., 73.

64. Graeme Wynn, "A Region of Scattered Settlements and Bounded Possibilities: Northeastern North America, 1775–1800," *Canadian Geographer* 31 (1987): 333; Gwyn, "Economic Fluctuations in Nova Scotia," 86. Nova Scotia and Cape Breton received £152,300 sterling in the sixty years between 1756 and 1815. See ibid., 73; J. M. Bumsted, "Puritan and Yankee Redeviva," *Acadiensis* 2 (1972): 6.

65. Mather Byles to his sisters, July 10, 1783, MG 1, vol. 163, no. 1, in Nova Scotia Public Archives.

66. Wynn, "Region of Scattered Settlements," 326.

67. Graham, *Sea Power and British North America,* 49.

68. Ibid., 41, 35, 44, 56. During the late 1780s, Nova Scotia developed a shipbuilding industry. By 1786 sixteen vessels averaging more than seventy-five tons were built in Nova Scotia. The war with France slowed construction and left the industry in a prolonged slump. See ibid., 47.

69. Ibid., 72. By 1790 fish was being sent from the United States to the West Indies in American ships. See Wynn, "Region of Scattered Settlements," 327.

70. Graham, *Sea Power and British North America,* 201.

71. Ibid., 201, 206.

72. Joseph Galloway, Plan of Union, in *Anglo-American Union,* 114.

73. Quoted in Anglo-American Union, 39.

74. Joseph Galloway, "Plan of Union," in *Anglo-American Union,* 114.

75. Joseph Galloway, Plan of Union, in *Anglo-American Union,* 114.

76. Joseph Galloway, Plan of Union, 1779, Set Forth in a letter from Joseph Galloway to Lord George Germain, March 18, 1779, in *Anglo-American Union,* 122.

77. Joseph Galloway, letter to Charles Jenkinson, ca. 1780, in *Anglo-American Union*, 129.

78. Ibid., 136.

79. Galloway, Plan of Union, 1779, 117.

80. Galloway, letter to Jenkinson, ca. 1780, 137.

81. W. H. Nelson, "The Last Hope of American Loyalists," *Canadian Historical Review* 32 (1951): 34.

82. Darrel Butler, "Ward Chipman Senior: A Founding Father of New Brunswick," in *Eleven Exiles: Accounts of Loyalists of the American Revolution*, ed. Phyllis R. Blakeley and John N. Grant (Toronto: Dundurn, 1982), 147–48.

83. Jonathan Sewell to Edward Winslow, January 10, 1776, in Raymond, *Winslow Papers*.

84. Jonathan Sewell, Plan of Union, 1785, in *Anglo-American Union*, 158. This plan has been misattributed to Galloway and was written by Sewell.

85. Ibid., 157–58.

86. Ibid., 164.

87. Qtd. in Reginald George Trotter, *Canadian Federation: Its Origins and Achievement: A Study in Nation Building* (Toronto: Dent, 1924), 5.

88. Charles Inglis to Archbishop, April 20, 1789, MG1, vol. 479a, in NSA, 147.

89. Charles Inglis to Archbishop, March 18, 1789, MG1, vol. 479a, in NSA, 144.

90. Charles Inglis to Governor William Macarmick. March 18, 1789, MG1 vol. 479a, in NSA, 152.

91. Nova Scotia Charter, 1785, MG 23 C 20, in Nova Scotia Public Archives.

92. L. F. S. Upton, *Loyal Whig: William Smith of New York and Quebec* (Toronto: University of Toronto Press, 1969), 193; Oscar Zeichner, "Documents: William Smith's "Observations on America","" *New York History* XXIII (1942), 339.

93. Sewell and Robinson, 1824 Plan of Union, 37.

94. Ibid., 38.

95. Ibid., 41.

96. Qtd. in Edward C. Papenfuse, "Economic Analysis and Loyalist Strategy during the American Revolution: Robert Alexander's Remarks on the Economy of the Peninsula or Eastern Shore of Maryland," *Maryland Historical Magazine* 68 (1973): 174.

Robert McClure Calhoon

1. Warren R. Hofstra, ed., *Ulster to America: The Scots-Irish Migration Experience, 1680–1830* (Knoxville: University of Tennessee Press, 2012). Robert Calhoon's contribution, "Historical Political Moderation in the Ulster-to-America Diaspora," can be found on pp. 233–50.

2. For the most notable example of this genre of writing, see James Webb, *Born Fighting: How the Scots-Irish Shaped a Nation* (New York: Broadway Books, 2004), and also Rory Fitzpatrick, *God's Frontiersmen: The Scots-Irish Epic* (London: Weidenfeld & Nicholson, 1989); Billy Kennedy, *The Making of America: How the Scots-Irish Shaped a Nation* (Belfast: Ambassador International, 2001); and Billy Kennedy, *Our Most Priceless Heritage: The Lasting Legacy of the Scots-Irish in America* (Belfast: Ambassador International, 2005).

3. Robert M. Calhoon, *Political Moderation in America's First Two Centuries* (Cambridge: Cambridge University Press, 2009), 6.

4. Ibid., 8.

5. Ibid., 9.

6. Ibid., 12.

7. Ibid., 151.

8. Ibid.

9. David Cannadine, *Mellon: An American Life* (New York: Knopf, 2006), 23–24.

10. Marguerite Ross Howell, "Bibliographical Pathways to the Backcountry: Historical Writings of Robert M. Calhoon," *Journal of Backcountry Studies* 7 (Fall 2012), http://libjournal.uncg.edu/jbc/article/view/569/329. (accessed January 1, 2017). The quotation is Calhoon's and comes from the introduction to this article.

11. Ibid.

12. Joshua Shiver, "Interview with Robert M. Calhoon," November 3, 2006, 4, UNCG in the 1960s Oral History Collection, http://libcdm1.uncg.edu/cdm/ref/collection/ui/id/59847 (accessed February 9, 2018).

13. Howell, "Bibliographical Pathways."

14. Ibid.

15. Shiver, "Interview," 15–16.

16. Ibid., 16.

17. William Link, "Interview with Robert Calhoon," February 1, 1990, 2, UNCG Centennial Oral History Project Collection, http://libcdm1.uncg.edu/cdm/ref/collection/ui/id/59724 (accessed February 9, 2018).

18. Ibid., 4.

19. Ibid., 13.

20. Shiver, "Interview," 6.

21. Ibid., 14.

22. Link, "Interview," 15–16.

List of Contributors

REBECCA BRANNON is an associate professor of history at James Madison University. She is the author of *From Revolution to Reunion: The Reintegration of the South Carolina Loyalists* (2016), which won the 2016 George C. Rogers Jr. Award and was listed as one of the 100 Best Books on the American Revolution by the Journal of the American Revolution.

C. L. "CHIP" BRAGG is a practicing anesthesiologist in Thomasville, Georgia. He is the author of *Crescent Moon over Carolina: William Moultrie and American Liberty* (2013) and *Martyr of the American Revolution: The Execution of Isaac Hayne, South Carolinian* (2017).

EILEEN KA-MAY CHENG teaches history at Sarah Lawrence College. She is the author of *The Plain and Noble Garb of Truth: Nationalism and Impartiality in American Historical Writing, 1784–1860* (2008) and *Historiography: An Introductory Guide* (2012). She is currently working on a book project on Loyalist historians of the American Revolution and their legacy.

RUMA CHOPRA is professor of history at San Jose State University. She is the author *of Almost Home: Maroons Between Slavery and Freedom in Jamaica, Nova Scotia, and Sierra Leone* (2018). She has also written *Unnatural Rebellion: Loyalists in New York City during the Revolution* (2011) and *Choosing Sides: Loyalists in Revolutionary America* (2013).

AARON N. COLEMAN is associate professor of history and chair of the History and Political Science Department at the University of the Cumberlands. He is the author of *The American Revolution, State Sovereignty, and the American Constitutional Settlement, 1765–1800* (2016) and coeditor of *Debating Federalism: From the Founding to Today* (forthcoming). His current book project, under contract with Manchester University Press, is titled *Understanding the American Founding*.

SALLY E. HADDEN is the author of *Slave Patrols: Law and Violence in Virginia and the Carolinas* (2003) and coeditor of *Signposts: New Directions in Southern Legal History* (2013) and *A Companion to American Legal History* (2013). She is completing a history of eighteenth-century lawyers in early America, and she is also cowriting (with Maeva Marcus) a history the earliest US Supreme Court. Hadden has been a member of the history department of Western Michigan University since 2010.

WARREN R. HOFSTRA is Stewart Bell Professor of History at Shenandoah University. He is the author of several books, including *The Planting of New Virginia: Settlement and Landscape in the Shenandoah Valley* (2004). He is the editor of *Ulster to America: The Scots-Irish Migration Experience, 1680–1830* (2011).

BONNIE HUSKINS teaches history at St. Thomas University and the University of New Brunswick at Fredericton, where she is also Loyalist studies coordinator. She has published on the Loyalists in Shelburne, Loyalist freemasons, and Loyalist and Acadian commemorations, and is pursuing ongoing research projects on Loyalist sociability patterns and the life and career of eighteenth-century British military engineer William Booth.

GREGORY KNOUFF is professor of history at Keene State College in New Hampshire. He is the author of *The Soldiers' Revolution: Pennsylvanians in Arms and the Forging of Early American Identity* (2004).

CHRISTOPHER F. MINTY is assistant editor at The Adams Papers Editorial Project at the Massachusetts Historical Society. He received his PhD from the University of Stirling and has published in *New York History*, the *Long Island History Journal*, and *Early American Studies*. He is working on two projects, one of which focuses on the origins of Loyalism in New York City. The second is a coedited documentary edition of Rev. Myles Cooper's correspondence during the Revolutionary War.

JOSEPH S. MOORE is associate professor of history and department chair at Gardner-Webb University, where he has also served as Special Assistant to both the President and the Provost. His writings have appeared in *Slavery & Abolition*, *The New York Times*, and a range of journals and newspapers. He is the author of *Founding Sins: How a Group of Antislavery Radicals Fought to Put Christ into the Constitution.*

BRETT PALFREYMAN is an assistant professor at Wagner College. He is currently working on book projects about the reintegration of Loyalists after the American Revolution and the history of beer and brewing in New York City.

KACY DOWD TILLMAN is an associate professor of English and writing and associate director of the Honors Program at the University of Tampa. She studies early American life writing, particularly women's letters and diaries of the American Revolution, a subject about which she has published in *Early American Literature, Tulsa Studies in Women's Literature*, and *Literature of the Early American Republic*. She is currently working on her manuscript, "Stripped and Script: Loyalist Women Writers of the American Revolution."

CATHERINE M. A. COTTREAU-ROBINS, PhD is the curator of archaeology for the Nova Scotia Museum. Her curatorial work connects with the full range of archaeological time periods in the Atlantic Northeast from the Paleo-Indian to the early twentieth century. Her specific research focus areas include slavery in Nova Scotia following the American Revolution, urban archaeology, and the classification of copper artifacts from precontact and protohistoric archaeological sites.

TAYLOR STOERMER is a lecturer in museum studies at the John Hopkins University. Formerly he was an instructor of Public History and Graduate School fellow at Harvard University and the chief historian at Colonial Williamsburg.

CHRISTOPHER SPARSHOTT is assistant professor in residence at Northwestern University in Qatar. He completed his dissertation, "The Popular Politics of Loyalist during the American Revolution, 1774–1790," at Northwestern University in 2007.

CAROLE W. TROXLER, Elon University, primarily studies the impacts of the American Revolution in the southern backcountry, Maritime Canada, and the Bahamas. Her articles feature white and black allegedly "Loyalist" persons, settlements, and themes. She received the Christopher Crittenden Award in 2010. Her latest backcountry book is *Farming Dissenters: The Regulator Movement in North Carolina* (2011).

Index